Controversies in
International Relations Theory

REALISM AND THE NEOLIBERAL CHALLENGE

Controversies in International Relations Theory

REALISM AND THE NEOLIBERAL CHALLENGE

Charles W. Kegley Jr.
University of South Carolina

Australia • Canada • Mexico • Singapore • Spain • United Kingdom • United States

Executive editor: Don Reisman
Manager, publishing services: Emily Berleth
Publishing services associate: Kalea Chapman
Project management: Till & Till, Inc.
Production supervisor: Joe Ford
Text design: Russell Till
Cover design: Marek Antoniak

Wadsworth Group/Thomson Learning
10 Davis Drive
Belmont CA 94002-3098
USA

For information about our products, contact us:
Thomson Learning Academic Resource Center
1-800-423-0563
http://www.wadsworth.com

For permission to use material from this text, contact us by
Web: http://www.thomsonrights.com
Fax: 1-800-730-2215
Phone: 1-800-730-2214

Printed in the United States of America
10 9 8 7 6 5 4 3 2

ISBN:0-312-09653-4
Library of Congress Catalog Card Number: 94-65226

Acknowledgments
It is a violation of the law to reproduce these
selections by any means whatsoever without the written permission
of the copyright holder.

Ole R. Holsti. "Theories of International Relations and Foreign Policy: Realism and Its Challengers." Originally titled "Models of International Relations and Foreign Policy," in *Diplomatic History*. 13(1): 15–43. Reprinted with permission.

Kenneth N. Waltz. "Realist Thought and Neorealist Theory." Originally appeared in *Journal of International Affairs*, Volume 44 (Spring/Summer 1990). Reprinted with permission of *Journal of International Affairs* and the Trustees of Columbia University in the city of New York.

Michael W. Doyle, "Exploring Liberalism and World Politics." Originally appeared in *American Political Science Review* (December 1986). Reprinted with permission.

Joseph M. Grieco. "Anarchy and the Limits of Cooperation: A Realist Critique of the Newest Liberal Institutionalism." Originally appeared in *International Organization*, Volume 42 (Summer 1988). Copyright 1988 by the World Peace Foundation and Massachusetts Institute of Technology. Reprinted with permission of The MIT Press.

FOR EUGENE R. WITTKOPF

—my respected colleague and my valued friend

Preface

The rationale for the book is simple: To come to grips with contemporary theoretical inquiry in world affairs, it is worthwhile to begin with an appreciation of the factors that promote revisions in the ways international phenomena are interpreted. There are controversies about everything; struggles for "hegemony" among contending traditions in the study of international relations are no exception. Most recently, in the aftermath of the Cold War, students of international relations have begun to explore the formerly heretical idea that the study of international affairs now warrants, in place of realism and neorealism, a reconstructed paradigm inspired by the ideas associated with the liberal legacy. Hence, it is important for students and scholars to be provided with readings that can allow them to understand the discourse this challenge has provoked, the issues over which theoretical debate centers, and the prospects for adjusting the theoretical lens through which contemporary international events are perceived.

The essays in this anthology introduce the rich diversity of thought within both the realist/neorealist and the liberal/neoliberal perspectives. They are written to illuminate the differences and commonalities that exist about the ways theoreticians are now interpreting contemporary international developments from these perspectives. As such, they help define the range of viewpoints associated with each orientation. The book therefore allows the current manifestation of the realist-liberal debate to be understood, without violating the eclectic nature of the intellectual sources from which both traditions spring or masking the many ways in which realist/neorealist and liberal/neoliberal approaches overlap.

If this book succeeds in its primary goals, it will (1) introduce the major assumptions underlying the two major theoretical traditions in international relations inquiry, (2) stimulate thoughtful discussion about the future direction of international relations theorizing, (3) help to identify the research questions and principal global issues that will command attention in the twilight of the twentieth century, (4) suggest why a synthesis of realist and liberal theories is needed and possible given their shared concerns, and (5) provoke analysis of how such an integration might be approached.

Many people contributed to the development of this volume, and their contribution should be acknowledged. In particular, I would like to thank Hayward R. Alker, W. Ladd Hollist, Steven W. Hook, Pamela R. Howard,

Gregory A. Raymond, Neil R. Richardson, Harvey Starr, John A. Vasquez, and Eugene R. Wittkopf for their helpful advice on an earlier version of the Presidential Address to the International Studies Association from which this project emanated. David P. Forsythe, University of Nebraska; Eric Mlyn, University of North Carolina, Chapel Hill; Patrick M. Morgan, University of California, Irvine; Neil R. Richardson, University of Wisconsin, Madison; John A. Rothgeb, Miami University; Randolph M. Silverson, University of California, Davis; Herbert K. Tillema, University of Missouri, Columbia; and John A. Vasquez, Vanderbilt University, also provided insightful commentary and constructive criticism on earlier versions of the manuscript; the contributors are to be thanked for the professional response they made to these recommendations in revising their chapters. Shannon Lindsey Blanton, Jean A. Garrison, and Pamela R. Howard also provided valuable research assistance, and the supportive environment provided the editor by Linda S. Schwartz was instrumental to the book's completion. So, too, was the production management provided by Russ Till and the editorial work of Suzanne Mieso. And this book could not have been produced without the dedicated and professional word processing of Christina J. Payne, whose patience with me and my compulsions knows no limit. I also wish to thank my friends at St. Martin's Press, Don Reisman, senior editor, and Mary Hugh Lester, associate editor, for their faith in this venture and their support for its production.

Contents

CHAPTER 1

The Neoliberal Challenge to Realist Theories of World Politics: An Introduction

CHARLES W. KEGLEY JR.

I would rather be defeated in a cause that will ultimately triumph,
than to win in a cause that will ultimately be defeated.
—WOODROW WILSON

This book is designed to provide an introduction to the contemporary state of theoretical activity in international relations. To that end, it proceeds from a basic assumption: Since its advent as a discipline, theoretical debate has ranged primarily within the boundaries defined by the discourse between the realist and liberal visions. To a large degree, this division encompasses most of the other theoretical variants that have arisen at one time or another (Holsti, 1974; Ferguson and Mansbach, 1988; Kauppi and Viotti, 1992). The debate between these traditions "has permeated the last four centuries" (Banks, 1986: 9), and now continues to do so more animatedly than ever.

Controversies in International Relations Theory is not meant to provide a broad, comparative overview of international relations theory. It does not try to cover every unfolding intellectual movement, or even introduce an overarching sampling of the many issues that are of interest to international relations scholars. It therefore does not purport to examine every controversy. Instead, it focuses selectively on what is arguably the hottest topic in international relations theory today: the challenge to the dominant realist paradigm that is currently being mounted from diverse perspectives grounded in the liberal—or its subset, the so-called "idealist"—theoretical orientation. Without apologies, the book pursues the current state of theorizing activity within a confined parameter.

1

To introduce contemporary international relations theory by juxtaposing the field's two major conceptual approaches thus is not to suggest that this prism is adequate for capturing all the controversies in contemporary theoretical discourse. It is merely meant as a way of capturing the key cleavage in which that activity is centered, while also showing how the two most popular theoretical perspectives overlap and reinforce each other by speaking to common concerns and issues (Kegley, 1994b; Palan and Blair, 1993). The presentation does so without claiming to achieve a perfect balance between these contending schools, leaning toward an examination of neoliberalism because it is much less developed and known.

The need for such a book is rationalized by several concerns. Foremost is the question of whether the international relations discipline as currently configured is "an asset or a liability." Arguing on behalf of the latter, Michael Banks frames the issue by contending that

> The realist–idealist debate is the most significant because it gave us structures and institutions which still operate. It has also endowed us with a durable vocabulary, some of which has become extremely damaging. Such notions as reason of state, balance of power, and national security dominate our thinking and cripple our creativity. It is unfortunate that we seem to have retained the worst of the realist–idealist argument and lost the best part of it. (Banks, 1986: 11)

If Banks is correct in arguing that the "entire set of liberal–progressive–idealist ideas has been neglected in our own time," rendering the discipline "intellectually totalitarian, dominated by one school of thought," then the theoretical study of international relations is, indeed, in trouble, and a need exists to redress the balance. Putting recent efforts to do so into perspective is a need which this book seeks to meet.

This goal is related to the book's secondary objective—to make available theoretical writings about contemporary international trends that can facilitate an "exchange between the liberals on the one hand, and the realists on the other." The readings and reflections are designed to provoke consideration of whether a "full-scale criticism of [realism] from a liberal perspective" (Banks, 1986: 11, 13) might provide the necessary medicine to free realism from the intellectual closure that was prevalent during the frigid Cold War.

Thus, *Controversies in International Relations Theory: Realism and the Neoliberal Challenge* presents original or especially revised essays by leading scholars that probe prevailing developments in light of the realist and liberal theoretical debate that has recently ignited with renewed heat. These contributions describe the realist principles and theories to which the new liberal theorists are reacting, as well as realists' responses to their challenge. Hence, the neoliberal challenge is placed against the backdrop of the realist tradition, so that the controversies in the discourse can be identified and the dialogue can be broadened.

DEFINING REALISM AND LIBERALISM

It is axiomatic that for this book's pedagogical goals to be serviced, readers need to be exposed to the assumptions underlying both the realist and liberal–idealist theoretical heritage. The readings in this anthology provide that background, which broadens the kind of definitions some texts provide (see Box 1.1).

However, as the authors of these summaries make clear, and as shall be elaborated in the Introduction to Part I, the definition of both realist and liberal theory is itself a subject of considerable controversy and contention. Agreement on the core premises that underlie either of these traditions, or international relations theory generally, does not exist. As any entrant to the formal study of international relations soon discovers, a consensus does not even exist about what a theory is or what objectives theoretical inquiry should primarily pursue. Disagreements about the nature, types, and appropriate objectives of theory abound. The study of world politics is as much a contest about the politics of meaning as it is a conflict about politics within the world. This is a barrier to communication and understanding. To overcome it, students need to begin with appreciation of the differences that divide scholars about the definition of the theories in their field.

In order to help reduce these semantic problems, *Controversies in International Relations Theory* frames the contemporary realist and liberal theoretical debate and the diversity of opinion extant about the purpose of theoretical inquiry by breaking these traditions into their discrete component varieties. Realism and neorealism, as well as liberalism and its idealist derivative and neoliberal reformulations, and other theoretical challengers, will be distinguished (see Part I in particular).

To make the relevance of these theoretical movements to real-world events clear, the contributors rely on them and the definitions they prescribe to interpret some of the principal issues and substantive problems in today's world. The book thus takes as its point of departure the propensity for the themes and postulates emphasized by theoreticians to change over time in conjunction with changes in international circumstances. This, we can confidently assert, is now occurring again.

To introduce the current phase of the continuing realist liberal controversy, we need to look briefly at the thinking that now motivates realism's challengers. As a preface to the essays that follow, in this introductory chapter we will describe the current climate of international theoretical activity. Let us suggest why debate about whether it is time to revise, reconstruct, or, more boldly, reject orthodox realism has become so intense and why this controversy preoccupies so many theoreticians.

BOX 1.1
What Are Liberal Idealism and Realism?

The Liberal/Idealist World View

Idealists hold divergent views of world politics. What joins them is their shared assumptions about reality and the homogeneity of their conclusions. Collectively, idealists embrace a world view based on the following beliefs:

1. Human nature is essentially "good" or altruistic and people are therefore capable of mutual aid and collaboration.
2. The fundamental human concern for the welfare of others makes progress possible (that is, the Enlightenment's faith in the possibility of improving civilization was reaffirmed).
3. Bad human behavior is the product not of evil people but of evil institutions and structural arrangements that motivate people to act selfishly and to harm others—including making war.
4. War is not inevitable and its frequency can be reduced by eradicating the anarchical conditions that encourage it.
5. War and injustice are international problems that require collective or multilateral rather than national efforts to eliminate them.
6. International society must reorganize itself institutionally to eliminate the anarchy that makes problems such as war likely.
7. This goal is realistic because history suggests that global change and cooperation are not only possible but empirically pervasive.

The Realist World View

As applied to twentieth-century world politics, realism views nation-states as the principal actors in world politics, for they answer to no higher political authority. Moreover, conflicts of interests among them are assumed to be inevitable. Realism also emphasizes the way the (perceived) realities of international politics dictate the choices that foreign policymakers, as rational problem solvers, must make. States are the superordinate actors on the world's stage. The purpose of statecraft is national survival in a hostile environment. No means is more important to that end than the acquisition of *power*. And no principle is more important than *self-help*—the ultimate dependence of the state on its own resources to promote its interests and protect itself. State *sovereignty*, a cornerstone of international law, enshrines this perspective, giving heads of state the freedom—and responsibility—to do whatever is necessary to advance the state's interests and survival. Respect for moral principles is a wasteful and dangerous interference in the rational pursuit of national power.

    To the realist, therefore, questions about the relative virtues of the values within this or that *ism* (ideological system) cannot be allowed to interfere with sound policy making. The ideological preferences of states are neither good nor bad; what matters is whether one's self-interest is served. Accordingly, the game of international politics takes place under conditions of permanent anarchy and revolves around the pursuit of power: acquiring it, increasing it, projecting it, and using it to bend others to one's will.

At the risk of oversimplification, realism's message can be summarized in the form of ten assumptions and related propositions:

1. A reading of history teaches that people are by nature sinful and wicked.
2. Of all of people's evil ways, no sins are more prevalent, inexorable, or dangerous than are their instinctive lust for power and their desire to dominate others.
3. The possibility of eradicating the instinct for power is a utopian aspiration.
4. Under such conditions international politics is, as the English sixteenth-century philosopher Thomas Hobbes put it, a struggle for power, "a war of all against all."
5. The primary obligation of every state in this environment—the goal to which all other national objectives should be subordinated—is to promote the "national interest," defined as the acquisition of power.
6. The anarchical nature of the international system necessitates the acquisition of military capabilities sufficient to deter attack by potential enemies.
7. Economics is less relevant to national security than military might and is important primarily as a means to acquiring national power and prestige.
8. Allies might increase the ability of a state to defend itself, but their loyalty and reliability should not be assumed.
9. Never entrust the task of self-protection to international organizations or to international law.
10. If all states seek to maximize power, stability will result from maintaining a *balance of power*, lubricated by fluid alliance systems.

—Abridged and modified from Charles W. Kegley Jr. and Eugene R. Wittkopf (1995)

INTERNATIONAL RELATIONS THEORY AFTER THE COLD WAR: REALISM'S ERODING POWER?

Those advocating new or resurgent liberal–idealist theoretical departures differ among themselves in focus and motive, for those challenging realism are not part of a homogeneous, coherent intellectual movement. Because they have no single, unified voice, critics of realism question various facets of realism's message.

We must be sensitive to the challengers' differences in outlook. Yet realism's critics agree on some aspects of its purported deficiencies. Let us enumerate six of their complaints.

The Challengers to Realism: Criticisms

First, those mounting the challenges fault realism's poor *predictive* power. Since the eve of the Second World War, realism has been by far the most popular theoretical perspective for viewing world affairs. Leaders and scholars alike organized their thoughts and images almost exclusively in terms of this dominant paradigm. This reliance on realism to explain and predict international developments was understandable. Realism found a fertile ground in which to flourish during the conflict-ridden fifty-year period between 1939 and 1989. The lust for power, appetite for imperial expansion and struggle for hegemony, a pervasive arms race, and obsession with military security were in strong evidence. Realism accounted for these phenomena better than did any other theoretical perspective.

Yet when conditions change, a prevailing paradigm can function like a badly warped piano—the players tend to hit dead keys. With the Cold War's end, events and developments occurred that did not fit with realist theory's expectations. Realism and neorealism did not anticipate the Soviet Union's voluntary retreat from empire, deep disarmament cuts, the democratic revolutions that swept the world, or the surge of global cooperation, integration, and change generally (Scholte, 1993: 8). To critics, reliance on an unreconstructed realism is similarly likely to compromise the capacity to predict subsequent developments in world affairs.

Second, realism's challengers question its *descriptive* power. Like Georgia O'Keeffe's complaint regarding art that "nothing is less real than realism," so, today, some scholars see intellectual reasons to ask if that characterization also applies to realist theories of international relations. For example, Stanley Hoffmann (in Friedman, 1993: E5) concludes that "this wisdom [that] calls itself 'realism' . . . is utter nonsense today." Because "somehow the reality falls through the interstices of [realist] theories, [critics recommend that] political scientists [should] ask why their generalizations fail when they are confronted with something new. . . ." (Draper, 1992: 8).

Third, to realism's challengers, the field of study cannot rest contently in reaffirmation of familiar realist premises and rejection of new ones without first demonstrating either the advantages of the old or the inadequacies of the new. It must face the question of whether realism can account meaningfully for the new issues and cleavages that define today's global agenda. In the critics' view, in the wake of the Cold War conflict a window has opened to expose a view of international relations that realism largely ignores. "The problem . . . today . . . is not new challengers for hegemony; it is the new challenge of transnational interdependence" (Nye, 1992: 320), and it appears probable that "welfare, not warfare, will shape the rules [and] global threats like ozone holes and pollution will dictate the agenda" (Joffe, 1992: 35).[1]

---

[1] Among the pressing but heretofore neglected problems are acid rain, the AIDS epidemic, international drug trafficking, the depletion of the earth's finite resources, global warming propelled by the greenhouse effect and deforestation, exponential population growth, hypernationalism and ethnic conflict, chronic international debt, the specter of another worldwide economic depression fostered by neomercantilistic protectionism, the widening disparity between the affluent North and the impoverished South, the global refugee problem, and the failure to protect human rights.

As a result of the pressures of these changes in *global issues*, the broadened global agenda goes beyond what realism can realistically be expected to address: "International relations have parts which realist theory cannot reach" (Scholte, 1993: 8). As one critic complains, "realist preoccupations operate as a gigantic distraction from the deeper challenges associated with [the] political, economic, and social restructuring [occurring]" (Falk, 1992: 227). Given this limitation, "the approach of classical realism," Robert Jervis (1992: 266) predicts, "will not be an adequate guide for the future of international politics. . . ."

Fourth, mounting "proof" has accumulated that "the realist paradigm does not properly either describe or explain the world" (Banks, 1986: 16). An impressive body of *empirical research* has aggregated to reveal realism's "failure to provide an adequate understanding of the dynamics of peace and war [which are] at the heart of the paradigm (on the topics that realism claims to provide the best answers). . . . The dominant realist paradigm . . . has simply not been up to the task. It has not been able to explain inconsistencies in a satisfactory manner," and this failure, John A. Vasquez (1993: 3–4, 10, 85) summarizes, has suggested that "an entirely new theoretical approach may be needed, one that will put both existing findings and unresolved questions into a perspective that makes sense of both."

Fifth, the recent wave of neoliberal critiques derives from *intellectual antecedents*. Long before the Cold War began to thaw—in the period where realism appeared apt, applicable, and accurate—many scholars warned that realism was incomplete, misdirected, nonrigorous, conceptually confused, riddled with anomalies it could not explain, and incapable methodologically of finding answers to the questions it advanced for analyses.[2]

The current surge of complaint is fueled by these pioneering attacks on the "power of power politics" (Vasquez, 1983) and "the costs of realism" (Rothstein, 1972) and the warnings made long ago that realism's basic premises should be abandoned in favor of a truly different paradigm (Deutsch et al., 1957; Keohane and Nye, 1971; Burton et al., 1974; Mansbach and Vasquez, 1981). The important contributions within this invisible college in the 1970s focused on international integration, interdependence, and regimes. They paved the way for an intellectual climate that now is receptive to consideration of a new paradigm, as much as did the rise of trends that realism predicted would not take root and the ascendance of questions for which realism had no satisfactory answers.

Sixth, critics aver that realism is poor for *prescribing policy*. As one challenger laments, realism predicts consequences

---

[2] Elaborating why "a realist perspective constrict[s] our understanding of international politics," Justin Rosenberg (1990: 285–86, 289, 291) notes that "its deepest assumptions are grounded in ideological needs," that "the premises of realism [are] ensnared from the start in circular arguments [that] can legitimate just about any course of action," and that realist theory employs "a definition of power which produces . . . unfalsifiable hypothes[es]."

for its policies [that] do not occur. The scientific inaccuracy of realism is evident in the fact that the practices it recommends for dealing with war-threatening situations do not lead to peace but to war; indeed they often increase the prospect of war. This indicates that the underlying theory of war and peace from which these practices are derived is flawed. (Vasquez, 1993: 89)

These reawakened liberal theorists warn that if policymakers steadfastly seek to navigate the uncharted seas of the post–Cold War disorder with a realist cartography, their blind devotion could compromise their ability to prescribe viable policy paths to a more orderly and just global system.[3] Alexander George's (1993) critique of neorealism's severe limitations as a policy-relevant theory is but one among many recent attacks of realism's policy usefulness (for example, see Hitchens, 1991).

A theory of international relations needs to perform four principal tasks. It should describe, explain, predict, and prescribe. On each of these, critics complain that realism is deficient and scientifically unsophisticated. Because of these alleged inadequacies, critics maintain that realism and neorealism not only misunderstand the present but also "systematically misconceive the past" (Kratochwil, 1993: 69); "for many students [they are] a research enterprise in crisis" (James, 1993: 132).

As liberal theorists challenging realism warn, if an increasingly outmoded paradigm is religiously worshipped and new rationales are concocted for old theoretical practices, our ability to prepare productively for the emerging new realities will diminish. "It is time," they contend (Kober, 1990: 9), "for a new, more rigorous idealist alternative to realism."

Realism's Fading Relevance?

Indicators abound that realism might be losing its grip on the imagination of those writing in our field and on policymakers' thinking. Attacks on "the poverty" of conventional realism (Krauthammer, 1986; Weigel, 1993) and on the "poverty of neorealism" (Ashley, 1984) have become a growth industry. Revealingly, the leading periodical home for the expression of realist interpretations of world affairs, *The National Interest*, found it necessary to "reconsider realism's relevance" in a symposium in its winter 1992–1993 issue by confronting directly the question "Is Realism Finished?" (Zakaria, 1992–1993).

---

[3] These proponents argue that

idealism provides a fundamental challenge to realism and geopolitics [and] it is no longer possible to dismiss idealists as utopian dreamers who do not understand the harsh reality of power. On the contrary, idealists can respond that it is realists and geopoliticians who have oversimplified the concept of power and misunderstood the lessons of history. The debate between them is of critical importance in formulating policy to respond to the revolutionary changes now confronting the world. (Kober, 1990: 16)

As one realist, Charles Krauthammer, summarizes the prevailing mood,

[Since] publication [in 1948] of the realist classic, Hans Morgenthau's *Politics Among Nations*, the fortunes of the realist school have fluctuated. . . . Realism finds itself at a historically awkward moment. It was born in opposition to Wilsonian utopianism. It flourished as a critique of liberal internationalism. [But after Vietnam the liberal consensus collapsed, and now] we may . . . see a fracturing of the realist school paralleling the fracture of liberal internationalism. (Krauthammer, 1986: 14, 22)

Contemporary dissatisfaction with realism is reflected in the current wave of theoretical analyses that ask "what's the matter with realism?" (Rosenberg, 1990), call for the discovery of "the real realism" (Griffiths, 1992), recommend efforts to "rethink neorealism" (Buzan, Jones, and Little, 1993), and request that realism be brought "up to date" (Singer and Wildavsky, 1993: 187) and that neorealism be "elaborated" (James, 1993). Many now urge that realpolitik not just be "revisited" (Jensen and Faulkner, 1992), but fundamentally "reformulated" (Niou, Ordeshook, and Rose, 1991; Niou and Ordeshook, 1993). These contemporary calls range from espousal of a revised realism from a feminist perspective (Tickner, 1991; Enloe, 1993) to its reconstruction through the kind of rigorous analysis (Cusack and Stoll, 1990, 1992) that would enable empirical research to modernize realist theory, which remains "oblivious to the modern currents of scholarship that might inform it" (Wayman and Diehl, 1994: 1). The challengers all follow the principle that paradigm changes should occur when anomalies accumulate that contradict a prevailing paradigm's core assumptions (Kuhn, 1962) and when substantial evidence is produced that is inconsistent with the paradigm's premises (Lakatos, 1978).

WILSONIAN LIBERALISM REDISCOVERED

Driving much of the escalating expressions of dissatisfaction with realism is growing awareness of the profoundly altered attributes of the post–Cold War setting. In the wake of that hegemonic struggle, increasing numbers of theorists have recommended examining whether an image of world politics consistent with that portrayed by Woodrow Wilson seventy-five years ago has now become applicable and appropriate.

To their eyes, Wilson was in many ways a visionary. At the end of World War I he responded to the challenge to establish a peace. Yet in his endeavors Wilson conceived of a world that did not yet exist, that was still in its incipient stage of development (Knock, 1992). Consequently, Wilson was regarded by his contemporaries as quixotic about the prospects for international cooperation and change and was dismissed by a subsequent generation of disillusioned realists who thought him naive. Looking back, Wilson's quest to "stiffen . . .

moral purpose with a sense of responsibility for the practical consequences of ideals" (Osgood, 1953: 295) was arguably premature.

But now, as many of the essays in this book argue, the long-term trajectories in world affairs have converged to create a transformed international system. Wilson's ideas and ideals now appear less unrealistic and more compelling. Old ideas are new again. Our professional journals now frequently take seriously "neo-Wilsonian" idealism (Fukuyama, 1992a), "idealpolitik" (Kober, 1990), "neo-idealism" (Kegley, 1988, 1993), and "neoliberalism" (Nye, 1988) or its derivative "neoliberal institutionalism" (Grieco, 1990) and treat "the recovery of liberalism" (Little, 1993) as a needed theoretical objective. The "neoliberal challenge and neorealist response" has become a heated "contemporary debate" (Baldwin, 1993). The reawakened interest in the Wilsonian world view (Tucker, 1992, 1992–1993; Shimko, 1992) indicates that our profession has responded to John Lewis Gaddis's (1990: 58) plea that we give Wilson's vision "the fair test it has never received."

Core Components of Neoliberal Theorizing

Many scholars are already actively engaged in research that tests propositions derived from the Wilsonian liberal vision. Indeed, as the essays in this book reflect, the questions and puzzles that now dominate research and theorizing read like they were lifted from Wilson's Fourteen Points speech to the U.S. Senate on January 22, 1917. Collectively, they define the principles central to the neoliberal/neoidealist critique of realism and can be used as a benchmark for analyzing the contemporary challenge to realism. Consider the following indicators.

- **Item:** The march of democracy, its causes and consequences, has been rediscovered and made the focal point for analysis. In 1992 and 1993, three of the field's leading journals—*International Interactions*, the *Journal of Conflict Resolution*, and the *Journal of Peace Research*—devoted special issues to the impact of democracy and secondarily to the evaluation of democratization's "consequences for neorealist thought" (Sørensen, 1992). Much of this analysis centered on Wilson's proposition that making the world safe for democracy would make "the world fit and safe to live in" (Chan, 1993; Dixon, 1994; Doyle, 1986, 1991; Huntington, 1991; Lake, 1992; Morgan and Schwebach, 1992; Ray, 1994; Robbins, 1991; Russett, 1993; Starr, 1992).

  This extensive research has strengthened confidence in Wilson's expectation that democracies promote peace. The evidence that democracies almost never wage war against each other is "as close as anything we have to an empirical law in international relations" (Levy, 1989: 270). To some, these results expose "the fallacy of political realism" (Nincic, 1992) and support the validity of Wilsonian idealism rooted in Kantian liberalism by suggesting that "domestic politics play a much larger role in national security policy than is generally believed by realists and neorealist theorists" (Bueno de Mesquita, Siverson, and Woller, 1992: 638).

■ *Item:* Wilson's championed but neglected principle, *self-determination*, is once again a topic of searching scrutiny. Realism's worship of the nation-state as the only legitimate political authority on the world's stage to which all other supranational and subnational units are subservient has been undercut by the growth worldwide of strident public challenges to governments' authority and legitimacy (Rosenau, 1990). Some see localized empowerment portending "the twilight of sovereignty" (Wriston, 1992).

Wilson anticipated this development. He not only had important things to say about the conflict then raging in the Balkans but more generally (Point V) about "the principle that, in determining all such questions of sovereignty, the interests of the populations concerned must have equal weight with the equitable claims of the government whose title is to be determined."

■ *Item:* "With the growth of private cross-border communications and organizations, and with the rise of economic interdependence, the 'hard shell' of the state has crumbled" (Lake, 1993: 772). Governments are not untouchable. There is evident "a devolution of power not only upward toward supranational bodies and outward toward commonwealths and common markets but also downward toward freer, more autonomous units of administration" (Talbott, 1992: 71).

Contrary to the expectations generated by the state-centric or "unitary actor" model of structural realism, when the layers that realism enshells around the nation-state are peeled away, we discover that what happens *within* countries can change the geopolitical map of the globe.[4] People matter and, as evidence shows, public opinion counts (Russett, 1990; Wittkopf, 1990); public sentiment is captured instantaneously in our age of global communications knit together by cables, the airwaves, and the fax machine. The distinction between domestic and foreign affairs has broken down, and as a result neoliberals have made "the growing irrelevance of borders" (Cooper, 1993: 18) an object of inquiry. This also follows Wilson's belief that lowering barriers between countries would be a barrier to warfare.

■ *Item:* As Wilson predicted but many realists deny, the motives that animate the goals of states are not immutable. They *can* change. There are

---

[4] Perhaps the best illustration of the inadequacy of realism's billiard-ball model is the fall of the Soviet Union. The USSR did not crumble simply due to the intimidating military capabilities of its external adversaries, as many realists claim (Kegley 1994a; Lebow and Stein, 1994). Soviet leaders abandoned the realist perspective that had previously governed much of Soviet policy making. Because the change in grand strategy was determined as much by domestic politics as by international pressures, "departures from realist expectations are in fact essential to an understanding of the dynamics of war and peace" (Rosecrance and Stein, 1993: 12); the internal sources of foreign policy change cannot be ignored.

good reasons for questioning the realist belief "that if a nation was (much) more powerful than its neighbors it would use its power to control or conquer them" (Singer and Wildavsky, 1993: 5). Many states long ago lost their appetite for territorial conquest and colonialism. "There are many precedents for countries with long histories of imperialism giving up their empires . . . more or less voluntarily. . . . Hyper-realism, in other words, is not terribly realistic about the changing nature of modern states and the kinds of aspirations they entertain" (Fukuyama, 1992a: 27–28).

■ *Item:* Disarmament has ceased to be a mere slogan and instead has gained recognition as a viable path to common security. The formerly unimaginable has occurred as disarmament agreements of unprecedented magnitude have been negotiated. The post–Cold War arms race in reverse was unanticipated by realist theories, which hold reductions in arsenals as anathema. Yet powerful states did what some realists claimed they could not, and cautioned they must not, do: They agreed voluntarily to diminish their military power. By accepting deep cuts in their strategic arsenals, Russia and the United States violated the realist's first rule that states should always "increase [military] capabilities and fight rather than fail to increase capabilities" (Kaplan, 1957: 23).

Scholars and leaders now question the assumption that the power to destroy equals the power to control. Rather, they now focus on the inverse correlation between military expenditures and both economic growth (Kennedy, 1987) and national security (Johansen, 1991). The costs of arms races and their contribution to the international security dilemma (Wallace, 1979; Herz, 1950) are no longer regarded as liberal propositions unworthy of rigorous treatment; the causes and consequences of arms races and disarmament have become a hot research topic (Hammond, 1993).

Whatever the circumstantial sources for this change in thinking, its intellectual roots are deep. Proposals to take disarmament seriously stem from many antecedents as far back as the biblical injunction for nations to beat their swords into plowshares, but were given especially vocal expression in Wilson's conviction (Point IV) that "the programme of the world's peace" requires that "adequate guarantees [be] given and taken that national armaments will be reduced to the lowest point consistent with domestic safety."

■ *Item:* The economic underpinnings of international behavior are now receiving increasing emphasis (Sorensen, 1992). The attention departs from realpolitik's view of economic power as of secondary importance, useful primarily because it can be converted into military power (Gowa and Mansfield, 1993). Liberals fault realism for not perceiving economic welfare as a vital autonomous state objective; for not seeing economic power and interdependence as a viable road to peace; and for ignoring the economic consequences of capitalism that modern-world-system (Wallerstein, 1980) and dependency theorists (Packenham, 1992) regard as so important. More specifically, not only are liberals giving renewed consideration to the commercial paths to world order that Immanuel Kant advocated in the eighteenth century (Rosecrance, 1986; Nye, 1988), but they are also giving heightened consideration to the consequences for economic growth and for international peace of market-oriented systems and free trade through the abolition of protective tariffs (Fukuyama, 1992b). These inquiries take implicit cognizance of Wilson's belief (Point III) that peace could be fostered by "the removal, so far as possible, of all economic barriers and the establishment of an equality of trade conditions among all the nations consenting to the peace and associating themselves for its maintenance."

■ *Item:* International organization has been rediscovered. Freed from Cold War paralysis, the United Nations has begun to flex its muscle, and substantial enthusiasm has grown about its capacity (and that of other intergovernmental organizations) to preserve peace (Carlsson, 1992; Gregg, 1993; Rochester, 1993). Note that this is also anathema to the realist dictum that states should "constrain actors who subscribe to supranational organizational principles" (Kaplan, 1957: 23). Realism failed to appreciate the extent to which states could see their interests served by the pooling of their sovereignty and the voluntary integration of their economies—an anomaly in Europe that reduces confidence in some realists' contention that competition will always supersede cooperation in an anarchic system (Kegley, 1991b). But instead, today we witness the continuing expansion of the authority of supranational organizations and hear many who agree with President Clinton (in Brooks, 1992: A12) that "multilateral action holds promise as never before"—that there exists an opportunity "to reinvent the institutions of collective security."

Such proposals, like those during World War I on behalf of a "league to enforce peace" and a "steadfast concert for peace," are today informed by theories and evidence about the demonstrable pacific influence of concerts and other collective security mechanisms (Hendrickson, 1993; Kupchan and Kupchan, 1992; Rosecrance, 1992). Here again, we detect a loud echo of Wilson's contention (Point XIV) that "A general association of nations must be formed under specific covenants for the purpose of affording mutual guarantees of political independence and the territorial integrity of great and small states alike."

■ *Item:* Support for strengthening international law has grown visibly (Moynihan, 1990; Burley, 1992). Despite the realist assertions that international law is merely a tool for the strong to exploit the weak (Morgenthau, 1985), that states use international law propagandistically to get what they can and justify what they have obtained (Wright, 1953), and that a legalistic posture toward policy choice should be avoided (Kennan, 1951), the evidence that most states voluntarily adhere to international law even in circumstances where compliance runs counter to their immediate self-interests (Jones, 1991; Joyner, 1995) contradicts these claims and conclusions. Peace through international law, as well, is consistent with Wilson's program, as captured (Point I) by his plea for "open covenants, openly arrived at" and his emphasis (Point VIII) on the importance of restoring "confidence among the nations in the laws which they have themselves set and determined for . . . their relations with one another."

- *Item:* Neoliberals have recently given great emphasis to bilateral and multilateral diplomacy for the promotion and protection of human rights. They have brought the topic of humanitarian intervention into the spotlight and "out of the cold" (Hoffmann, 1993b; Stedman, 1993). This, too, returns inquiry to a focus on concerns central to idealists in the liberal tradition of Wilson.
- *Item:* Neoliberals have placed morality in statecraft center stage. Although many realists operate from strong normative convictions (see Rosenthal, 1991), in general the classic posture of realists toward ethics is one of indifference, disdain, and disrespect,[5] and is at odds with the normative principle of reciprocity at the heart of international law and ethics (Leng, 1993).

Animating much of the neoliberal normative theorizing evident today is the desire to give "the power of principle in a pluralistic world" (Kegley, 1992b) and the long-repudiated idea of "moral progress" (Ray, 1989; Mueller, 1992) renewed respect, while assigning to David Hume's (1965: 507) eighteenth-century focus on the causal importance of "the spirit of the age" greater explanatory power than most realist theories give to the shifting climate of moral opinion. This effort joins those who criticize realism "for being amoral, and perhaps even immoral, in its elevation of the national interest over other ethical principles" (Lake, 1993: 773).

To Wilson's disappointment, his program did not prescribe principles that fit the times in which he lived. Wilson's ideas and ideals were at odds with the deeper realities of his time. Yet they seem to have transcended his time and place and find relevance in the new post–Cold War realities. "Utopias are not fairytales but rich views of constructive ideas that can gradually come true" (Beer, 1993: 540). It is ironic that, as the world breaks from the grip of the past, Wilson's vision has at last come into fashion, and now, eight decades later, "there are good reasons for examining aspects of the liberal international legacy once again" (Fukuyama, 1992a: 28).

Realism's Abiding Relevance?

However propitious prevailing trends may appear for a revival of liberal theories of world politics, there are good reasons not to rush prematurely into

[5] "The realist approach opens the door to a purely amoral foreign policy" (Gordis, 1984: 36), indeed, "holds international politics to be beyond the concern of morality" (Suganami, 1983: 35). *Raison d'état* overrides a moral concern in the realist account (Sabia, 1991; see also Loriaux, 1992).

acceptance of this recently rediscovered body of theory. As many of the essays in this anthology show, despite international change and cooperation some recent developments do not fit the world Wilson visualized. It is too early to tell if the emerging world will be cast more in the Wilsonian than in the realist images. After all, the Cold War is barely over and we face great uncertainty about which of the countervailing trends unfolding in world affairs will dominate.

The sea changes caused by the end of the Cold War again raise the questions "What is new?" and "What is constant?" (Jervis, 1991–1992: 46). Until it becomes clear which new trends in international relations will continue, it may be premature to judge whether realism's paradigmatic axioms no longer serve its descriptive, explanatory, predictive, and prescriptive purposes well. It is only a possibility, but not a certainty, that the world will develop in a way that will no longer fit with the realist paradigm. It could be that today's global gyrations are a temporary aberration caused by a stray magnet. Since we cannot assuredly know if the theoretical compass will need to be adjusted, the realist–liberal debate will continue.

Rather than accommodating the liberal vision, some trends suggest that realism, not Wilsonian idealism, will remain the most useful guide for the future. In this context, consider that

- The capacity of the great powers to avoid war with each other for the longest period in modern history notwithstanding, the promising indicators of war's obsolescence (Mueller, 1989) do *not* necessarily presage "that traditional considerations of *Machtpolitik* will lose or have lost their primacy; that force, in other words, is finished" (Cohen, 1992: 34). "Realist thought and practice depend on the possibility, if not the threat or actuality, of war. If it recedes far into the background among the developed countries, much new thinking will be required" (Jervis, 1992: 266–67). But we have no assurance, if past history remains a guide to the future, that great-power war *will* recede into oblivion. Should we witness the advent of a new multipolar system, renewed conflict and even war are eventually likely, and realism enriched by neorealism will remain the most compelling framework to assess the dynamics that will surround the great powers' probable interactions (Kegley and Raymond, 1994; Pollins, 1994).
- The collapse of Balkan order raises questions about the "end of history" (Fukuyama, 1989) and the growth of public support for democratic nonviolence. The ethnic clashes in the Balkans are parts of a larger epidemic of localized chaos and nationalistic confrontations. There is a possibility that much of Eurasia will confront similar convulsions and that "the democratic revolutions [since 1989] are being transformed into something ugly and dangerous" (Kober, 1993: 63). The stubborn propensity for differences to divide need not undermine faith in the Wilsonian argument, but it demands that its postulates be treated warily.

- It is unclear in a world in which "fewer than 10 percent of the 186 countries on earth are ethnically homogeneous" (Talbott, 1992: 70) whether Wilsonian self-determination constructively reduces or destructively encourages the militant quest of grievance groups for national independence. "Acceptance of the principle of ethnic homogeneity as a criterion for new statehood," warns Paul C. Warnke (1993: C1), could dangerously encourage "a multitude of mini-states whose whole reason for existence would be common religion or ethnicity." On the principle of self-determination, Wilson may thus yet prove to have been most misguided, for the belligerent pursuit of ethnic-group self-determination has accelerated the disintegrating fragmentation, barbarity, and bloodshed so prevalent today (Moynihan, 1993). It is ironic that internal wars have increased worldwide at the very time that the danger of an apocalyptic war between the great powers has decreased dramatically.
- Despite the European Union's expansion in May 1994 to sixteen members, its hesitation in its drive for political integration, its impotence over management of the Yugoslavian breakup, and its continuing conflicts over economic coordination suggest a slowing of momentum toward European confederation. Many of the ambitious integrative objectives of the Maastricht Accords are likely to remain the subject of intense criticism among various publics, which "find it difficult to identify with a 'Europe' that remains a purely economic and bureaucratic construction and shows few signs of becoming a nation" (Hoffmann, 1993a: 31).
- The superpowers' progress in arms reductions has been offset by the alarming race for sophisticated weapons of mass destruction by emerging regional powers. The nuclear shadow has not dissipated, and there is great danger that the Nuclear Nonproliferation Treaty will not be renewed in 1995 if, as announced, North Korea and other nuclear aspirants pull out of the nonproliferation regime. "The new nuclear menace" (Zuckerman, 1993) portends an abiding future for realism's preoccupation with the consequences of redistributions in global military capabilities.
- Macroeconomic trends point toward free markets *within* regional blocs (including that now established in North America) but continuing, if not intensifying, competitive protectionism *among* them (Thurow, 1992). The free-trade alliance is fragile, and in an economic downslide the recently negotiated agreements to lower barriers to trade could collapse.
- Despite the attractions of liberal tenets, its proponents have often engaged in illiberal diplomatic practices. "Even nineteenth-century Britain and America, portrayed in economic lore as the most virtuously laissez-faire of rising economies, were never free traders" (Mead, 1993: 61). Moreover, liberalism provides no automatic panacea for unprincipled actions, as the illicit military interventions that Wilson himself authorized in Mexico and lamely rationalized as promotive of democracy illustrate. Indeed, the moral crusading and interventionism that have sometimes been followed by outbursts of idealism are, as George F. Kennan (1951) warned, as

dangerous as is the ruthless exercise of power that realpolitik can rational-ize. Accordingly, the sins of liberal states in the international arena should be acknowledged, and faith in liberalism should be suspended until we have a basis for confidence that these states can overcome these excesses and the interventionism they are prone to practice when overcome by "unreflective, overweening moralism" (Krauthammer, 1993: 74; see also Herz, 1950; Stedman, 1993).

RETHINKING THE REALIST–NEOLIBERAL DIVISION

The foregoing countervailing and discouraging developments suggest not the need for the unrestrained re-embrace of realism alongside the repudiation of the new liberal approaches, but for a melding of the two. The post–Cold War setting described by the essays in this book will challenge students and scholars to resume the search (recall Herz, 1951; Wright, 1952) for that hybrid combi-nation of both realist and liberal concepts around which a new paradigm might be organized. The global system's evolving character encourages considering how a reconstructed theory that integrates the most relevant features of both theoretical traditions might be built, or, alternatively, if an altogether different theoretical framework that transcends them needs to be constructed.

In part to facilitate that theory-building exercise and in part to expose the range of theoretical discourse surrounding this task, the essays in *Contro-versies in International Relations Theory: Realism and the Neoliberal Chal-lenge* force examination of today's changing circumstances and the major con-troversies on the central issues in world affairs, in light of both the traditional realist and new liberal perspectives. We turn in Part I to consider more closely the differences between realism and its neoliberal (and other) challengers and the issues about which proponents are presently debating.

REFERENCES

Ashley, Richard K. (1984) "The Poverty of Neorealism," *International Organization* 38 (Spring): 255–86.
Baldwin, David A., ed. (1993) *Neorealism and Neoliberalism: The Contemporary Debate*. New York: Columbia University Press.
Banks, Michael. (1986) "The International Relations Discipline: Asset or Liability for Conflict Resolution?" pp. 5–27 in Edward E. Azar and John W. Burton, eds., *International Conflict Resolution*. Boulder, Colo.: Lynne Rienner.
Beer, Francis A. (1993) Review of Richard Falk, *Explorations at the Edge of Time*, *American Political Science Review* 87 (June): 540.
Brooks, David. (1992) "It's a Bird, It's a Plane, It's Multilateral Man!" *The Wall Street Journal* (September 12): A12.

Bueno de Mesquita, Bruce, and David Lalman. (1992) *War and Reason: Domestic and International Imperatives.* New Haven, Conn.: Yale University Press.

Bueno de Mesquita, Bruce, Randolph M. Siverson, and G. Woller. (1992) "War and the Fate of Regimes: A Comparative Analysis," *American Political Science Review* 86 (March): 638–46.

Burley, Anne-Marie. (1992) "Liberal States: A Zone of Law." Paper presented to the Annual Meeting of the American Political Science Association, September 3–6, Chicago.

Burton, John W., A. J. R. Groom, C. R. Mitchell, and A. V. S. Dereuck. (1974) *The Study of World Society: A London Perspective.* Pittsburgh: The International Studies Association.

Buzan, Barry, Charles Jones, and Richard Little. (1993) *The Logic of Anarchy: Rethinking Neorealism.* New York: Columbia University Press.

Carlsson, Ingvar. (1992) "A New International Order Through the United Nations," *Security Dialogue* 23 (December): 7–11.

Chan, Steve, guest ed. (1993) "Democracy and War: Research and Reflections," *International Interactions* 18 (No. 1): 195–282.

Cohen, Eliot A. (1992) "The Future of Military Power: The Continuing Utility of Force," pp. 33–40 in Charles W. Kegley Jr. and Eugene R. Wittkopf, eds., *The Global Agenda*, 3rd ed. New York: McGraw-Hill.

Cooper, Robert. (1993) "Is There a New World Order?" pp. 8–24 in Seizaburo Sato and Trevor Taylor, eds., *Prospects for World Order.* London: Royal Institute of International Affairs.

Cusack, Thomas C., and Richard J. Stoll. (1992) "The Security Predicament: Assessing the Effectiveness of Realist and Idealist Principles in Interstate Politics." Berlin: International Relations Research Group, Wissehschaftszentrum Berlin für Sozialforschung.

———. (1990) *Exploring Realpolitik.* Boulder, Colo.: Lynne Rienner.

Deutsch, Karl W., et al. (1957) *Political Community and the North Atlantic Area.* Princeton, N.J.: Princeton University Press.

Dixon, William J. (1994) "Democracy and the Peaceful Settlement of International Conflict," *American Political Science Review* 88 (March): 14–32.

Doyle, Michael W. (1991) "The Voice of the People: Political Theorists on the International Implications of Democracy." Paper presented to "The Transformation of the International System and International Relations Theory" Conference, Cornell University, October 18–19.

———. (1986) "Liberalism and World Politics," *American Political Science Review* 80 (December): 1151–69.

Draper, Theodore. (1992) "Who Killed Soviet Communism?" *New York Review of Books* 39 (June 11): 7–14.

Enloe, Cynthia. (1993) *The Morning After: Sexual Politics at the End of the Cold War.* Berkeley: University of California Press.

Falk, Richard A. (1992) *Explorations at the Edge of Time: The Prospects for World Order.* Philadelphia: Temple University Press.

Ferguson, Yale H., and Richard W. Mansbach. (1988) *The Elusive Quest: Theory and International Politics.* Columbia: University of South Carolina Press.

Friedman, Thomas L. (1993) "Friends Like Russia Make Diplomacy a Mess," *New York Times* (March 28): E5.

Fukuyama, Francis. (1992a) "The Beginning of Foreign Policy," *The New Republic* 207 (August 17 and 24): 24–32.

———. (1992b) *The End of History and the Last Man.* New York: Free Press.

———. (1989) "The End of History?" *The National Interest* 16 (Summer): 3–16.

Gaddis, John Lewis. (1990) "Coping with Victory," *The Atlantic Monthly* 265 (May): 49–60.

George, Alexander L. (1993) *Bridging the Gap: Theory and Practice in Foreign Policy.* Washington, D.C.: U.S. Institute of Peace.

Gordis, Robert. (1984) "Religion and International Responsibility," pp. 33–49 in Kenneth W. Thompson, ed., *Moral Dimensions of American Foreign Policy.* New Brunswick, N.J.: Transaction Books.

Gowa, Joanne, and Edward D. Mansfield. (1993) "Power Politics and International Trade," *American Political Science Review* 87 (June): 408–20.

Gregg, Robert W. (1993) *About Face?: The United States and the United Nations.* Boulder, Colo.: Lynne Rienner.

Grieco, Joseph M. (1990) *Cooperation among Nations.* Ithaca, N.Y.: Cornell University Press.

Griffiths, Martin. (1992) "Order and International Society: The Real Realism?" *Review of International Studies* 18 (July): 217–40.

Hammond, Grant T. (1993) *Plowshares into Swords: Arms Races in International Politics, 1840–1991.* Columbia: Univerity of South Carolina Press.

Hendrickson, David C. (1993) "The Ethics of Collective Security," *Ethics and International Affairs* 7: 1–15.

Herz, John. (1951) *Political Realism and Political Idealism.* Chicago: University of Chicago Press.

———. (1950) "Idealist Internationalism and the Security Dilemma," *World Politics* 2 (January): 157–80.

Hitchens, Christopher. (1991) "Why We Are Stuck in the Sand: Realpolitik in the Gulf—A Game Gone Tilt," *Harper's* 282 (January): 70–74, 78.

Hoffmann, Stanley. (1993a) "Goodbye to a United Europe?" *The New York Review of Books* 40 (May 27): 27–32.

———. (1993b) "Out of the Cold: Humanitarian Intervention in the 1990s," *Harvard International Review* 26 (Fall): 8–9, 62.

Holsti, Ole R. (1974) "The Study of International Politics Makes Strange Bedfellows," *American Political Science Review* 68 (March): 217–42.

Hume, David. (1965) *Essential Works.* Edited by Ralph Cohen. New York: Bantam Books.

Huntington, Samuel P. (1991) *The Third Wave: Democratization in the Late Twentieth Century.* Norman: University of Oklahoma Press.

James, Patrick. (1993) "Neorealism as a Research Enterprise: Toward Elaborated Structural Realism," *International Political Science Review* 14 (No. 2): 123 48.

Jensen, Kenneth M., and Elizabeth P. Faulkner, eds. (1992) *Morality and Foreign Policy: Realpolitik Revisited.* Washington, D.C.: U.S. Institute of Peace.

Jervis, Robert. (1992) "A Usable Past for the Future," pp. 257–68 in Michael J. Hogan, ed., *The End of the Cold War: Its Meaning and Implications.* New York: Cambridge University Press.

———. (1991–1992) "The Future of World Politics: Will It Resemble the Past?" *International Security* 16 (Winter): 39–73.

Joffe, Josef. (1992) "Entangled Forever," pp. 33–39 in Charles W. Kegley Jr. and Eugene R. Wittkopf, eds., *The Future of American Foreign Policy*. New York: St. Martin's Press.

Johansen, Robert C. (1991) "Do Preparations for War Increase or Decrease National Security?" pp. 224–44 in Charles W. Kegley Jr., ed., *The Long Postwar Peace*. New York: HarperCollins.

Jones, Dorothy V. (1991) *Code of Peace: Ethics and Security in the World of Warlord States*. Chicago: University of Chicago Press.

Joyner, Christopher C. (1995) "The Reality and Relevance of International Law in the Post–Cold War Era," forthcoming in Charles W. Kegley Jr. and Eugene R. Wittkopf, eds., *The Global Agenda*, 4th ed. New York: McGraw-Hill.

Kaplan, Morton A. (1957) *System and Process in International Politics*. New York: Wiley.

Kauppi, Mark V., and Paul R. Viotti. (1992) *The Global Philosophers: World Politics in Western Thought*. New York: Lexington Books.

Kegley, Charles W., Jr. (1994a) "How Did the Cold War Die? Principles for an Autopsy," *Mershon International Studies Review* 38, Supplement 1 (March): 11–41.

_____. (1994b) "Redirecting Realism," *International Studies Notes* 19 (Winter): 7–9.

_____. (1993) "The Neoidealist Moment in International Studies? Realist Myths and the New International Realities," *International Studies Quarterly* 37 (June): 131–46.

_____. (1992a) "The Long Postwar Peace during the Cold War: Some New Conventional Wisdoms Reconsidered," *Jerusalem Journal of International Relations* 14 (December): 1–18.

_____. (1992b) "The New Global Order: The Power of Principle in a Pluralistic World," *Ethics and International Affairs* 6: 21–42.

_____, ed. (1991a) *The Long Postwar Peace: Contending Explanations and Projections*. New York: HarperCollins.

_____. (1991b) "The New Containment Myth: Realism and the Anomaly of European Integration," *Ethics and International Affairs* 5: 99–114.

_____. (1988) "Neo-Idealism: A Practical Matter," *Ethics and International Affairs* 2: 173–97.

Kegley, Charles W., Jr., and Gregory A. Raymond. (1994) *A Multipolar Peace? Great-Power Politics in the Twenty-first Century*. New York: St. Martin's Press.

_____. (1992) "Must We Fear a Post–Cold War Multipolar System?" *Journal of Conflict Resolution* 36 (September): 573–85.

_____. (1990) *When Trust Breaks Down: Alliance Norms and World Politics*. Columbia: University of South Carolina Press.

Kegley, Charles W., Jr., and Eugene R. Wittkopf. (1995) *World Politics: Trend and Transformation*, 5th ed. New York: St. Martin's Press.

Kennedy, Paul. (1987) *The Rise and Fall of the Great Powers*. New York: Random House.

Kennen, George F. (1951) *American Diplomacy, 1900–1950*. Chicago: University of Chicago Press.

Keohane, Robert O., ed. (1986) *Neorealism and Its Critics*. New York: Columbia University Press.

Keohane, Robert O., and Joseph S. Nye, Jr. (1989) *Power and Interdependence*, 2nd ed. Glenview, Ill.: Scott, Foresman/Little, Brown.

––––––. (1971) *Transnational Relations and World Politics*. Cambridge, Mass.: Harvard University Press.

Knock, Thomas J. (1992) *To End All Wars: Woodrow Wilson and the Quest for a New World Order*. New York: Oxford University Press.

Kober, Stanley. (1993) "Revolutions Gone Bad," *Foreign Policy* 91 (Summer): 63–83.

––––––. (1990) "Idealpolitik," *Foreign Policy* 79 (Summer): 3–24.

Kratochwil, Friedrich. (1993) "The Embarrassment of Changes: Neo-Realism as the Science of *Realpolitik* without Politics," *Review of International Studies* 19 (January): 63–80.

Krauthammer, Charles. (1993) "How the Doves Became Hawks," *Time* (May 17): 74.

––––––. (1986) "The Poverty of Realism," *The New Republic* 194 (February 17): 14–22.

Kuhn, Thomas S. (1962) *The Structure of Scientific Revolutions*. Chicago: University of Chicago Press.

Kupchan, Charles A., and Clifford A. Kupchan. (1992) "A New Concert of Europe," pp. 249–60 in Graham T. Allison and Gregory F. Treverton, eds., *Rethinking America's Security: Beyond Cold War to New World Order*. New York: W. W. Norton.

Lakatos, Imre. (1978) "Falsification and the Methodology of Scientific Research Programmes," pp. 91–196 in Imre Lakatos and Alan Musgrave, eds., *Criticism and the Growth of Knowledge*. London: Cambridge University Press.

Lake, David A. (1993) "Realism," pp. 771–73 in Joel Krieger, ed., *The Oxford Companion to Politics of the World*. New York: Oxford University Press.

––––––. (1992) "Powerful Pacifists: Democratic States and War," *American Political Science Review* 86 (March): 24–37.

Lebow, Richard Ned, and Janice Gross Stein. (1994) *We All Lost the Cold War*. Princeton, N.J.: Princeton University Press.

Leng, Russell J. (1993) *Interstate Crisis Behavior, 1816–1980: Realism vs. Reciprocity*. Cambridge: Cambridge University Press.

Levy, Jack S. (1989) "The Causes of War: A Review of Theories and Evidence," pp. 209–333 in Philip E. Tetlock, Jo L. Husbands, Robert Jervis, Paul C. Stern, and Charles Tilly, eds., *Behavior, Society, and Nuclear War*, Vol. I. New York: Oxford University Press.

Little, David. (1993) "The Recovery of Liberalism," *Ethics and International Affairs* 7: 171–201.

Loriaux, Michael. (1992) "The Realists and Saint Augustine: Skepticism, Psychology, and Moral Action in International Relations Thought," *International Studies Quarterly* 36 (December): 401–20.

Mansbach, Richard W., and John A. Vasquez. (1981) *In Search of Theory: A New Paradigm for Global Politics*. New York: Columbia University Press.

Mead, Walter Russell. (1993) "Why the Deficit Is a Godsend, and Five Other Economic Heresies," *Harper's* 286 (May): 56–63.

Morgan, T. Clifton, and Valerie L. Schwebach. (1992) "Take Two Democracies and Call Me in the Morning: A Prescription for Peace?" *International Interactions* 17 (No. 4): 305–20.

Morgenthau, Hans J. (1985) *Politics among Nations: The Struggle for Power and Peace*, 6th ed. Rev. by Kenneth W. Thompson. New York: Alfred A. Knopf.

Moynihan, Daniel P. (1993) *Pandemonium: Ethnicity in International Relations*. New York: Cambridge University Press.

––––––. (1990) *On the Law of Nations*. Cambridge, Mass.: Harvard University Press.

Mueller, John. (1992) "On the Obsolescence of Major War," pp. 41–52 in Charles W. Kegley Jr. and Eugene R. Wittkopf, eds., *The Global Agenda*, 3rd ed. New York: McGraw-Hill.

———. (1989) *Retreat from Doomsday: The Obsolescence of Major War*. New York: Basic Books.

Nincic, Miroslav. (1992) *Democracy and Foreign Policy: The Fallacy of Political Realism*. New York: Columbia University Press.

Niou, Emerson M. S., and Peter C. Ordeshook. (1993) "Less Filling or Tastes Great? The Realist–Liberal Debate." Paper presented at the Annual Meetings of the Midwest Political Science Association, April 15–17, Chicago.

Niou, Emerson, Peter C. Ordeshook, and Gregory F. Rose. (1991) "Realism versus Neoliberalism: A Formulation," *American Journal of Political Science* 35 (May): 481–511.

Nye, Joseph S., Jr. (1992) "The Misleading Metaphor of Decline," pp. 309–20 in Charles W. Kegley Jr. and Eugene R. Wittkopf, eds., *The Global Agenda*, 3rd ed. New York: McGraw-Hill.

———. (1988) "Neorealism and Neoliberalism," *World Politics* 40 (January): 235–51.

Osgood, Robert E. (1953) *Ideals and Self-Interest in America's Foreign Relations: The Great Transformation of the Twentieth Century*. Chicago: University of Chicago Press.

Packenham, Robert. (1992) *The Dependency Movement: Scholarship and Politics in Dependency Studies*. Cambridge, Mass.: Harvard University Press.

Palan, Ronen P., and Brook M. Blair. (1993) "On the Idealist Origins of the Realist Theory of International Relations," *Review of International Studies* 19 (October): 385–99.

Pollins, Brian. (1994) "Cannons and Capital: The Use of Coercive Diplomacy by Major Powers in the 20th Century," forthcoming in Frank W. Wayman and Paul F. Diehl, eds., *Reconstructing Realpolitik*. Ann Arbor: University of Michigan Press.

Ray, James Lee. (1994) *Democracy and International Conflict: An Evaluation of the Democratic Peace Proposition*. Columbia: University of South Carolina Press.

———. (1989) "The Abolition of Slavery and the End of International War," *International Organization* 43 (Summer): 405–39.

Robbins, James. (1991) "Foreign Policy and Limited Government: Towards a Muscular Libertarianism," *Orbis* 35 (Fall): 533–47.

Rochester, J. Martin. (1993) *Waiting for the Millennium: The United Nations and the Future of World Order*. Columbia: University of South Carolina Press.

Rosecrance, Richard. (1992) "A New Concert of Powers," *Foreign Affairs* 71 (Spring): 64–82.

———. (1986) *The Rise of the Trading State: Commerce and Conquest in the Modern World*. New York: Basic Books.

Rosecrance, Richard, and Arthur A. Stein. (1993) "Beyond Realism: The Study of Grand Strategy," pp. 3–21 in Richard Rosecrance and Arthur A. Stein, eds., *The Domestic Bases of Grand Strategy*. Ithaca, N.Y.: Cornell University Press.

Rosenau, James N. (1990) *Turbulence in World Politics: A Theory of Change and Continuity*. Princeton, N.J.: Princeton University Press.

Rosenberg, Justin. (1990) "What's the Matter with Realism?" *Review of International Studies* 16 (April): 285–303.

Rosenthal, Joel H. (1991) *Righteous Realists: Political Realism, Responsible Power, and American Culture in the Nuclear Age*. Baton Rouge: Louisiana State University Press.

Rothstein, Robert L. (1972) "On the Costs of Realism," *Political Science Quarterly* 87 (September): 347–62.

Russett, Bruce M. (1993) *Grasping the Democratic Peace: Principles for a Post–Cold War World.* Princeton, N.J.: Princeton University Press.

———. (1990) *Controlling the Sword: The Democratic Governance of National Security.* Cambridge, Mass.: Harvard University Press.

Sabia, Daniel R., Jr. (1991) "Reason of State, Machiavelli, and Conceptions of the Relationship between Politics and Morality." Paper presented at the Annual Meeting of the Southern Political Science Association, November 7, Tampa, Florida.

Scholte, Jan Aart. (1993) "From Power Politics to Social Change: An Alternative Focus for International Studies," *Review of International Studies* 19 (January): 3–21.

Shimko, Keith L. (1992) "Realism, Neoliberalism, and American Liberalism," *The Review of Politics* 54 (Spring): 281–301.

Singer, Max, and Aaron Wildavsky. (1993) *The Real World Order.* Chatham, N.J.: Chatham House.

Snyder, Jack. (1991) *Myths of Empire: Domestic Politics and International Ambition.* Ithaca, N.Y.: Cornell University Press.

Sørensen, Georg. (1992) "Kant and Processes of Democratization: Consequences for Neorealist Thought," *Journal of Peace Research* 29 (November): 397–414.

Sorensen, Theodore C. (1992) "Rethinking National Security: Democracy and Economic Independence," pp. 74–84 in Charles W. Kegley Jr. and Eugene R. Wittkopf, eds., *The Future of American Foreign Policy.* New York: St. Martin's Press.

Starr, Harvey. (1992) "Why Don't Democracies Fight One Another? Evaluating the Theory-Findings Feedback Loop," *Jerusalem Journal of International Relations* 14 (December): 41–59.

Stedman, Stephen John. (1993) "The New Interventionists," *Foreign Affairs* 72 (No. 1): 1–16.

Stein, Arthur A. (1991) *Why Nations Cooperate: Circumstance and Choice in International Relations.* Ithaca, N.Y.: Cornell University Press.

Suganami, Hidemi. (1983) "A Normative Enquiry in International Relations: The Case of 'Pacta Sunt Servanda'," *Review of International Studies* 9 (January): 35–54.

Talbott, Strobe. (1992) "The Birth of the Global Nation," *Time* (July 20): 70–71.

Thurow, Lester C. (1992) *Head to Head: Coming Economic Battles among Japan, Europe, and America.* New York: William Morrow.

Tickner, Ann J. (1991) "Hans Morgenthau's Principles of Political Realism: A Feminist Reformulation," pp. 27–40 in Rebecca Grant and Kathleen Newland, eds., *Gender and International Relations.* Bloomington: Indiana University Press.

Tucker, Robert W. (1992) "Brave New World Orders: Woodrow Wilson, George Bush, and the 'Higher Realism'," *The New Republic* 206 (February–May): 24–34.

———. (1992–1993) "Realism and the New Consensus," *The National Interest* 30 (Winter): 33–36.

Vasquez, John A. (1993) *The War Puzzle.* Cambridge: Cambridge University Press.

———. (1983) *The Power of Power Politics: A Critique.* New Brunswick, N.J.: Rutgers University Press.

Wallace, Michael D. (1979) "Arms Races and Escalation," *Journal of Conflict Resolution* 23 (March): 3–16.

Wallerstein, Immanuel. (1980) *The Modern World System II.* New York: Academic Press.

Warnke, Paul C. (1993) "Who Needs NATO?" *The Washington Post* (May 23): C1, C2.

Wayman, Frank, and Paul Diehl, eds. (1994) *Reconstructing Realpolitik.* Ann Arbor: University of Michigan Press.

Wayman, Frank, and Paul Diehl, eds. (1994) *Reconstructing Realpolitik*. Ann Arbor: University of Michigan Press.

Weigel, George. (1993) "The Poverty of Conventional Realism," pp. 67–87 in Michael Cromartie, ed., *Might and Right after the Cold War*. Washington, D.C.: University Press of America.

Wittkopf, Eugene R. (1990) *Faces of Internationalism: Public Opinion and American Foreign Policy*. Durham, N.C.: Duke University Press.

Wright, Quincy. (1953) "The Outlawry of War and the Law of War," *American Journal of International Law* 47 (July): 365–76.

———. (1952) "Realism and Idealism in International Politics," *World Politics* 5 (January): 116–29.

Wriston, Walter B. (1992) *The Twilight of Sovereignty*. New York: Charles Scribner's Sons.

Zakaria, Fareed. (1992–1993) "Is Realism Finished?" *The National Interest* 30 (Winter): 21–32.

Zuckerman, Lord. (1993) "The New Nuclear Menace," *The New York Review of Books* 40 (June 24): 14–19.

The Foundations of International Relations Theory and the Resurrection of the Realist–Liberal Debate

To interpret today's theoretical dialogue, we must first summarize the divergent realist and liberal traditions on which theorists necessarily rely, as well as the neorealist and neoliberal departures that have recently emerged to inform contemporary theorizing. In Part I we will examine these foundations and the discourse that has arisen between realists and their challengers.

The divergent thinking and policy advice of realism defies simple characterization. It is less a single school of thought than an attribute of thought (Berki, 1981; see also Gilpin, 1984; Kauppi and Viotti, 1992; Smith, 1986). Recognizing this, the essays in Part I dissect the rich diversity of ideas and modes of thinking encompassed by the texts and subtexts in the realist and neorealist perspectives that have dominated the theoretical analysis of world affairs since World War II. These essays also explain the commonalities across the types of realism that make it possible to argue that "realism is a school whose members harbour shared assumptions about the primacy of states as international actors, the separation of domestic and international politics, and who describe the latter in terms of anarchy and a concomitant ubiquitous struggle for power and security" (Griffiths, 1992: 217; see also James, 1989).

The first essay, "Theories of International Relations and Foreign Policy: Realism and Its Challengers" by Ole R. Holsti, does so by placing realism and neorealism into context with the other major theoretical orientations in the study of world politics with which they are today contending, and with which they share much in common and to which they are in discourse. As such, Holsti's essay is a primer on the current state of international relations theory, serving as an overview and introduction to the proliferation of approaches in recent years.

Holsti first revisits the key assumptions of classical and modern realism and its neorealist extension as a way of not only summarizing their theoretical orientation but also as a way of identifying their limitations. His chapter also shows how prevailing macro trends in the international system have strengthened confidence in liberal theories while concomitantly reducing confidence in the realist accounts. Specifically, realism's contribution has been to provide a framework to explain World War II and the Cold War, but Holsti laments that its focus on the nation-state, war, security, and survival fails to illuminate the degree to which welfare, modernization, the environment, and the threats arising from a multiplicity of problems beyond military security are equally important in world affairs. The new variants of liberal theories, in contrast, make these issues the center of their attention, for, as Holsti's chapter explains in detail,

> Liberalism shares with realism the stress on explaining the behavior of separate and typically self-interested units of action, but from the standpoint of international relations, there are three critical differences between these schools of thought. First, liberalism focuses not merely on states but on privately organized social groups and firms. The transnational as well as domestic activities of these groups and firms are important for liberal analysts, not in isolation from the actions of states but in conjunction with them. Second, in contrast to realism, liberalism does not emphasize the significance of military force, but rather seeks to discover ways in which separate actors, with distinct interests, can organize themselves to promote economic efficiency and avoid destructive physical conflict, without renouncing either the economic or political freedoms that liberals hold dear. Finally, liberalism believes in at least the possibility of cumulative progress, whereas realism assumes that history is not progressive. (Keohane, 1992a: 174)

Given these differences, Holsti suggests that they render liberalism an increasingly useful model of international relations. As he observes,

> The liberal models have several important virtues. They recognize that international behavior and outcomes arise from a multiplicity of motives, not merely security, at least if security is defined solely in military or strategic terms. They also alert us to the fact that important international processes and conditions originate not only in the actions of nation-states but also in the aggregated behavior of other actors. These models not only enable the analyst to deal with a broader agenda of critical issues but, more importantly, they force one to contemplate a much richer menu of demands, processes, and outcomes than would be derived from power-centered realist models. Stated differently, liberal theories are more sensitive to the possibility that politics of trade, currency, immigration, health, the environment, and the like may significantly and systematically differ from those typically associated with security issues.

Holsti's overview does not stop at this provocative thesis, however. To provide a more complete account of the diverse challenges to the grip of realism (and Marxist/World System/Dependency models) on the theoretical study of world politics, Holsti next broadens the picture by discussing the premises of three "decision-making" approaches (bureaucratic politics, group dynamics, and individual decision making), all of which share a skepticism about the adequacy of realism and other accounts that neglect the impact of political processes *within* the units that comprise the system. As he shows, because they lead to different conclusions, two different dependent variables need to be distinguished—foreign policy decisions by states and the outcomes of relations between states. These counterpoints to realism, Holsti explains, stem from the liberal tradition's stress on the potency of domestic pressures as influences on foreign policy decisions and, Holsti argues, represent in their own way another challenge to the utility of the realist and neorealist models. This survey thus highlights the importance of different levels of analysis in differing approaches.

In a creative concluding assessment, Holsti offers some speculations about the impact of recent events on the relative advantages and disadvantages of these contending theoretical positions, which underscore the extent to which "contemporary controversies are extensions of old disputes" (Keohane, 1992b: 1112). Holsti cautiously counsels against the temptation to assume that presently unfolding trends are permanent and, in so arguing, suggests the reasons why "the venerable debate between realists and liberals" will continue. Still, in demonstrating why "liberal theories have generally fared better, at least for explaining relations among the industrial democracies," Holsti's critical summary of theories of international relations and foreign policy and the factors that shape their popularity indicates that the challenge to realism is likely to expand and intensify.

The next chapter, by Kenneth N. Waltz, expands on Holsti's introduction by developing in greater detail the *neorealist* theory Waltz pioneered that continues to command a wide following. In "Realist Thought and Neorealist Theory," Waltz shows why the need existed for a systematic *theory* of international politics that extended beyond the preexisting inconsistent collection of classical realist *thoughts* and why his innovative neorealist departure in theory building (Waltz, 1979) was warranted.

Realists such as Raymond Aron and Hans Morgenthau failed to go beyond conjectural and impressionistic argumentation, Waltz maintains, in part because their exaggeration of the role of accidental and unexpected events deterred them from searching for a theory that could specify patterns in the relative importance of causal factors. To rectify the inconsistencies pervading realist thinking, Waltz demonstrates that it *is* possible to do what traditional realists "believed to be impossible for students of international politics to accomplish": Construct a nomothetic theory that deals in regularities and repetitions and that traces the important linkages which connect them. "Neorealism's response [was] that, while difficulties abound, some that seem most daunting lie in misapprehensions about theory."

Clarifying the requirements of theory, Waltz's new realism—in contrast to the old—begins by proposing a solution to the problem of distinguishing between internal and external factors in international politics. Arguing that structural and unit levels are at once distinct and connected, Waltz avers how a neorealist theory that makes their relationships salient can enhance the predictive power of classical realism while also capturing the complexity that surrounds entangled causal relationships among variables in world politics, so as to alter the appearance of the whole field of inquiry.

Neorealism's revision of classical realism also entails a conceptualization of international politics as a *system* whose structure is defined by the anarchy and the distribution of capabilities across the units within it. Reconceiving "the causal link between interacting units and international outcomes," the new realism posits that variations in structures influence the subsequent inter-actions of the units and the outcomes they produce. In addition, neorealism explains power without reference to human nature or volition, simply (that is, parsimoniously) as the consequence of the changes in the ways the capabil-ities of states are distributed. Finally, neorealist theories break from realism and confront the "agent-structure" problem (Dessler, 1989) by operating from the assumption that the system's structure greatly affects the behavior of the states within it because of the powerful constraints it places upon them. Neorealism thereby proposes a macrotheoretical solution to the micro account of realism that focuses on unit- and individual-level explanations.

The departure is significant, for the new realism demonstrates how the barriers of the "ideology" (Rosenberg, 1990: 296) of the old realism to the construction of a theory of international politics might be overcome and suggests why that theory might advance understanding of both the changes and continuities that occur in international politics. As a consequence, neore-alism, like the realism that preceded it, represents a major school of thought to which neoliberal and other challengers must respond in their quest for a theory that can better account for the emerging international realities.

The Holsti and Waltz overviews of the realist and neorealist foundations of contemporary international relations theory set the stage for consideration of the liberal tradition and the wave of recent rediscovery that has led to its resurrection. In "Liberalism and World Politics Revisited," Michael W. Doyle revises and updates his well-received account (Doyle, 1986) that played such a catalytic part in expanding the theoretical discourse beyond the confines of realist thought and neorealist theory.

Summarizing how real-world events and empirical research have symbi-otically strengthened confidence in liberal theories of international relations, Doyle takes as his test case the traditional liberal claim that democratic gov-ernments exercise "restraint" and "peaceful intentions" in their foreign policy conduct. Doyle first addresses and discards two orientations that rest on fundamentally different premises: Joseph Schumpeter's "liberal pacifism," which describes capitalism and democracy as forces for peace because human interests are served by peaceful trade, and Niccoló Machiavelli's contrasting "liberal imperialism," which concludes that, because citizens act primarily from their desire to rule and their fear of being dominated, republican governments are prone to wage war abroad.

This contradiction between liberal pacifism and liberal imperialism might be expected to erode confidence in liberal prescriptions. But Doyle argues that rejection is unwarranted, and, the sometimes fragility of democratic governance and pacificity (Fuller, 1991) notwithstanding, "liberalism does leave a coherent legacy on foreign affairs." The basis resides in the belief expressed by Immanuel Kant and other liberal republicans that "liberal states are different" because "they are indeed peaceful." To Kant's vision, citizens are capable in a democracy of "appreciating the moral equality of all individuals and of treating other individuals as ends rather than as means," and democracies practice peaceful relations with other democracies because they "exercise democratic caution and are capable of appreciating the international rights of foreign republics." However, they are "prone to make war" with nonrepublics. To Doyle, therefore, liberalism leaves two legacies: First, liberal democracies have demonstrated over the centuries a growing capacity to establish a separate peace among themselves. Second, liberal states are also prone, as Kant feared, to find liberal justifications for waging wars against nonliberal states.

Doyle concludes by exploring why the opportunities and constraints that flow from these empirical regularities indicate that liberal theories are relevant to contemporary world politics. He argues that the differences among the three liberal philosophies he reviews (liberal pacifism, liberal imperialism, and Kant's liberal internationalism) are not arbitrary. Because they are rooted in differing conceptions of the citizen and the state, they lead to conclusions that allow an "important analytic theory of international politics" to result by helping us "to understand the interactive nature of international relations" and to overcome the inability of realist and marxist theories to explain "the separate peace maintained by more than 150 years among states sharing one particular form of government—liberal principles and governance." Hence, Doyle shows why "Kant's argument for the combined effect of structures, norms, and interests warrants our attention" and can serve as the springboard for the revival of liberal interpretations of world affairs. In so doing, he also shows why, as Robert O. Keohane (1992a: 166) put it, "liberalism—or at any rate, a certain strand of liberalism—is more sophisticated than many of its critics have alleged."

In "Liberal International Theory: Common Threads, Divergent Strands," Mark W. Zacher and Richard A. Matthew stretch this profile still further by differentiating among the myriad characteristics of liberal theories in order to isolate those dimensions that are shared from those that depart in different directions. The result is a map of the diverse schools of thought within the rich liberal tradition, in which the roots and core principles of each strand are summarized and analyzed. The synthesis and classifications place into context, in broad strokes, the entire theoretical edifice on which liberal international theory rests, with its component parts broken by a typology that enables the commonality and diversity of the liberal tradition to be appreciated and rendered amenable to closer inspection.

Consider more closely the comprehensive survey of liberal international theory and its literature that Zacher and Matthew provide and the classification scheme they use to summarize it. Their approach first compares liberal theories with the realist and marxist theories with which they are conventionally placed in contention and shows how many of their key features overlap in complicated ways. Next, Zacher and Matthew focus on the historical and recent evolution of liberal international theory, in order to suggest avenues for future research and to evaluate the potential of liberal and neoliberal challengers to realism (and marxism) for guiding international relations scholarship.

To better enable the reader "to judge whether liberal international theory offers a viable alternative to the dominant variants of realism and marxism," Zacher and Matthew then explore liberalism's central theses and build a convincing argument that its tenets about the importance of and prospects for international peace and cooperation can be profitably viewed as independent "aspects of the process of modernization." Specifically, they show that the key components of the process are connected by liberal theory's common orientation toward liberal democracy, commercial and military interdependence, cognitive progress, international sociological integration, and international institutions. But there is more. Beyond this identification of liberal and neoliberal theory's common threads, Zacher and Matthew reveal how they spread in five divergent strands: (1) republican liberalism, (2) interdependence liberalism, (3) cognitive liberalism, (4) sociological liberalism, and (5) institutional liberalism. This typology and overview thus highlight the different colorations of a body of theory that ultimately converge on a concern for "enhancing the security, prosperity, and human rights of individuals. While analyses often focus on state interests and interstate interactions, the lens through which they are viewed by liberals is how they affect the material and moral conditions of humans."

This conceptualization of liberal and neoliberal theories serves this book's pedagogical purposes well. It organizes a rich and eclectic body of evolving theory systematically, so the core elements can be located across the disparate ideas associated with it. Indeed, the conceptualization and summary of liberal international theories provide a categorization through which the different components separately examined in subsequent chapters can be placed. This allows their connections to liberalism's diverse background to be recognized and enables other neoliberal approaches, such as feminist theory's critique of realism (Enloe, 1993; Tickner, 1992), to be evaluated. The chapter also services this book's research and theoretical aim by confronting head-on the vital question: Can liberal international theory stand on its own as a comprehensive theoretical framework, or must it be integrated with other theories to develop such a framework?

Their answer is controversial, but constructive. Maintaining that it is possible that "international relations scholars have not recognized what is the central theoretical paradigm in their midst," Zacher and Matthew submit that liberalism can stand on its own because it provides the key to understanding what is central—that "world politics is about evolution" and that scholars "should be fascinated about all dimensions of that evolution." Hence, they conclude,

> If liberals integrate insights from other theories into their analyses, their theoretical positions do not become less liberal as long as they adhere to the central assumptions of liberal international theory. At the core what makes international relations scholars liberals is that they think that international politics is about the changing interests of the inhabitants of states (or other entities) and that the underlying forces of change are creating opportunities for increased cooperation and a greater realization of peace, welfare, and justice.

Clearly, this is a powerful argument on behalf of the advantages for a neoliberal challenge to the realist paradigm.

To enable the reader to better evaluate that argument, *Controversies in International Relations Theory* concludes Part I's introduction to contemporary theorizing by providing an essay that describes the axes on which the debate between realists and the new liberal theorists presently revolves and prescribes a controversial path toward which future theoretical activity should be directed—the retention of realism. In "Anarchy and the Limits of Cooperation: A Realist Critique of the Newest Liberal Institutionalism," Joseph M. Grieco mounts a realist response to the neoliberal challenge. Abridging and revising his well-known essay, Grieco challenges neoliberalism's thesis that states "can work together and can do so especially with the assistance of international institutions." This critique is necessary, Grieco contends, because "if neoliberal institutionalists are correct, they they have dealt realism a major blow while providing the intellectual justification for treating their own approach, and the tradition from which it emerges, as the most effective for understanding world politics."

To Grieco, this challenge is not as threatening as neoliberals would like to assume because the new liberalism fails to take sufficient account of the extent to which international anarchy constrains the willingness of states to cooperate; therefore neoliberal institutionalism's optimism about international cooperation is likely to be proven wrong.

To build his case why this conclusion is warranted, Grieco provides a penetrating summary of the major propositions advanced by liberalism, neoliberal institutionalism, and realism; the assumptions that propel their respective inquiries; and the literature that informs their conclusions. These comparisons pinpoint the differences among the perspectives (see Box 2.1 for another contrast). Grieco summarizes the key difference by concluding that whereas "neoliberals begin with assertions of acceptance of several key realist propositions," the logic of their argument ends "with a rejection of realism" and its stress upon the inhibiting "effects of anarchy on the willingness of states to cooperate."

BOX 2.1
Neoliberalism and Neorealism: Contrasting the Terms of the Contemporary Debate

Six focal points . . . characterize the current debate between neoliberalism and neorealism.

- *The Nature and Consequences of Anarchy.* Although no one denies that the international system is anarchical in some sense, there is disagreement as to what this means and why it matters. . . .
- *International Cooperation.* Although both sides agree that international cooperation is possible, they differ as to the ease and likelihood of its occurrence. . . .
- *Relative versus Absolute Gains.* Although it would be misleading to characterize one side as concerned with relative gains and the other as concerned only with absolute gains, the neoliberals have stressed the absolute gains [and common interests] from international cooperation, while the neorealists have emphasized relative gains [by assuming that actors will ask, "Who will gain more?"].
- *Priority of State Goals.* Neoliberals and neorealists agree that both national security and economic welfare are important, but they differ in relative emphasis on these goals [with neoliberals stressing the latter and neorealists the former].
- *Intentions versus Capabilities.* Contemporary neorealists . . . emphasize capabilities more than intentions [whereas neoliberals emphasize] intentions, interests, and information [instead of] the distribution of capabilities. . . .
- *Institutions and Regimes.* Both neorealists and neoliberals recognize the plethora of international regimes and institutions that have emerged since 1945. They differ, however, with respect to the significance of such arrangements. . . .

— David A. Baldwin (1993: 4–8)

To Grieco's reasoning, this profound divergence leads to unfortunate consequences because "neoliberal institutionalism understates the range of uncertainties and risks states believe they must overcome to cooperate with others." Hence, because realism specifies a wider range of systemic-level constraints on cooperation than does neoliberalism, Grieco concludes that realism is likely to offer the most compelling explanation of when international cooperation can occur.

Still, Grieco acknowledges that the international political economy remains a neoliberalist preserve because it provides a cogent explanation of the maintenance of cooperative economic relationships among the advanced democracies. This subset of states accordingly provides an opportunity to design "crucial experiments" to test the neoliberal theory that these states have the broadest range of common political, military, and economic interests and the greatest prospect of realizing absolute gains through joint action. But holding to his thesis, Grieco predicts that "these tests are likely to demonstrate that realism offers the most effective understanding of the problem of international cooperation" even in this domain, while acknowledging that this kind of empirical confirmation "would certainly not mark the end of the liberal institutionalist challenge to realism."

Grieco's nuanced explication of why the newest liberal theorizing fails to transcend the central barriers inherent in its posture thus joins other realists and neorealists (Waltz, 1979; Zakaria, 1992–1993) in pessimistically doubting the capacity for international relations to transcend the "politics as usual" that has governed it throughout most recorded history. As such, his essay, and the others in Part I, demonstrate that the current controversies in international relations theory are extensions of debates whose origins are rooted in centuries past and that they are unlikely to be easily resolved. The community effort by scholars to discover a theory that can account for the multidimensional dynamics of international behavior will continue. Beyond expanding our awareness of the roots of contemporary controversies, these essays also bring to the surface the cleavages that crisscross the new realist and liberal efforts to comprehend theoretically the evolving pattern of international relations.

REFERENCES

Baldwin, David A. (1993) "Neoliberalism, Neorealism, and World Politics," pp. 3–25 in David A. Baldwin, ed., Neorealism and Neoliberalism. New York: Columbia University Press.

Berki, R. N. (1981) On Political Realism. London: J. M. Dent and Sons.

Dessler, David. (1989) "What's at Stake in the Agent-Structure Debate?" International Organization 43 (Summer): 441–73.

Doyle, Michael W. (1986) "Liberalism and World Politics," American Political Science Review 80 (December): 1151–69.

Enloe, Cynthia. (1993) The Morning After: Sexual Politics at the End of the Cold War. Berkeley: University of California Press.

Fuller, Graham E. (1991) The Democracy Trap: Perils of the Post–Cold War World. New York: Dutton.

Gilpin, Robert. (1984) "The Richness of the Tradition of Political Realism," International Organization 38 (Spring): 287–304.

Griffiths, Martin. (1992) "Order and International Society: The Real Realism?" Review of International Studies 18 (July): 217–40.

James, Alan. (1989) "The Realism of Realism: The State in the Study of International Relations," Review of International Studies 15 (July): 215–29.

Kauppi, Mark V., and Paul R. Viotti. (1992) The Global Philosophers: World Politics in Western Thought. New York: Lexington Books.

Keohane, Robert O. (1992a) "International Liberalism Reconsidered," pp. 165–94 in John Dunn, ed., The Economic Limits to Modern Politics. Cambridge: Cambridge University Press.

————. (1992b) Review of Martin Wight, *International Theory: The Three Traditions*, *American Political Science Review* 86 (December): 1112–13.

Rosenberg, Justin. (1990) "What's the Matter with Realism?" *Review of International Studies* 16 (April): 285–303.

Smith, Michael Joseph. (1986) *Realist Thought from Weber to Kissinger*. Baton Rouge: Louisiana State University Press.

Tickner, J. Ann. (1992) *Gender in International Relations: Feminist Perspectives on Achieving Global Security*. New York: Columbia University Press.

Waltz, Kenneth N. (1979) *Theory of International Politics*. Reading, Mass.: Addison-Wesley.

Zakaria, Fareed. (1992–1993) "Is Realism Finished?" *The National Interest* 30 (Winter): 21–32.

CHAPTER 2

Theories of International Relations and Foreign Policy: Realism and Its Challengers*

OLE R. HOLSTI

Scholars and statesmen, philosophers and reformers have long debated the question of how best to understand relations among nations, but discussions among proponents of alternative theories have always gained intensity in times of profound turmoil and change. In our own century, the cataclysm of World War I resurfaced and intensified the dialogue between such liberals as Woodrow Wilson, who sought to create a new world order anchored in the League of Nations, and realists, exemplified by Georges Clemenceau, who sought to use more traditional means to assure their nations' security. World War II renewed that debate, but the events leading up to that conflict and the Cold War that emerged almost immediately after the guns had stopped firing in 1945 seemed to provide ample evidence to tip the balance strongly in favor of the realist vision of international relations.

In the meanwhile, the growth of Soviet power, combined with the disintegration of the great colonial empires that gave rise to the emergence of some one hundred newly independent nations, gave prominence to still another perspective on world affairs, most variants of which drew to some extent on the writings of Marx and Lenin. More recent events, including the disintegration of the Soviet Union, the end of the Cold War, the reemergence of inter- and intranational ethnic conflicts that had been suppressed during the Cold War, the Persian Gulf War, the continuing economic integration of

* This chapter draws heavily on my essay "Models of International Relations and Foreign Policy," *Diplomatic History* (Winter, 1989). Alexander L. George, Joseph Grieco, Michael J. Hogan, Timothy Lomperis, Roy Melbourne, James N. Rosenau, and Andrew M. Scott kindly provided very helpful comments and suggestions on early drafts of that essay.

Europe, and the declining international economic position of the United States, have stimulated new debates (including this book) on theories of international relations and foreign policy. This chapter summarizes three prominent schools of thought that place primary explanatory emphasis on features of the international system. The following section discusses several "decision-making" approaches, all of which share a skepticism about the adequacy of theories that focus on the structure of the international system while neglecting political processes within units that comprise the system. A speculative conclusion assesses the impact of recent events on the several theoretical positions.

Three limitations should be stated at the outset. Each of the systemic and decision-making approaches described below is a composite of several models; limitations of space have made it necessary to focus on the common denominators rather than on subtle differences among them. This discussion will also avoid purely methodological issues and debates, for example, what Stanley Hoffmann (1977: 54) calls "the battle of the literates versus the numerates." Finally, "formal" or mathematical approaches of international relations (Richardson, 1960a, 1960b; Rapoport, 1957; Bueno de Mesquita, 1981, 1985; Niou et al., 1989) are neglected here, as are recent "postmodern" approaches (P. Rosenau, 1990).

Because "classical realism" is the most venerable and persisting model of international relations, it provides a good starting point and base line for comparison with competing models. Robert Gilpin (1981) may have been engaging in hyperbole when he questioned whether our understanding of international relations has advanced significantly since Thucydides, but one must acknowledge that the latter's analysis of the Peloponnesian War includes concepts that are not foreign to contemporary students of balance-of-power politics. There have always been Americans such as Alexander Hamilton who viewed international relations from a realist perspective, but its contemporary intellectual roots are largely European. Three important figures probably had the greatest impact on American scholarship: the historian E. H. Carr (1939), the geographer Nicholas Spykman (1942), and the political theorist Hans J. Morgenthau (1973). Other Europeans who have contributed significantly to realist thought include John Herz (1959), Raymond Aron (1966), Hedley Bull (1977), and Martin Wight (1973), while notable Americans of this school include scholars Arnold Wolfers (1962) and Norman Graebner (1984), as well as diplomat George F. Kennan (1951), journalist Walter Lippmann (1943), and theologian Reinhold Niebuhr (1945).

Although realists do not constitute a homogeneous school—any more than do any of the others discussed in this essay—most of them share at least five core premises about international relations. To begin with, they consider the central questions to be the causes of war and the conditions of peace. They also regard the structure of the system as a necessary if not always sufficient explanation for many aspects of international relations. According to classical realists, "structural anarchy," or the absence of a central authority to settle disputes, is the essential feature of the contemporary system. It gives rise to the "security dilemma": In a self-help system, one nation's search for security often leaves its current and potential adversaries insecure; any nation that strives for absolute security leaves all others in the system absolutely insecure; and it can provide a powerful incentive for arms races and other types of hostile interactions. Consequently, the question of *relative* capabilities is a crucial factor. Efforts to deal with this central element of the international system constitute the driving force behind the relations of units within the system; those that fail to cope will not survive. Thus, unlike "idealists" or "liberals," classical realists view conflict as a natural state of affairs rather than a consequence that can be attributed to historical circumstances, evil leaders, flawed sociopolitical systems, or inadequate international understanding and education.

A third premise that unites classical realists is their focus on geographically based groups as the central actors in the international system. During other periods the primary entities may have been city-states or empires, but at least since the Treaties of Westphalia (1648), nation-states have been the dominant units.

Classical realists also agree that state behavior is rational. The assumption behind this fourth premise is that states are guided by the logic of the "national interest," usually defined in terms of survival, security, power, and relative capabilities. To Morgenthau (1973: 5, 3), for example, "rational foreign policy minimizes risks and maximizes benefits." Although the national interest may vary according to specific circumstances, the similarity of motives among nations permits the analyst to reconstruct the logic of policymakers in their pursuit of national interests—what Morgenthau called the "rational hypothesis"—and to avoid the fallacies of "concern with motives and concern with ideological preferences."

Finally, the nation-state can also be conceptualized as a unitary actor. Because the central problems for states are starkly defined by the nature of the international system, their actions are primarily a response to external rather than domestic political forces. At best, the latter provide very weak explanations for external policy. According to Stephen Krasner (1978: 33), for example, the state "can be treated as an autonomous actor pursuing goals associated with power and the general interest of the society." However, classical realists sometimes use domestic politics to explain deviations from rational policies.

Realism has been the dominant model of international relations during recent decades, perhaps in part because it seemed to provide a useful framework for understanding World War II and the Cold War. Nevertheless, the classical versions articulated by Morgenthau and others have received a good deal of critical scrutiny. The critics have included scholars who accept the basic premises of realism but who found that in at least four important respects these theories lacked sufficient precision and rigor.

CRITIQUES OF CLASSICAL REALISM

Classical realism has usually been grounded in a pessimistic theory of human nature, either a theological version (e.g., St. Augustine and Reinhold Niebuhr) or a secular one (e.g., Machiavelli, Hobbes, and Morgenthau). Egoism and self-interested behavior are not limited to a few evil or misguided leaders, as the idealists would have it, but are basic to *homo politicus* and thus are at the core of a realist theory. But because human nature, if it means anything, is a constant rather than a variable, it is an unsatisfactory explanation for the full range of international relations. If human nature explains war and conflict, what accounts for peace and cooperation? In order to avoid this problem, most modern realists have turned their attention from human nature to the structure of the international system to explain state behavior. In addition, critics have noted a lack of precision and even contradictions in the way classical realists use such concepts as "power," "national interest," and "balance of power" (Claude, 1962; Rosenau, 1968; George and Keohane, 1980; Haas, 1953; and Zinnes, 1967). They also see possible contradictions between the central descriptive and prescriptive elements of classical realism. On the one hand, nations and their leaders "think and act in terms of interests defined as power," but, on the other, statesmen are urged to exercise prudence and self-restraint, as well as to recognize the legitimate national interests of other nations (Morgenthau, 1973: 5). Obviously, then, power plays a central role in classical realism. But the correlation between the relative power balance and political outcomes is often less than compelling, suggesting the need to enrich analyses with other variables. Moreover, the distinction between "power as capabilities" and "usable options" is especially important in the nuclear age.

While classical realists have typically looked to history, philosophy, and political science for insights and evidence, the search for greater precision has led many modern realists to look elsewhere for appropriate models, analogies, metaphors, and insights. The discipline of choice is often economics, from which modern realists have borrowed such tools and concepts as rational choice, expected utility, theories of firms and markets, bargaining theory, and game theory. Contrary to the assertion of some critics (Ashley, 1984), however, modern realists *share* rather than reject the core premises of their classical predecessors.

The quest for precision has yielded a rich harvest of theories and models, and a somewhat less bountiful crop of supporting empirical applications. Drawing in part on game theory, Morton Kaplan described several types of international systems—for example, balance of power, loose bipolar, tight bipolar, universal, hierarchical, and a unit-veto system in which any action requires the unanimous approval of all its members. He then outlined the essential rules that constitute these systems. For example, the rules for a balance of power system are:

(1) Increase capabilities, but negotiate rather than fight. (2) Fight rather than fail to increase capabilities. (3) Stop fighting rather than eliminate an essential actor. (4) Oppose any coalition or single actor that tends to assume a position of predominance within the system. (5) Constrain actors who subscribe to supranational organizational principles. (6) Permit defeated or constrained essential actors to reenter the system." (Kaplan, 1957: 23)

Richard Rosecrance (1963, 1966), J. David Singer (1963), Karl Deutsch and Singer (1964), Bruce Russett (1963), and many others (Waltz, 1964; Scott, 1967), although not necessarily realists, also have developed models that seek to understand international relations by virtue of system-level explanations. Andrew M. Scott's (1967) survey of the literature, which yielded a catalog of propositions about the international system, also illustrates the quest for greater precision in systemic models.

Kenneth Waltz's *Theory of International Politics* (1979), the most prominent effort to develop a rigorous and parsimonious model of "modern" or "structural" realism, has tended to define the terms of recent theoretical debates. It follows and builds upon another enormously influential book in which Waltz (1959) developed the Rousseauian position that a theory of war must include the system level (the "third image") and not just first (theories of human nature) or second (state attributes) images. Why war? Because there is nothing in the system to prevent it. *Theory of International Politics* is grounded in analogies from microeconomics: International politics and foreign policy are analogous to markets and firms. Oligopoly theory is used to illuminate the dynamics of interdependent choice in a self-help anarchical system. Waltz explicitly limits his attention to a structural theory of international systems, eschewing the task of linking it to a theory of foreign policy. Indeed, he doubts that the two can be joined in a single theory and is highly critical of many system-level analysts, including Morton Kaplan, Stanley Hoffmann, Richard Rosecrance, Karl Deutsch and J. David Singer, and others, charging them with various errors, including "reductionism"; that is, defining the system in terms of the attributes or interactions of the units.

In order to avoid reductionism and to gain rigor and parsimony, Waltz (1979: 82–101) erects his theory on the foundations of three core propositions that define the structure of the international system. The first concentrates on the principles by which the system is ordered. The contemporary system is anarchic and decentralized rather than hierarchical; although differing in many respects, each unit (state) is formally equal. Because Waltz strives for a universal theory that is not limited to any era, he uses the term "unit" to refer to the constituent members of the system; in the contemporary system these are states, but in order to reflect Waltz's intent more faithfully, the term "unit" is used here. A second defining proposition is the character of the units. An anarchic system is composed of similar sovereign units and therefore the functions that they perform are also similar rather than different; for example, all have the task of providing for their own security. In contrast, a hierarchical system would be characterized by some type of division of labor, as is the case in domestic politics. Finally, there is the distribution of capabilities among units in the system. Although capabilities are a unit-level attribute, the distribution of capabilities is a system-level concept.

A change in any of these elements constitutes a change in system structure. The first element of structure as defined by Waltz is a quasi-constant because the ordering principle rarely changes, and the second element drops out of the analysis because the functions of units are similar as long as the system remains anarchic. Thus, the last of the three attributes, the distribution of capabilities, plays the central role in Waltz's model.

Waltz (1970, 1981) uses his theory to deduce the central characteristics of international relations. These include some nonobvious propositions about the contemporary international system. For example, with respect to system stability (defined as maintenance of its anarchic character and no consequential variation in the number of major actors) he concludes that (1) because the bipolar system reduces uncertainty, it is more stable than alternative structures; (2) interdependence has declined rather than increased during the twentieth century, a tendency that has actually contributed to stability; and (3) the proliferation of nuclear weapons may contribute to rather than erode system stability.

Unlike some system-level models, Waltz's effort to bring rigor and parsimony to realism has stimulated a good deal of further research, but it has not escaped controversy and criticism (Grieco, 1990; Walt, 1987; Keohane, 1986). Leaving aside highly charged polemics—for example, that Waltz and his supporters are guilty of engaging in a "totalitarian project of global proportions" (Ashley, 1984: 228)—most of the vigorous debate has centered on four alleged deficiencies relating to interests and preferences, system change, misallocation of variables between the system and unit levels, and an ability to explain outcomes in generalities only.

Specifically, a spare structural approach suffers from an inability to identify adequately the nature and sources of interests and preferences because these are unlikely to derive solely from the structure of the system. Ideology or domestic considerations may often be at least as important. Consequently, the model is also unable to specify how interests and preferences may change. The three defining characteristics of system structure are too general, moreover, and thus they are not sufficiently sensitive to specify the sources and dynamics of system change. The critics buttress their claim that the model is too static by pointing to Waltz's assertion that there has been only a single structural change in the international system during the past three centuries.

Another drawback is the restrictive definition of system properties, which leads Waltz to misplace, and therefore neglect, elements of international relations that properly belong at the system level. Critics have focused on his treatment of the destructiveness of nuclear weapons and interdependence. Waltz labels these as unit-level properties, whereas some of his critics assert that they are in fact attributes of the system.

Finally, the distribution of capabilities explains outcomes in international affairs only in the most general way, falling short of answering the questions that are of central interest to many analysts. For example, the distribution of power at the end of World War II would have enabled one to predict the rivalry that emerged between the United States and the Soviet Union (as de Tocqueville did more than a century earlier), but it would have been inadequate for explaining the pattern of relations between these two nations—the Cold War rather than withdrawal into isolationism by either or both, a division of the world into spheres of influence, or World War III. In order to do so, it is necessary to explore political processes *within* states—at minimum within the United States and the USSR—as well as *between* them.

Robert Gilpin (1981: 10–11) shares with Waltz the core assumptions of modern realism, but his study of *War and Change in World Politics* also attempts to cope with some of the criticism leveled at Waltz's theory by focusing on the dynamics of system change. Drawing upon both economic and sociological theory, his model is based on five core propositions. The first is that the international system is stable—in a state of equilibrium—if no state believes that it is profitable to attempt to change it. Secondly, a state will attempt to change the status quo of the international system if the expected benefits outweigh the costs; that is, if there is an expected net gain for the revisionist state. Related to this is the proposition that a state will seek change through territorial, political, and economic expansion until the marginal costs of further change equal or exceed the marginal benefits. Moreover, when an equilibrium between the costs and benefits of further change and expansion is reached, the economic costs of maintaining the status quo (expenditures for military forces, support for allies, etc.) tend to rise faster than the resources needed to do so. An equilibrium exists when no powerful state believes that a change in the system would yield additional net benefits. Finally, if the resulting disequilibrium between the existing governance of the international system and the redistribution of power is not resolved, the system will be changed and a new equilibrium reflecting the distribution of relative capabilities will be established.

Unlike Waltz, Gilpin (1981, chap. 4) includes state-level processes in order to explain change. Differential economic growth rates among nations (a structural–systemic-level variable) play a vital role in his explanation for the rise and decline of great powers, but his model also includes propositions about the law of diminishing returns on investments, the impact of affluence on martial spirits and on the ratio of consumptions to investment, and structural change in the economy (see also Kennedy, 1987). Table 2.1 summarizes some key elements of realism. It also contrasts them to two other system-level models of international relations—the liberal and the World System models, to which we now turn our attention.

TABLE 2.1
Three Models of the International System

	Realism	Liberalism	World System
Type of model	Classical: descriptive and normative Modern: deductive	Descriptive and normative	Descriptive and normative
Central problems	Causes of war Conditions of peace	Broad agenda of social, economic, and environmental issues arising from gap between demands and resources	Inequality and exploitation Uneven development
Conception of current international system	Structural anarchy	Global society Complex interdependence (structure varies by issue-area)	World capitalist system
Key actors	Geographically based units (tribes, city-states, nation-states, etc.)	Highly permeable nation-states *plus* a broad range of nonstate actors, including IOs, IGOs, NGOs, and individuals[a]	Classes and their agents
Central motivations	National interest Security Power	Human needs and wants	Class interests
Loyalties	To geographically based groups (from tribes to nation-states)	Loyalties to nation-state declining To emerging global values and institutions that transcend those of the nation-state and/or to subnational groups	To class values and interests that transcend those of the nation-state
Central processes	Search for security and survival	Aggregate effects of decisions by national and nonnational actors How units (not limited to nation-states) cope with a growing agenda of threats and opportunities arising from human wants	Modes of production and exchange International division of labor in a world capitalist system
Likelihood of system transformation	Low (basic structural elements of system have revealed an ability to persist despite many other kinds of changes)	High in the direction of the model (owing to the rapid pace of technological change, etc.)	High in the direction of the model (owing to inherent contradictions within the world capitalist system)
Sources of theory, insights, and evidence	Politics History Economics (especially "modern" realists)	Broad range of social sciences Natural and technological sciences	Marxist–Leninist theory (several variants)

[a] IO = International Organization; IGO = Intergovernmental Organization; NGO = Nongovernmental Organization.

LIBERAL THEORIES

Just as there are variants of realism, there are several liberal theories, but this discussion focuses on two common denominators. They all challenge the first and third core propositions of realism identified earlier, asserting that inordinate attention to the war/peace issue and the nation-state renders it an increasingly anachronistic model of global relations (Keohane and Nye, 1977; Morse, 1976; Rosenau, 1980; Mansbach and Vasquez, 1981; Scott, 1982; and J. Rosenau, 1990).

The agenda of critical problems confronting states has been vastly expanded during the twentieth century. Attention to the issues of war and peace is by no means misdirected according to proponents of a liberal perspective, but concerns for welfare, modernization, the environment, and the like are today no less potent sources of motivation and action. Indeed many liberals define security in terms that are broader than the geopolitical–military spheres, and they emphasize the potential for cooperative relations among nations. Institution building to reduce uncertainty and fears of perfidy; improved international education and communication to ameliorate fears and antagonisms based on misinformation and misperceptions; and the positive-sum possibilities of such activities as trade are but a few of the ways, according to liberals, by which nations may jointly gain and thus mitigate, if not eliminate, the harshest features of international relations emphasized by the realists. Finally, the diffusion of knowledge and technology, combined with the globalization of communications, has vastly increased popular expectations. The resulting demands have outstripped resources and the ability of existing institutions—notably the nation-state—to cope effectively with them. Interdependence arises from an inability of even the most powerful states to cope, or to do so unilaterally or at acceptable levels of cost and risk, with issues ranging from trade to AIDS and immigration to environmental threats.

Paralleling the widening agenda of critical issues is the expansion of actors whose behavior can have a significant impact beyond national boundaries; indeed, the cumulative effects of their actions can have profound consequences for the international system. Thus, although nation-states continue to be important international actors, they possess a declining ability to control their own destinies. The aggregate effect of actions by multitudes of nonstate actors can have potent effects that transcend political boundaries. These may include such powerful or highly visible nonstate organizations as Exxon, the Organization of Petroleum Exporting Countries, or the Palestine Liberation Organization. On the other hand, the cumulative effects of decisions by less powerful or less visible actors may also have profound international consequences. For example, decisions by thousands of individuals, mutual funds, banks, pension funds, and other financial institutions to sell securities on 19 October 1987 not only resulted in an unprecedented "crash" on Wall Street, but within hours its consequences were felt throughout the entire global financial system. Governments might take such actions as loosening credit or even closing exchanges, but they were largely unable to contain the effects of the panic.

The widening agenda of critical issues, most of which lack a purely national solution, has also led to creation of new actors that transcend political boundaries; for example, international organizations, transnational organizations, non-government organizations, multinational corporations, and the like. Thus, not only does an exclusive focus on the war/peace issue fail to capture the complexities of contemporary international life but it blinds the analyst to the institutions, processes, and norms that permit cooperation and significantly mitigate some features of an anarchic system. In short, according to liberal perspectives, an adequate understanding of the emergent global system must recognize that no single model is likely to be sufficient for all issues and that if it restricts attention to the manner in which states deal with traditional security concerns, it is more likely to obfuscate rather than clarify the realities of contemporary world affairs.

The liberal models have several important virtues. They recognize that international behavior and outcomes arise from a multiplicity of motives, not merely security, at least if security is defined solely in military or strategic terms. They also alert us to the fact that important international processes and conditions originate not only in the actions of nation-states but also in the aggregated behavior of other actors. These models not only enable the analyst to deal with a broader agenda of critical issues but, more importantly, they force one to contemplate a much richer menu of demands, processes, and outcomes than would be derived from power-centered realist models. Stated differently, liberal theories are more sensitive to the possibility that politics of trade, currency, immigration, health, the environment, and the like may significantly and systematically differ from those typically associated with security issues.

On the other hand, some liberal analysts underestimate the potency of nationalism and the durability of the nation-state. Almost three decades ago one of them wrote that "the nation is declining in its importance as a political unit to which allegiances are attached" (Rosenau, 1968: 39; see also Rosecrance, 1986; Herz, 1957, 1968). Objectively, nationalism may be an anachronism but, for better or worse, powerful loyalties are still attached to nation-states. The suggestion that, because even some well-established nations have experienced independence movements among ethnic, cultural, or religious minorities, the sovereign territorial state may be in decline is not wholly persuasive. Indeed, that evidence perhaps points to precisely the opposite conclusion: In virtually every region of the world there are groups that seek to create or restore geographically based entities in which their members may enjoy the status and privileges associated with sovereign territorial statehood. Evidence from Poland to Palestine, Serbia to Sri Lanka, Estonia to Eritrea, Armenia to Afghanistan, and elsewhere seem to indicate that obituaries for nationalism may be somewhat premature.

The notion that such powerful non-national actors as major multinational corporations (MNCs) will soon transcend the nation-state seems equally premature (Vernon, 1971, 1991). International drug rings do appear capable of dominating such states as Colombia and Panama. However, the pattern of outcomes in confrontations between MNCs and states, including cases involving major expropriations of corporate properties, indicates that even relatively weak nations are not always the hapless pawns of the MNCs. Case studies by Joseph Grieco (1984) and Gary Gereffi (1983), among others, indicate that MNC–state relations yield a wide variety of outcomes.

Underlying the liberal critique of realist models is that the latter are too wedded to the past and are thus incapable of dealing adequately with change. For the present, however, even if global dynamics arise from multiple sources (including nonstate actors), the actions of nation-states and their agents would appear to remain the major sources of change in the international system. However, the last group of systemic models, the Marxist/World System/Dependency models—hereafter cited as World System models—downplay the role of the nation-state even further.

As in other parts of this essay, many of the distinctions among World System models are inevitably lost by treating them together and by focusing on their common features. These models challenge both the war/peace and state-centered features of realism, but they do so in ways that differ sharply from challenges of liberal theories (Galtung, 1971; Cockroft, Frank, and Johnson, 1972; Wallerstein, 1974a, 1974b; Chase-Dunn, 1979, 1981; Kubalkova and Cruickshank, 1985; and Denemark and Thomas, 1988). Rather than focusing on war and peace, World System models direct attention to quite different issues, including uneven development, poverty, and exploitation within and between nations. These conditions, arising from the dynamics of the modes of production and exchange, are basic, and they must be incorporated into any analysis of intra- and inter-nation conflict.

At a superficial level, according to adherents of these models, what exists today may be described as a system of nation-states. More fundamentally, however, the key groups within and between nations are classes and their agents: As Immanuel Wallerstein (1974a: 390) put it, "in the nineteenth and twentieth centuries there has been only one world system in existence, the world capitalist world economy." The "world capitalist system" is characterized by a highly unequal division of labor between the periphery and core. Those at the periphery are essentially the drawers of water and the hewers of wood whereas the latter appropriate the surplus of the entire world economy. This critical feature of the World System not only gives rise to and perpetuates a widening rather than narrowing gap between the wealthy core and poor periphery but also to a dependency relationship from which the latter are unable to break loose. Moreover, the class structure within the core, characterized by a growing gap between capital and labor, is faithfully reproduced in the periphery so that elites there share with their counterparts in the core an interest in perpetuating the system. Thus, in contrast to realist theories, World System models encompass and integrate theories of both the global and domestic arenas.

As has been the case with other systemic theories, World System models have been subjected to trenchant critiques (Smith, 1979; Zolberg, 1981). The state, nationalism, security dilemmas, and related concerns essentially drop out of these analyses; they are at the theoretical periphery rather than at the core: "Capitalism was from the beginning an affair of the world economy," Wallerstein (1974a: 401) asserts, "not of nation-states." A virtue of many World System models is that they take a long historical perspective on world affairs rather than merely focusing on contemporary issues. However, by neglecting nation-states and the dynamics arising from their efforts to deal with security in an anarchical system—or at best relegating these actors and motivations to a minor role—these models lose much of their appeal. Models of world affairs during the past few centuries that fail to give the nation-state a central role seem as incomplete as analyses of *Hamlet* that neglect the central character and his motivations.

Second, the concept of "world capitalist system" is central to these models, but its relevance for much of the twentieth century can be questioned. Whether this term accurately describes the world of the 1880s could be debated, but its declining analytical utility or even descriptive accuracy for international affairs of the post–World War II period seems clear. Thus, one could question Wallerstein's assertion (1974a: 412) two decades ago that "there are today no socialist systems in the world economy any more than there are feudal systems because there is only *one world system*. It is a world economy and it is *by definition capitalist* in form." Where within a system so defined would we have located the USSR or Eastern Europe? During the Cold War this area included enough industrial nations that it hardly seems to belong in the periphery. Yet to place these states in the core of a "world capitalist system" would require conceptual gymnastics of a high order. Would it have increased our analytical capabilities to have described the USSR and East European countries as "state capitalists"? Where would we have located China? How do we explain dynamics within the "periphery," or the differences between rapid-growth Asian nations such as South Korea, Taiwan, or Singapore and their slow-growth neighbors in Bangladesh, North Korea, and the Philippines? The inclusion of a third structural position—the "semiperiphery"—does not wholly answer these questions.

Third, World System models have considerable difficulty in explaining relations between noncapitalist nations during the Cold War—for example, between the USSR and its East European neighbors or China—much less outright conflict between them. Indeed, advocates of these models have usually restricted their attention to West–South relations, eschewing analyses of East–East or East–South relations. Would one have gained greater and more general analytical power by using the lenses and language of marxism or of realism to describe relations between the USSR and Eastern Europe, the

USSR and Third World nations, China and Vietnam, India and Sri Lanka, or Vietnam and Kampuchea? Were these relationships better described and understood in terms of such World System categories as "class" or such realist ones as "relative capabilities"?

Finally, the earlier observations about the persistence of nationalism as an element of international relations seem equally appropriate here. Perhaps national loyalties can be dismissed as prime examples of "false consciousness," but even in areas that experienced almost two generations of one-party Communist rule, as in Poland, evidence that feelings of transnational solidarity with workers in other socialist nations have replaced nationalist sentiments is in short supply.

DECISION-MAKING CHALLENGES TO REALISM

Many advocates of realism recognize that it cannot offer fine-grained analyses of foreign policy behavior, and, as noted earlier, Waltz denies that it is desirable or even possible to combine theories of international relations and foreign policy. Decision-making models challenge the premise that it is fruitful to conceptualize the nation as a unitary rational actor whose behavior can adequately be explained by reference to the system structure—the second, fourth, and fifth realist propositions identified earlier—because individuals, groups, and organizations acting in the name of the state are also sensitive to pressures and constraints other than international ones, including elite maintenance, electoral politics, public opinion, pressure group activities, ideological preferences, and bureaucratic politics. Such core concepts as "the national interest" are not defined solely by the international system, much less by its structure alone, but they are also likely to reflect elements within the domestic political arena. Thus, rather than assuming with the realists that the state can be conceptualized as a "black box"—that the domestic political processes are both hard to comprehend and generally superfluous for explaining its external behavior—decision-making analysts believe one must indeed take these internal processes into account, with special attention directed at decision makers and their "definitions of the situation" (Snyder, Bruck, and Sapin, 1962). In order to reconstruct how nations deal with each other, it is necessary to view the situation through the eyes of those who act in the name of the nation-state: decision makers, and the group and bureaucratic–organizational contexts within which they act. Table 2.2 provides an overview of three major types of decision-making models.

Traditional models of complex organizations and bureaucracy emphasize the positive contributions to be expected from a division of labor, hierarchy, and centralization, coupled with expertise, rationality, and obedience. Such models assume that clear boundaries should be maintained between politics and decision making, on the one hand, and administration and implementation

TABLE 2.2
Three Models of Decision Making

	Bureaucratic Politics	Group Dynamics	Individual Decision Making
Conceptualization of decision making	Decision making as the result of bargaining within bureaucratic organizations	Decision making as the product of group interaction	Decision making as the result of individual choice
Premises	Central organizational values are imperfectly internalized Organizational behavior is political behavior Structure and standard operating procedures affect substance and quality of decisions	Most decisions are made by small elite groups Group is different than the sum of its members Group dynamics affect substance and quality of decisions	Importance of subjective appraisal (definition of the situation) and cognitive processes (information processing, etc.)
Constraints on rational decision making	Imperfect information, resulting from centralization, hierarchy, and specialization Organizational inertia Conflict between individual and organizational utilities Bureaucratic politics and bargaining dominate decision making and implementation of decisions	Groups may be more effective for some tasks, less for others Pressures for conformity Risk-taking propensity of groups (controversial) Quality of leadership "Groupthink"	Cognitive limits on rationality Information processing distorted by cognitive consistency dynamics (unmotivated biases) Systematic and motivated biases in causal analysis Individual differences in abilities related to decision making (e.g., problem-solving ability, tolerance of ambiguity, defensiveness and anxiety, information seeking, etc.)
Sources of theory, insights, and evidence	Organization theory Sociology of bureaucracies Bureaucratic politics	Social psychology Sociology of small groups	Cognitive dissonance Cognitive psychology Dynamic psychology

on the other. Following pioneering works by Chester I. Barnard (1938), Herbert Simon (1957), James G. March and Simon (1958), and others, more recent theories depict organizations quite differently. The central premise is that decision making in bureaucratic organizations is not constrained only by the legal and formal norms that are intended to enhance the rational and eliminate the capricious aspects of bureaucratic behavior. Rather, most complex organizations are seen as generating serious "information pathologies" (Wilensky, 1967). There is an *emphasis* upon rather than a denial of the political character of bureaucracies, as well as on other "informal" aspects of organizational behavior. Complex organizations are composed of individuals and units with conflicting perceptions, values, and interests that may arise from parochial self-interest ("what is best for my bureau is also best for my career") and also from different perceptions of issues arising ineluctably from a division of labor ("where you stand depends on where you sit"). Organizational norms and memories, prior policy commitments, normal organizational inertia, routines, and standard operating procedures may shape and perhaps distort the structuring of problems, channeling of information, use of expertise, and implementation of executive decisions. The consequences of bureaucratic politics within the executive branch or within the government as a whole may significantly constrain the manner in which issues are defined, the range of options that may be considered, and the manner in which executive decisions are implemented by subordinates. Consequently, organizational decision making is essentially political in character, dominated by bargaining for resources, roles, and missions, and by compromise rather than analysis (Kissinger, 1960; Allison, 1971; Allison and Halperin, 1972; and Halperin, 1974).

Perhaps because of the dominant position of the realist perspective, most students of foreign policy have only recently incorporated bureaucratic–organizational models and insights into their analyses. An ample literature on budgeting, weapons acquisitions, military doctrine, and similar situations confirms that foreign and defense policy bureaucracies rarely conform to the Weberian "ideal type" of rational organization (see for example, Williamson, 1969; Lauren, 1975; and Posen, 1984). Some analysts assert that crises may provide the motivation and means for reducing some of the nonrational aspects of bureaucratic behavior. Crises are likely to push decisions to the top of the organization where higher quality of intelligence is available; information is more likely to enter the top of the hierarchy directly, reducing the distorting effects of information processing through several levels of the organization; and broader, less parochial values may be invoked. Short decision time in crises reduces the opportunities for decision making by bargaining, log rolling, incrementalism, lowest-common-denominator values, "muddling through," and the like (Wilensky, 1967; Lowi, 1969; and Verba, 1961).

However, even studies of international crises from a bureaucratic–organizational perspective are not uniformly sanguine about decision making in such circumstances (Hermann, 1963). Graham T. Allison's (1971) analysis of the Cuban missile crisis identified several critical bureaucratic malfunctions concerning dispersal of American aircraft in Florida, the location of the naval blockade, and grounding of weather-reconnaissance flights from Alaska that might stray over the Soviet Union. Richard Neustadt's (1970) study of two crises involving the United States and Great Britain revealed significant misperceptions of each other's interests and policy processes. And an examination of three American nuclear alerts found substantial gaps in understanding and communication between policymakers and the military leaders who were responsible for implementing the alerts (Sagan, 1985).

Critics of some organizational–bureaucratic models and the studies employing them have focused on several points (Rothstein, 1972; Krasner, 1972; Art, 1973; Ball, 1974; and Perlmutter, 1974). They point out, for instance, that the emphasis on bureaucratic bargaining fails to differentiate adequately between the positions of the participants. In the American system, the president is not just another player in a complex bureaucratic game. Not only must he ultimately decide but he must also select who the other players will be, a process that may be crucial in shaping the ultimate decisions. If General Matthew Ridgway and Attorney General Robert Kennedy played key roles in the American decisions not to intervene in Indochina in 1954 or not to bomb Cuba in 1962, it was because Presidents Eisenhower and Kennedy chose to accept their advice rather than that of other officials. Also the conception of bureaucratic bargaining tends to emphasize its nonrational elements to the exclusion of genuine intellectual differences that may be rooted in broader concerns—including disagreements on what national interests, if any, are at stake in a situation—rather than narrow parochial interests. Indeed, properly managed, decision processes that promote and legitimize "multiple advocacy" among officials may facilitate high-quality decisions (George, 1972).

These models may be especially useful for understanding the slippage between executive decisions and foreign policy actions that may arise during *implementation*, but they may be less valuable for explaining the decisions themselves. Allison's (1971) study of the Cuban missile crisis does not indicate an especially strong correlation between bureaucratic roles and evaluations of the situation or policy recommendations, as predicted by his "Model III" (bureaucratic politics), and recent evidence about deliberations during the crisis does not offer more supporting evidence for that model (Welch and Blight, 1987–1988; Bundy and Blight, 1987–1988; and Blight and Welch, 1989). On the other hand, Allison does present some compelling evidence concerning policy implementation that casts considerable doubt on the adequacy of "Model I" (the realist conception of the unitary rational actor).

Another decision-making model supplements bureaucratic–organizational models by narrowing the field of view to top policymakers. This approach lends itself well to investigations of foreign policy decisions, which are usually made in a small-group context. Some analysts have drawn upon sociology and social psychology to assess the impact of various types of group dynamics on decision making (de Rivera, 1968; Paige, 1968; Janis, 1972, 1982; Hermann, Hermann, and Hagan, 1987). Underlying these models are the premises that the group is not merely the sum of its members (thus decisions emerging from the group are likely to be different than what a simple aggregation of individual preferences and abilities might suggest), and group dynamics, the interactions among its members, can have a significant impact on the substance and quality of decisions.

Groups often perform better than individuals in coping with complex tasks due to diverse perspectives and talents, an effective division of labor, and high-quality debates centering on evaluations of the situation and policy recommendations for dealing with it. Groups may also provide decision makers with emotional and other types of support that may facilitate coping with complex problems. On the other hand, they may exert pressures for conformity to group norms, thereby inhibiting the search for information and policy options or cutting it off prematurely, ruling out the legitimacy of some options, curtailing independent evaluation, and suppressing some forms of intragroup conflict that might serve to clarify goals, values, and options. Classic experiments by the psychologist Solomon Asch revealed the extent to which group members will suppress their beliefs and judgments when faced with a majority adhering to the contrary view, even a counterfactual one (Festinger, 1965; Asch, 1953, 1965).

Drawing upon a series of historical case studies, social psychologist Irving L. Janis (1972, 1982, and a critique in Etheredge, 1985) has identified a different variant of group dynamics, which he labeled "groupthink" to distinguish it from the more familiar type of conformity pressure on "deviant" members of the group. Janis challenged the conventional wisdom that strong cohesion among the members of a group invariably enhances performance. Under certain conditions, strong cohesion can markedly degrade the group's performance in decision making. Thus, the members of a cohesive group may, as a means of dealing with the stresses of having to cope with consequential problems and in order to bolster self-esteem, increase the frequency and intensity of face-to-face interaction. This results in a greater identification with the group and less competition within it. The group dynamics of what Janis called "concurrence seeking" may displace or erode reality testing and sound information processing and judgment. As a consequence, groups may be afflicted by unwarranted feelings of optimism and invulnerability, stereotyped images of adversaries, and inattention to warnings. Janis's analyses (1982: 260–76) of both "successful" (the Marshall Plan, the Cuban missile crisis) and "unsuccessful" (The Munich Conference of 1938, Pearl Harbor, the Bay of Pigs invasion) cases indicate that "groupthink" or other decision-making pathologies are not inevitable, and he developed some guidelines for avoiding them.

Still other decision-making analysts focus on the individual. Many approaches to the policymaker emphasize the gap between the demands of the classical model of rational decision making and the substantial body of theory and evidence about various constraints that come into play in even relatively simple choice situations (Abelson and Levi, 1985; Jervis, 1976; Steinbruner, 1974; and Axelrod, 1976). The more recent perspectives, drawing upon cognitive psychology, go well beyond some of the earlier formulations that drew upon psychodynamic theories to identify various types of psychopathologies among political leaders: paranoia, authoritarianism, and the displacement of private motives on public objects, among others (Lasswell, 1930). These more recent efforts to include the information-processing behavior of the decision maker in foreign policy analyses have been directed at the cognitive and motivational constraints that, in varying degrees, affect the decision-making performance of "normal" rather than pathological subjects. Thus, attention is directed to all leaders, not merely those, such as Hitler or Stalin, who display evidence of clinical abnormalities.

The major challenges to the classical model have focused on limited human capabilities for performing the tasks required by objectively rational decision making. The cognitive constraints on rationality include limits on the individual's capacity to receive, process, and assimilate information about the situation; an inability to identify the entire set of policy alternatives; fragmentary knowledge about the consequences of each option; and an inability to order preferences on a single utility scale (March and Simon, 1958: 113). These have given rise to several conceptions of the decision maker's strategies for dealing with complexity, uncertainty, incomplete or contradictory information, and, paradoxically, information overload. They variously characterize the individual as a problem solver, naive or intuitive scientist, cognitive balancer, dissonance avoider, information seeker, cybernetic information processor, and reluctant decision maker.

Three of these conceptions seem especially relevant for foreign policy analysis. The first views the decision maker as a "bounded rationalist" who seeks satisfactory rather than optimal solutions. As Herbert Simon (1957: 198) has put it, "The capacity of the human mind for formulating and solving complex problems is very small compared with the size of the problem whose solution is required for objectively rational behavior in the real world—or even a reasonable approximation of such objective rationality." Moreover, it is not practical for the decision maker to seek optimal choices; for example, because of the costs of searching for information. Related to this is the more recent concept of the individual as a "cognitive miser," one who seeks to simplify complex problems and to find short cuts to problem solving and decision making.

Another approach is to look at the decision maker as an "error-prone intuitive scientist" who is likely to commit a broad range of inferential mistakes. Thus, rather than emphasizing the limits on the search for policy options, information processing, and the like, this conception views the decision maker as the victim of flawed heuristics or decision rules who uses data poorly. There are tendencies to underuse rate data in making judgments, believe in the "law of small numbers," underuse diagnostic information, overweight low probabilities and underweight high ones, and violate other requirements of consistency and coherence. These deviations from classical decision theory are traced to the psychological principles that govern perceptions of problems and evaluations of options (Tversky and Kahneman, 1981; Kahneman and Tversky, 1973; and Kahneman, Slovic, and Tversky, 1982).

The final perspective emphasizes the motivational forces that will not or cannot be controlled (Janis and Mann, 1977; Steiner, 1983; and Lebow, 1981). Decision makers are not merely rational calculators; important decisions generate conflict, and a reluctance to make irrevocable choices often results in behavior that reduces the quality of decisions. These models direct the analyst's attention to policymakers' belief systems, images of relevant actors, perceptions, information processing strategies, heuristics, certain personality traits (ability to tolerate ambiguity, cognitive complexity, etc.), and their impact on decision making.

Despite this diversity of perspectives and the difficulty of choosing between cognitive and motivational models, there has been some convergence on several types of constraints that may affect decision processes (Kinder and Weiss, 1978; Holsti, 1976). One involves the consequences of efforts to achieve cognitive consistency on perceptions and information processing. Several kinds of systematic bias have been identified in both experimental and historical studies. Policymakers have a propensity to assimilate and interpret information in ways that conform to rather than challenge existing beliefs, preferences, hopes, and expectations. They may deny the need to confront tradeoffs between values by persuading themselves that an option will satisfy all of them, or they may indulge in rationalizations to bolster the selected option while denigrating those that were not selected.

An extensive literature on styles of attribution has revealed several types of systematic bias in causal analysis. Perhaps the most important for foreign policy analysis is the basic attribution error—a tendency to explain the adversary's behavior in terms of his characteristics (for example, inherent aggressiveness or hostility) rather than in terms of the context or situation, while attributing one's own behavior to the latter (for example, legitimate security needs arising from a dangerous and uncertain environment) rather than to the former. A somewhat related type of double standard has been noted by George Kennan (1978: 87–88): "Now is it our view that we should take account only of their [Soviet] capabilities, disregarding their intentions, but we should expect them to take account only for our supposed intentions, disregarding our capabilities?"

Analysts also have illustrated the effect on decisions of policymakers' assumptions about order and predictability in the environment. Whereas a policymaker may have an acute appreciation of the disorderly environment in which he or she operates (arising, for example, from domestic political processes), there is a tendency to assume that others, especially adversaries, are free of such constraints. Graham T. Allison (1971), Robert Jervis (1976), and others have demonstrated that decision makers tend to believe that the realist "unitary rational actor" is the appropriate representation of the opponent's decision processes and, thus, whatever happens is the direct result of deliberate choices. For example, the hypothesis that the Soviet destruction of KAL flight 007 may have resulted from intelligence failures or bureaucratic foul-ups, rather than from a calculated decision to murder civilian passengers, was either not given serious consideration or it was suppressed for strategic reasons (Hersh, 1986).

Drawing on a very substantial experimental literature, several models linking crisis-induced stress to decision processes have been developed and used in foreign policy studies (Hermann, 1972; Hermann and Hermann, 1975; Hermann, 1979; Holsti, 1972; and Holsti and George, 1975). Irving L. Janis and Leon Mann (1977: 3) have developed a more general conflict-theory model that conceives of man as a "reluctant decision maker" and focuses upon "when, how and why psychological stress generated by decisional conflict imposes limitations on the rationality of a person's decisions." One may employ five strategies for coping with a situation requiring a decision: unconflicted adherence to existing policy, unconflicted change, defensive avoidance, hypervigilance, and vigilant decision making. The first four strategies are likely to yield low-quality decisions due to incomplete search for information, inadequate appraisal of the situation and options, and poor contingency planning, whereas vigilant decision making, characterized by a more adequate performance of vital tasks, is more likely to result in a high-quality choice. Decision styles are affected by information about risks, expectations of finding a better option, and time for adequate search and deliberation.

A final approach attempts to show the impact of personal traits on decision making. There is no shortage of typologies linking leadership traits to decision-making behavior, but systematic research demonstrating such links is in much shorter supply. Still, some efforts have borne fruit. Margaret G. Hermann (1980, 1984) has developed a scheme for analyzing leaders' public statements of unquestioned authorship for eight variables: nationalism, belief in one's ability to control the environment, need for power, need for affiliation, ability to differentiate environments, distrust of others, self-confidence, and task emphasis. The scheme has been tested with impressive results on a broad range of contemporary leaders. Alexander L. George (1969) has reformulated Nathan Leites's (1951) concept of "operational code" into five philosophical and five instrumental beliefs that are intended to describe politically relevant core beliefs, stimulating a number of empirical studies and, more recently, further significant conceptual revisions (Walker, 1977, 1983). Finally several psychologists have developed and tested the concept of "integrative complexity," defined as the ability to make subtle distinction along multiple dimensions, flexibility, and the integration of large amounts of diverse information to make coherent judgments. A standard content analysis technique has been used for research on documentary materials generated by top decision makers in a wide range of international crises, including World War I, Cuba (1962), Morocco (1911), Berlin (1948–1949 and 1961), Korea, and the Middle East wars of 1948, 1956, 1967, and 1973 (Suedfeld and Tetlock, 1977; Suedfeld, Tetlock, and Ramirez, 1977; Raphael, 1982; and Tetlock, 1985).

Decision-making approaches clearly permit the analyst to overcome many limitations of the systemic models described earlier, but not without costs. Those described here impose increasingly heavy data burdens on the analyst. Moreover, there is a danger that adding levels of analysis may result in an undisciplined proliferation of variables with at least two adverse consequences: It may become increasingly difficult to determine which are more or less important, and ad hoc explanations for individual cases erode the possibilities for broader generalizations across cases. However, well-designed, multicase, decision-making studies indicate that these and other traps are avoidable (George and Smoke, 1974; Smoke, 1977; Snyder and Diesing, 1977; Brecher and Geist, 1980; Lebow, 1981; Eckstein, 1975; and George, 1979).

The study of international relations and foreign policy has always been an eclectic undertaking, with extensive borrowing from disciplines other than political science and history (Wright, 1955). The primary differences today tend to be between two broad approaches. Analysts of the first school focus on the structure of the international system, often borrowing from economics for models, analogies, insights, and metaphors, with an emphasis on *rational preferences and strategy* and how these tend to be shaped and constrained by the structure of the international system. Decision-making analysts, meanwhile, display a concern for domestic political processes and tend to borrow from social psychology and psychology in order to understand better the *limits and barriers* to information processing and rational choice. For many purposes both approaches are necessary and neither is sufficient. Neglect of the system structure and its constraints may result in analyses that depict policymakers as relatively free agents with an almost unrestricted menu of choices, limited only by the scope of their ambitions and the resources at their disposal. At worst, this type of analysis can degenerate into Manichean explanations that depict foreign policies of the "bad guys" as the external manifestation of flawed leaders or domestic structures, whereas the "good guys" only react from necessity. Radical-right explanations of the Cold War usually depicted Soviet policies as driven by inherently aggressive totalitarian communism and the United States as its blameless victim; radical-left explanations tended to be structurally similar, with the roles of aggressor and victim reversed (Holsti, 1974).

Conversely, neglect of foreign policy decision making not only leaves one unable to explain the dynamics of the international relations, but many important aspects of a nation's external behavior will be inexplicable. Advocates of realism have often argued its superiority for understanding the "high" politics of deterrence, containment, alliances, crises, and wars, if not necessarily for "low" politics. But there are several rejoinders to this line of reasoning. First, the low politics of trade, currencies, and other issues that are almost always highly sensitive to domestic pressures are becoming an increasingly important element of international relations. Second, the growing literature on the putative domain *par excellence* of realism—security issues—raises substantial doubts about the universal validity of the realist model even for these issues (in addition to the previously cited literature on war, crises, and deterrence, see Betts, 1987; Jervis, Lebow, and Stein, 1985; and Lebow, 1987). Finally, exclusive reliance on realist models and their assumptions of rationality may lead to unwarranted complacency about dangers in the international system. Nuclear weapons and other features of the system have no doubt contributed to the "long peace" among major powers (Gaddis, 1986). At the same time, however, a narrow focus on power balances, "correlations of forces," and other features of the international system will result in neglect of dangers—for example, the command, communication, control, intelligence problem or inadequate information processing—that can only be identified and analyzed by a decision-making perspective (Bracken, 1983; Blair, 1985; Steinbruner, 1981–1982; Sagan, 1985; and George, 1980).

This observation parallels that made three decades ago by the foremost contemporary proponent of realism: The third image (system structure) is necessary for understanding the context of international behavior, whereas the first and second images (decision makers and domestic political processes) are needed to understand dynamics within the system (Waltz, 1959: 238). But to acknowledge the existence of various levels of analysis is not enough. *What* the investigator wants to explain and the *level of specificity and comprehensiveness* to be sought should determine which level(s) of analysis are relevant and necessary. In this connection, it is essential to distinguish two different dependent variables: foreign policy decisions by states, on the one hand, and the outcomes of policy and interactions between two or more states, on the other. If the goal is to understand the former—foreign policy decisions—Harold and Margaret Sprout's (1957) notion of "psychological milieu" is relevant and sufficient; that is, the objective structural variables influence the decisions via the decision maker's perception and evaluation of those "outside" variables. However, if the goal is to explain outcomes, the "psychological milieu" is quite inadequate; the objective factors, even if misperceived or misjudged by the decision maker, will influence the outcome. Students of international relations are increasingly disciplining their use of multiple levels of analysis in studying outcomes that cannot be adequately explained via only a single level (for example, Yoffie, 1983; Odell, 1982; Larson, 1985; Snyder, 1984; Aggarwal, 1985; Posen, 1984; and Walt, 1987).

CONCLUSION

A renowned diplomatic historian has asserted that most theories of international relations flunked a critical test by failing to forecast the end of the Cold War (Gaddis, 1992–1993). This conclusion speculates on the related question of how well the theories discussed above might help us to understand international politics in the post–Cold War world. Dramatic events since the late 1980s would appear to have posed serious challenges for several theories, but one should be wary about writing premature obituaries for any of them. The importance of recent developments notwithstanding, one should avoid "naive (single case) falsification" of major theories. Further, less than six years after the Berlin Wall came down and less than four years after dissolution of the Soviet Union, some caution about declaring that major events and trends are irreversible seems warranted.

Because recent debates on the theories of international politics have often centered on realism, especially structural realism, most of these comments will focus on that approach. However, a few comments on the other two systemic theories may also be in order. Events of the past decade have not been kind to theories that draw at least in part from the works of Marx and Lenin, including World System approaches. This is not the place to engage in detailed analyses of the relative performance of centrally planned and market economics, either in the developed or developing worlds, but recent trends would appear to favor the latter by a wide margin. Moreover, we may gain greater leverage for understanding inter- and intrastate conflict in much of the "second" and "third" worlds by focusing on ethnic, nationalist, and religious passions rather than on the clash of class-based material interests. Nevertheless, we may expect materialist interpretations of world politics to persist, if only because their adherents may justly argue that theirs is a long-term perspective that should not be judged merely by specific events or short-term trends.

Liberal theories have generally fared better, at least for explaining relations among the industrial democracies. Progress toward economic unification of Europe, although not without detours and setbacks, would appear to provide significant support for the liberal view that, even in an anarchic world, major powers may find ways of cooperating and overcoming the constraint of the "relative gains" problem. Moreover, Wilson's thesis that a world of democratic nations will be more peaceful has stood the test of time rather well, at least in the sense that democratic nations don't go to war with each other (Doyle, 1983, 1986). His diagnosis that self-determination also supports peace may be correct in the abstract, but universal application of that principle is neither possible nor desirable, if only because it would result in immense bloodshed; the peaceful divorces of Norway and Sweden in 1905 and of the Czech Republic and Slovakia in 1992 are unfortunately not the norm. Although it appears that economic interests have come to dominate nationalist, ethnic, or religious passions among the industrial democracies, the evidence is far less assuring in other areas, including parts of the former Soviet Union, Central Europe, the Middle East, South Asia, and elsewhere.

Recent events appear to have created an especially acute challenge to structural realism. Although structural realism provides a parsimonious and elegant theory, its deficiencies are likely to become more rather than less apparent in the post–Cold War world. Its weaknesses in dealing with questions of system change and in specifying policy preferences other than survival and security are likely to be magnified. Moreover, whereas classical realism espouses a number of attractive prescriptive features (caution, humility, warnings against mistaking one's preferences for the moral laws of the universe), neorealism is an especially weak source of policy-relevant theory (George, 1993). Indeed some of the prescriptions put forward by neorealists seem reckless; for example, the suggestion to let Germany join the nuclear club (Mearsheimer, 1990). In addition to European economic cooperation, specific events that seem inexplicable by structural realism include Soviet acquiescence in the collapse of its empire and peaceful transformation of the system structure. These developments are especially telling because structural realism is explicitly touted as a theory of major powers (Waltz, 1979). Consequently, even as distinguished a realist as Robert Tucker (1992–1993: 36) has characterized the structural version of realism as "more questionable than ever."

More important, even though the international system remains anarchic, the possibility of war among major powers cannot wholly be dismissed, and proliferation may place nuclear weapons in the hands of leaders with little stake in maintaining the status quo, the constraints imposed by systemic imperatives on foreign policy choices are clearly eroding. National interests and even national security increasingly have come to be defined in ways that transcend the military/strategic concerns that are at the core of realist theory. Well before the disintegration of the Soviet Union, an Americans Talk Security survey revealed that the perceived threat to national security from "Soviet aggression around the world" ranked in a seventh-place tie with the "greenhouse effect" and well behind a number of post–Cold War, nonmilitary threats (ATS, 1988). Trade, drug trafficking, immigration, the environment, and AIDS are among the nonmilitary issues that regularly appear on lists of top national security threats as perceived by both mass publics and elites.

The expanded agenda of national interests, combined with the trend toward greater democracy in many parts of the world, suggests that we are entering an era in which the balance between the relative potency of systemic and domestic forces in shaping and constraining foreign policies is moving toward the latter. Such issues as trade, immigration, and others can be expected to enhance the impact of domestic actors—including public opinion, and ethnic, religious, economic, and perhaps even regional pressure groups—while reducing the ability of executives to dominate policy processes on the grounds, so frequently invoked during the Cold War, that the adept pursuit of national security requires secrecy, flexibility, and the ability to act with speed. In short, we are likely to see the increasing democratization of foreign policy in the post–Cold War era. And that brings us back to the point at which we started, for the relationship between democracy and foreign policy is another of the issues on which realists and liberals are in sharp disagreement. Realists such as de Tocqueville, Morgenthau, Lippmann, Kennan, and many others share a profound skepticism about the impact of democratic political processes, and especially of public opinion, on the quality and continuity of foreign policy. In contrast, liberals in the Kant–Wilson tradition maintain that more democratic foreign policy processes contribute to peace and stability in international politics. Thus, if domestic politics does in fact come to play an increasingly important role in shaping post–Cold War era foreign policies, that development will ensure continuation of the venerable debate between realists and liberals.

REFERENCES

Abelson, Robert, and A. Levi. (1985) "Decision Making and Decision Theory," in Gardner Lindzey and Elliott Aronson, eds., *Handbook of Social Psychology*, 3rd ed., vol. 1. New York: Random House.

Aggarwal, Vinod K. (1985) *Liberal Protectionism: The International Politics of Organized Textile Trade*. Berkeley: University of California Press.

Allison, Graham T. (1971). *Essence of Decision: Explaining the Cuban Missile Crisis*. Boston: Little, Brown.

Allison, Graham T., and Morton Halperin. (1972) "Bureaucratic Politics: A Paradigm and Some Policy Implications," *World Politics* 24: 40–79.

Americans Talk Security. (1988) *Attitudes Concerning National Security: National Survey No. 9*. Winchester, Mass.: ATS.

Aron, Raymond. (1966) *Peace and War*. Garden City, N.Y.: Doubleday.

Art, Robert J. (1973) "Bureaucratic Politics and American Foreign Policy: A Critique," *Policy Sciences* 4: 467–90.

Asch, Solomon. (1965) "Opinions and Social Pressure," in A. Paul Hare, Edgar G. Borgotta, and Robert F. Bates, eds., *Small Groups: Studies in Social Interaction*. New York: Knopf.

———. (1953) "Effects of Group Pressures upon Modification and Distortion of Judgment," in Dorwin Cartwright and A. Zander, eds., *Group Dynamics: Research and Theory*. Evanston, Ill.: Row, Peterson.

Ashley, Richard K. (1984) "The Poverty of Neo-Realism," *International Organization* 38: 225–86.

Axelrod, Robert. (1976) *The Structure of Decision*. Princeton, N.J.: Princeton University Press.

Ball, Desmond J. (1974) "The Blind Men and the Elephant: A Critique of Bureaucratic Politics Theory," *Australian Outlook* 28: 71–92.

Barnard, Chester. (1938) *Functions of the Executive*. Cambridge Mass.: Harvard University Press.

Betts, Richard. (1987) *Nuclear Blackmail and Nuclear Balance*. Washington D.C.: Brookings Institution.

Blair, Bruce. (1985) *Strategic Command and Control*. Washington, D.C.: Brookings Institution.

Blight, James, and David Welch. (1989) *On the Brink*. New York: Hill and Wang.

Bracken, Paul. (1983) *Command and Control of Nuclear Forces*. New Haven, Conn.: Yale University Press.

Brecher, Michael, and Barbara Geist. (1980) *Decisions in Crisis: Israel, 1967 and 1973*. Berkeley: University of California Press.

Bueno de Mesquita, Bruce. (1985) "The War Trap Revisited: A Revised Expected Utility Model," *American Political Science Review* 79: 156–77.

———. (1981) *The War Trap*. New Haven, Conn.: Yale University Press.

Bull, Hedley. (1977) *The Anarchical Society: A Study of Order in World Politics.* London: Macmillan.

Bundy, McGeorge, and James G. Blight. (1987–1988) "October 27, 1962: Transcripts of the Meetings of the ExComm," *International Security* 12: 30–92.

Carr, E. H. (1939) *Twenty Year Crisis.* London: Macmillan.

Chase-Dunn, Christopher. (1981) "Interstate System and Capitalist World-Economy: One Logic or Two?" *International Studies Quarterly* 25: 19–42.

———. (1979) "Comparative Research on World System Characteristics," *International Studies Quarterly* 23: 601–23.

Claude, Inis L. (1962) *Power and International Relations.* New York: Random House.

Cockroft, James, Andre Gunder Frank, and Dale L. Johnson. (1972) *Dependence and Under-Development.* New York: Anchor Books.

de Rivera, Joseph. (1968) *The Psychological Dimension of Foreign Policy.* Columbus, Ohio: C. E. Merrill.

Denemark, Robert A., and Kenneth O. Thomas. (1988) "The Brenner–Wallerstein Debates," *International Studies Quarterly* 28: 47–66.

Deutsch, Karl, and J. David Singer. (1964) "Multipolar Power Systems and International Stability," *World Politics* 16: 390–406.

Doyle, Michael. (1986) "Liberalism and World Politics," *American Political Science Review* 80: 1151–70.

———. (1983) "Kant, Liberal Legacies, and Foreign Affairs," *Philosophy and Public Affairs* 12: 205–35.

Eckstein, Harry. (1975) "Case Study and Theory in Political Science," in Fred I. Greenstein and Nelson W. Polsby, eds., *Handbook of Political Science.* Reading, Mass.: Addison-Wesley.

Etheredge, Lloyd. (1985) *Can Governments Learn?* New York: Pergamon Press.

Festinger, Leon. (1965) "A Theory of Social Comparison Processes," in A. Paul Hare, Edgar F. Borgatta, and Robert F. Bales, eds., *Small Groups: Studies in Social Interaction.* New York: Knopf.

Gaddis, John Lewis. (1992–1993) "International Relations Theory and the End of the Cold War," *International Security* 17: 5–58.

———. (1986) "The Long Peace: Elements of Stability in the Postwar International System," *International Security* 10: 99–142.

Galtung, John. (1971) "A Structural Theory of Imperialism," *Journal of Peace Research* 8: 81–117.

George, Alexander I. (1993) *Bridging the Gap: Theory and Practice in Foreign Policy.* Washington, D.C.: U.S. Institute of Peace.

———. (1980) *Presidential Decision Making in Foreign Policy: The Effective Use of Information and Advice.* Boulder, Colo.: Westview.

———. (1979) "Case Studies and Theory Development: The Method of Structured, Focused Comparison," in Paul Gordon Lauren, ed. *Diplomacy.* New York: Free Press.

———. (1972) "The Case for Multiple Advocacy in Making Foreign Policy," *American Political Science Review* 66: 751–85.

———. (1969) "The 'Operational Code': A Neglected Approach to the Study of Political Leaders and Decision Making," *International Studies Quarterly* 13: 190–222.

George, Alexander L., and Robert Keohane. (1980) "The Concept of National Interests: Uses and Limitations," in Alexander L. George, *Presidential Decision Making in*

Foreign Policy: The Effective Use of Information and Advice. Boulder, Colo.: Westview.

George, Alexander L., and Richard Smoke. (1974) *Deterrence in American Foreign Policy*. New York: Columbia University Press.

Gereffi, Gary. (1983) *The Pharmaceutical Industry and Dependency in the Third World*. Princeton, N.J.: Princeton University Press.

Gilpin, Robert. (1981) *War and Change in World Politics*. Cambridge: Cambridge University Press.

Graebner, Norman A. (1984) *America as a World Power: A Realist Appraisal from Wilson to Reagan*. Wilmington, Del.: Scholarly Resources.

Grieco, Joseph. (1990) *Cooperation among Nations*. Ithaca, N.Y.: Cornell University Press.

———. (1988) "Anarchy and the Limits of Cooperation: A Realist Critique of Neoliberal Institutionalism," *International Organization* 42: 485–507.

———. (1984) *Between Dependence and Autonomy*. Berkeley: University of California Press.

Haas, Ernst B. (1953) "The Balance of Power: Prescription, Concept or Propaganda?" *World Politics* 5: 442–77.

Halperin, Morton. (1974) *Bureaucratic Politics and Foreign Policy*. Washington, D.C.: Brookings Institution.

Hermann, Charles F. (1972) *International Crises: Insights from Behavioral Research*. New York: Free Press.

———. (1963) "Some Consequences of Crises Which Limit the Viability of Organizations," *Administrative Science Quarterly* 8: 61–82.

Hermann, Margaret G. (1984) "Personality and Foreign Policy Decision Making," in Donald Sylvan and Steve Chan, eds., *Foreign Policy Decision Making: Perception, Cognition, and Artificial Intelligence*. New York: Praeger.

———. (1980) "Explaining Foreign Policy Behavior Using Personal Characteristics of Political Leaders," *International Studies Quarterly* 24: 7–46.

———. (1979) "Indicators of Stress in Policy-makers during Foreign Policy Crises," *Political Psychology* 1: 27–46.

Hermann, Charles F., and Margaret G. Hermann. (1987) "Who Makes Foreign Policy Decisions and How: An Initial Test of Model." Paper presented to the Annual Meeting of the American Political Science Association, Chicago.

Hermann, Margaret G., and Charles F. Hermann. (1975) "Maintaining the Quality of Decision Making in Foreign Policy Crises," in *Report of the Commission on the Organization of the Government for the Conduct in Foreign Policy*, vol. 2. Washington, D.C.: U.S. Government Printing Office.

Hermann, Margaret G., Charles F. Hermann, and Joe D. Hagan. (1987) "How Decision Units Shape Foreign Policy Behavior," in Charles F. Hermann, Charles W. Kegley Jr., and James N. Rosenau, eds., *New Directions in the Study of Foreign Policy*. London: HarperCollins Academic.

Hersh, Seymour M. (1986) *The Target Is Destroyed*. New York: Random House.

Herz, John H. (1968) "The Territorial State Revisited: Reflections on the Future of the Nation-State," *Polity* 1: 12–34.

———. (1959) *International Politics in the Atomic Age*. New York: Columbia University Press.

———. (1957) "The Rise and Demise of the Territorial State," *World Politics* 9: 473–93.

Hoffmann, Stanley. (1977) "An American Social Science: International Relations," *Daedalus* 106: 41–60.

Holsti, Ole R. (1976) "Foreign Policy Formation Viewed Cognitively," in Robert Axelrod, ed., *Structure of Decision*. Princeton, N.J.: Princeton University Press.

———. (1974) "The Study of International Politics Makes Strange Bedfellows," *American Political Science Review* 68: 217–42.

———. (1972) *Crisis, Escalation, War*. Montreal: Queen's University Press.

Holsti, Ole R., and Alexander L. George. (1975) "The Effects of Stress on the Performance of Foreign Policy-Makers," *Political Science Annual*, vol. 6. Indianapolis: Bobbs-Merrill.

Janis, Irving L. (1982) *Groupthink*. Boston: Houghton Mifflin.

———. (1972) *Victims of Groupthink: A Psychological Study of Foreign Policy Decisions and Fiascos*. Boston: Houghton Mifflin.

Janis, Irving L., and Leon Mann. (1977) *Decision Making*. New York: Free Press.

Jervis, Robert. (1976) *Perception and Misperception in International Politics*. Princeton, N.J.: Princeton University Press.

Jervis, Robert, Richard Ned Lebow, and Janice G. Stein. (1985) *Psychology and Deterrence*. Baltimore: Johns Hopkins University Press.

Kahneman, Daniel, Paul Slovic, and Amos Tversky. (1982) *Judgment under Uncertainty: Heuristics and Biases*. Cambridge: Cambridge University Press.

Kahneman, Daniel, and Amos Tversky. (1973) "On the Psychology of Prediction," *Psychology Review* 80: 251–73.

Kaplan, Morton. (1957) *System and Process in International Politics*. New York: Wiley.

Kennan, George F. (1978) *The Cloud of Danger*. London: Hutchinson.

———. (1951) *American Diplomacy, 1900–1950*. Chicago: University of Chicago Press.

Kennedy, Paul. (1987) *The Rise and Fall of the Great Powers*. New York: Random House.

Keohane, Robert, ed. (1986) *Neorealism and Its Critics*. New York: Columbia University Press.

Keohane, Robert, and Joseph S. Nye Jr. (1977) *Power and Interdependence*. Boston: Little, Brown.

Kinder, Donald, and J. R. Weiss. (1978) "In Lieu of Rationality: Psychological Perspectives on Foreign Policy," *Journal of Conflict Resolution* 22: 707–35.

Kissinger, Henry A. (1960) "Conditions of World Order," *Daedalus* 95: 503–29.

Krasner, Stephen. (1978) *Defending the National Interest*. Princeton, N.J.: Princeton University Press.

———. (1972) "Are Bureaucracies Important?" *Foreign Policy* 7: 159–70.

Kubalkova, Vendulka, and A. A. Cruickshank. (1985) *Marxism and International Relations*. Oxford: Clarendon.

Larson, Deborah. (1985) *Origins of Containment: A Psychological Explanation*. Princeton, N.J.: Princeton University Press.

Lasswell, Harold. (1930) *Psychopathology and Politics*. Chicago: University of Chicago Press.

Lauren, Paul Gordon. (1975) *Diplomats and Bureaucrats*. Stanford, Calif.: Hoover Institute Press.

———, ed. (1979) *Diplomacy: New Approaches to History, Theory and Policy*. New York: Free Press.

Lebow, Richard Ned. (1987) *Nuclear Crisis Management: A Dangerous Illusion.* Ithaca, N.Y.: Cornell University Press.

———. (1981) *Between Peace and War.* Baltimore: Johns Hopkins University Press.

Leites, Nathan. (1951) *The Operational Code of the Politburo.* New York: McGraw-Hill.

Lippmann, Walter. (1943) *U.S. Foreign Policy: Shield of the Republic.* Boston: Little, Brown and Co.

Lowi, Theodore. (1969) *The End of Liberalism: Ideology, Policy and the Crisis of Public Authority.* New York: Norton.

Mansbach, Richard, and John Vasquez. (1981) *In Search of Theory: A New Paradigm for Global Politics.* New York: Columbia University Press.

March, James G., and Herbert Simon. (1958) *Organizations.* New York: Wiley.

Mearsheimer, John. (1990) "Back to the Future: Instability in Europe after the Cold War," *International Security* 15: 5–56.

Morgenthau, Hans J. (1973) *Politics among Nations,* 5th ed. New York: Knopf.

Morse, Edward. (1976) *Modernization and the Transformation of International Relations.* New York: Free Press.

Neustadt, Richard. (1970). *Alliance Politics.* New York: Columbia University Press.

Niebuhr, Reinhold. (1945) *The Children of Light and the Children of Darkness.* New York: Scribner.

Niou, Emerson, Peter C. Ordeshook, and G. F. Rose (1989). *The Balance of Power.* Cambridge: Cambridge University Press.

Nye, Joseph S., Jr. (1988) "Neorealism and Neoliberalism," *World Politics* 40: 235–51.

Odell, John. (1982). *U.S. International Monetary Policy: Markets, Power and Ideas as Sources of Change.* Princeton, N.J.: Princeton University Press.

Paige, Glenn D. (1968) *The Korean Decision.* New York: Free Press.

Perlmutter, Amos. (1974) "Presidential Political Center and Foreign Policy," *World Politics* 27: 87–106.

Posen, Barry. (1984) *The Sources of Military Doctrine.* Ithaca, N.Y.: Cornell University Press.

Rapoport, Anatol. (1957) "L. F. Richardson's Mathematical Theory of War," *Journal of Conflict Resolution* 1: 249–99.

Raphael, Theodore D. (1982) "Integrative Complexity Theory and Forecasting International Crises: Berlin 1946–1962," *Journal of Conflict Resolution* 26: 433–50.

Richardson, Lewis Fry. (1960a) *Arms and Insecurity.* Chicago: Quadrangle Press.

———. (1960b) *Statistics of Deadly Quarrels.* Chicago: Quadrangle Press.

Rosecrance, Richard. (1986) *The Rise of the Trading State.* New York: Basic Books.

———. (1966) "Bipolarity, Multipolarity, and the Future," *Journal of Conflict Resolution* 10: 314–27.

———. (1963) *Action and Reaction in International Politics.* Boston: Little, Brown.

Rosenau, James N. (1990) *Turbulence in World Politics.* Princeton, N.J.: Princeton University Press.

———. (1980) *The Study of Global Interdependence.* London: F. Pinter.

———. (1968) "National Interest," *International Encyclopedia of the Social Sciences,* vol. 11: 34–40. New York: Macmillan.

Rosenau, Pauline. (1990) "Once Again into the Breach: International Relations Confronts the Humanities," *Millenium* 19: 83–110.

Rothstein, Robert. (1972) *Planning, Prediction, and Policy-making in Foreign Affairs: Theory and Practice.* Boston: Little, Brown.

Rummel, Rudolph J. (1983) "Libertarianism and Violence," *Journal of Conflict Resolution* 27: 27–71.
Russett, Bruce M. (1963) "Toward a Model of Competitive International Politics," *Journal of Politics* 25: 226–47.
Sagan, Scott. (1985) "Nuclear Alerts and Crisis Management," *International Security* 9: 99–139.
Scott, Andrew M. (1982) *The Dynamics of Interdependence*. Chapel Hill: University of North Carolina Press.
––––––. (1967) *The Functioning of the International Political System*. New York: Macmillan.
Simon, Herbert. (1957) *Administrative Behavior*. New York: Macmillan.
Singer, J. David. (1963) "Inter-Nation Influence: A Formal Model," *American Political Science Review* 57: 420–30.
Smith, Tony. (1979) "The Underdevelopment of Development Literature: The Case of Dependency Theory," *World Politics* 31: 247–88.
Smoke, Richard. (1977) *War: Controlling Escalation*. Cambridge, Mass.: Harvard University Press.
Snyder, Glenn H., and Paul Diesing. (1977) *Conflict among Nations: Bargaining, Decision Making and System Structure in International Crises*. Princeton, N.J.: Princeton University Press.
Snyder, Jack. (1984) *The Ideology of the Offensive: Military Decision Making and the Disaster of 1914*. Ithaca, N.Y.: Cornell University Press.
Snyder, Richard C., H. W. Bruck, and Burton Sapin, eds. (1962) *Foreign Policy Decision Making*. New York: Free Press.
Sprout, Harold, and Margaret Sprout. (1957) "Environmental Factors in the Study of International Politics," *Journal of Conflict Resolution* 1: 309–28.
Spykman, Nicholas. (1942) *America's Strategy in World Politics*. New York: Harcourt, Brace and Co.
Steinbruner, John. (1974) *The Cybernetic Theory of Decision*. Princeton, N.J.: Princeton University Press.
––––––. (1981–1982) "Nuclear Decapitation," *Foreign Policy* 45: 16–28.
Steiner, Miriam. (1983) "World of Foreign Policy," *International Organization* 37: 373–414.
Stewart, Philip D., Margaret G. Hermann, and Charles F. Hermann. (1986) "The Politburo and Foreign Policy: Toward a Model of Soviet Decision Making." Paper presented to the Annual Meeting of International Society for Political Psychology, Amsterdam.
Suedfeld, Peter, and Philip Tetlock. (1977) "Integrative Complexity of Communications in International Crises," *Journal of Conflict Resolution* 21: 169–86.
Suedfeld, Peter, Philip Tetlock, and Carmenza Ramirez. (1977) "War, Peace and Integrative Complexity," *Journal of Conflict Resolution* 21: 427–42.
Tetlock Philip. (1985) "Integrative Complexity of American and Soviet Foreign Policy Rhetoric: A Time Series Analysis," *Journal of Personality and Social Psychology* 49: 1565–85.
––––––. (1979) "Identifying Victims of Groupthink from Public Statements of Decision Makers," *Journal of Personality and Social Psychology* 37: 1314–24.
Tucker, Robert W. (1992–1993) "Realism and the New Consensus," *National Interest* 30: 33–36.

Tversky, Amos, and Daniel Kahneman. (1981) "Judgment under Uncertainty," *Science* 211: 453–55.

Verba, Sidney. (1961) "Assumptions of Rationality and Non-Rationality in Models of the International System," *World Politics* 14: 93–117.

Vernon, Raymond. (1991) "Sovereignty at Bay: Twenty Years After," *Millenium* 20: 191–95.

———. (1971) *Sovereignty at Bay*. New York Basic Books.

Walker, Stephen G. (1983) "The Motivational Foundations of Political Belief Systems: A Re-Analysis of the Operational Code Construct," *International Studies Quarterly* 27: 179–202.

———. (1977) "The Interface between Beliefs and Behavior: Henry Kissinger's Operational Code and the Vietnam War," *Journal of Conflict Resolution* 21: 129–68.

Wallerstein, Immanuel. (1974a) *The Modern World-System*. New York: Academic Press.

———. (1974b) "The Rise and Future Demise of the World Capitalist System: Concepts for Comparative Analysis," *Comparative Studies in Society and History* 16: 387–415.

Walt, Steven M. (1987) *The Origin of Alliances*. Ithaca, N.Y.: Cornell University Press.

Waltz, Kenneth W. (1981) "The Spread of Nuclear Weapons: More May Be Better," *Adelphi Papers*, No. 171.

———. (1979) *Theory of International Politics*. Reading, Mass.: Addison-Wesley.

———. (1970) "The Myth of National Interdependence," in Charles P. Kindleberger, ed., *The International Corporation*. Cambridge, Mass.: M.I.T. Press.

———. (1964) "The Stability of a Bipolar World," *Daedalus* 93: 881–909.

———. (1959) *Man, the State, and War*. New York: Columbia University Press.

Welch, David A., and James G. Blight. (1987–1988) "An Introduction to the ExComm Transcripts," *International Security* 12: 5–29.

Wight, Martin. (1973) "The Balance of Power and International Order," in Alan James, ed., *The Bases of International Order*. London: Oxford University Press.

Wilensky, Harold. (1967) *Organizational Intelligence: Knowledge and Policy in Government and Industry*. New York: Basic Books.

Williamson, Samuel R., Jr. (1969) *The Politics of Grand Strategy: Britain and France Prepare for War, 1904–1914*. Cambridge, Mass.: Harvard University Press.

Wolfers, Arnold. (1962) *Discord and Collaboration*. Baltimore: Johns Hopkins University Press.

Wright, Quincy. (1955) *The Study of International Relations*. New York: Appleton-Century-Crofts.

Yoffie, David B. (1983) *Power and Protectionism: Strategies of the Newly Industrializing Countries*. New York: Columbia University Press.

Zinnes, Dina A. (1967) "An Analytical Study of the Balance of Power," *Journal of Peace Research* 3: 270–88.

Zolberg, Aristide. (1981) "Origins of the Modern World System: A Missing Link," *World Politics* 33: 253–81.

CHAPTER 3

Realist Thought and
Neorealist Theory*

KENNETH N. WALTZ[1]

I offer this essay as a contribution toward clarifying some problems in the framing and applying of international-political theory. I begin by looking at a theoretical breakthrough in a related field: economics. Realists and neorealists represent two of the major theoretical approaches followed by students of international politics in the past half century or so. They encountered problems similar to those the Physiocrats began to solve in France in the middle of the eighteenth century. Students of international politics have had an extraordinarily difficult time casting their subject in theoretical terms. Looking first at an example of comparable difficulties surmounted in a related field may be instructive.

HOW ECONOMIC THEORY BECAME POSSIBLE

Difficulties common to earlier economists and twentieth-century political scientists are revealed by examining Sir Josiah Child's (1740; see also Letwin, 1959) *A New Discourse*, written mainly in the years 1668 to 1670. Child dealt with a striking question. Why, he wondered, did the prosperity of the Dutch surpass that of the English? In casting about for an answer, he seized on what seemed to be a compelling fact: namely, that the Dutch rate of interest had been lower than the English rate. The reasoning used to establish the causal role of the rate of interest is correlative and sequential. Child tried to show

* This chapter is based on an essay that was originally published in the *Journal of International Affairs* 44 (Spring/Summer 1990): 21–37.
[1] I should like to thank David Schleicher for his help on this paper.

that the prosperity of various countries varies inversely with prevailing rates of interest. He then established the causal direction by arguing that the expected changes in the level of prosperity followed upon changes in rates of interest.

Child's work is the kind of pretheoretical effort that provides stimulus to, and material for, later theories. That is its merit. It is, however, the kind of work that can neither provide satisfactory explanations nor lead to the construction of theory. We can profit by noticing why this is so. Child tried to establish a necessary relation between the rate of interest and the level of prosperity. Other economists picked different factors as their favorite causes—the accumulation of bullion, the fertility of the population or the soil, the industry of the people, the level of rents, or whatever. But none was able to show why the relation between the chosen factor or factors and the condition to be accounted for necessarily held. Child, for example, could not supply an answer to this now obvious question: Why doesn't a rise in interest rates attract capital, ultimately lowering its price as with commodities? He could not say whether the association he claimed to have found was causal or coincidental. He could not say whether other factors in play may have caused interest rates and national prosperity to move in opposite directions. Innumerable explanations for the observed relation were available. Prephysiocratic economists could only cast about for sequences and associations that seemed to pertain within or across countries. They could at best hope to formulate plausible explanations of particular outcomes. They had no way of relating the parts of an economy to one another and to the economy as a whole.

The first step forward was, as it had to be, to invent the concept of an economy as distinct from the society and the polity in which it is embedded. Some will always complain that it is artificial to think of an economy separate from its society and polity. Such critics are right. Yet the critics miss the point. Theory is artifice. A theory is an intellectual construction by which we select facts and interpret them. The challenge is to bring theory to bear on facts in ways that permit explanation and prediction. That can only be accomplished by distinguishing between theory and fact. Only if this distinction is made can theory be used to examine and interpret facts.

In the pretheoretic era of economics, more and more information became available in the form of reported, or purported, facts, and more and more attempts were made to account for them. But differences of explanation remained unreconciled and explanations of particular processes and outcomes did not add up to an understanding of how a national economy works. In a remarkable survey in which the historical development, the sociological setting, and the scientific qualities of economic thought are brought together, Joseph Schumpeter described the best economic literature of that earlier time as having "all the freshness and fruitfulness of direct observation." But, he added, it also "shows all the helplessness of mere observation by itself" (Schumpeter, 1967: 24). Information accumulated, but arguments, even perceptive ones about propositions that might have been developed as theories, did not add up to anything more than ideas about particulars occasioned by current controversies.

Child was better than most economists of his day, although not as good as the best. The most creative economists were frustrated by the condition that Schumpeter described. The seventeenth-century economist Sir William Petty, for example, felt the frustration. Schumpeter (1967: 30) described him as creating "for himself theoretical tools with which he tried to force a way through the undergrowth of facts." To eliminate useless and misleading "facts" was an important endeavor, but not a sufficient one. What blocked the progress of economic understanding was neither too little nor too much knowledge but rather the lack of a certain kind of knowledge.

The answers to factual questions pose puzzles that theory may hope to solve and provide materials for theorists to work with. But the work begins only when theoretical questions are posed. Theory cannot be fashioned from the answers to such factual questions as: What follows upon, or is associated with, what? Instead, answers have to be sought to such theoretical questions as these: How does this thing work? How does it all hang together? These questions cannot usefully be asked unless one has some idea of what the "thing" or the "it" might be. Theory becomes possible only if various objects and processes, movements and events, acts and interactions are viewed as forming a domain that can be studied in its own right. Clearing away useless facts was not enough; something new had to be created. An invention was needed that would permit economic phenomena to be seen as distinct processes, that would permit an economy to be viewed as a realm of affairs marked off from social and political life.

This the Physiocrats first achieved. Francois Quesnay's famous economic table is a picture depicting the circulation of wealth among the productive and unproductive classes of society, but it is a picture of the unseen and the unseeable.[2] Certain cycles are well-known facts of economic life—cycles of sowing and harvesting, of mining, refining, forging, and manufacturing. But such a direct simplification of observable processes is not what Quesnay's table presents. It presents, instead, the essential qualities of an economy in picture form. The Physiocrats were the first to think of an economy as a self-sustaining whole made up of interacting parts and repeated activities. To do so, they had to make radical simplifications—for example, by employing a psychology that saw people simply as seeking the greatest satisfaction from the least effort. They invented the concepts they needed. Their notion of a "social product" can well be described as the intellectual creation of the unobservable and the nonexistent. No one can point to a social product. It is not an identifiable quantity of goods but is instead a concept whose validity can be established only through its role in a theory that yields an improved understanding of the economy.

[2] Francois Quesnay was the foremost Physiocrat. His *Tableau Oeconomique* was published in 1758.

The Physiocrats developed concepts comprising innumerable particularities and contingencies without examining them. Among these concepts were the durable notions of distribution and circulation. The quaint and crude appearance of some physiocratic ideas should not obscure the radical advance that their theory represented. Economists had found it hard to get a theoretical hold on their subject. In prephysiocratic economics, as Schumpeter said, "the connecting link of economic causality and an insight into the inner necessities and the general character of economics were missing. It was possible to consider the individual acts of exchange, the phenomenon of money, and the question of protective tariffs as economic problems, but it was impossible to see the total process which unfolds itself in a particular economic period. Before the Physiocrats appeared on the scene, only local symptoms on the economic body, as it were, had been perceived." Only the parts of an economy could be dealt with. It was therefore necessary, again in Schumpeter's words, "to derive an explanatory principle from each separate complex of facts—as if it were in a gigantic struggle with them—and it was at best possible merely to sense the great general contexts."

INTERNATIONAL POLITICS: BEYOND THE THEORETICAL PALE

What the Physiocrats did for economics is exactly what Raymond Aron and Hans Morgenthau, two of the most theoretically self-conscious traditional realists, believed to be impossible for students of international politics to accomplish. Aron drew a sharp distinction between the study of economics and the study of international politics. The latter he assigned to the category of history, which deals with unique events and situations, and of sociology, which deals with nonlogical actions and searches for general relations among them. In contrast to economics, Aron said international politics suffers from the following difficulties:

- Innumerable factors affect the international system and no distinction can be made between those that are internal and those that are external to it.
- States, the principal international actors, cannot be endowed with a single aim.
- No distinction can be drawn between dependent and independent variables.
- No accounting identities—such as investment equals savings—can be devised.
- No mechanism exists for the restoration of a disrupted equilibrium.
- There is no possibility of prediction and manipulation with identified means leading to specified goals (Aron, 1967: 185–206).

Do the reasons cited eliminate the possibility of devising a theory of international politics? If so, then economics would have been similarly hampered. Aron did not relate obvious differences between economics and politics to the requirements of theory construction. He merely identified differences, in the confident belief that because of them no international-political theory is possible.

Morgenthau's theoretical stance is similar to Aron's. Morgenthau dealt persuasively with major problems and with issues of enduring importance. He had the knack of singling out salient facts and constructing causal analyses around them. He sought "to paint a picture of foreign policy" that would present its "rational essence," abstracting from personality and prejudice, and, especially in democracies, from the importunities of popular opinion that "impair the rationality of foreign policy" (Morgenthau, 1973: 7). He was engaged, as it were, "in a gigantic struggle" with the facts, seeking "to derive an explanatory principle" from them. Like Petty, he forged concepts that might help him "force a way through the undergrowth of facts," such as "national interest" and "interest defined as power." Like Child, Morgenthau and other realists failed to take the fateful step beyond developing concepts to the fashioning of a recognizable theory.

Morgenthau (1973: 3) described his purpose as being "to present a theory of international politics." Elements of a theory are presented, but never a theory. Morgenthau at once believed in "the possibility of developing a rational theory" and remained deeply skeptical about that possibility. Without a concept of the whole, he could only deal with the parts. As is rather commonly done, he confused the problem of explaining foreign policy with the problem of developing a theory of international politics. He then concluded that international-political theory is difficult if not impossible to contrive (Morgenthau, 1970b: 253–58). He was fond of repeating Blaise Pascal's remark that the history of the world would have been different had Cleopatra's nose been a bit shorter, and then asking, "how do you systemize that?" (Morgenthau, 1970a: 78). His appreciation of the role of the accidental and the occurrence of the unexpected in politics dampened his theoretical aspirations.

Neorealism's response is that, while difficulties abound, some that seem most daunting lie in misapprehensions about theory. Theory obviously cannot explain the accidental or account for unexpected events. Theories deal in regularities and repetitions and are possible only if these can be identified. As a realist, Morgenthau (1973: 12) maintained "the autonomy of politics," but failed to develop the concept and apply it to international politics. A theory is a depiction of the organization of a domain and of the connections among its parts (Boltzman, 1960). A theory indicates that some factors are more important than others and specifies relations among them. In reality, everything is related to everything else, and one domain cannot be separated from others. Theory isolates one realm from all others in order to deal with it intellectually. To isolate a realm is a precondition to developing a theory that will explain what goes on within it. The theoretical ambitions of Morgenthau, as of Aron, were forestalled by his belief that the international-political domain cannot be marked off from others for the purpose of constructing a theory.

In summarizing Aron's argument, I have put the first three points in sequence because they are closely interrelated. The single word "complexity" suggests the impediment that concerns him. If "economic, political, and social variables" (Aron, 1967: 198) enter into the international system, as surely they do, if states have not one but many goals, as surely they have, if separating dependent from independent variables and distinguishing effects from causes is an uncertain undertaking, as surely it is—then one can never hope to fashion a theory.

Complexity, however, does not work against theory. Rather, theory is a means of dealing with complexity. Economists can deal with it because they long ago solved Aron's first problem. Given the concept of a market—a bounded economic domain—they have been able to develop further concepts and draw connections among them. Because realists did not solve the first problem, they could not satisfactorily deal with the next two. Men have many motives. If all or very many of them must always be taken into account, economic theory becomes impossible. "Economic man" was therefore created. Men were assumed to be single-minded, economic maximizers. An assumption or a set of assumptions is necessary. In making assumptions about men's (or states') motivations, the world must be drastically simplified; subtleties must be rudely pushed aside, and reality must be grossly distorted. Descriptions strive for accuracy; assumptions are brazenly false. The assumptions on which theories are built are radical simplifications of the world and are useful only because they are such. Any radical simplification conveys a false impression of the world.

Aron's second and third points must be amended. Actors cannot realistically be endowed with a single aim, but we can only know by trying whether or not they can usefully be so endowed for purposes of constructing a theory. Political studies are not different from other studies in the realm of human affairs. We can make bold assumptions about motives, we can guess which few of many factors are salient, we can arbitrarily specify relations of dependence and independence among variables. We may even expect that the more complex and intricate the matters being studied are, the stronger the urge "to be simple-minded" would become.[3]

If international politics is a recalcitrant realm for the theorist, then its special difficulties lie elsewhere than in the first three of Aron's points. Are they perhaps found in the last three? As the fourth of Aron's impediments to theory, I have listed the absence of "accounting identities" or, as others have put it, the lack of a unit of measure and a medium of exchange in which goals can be valued and instruments comparatively priced. Political capability and political effect, whether or not conceived of simply in terms of power, cannot be expressed in units, such as dollars, that would have clear meaning and be

---

[3] "To be simple-minded" is Anatol Rapoport's (1957: 275–76) first rule for the construction of mathematical models.

applicable to different instruments and ends. Yet one finds in Adam Smith, for example, no numbers that are essential to his theory. Indeed, one finds hardly any numbers at all, and thus no "accounting identities." That supply equals demand or that investment equals savings are general propositions or purported laws that theory may explain. Stating the laws does not depend on counting, weighing, or measuring anything. As Frank Knight well and rightly wrote:

> Pure theory, in economics as in any field, is abstract; it deals with forms only, in complete abstraction from content. On the individual side, economic theory takes men with (a) any wants whatever, (b) any resources whatever, and (c) any system of technology whatever, and develops principles of economic behaviour. The validity of its "laws" does not depend on the actual conditions or data with respect to any of these three elementary phases of economic action. (Knight, 1936: 281)

In politics, not everything can be counted or measured, but some things can be. That may be helpful in the application of theories but has nothing to do with their construction.

The fifth and sixth difficulties discovered by Aron seem to tell us something substantive about politics rather than about its amenability to theory and its status as science. In classical economic theory, no mechanism—that is, no agent or institution—restores a lost equilibrium. Classical and neoclassical economists were microtheorists—market and exchange relations emerge from the exercise of individual choice. The economy is produced by the interaction of persons and firms; it cannot be said to have goals or purposes of its own (Buchanan, 1966: 25–26). Governments may, of course, act to restore a lost equilibrium. So may powerful persons or firms within the economy. But at this point we leave the realm of theory and enter the realm of practice—or "sociology" as Aron uses the term. "Any concrete study of international relations is sociological," he avers (Aron, 1967: 198). The characteristic attaches to concrete studies and not simply to the study of international politics.

Aron (1967: 201; see also Morgenthau, 1970b: 253) identifies science with the ability to predict and control. Yet theories of evolution predict nothing in particular. Astronomers do predict (although without controlling), but what entitles astronomy to be called a science is not the ability to predict but the ability to specify causes, to state the theories and laws by which the predictions are made. Economic theory is impressive even when economists show themselves to be unreliable in prediction and prescription alike. Since theory abstracts from much of the complication of the world in an effort to explain it, the application of theory in any realm is a perplexing and uncertain matter.

Aron's first three problems can be solved, although in the realm of theory all solutions are tentative. Aron's last three difficulties are not impediments to the construction of theory but rather to its application and testing.

INTERNATIONAL POLITICS: WITHIN THE THEORETICAL PALE

The new realism, in contrast to the old, begins by proposing a solution to the problem of distinguishing factors internal to international-political systems from those that are external. Theory isolates one realm from others in order to deal with it intellectually. By depicting an international-political system as a whole, with structural and unit levels at once distinct and connected, neorealism establishes the autonomy of international politics and thus makes a theory about it possible.[4] Neorealism develops the concept of a system's structure which at once bounds the domain that students of international politics deal with and enables them to see how the structure of the system, and variations in it, affect the interacting units and the outcomes they produce. International structure emerges from the interaction of states and then constrains them from taking certain actions while propelling them toward others.

The concept of structure is based on the fact that units differently juxtaposed and combined behave differently and in interacting produce different outcomes. International structures are defined, first, by the ordering principle of the system, in our case anarchy, and second, by the distribution of capabilities across units. In an anarchic realm, structures are defined in terms of their major units. International structures vary with significant changes in the number of great powers. Great powers are marked off from others by the combined capabilities (or power) they command. When their number changes consequentially, the calculations and behaviors of states, and the outcomes their interactions produce, vary.

The idea that international politics can be thought of as a system with a precisely defined structure is neorealism's fundamental departure from traditional realism. The spareness of the definition of international structure has attracted criticism. Robert Keohane (1986: 191) asserts that neorealist theory "can be modified progressively to attain closer correspondence with reality." In the most sensitive and insightful essay on neorealism that I have read, Barry Buzan asks whether the logic of neorealism completely captures "the main features of the international political system." He answers this way:

> The criticisms of Ruggie, Keohane, and others suggest that it does not, because their concerns with factors such as dynamic density, information richness, communication facilities, and such like do not obviously fit into Waltz's ostensibly "systemic" theory. (Buzan, 1988: 35)

One wonders whether such factors as these can be seen as concepts that might become elements of a theory. "Dynamic density" would seem to be the most promising candidate. Yet dynamic density is not a part of a theory about one type of society or another. Rather it is a condition that develops in greater or

---

[4] Neorealism is sometimes referred to as structural realism. Throughout this chapter I refer to my own formulation of neorealist theory (see Waltz, 1979, chaps. 5 and 6).

lesser degree within and across societies. If the volume of transactions grows sufficiently, it will disrupt a simple society and transform it into a complex one. Dynamic density is not part of a theory of any society. Rather it is a social force developing in society that under certain circumstances may first disrupt and then transform it (Ruggie, 1986: 148–52; Waltz, 1979: 323–26). The "such likes" mentioned by Buzan would not fit into any theory. Can one imagine how demographic trends, information richness, and international institutions could be thrown into a theory? No theory can contain the "such likes," but if a theory is any good, it helps us to understand and explain them, to estimate their significance and to gauge their effects. Moreover, any theory leaves some things unexplained, and no theory enables one to move directly and easily from theory to application. Theories, one must add, are not useful merely because they may help one to understand, explain, and sometimes predict the trend of events. Equally important, they help one to understand how a given system works.

To achieve "closeness of fit" would negate theory. A theory cannot fit the facts or correspond with the events it seeks to explain. The ultimate closeness of fit would be achieved by writing a finely detailed description of the world that interests us. Nevertheless, neorealism continues to be criticized for its omissions. A theory can be written only by leaving out most matters that are of practical interest. To believe that listing the omissions of a theory constitutes a valid criticism is to misconstrue the theoretical enterprise.

The question of omissions arises because I limit the second term that defines structure to the distribution of power across nations. Now and then critics point out that logically many factors other than power, such as governmental form or national ideology, can be cast in distributional terms. Obviously so, but logic alone does not write theories. The question is not what does logic permit, but what does this theory require? Considerations of power dominate considerations of ideology. In a structural theory, states are differently placed by their power, and differences in placement help to explain both their behavior and their fates. In any political system, the distribution of the unit's capabilities is a key to explanation. The distribution of power is of special explanatory importance in self-help political systems because the units of the system are not formally differentiated with distinct functions specified as are the parts of hierarchic orders.

Barry Buzan (1988: 11) raises questions about the adequacy "of defining structure within the relatively narrow sectoral terms of politics." It may be that a better theory could be devised by differently drawing the borders of the domain to which it will apply, by adding something to the theory, by subtracting something from it, or by altering assumptions and rearranging the relations among a theory's concepts. But doing any or all of these things requires operations entirely different from the mere listing of omissions. Theory, after all, is mostly omissions. What is omitted cannot be added without thoroughly reworking the theory and turning it into a different one. Should one broaden the perspective of international-political theory to include economics? An international political-economic theory would presumably be twice as good as a theory of international politics alone. To fashion such a theory, one would have to show how the international political-economic domain can be marked off from others. One would first have to define its structure and then develop a theory to explain actions and outcomes within it. A political-economic theory would represent a long step toward a general theory of international relations, but no one has shown how to take it.

Those who want to disaggregate power as defined in neorealist theory are either calling for a new theory, while failing to provide one, or are pointing to some of the knotty problems that arise in the testing and application of theory. In the latter case, they, like Aron, confuse difficulties in testing and applying theory with the problem of constructing one.[5] Critics of neorealist theory fail to understand that a theory is not a statement about everything that is important in international-political life, but rather a necessarily slender explanatory construct. Adding elements of practical importance would carry us back from a neorealist theory to a realist approach. The rich variety and wondrous complexity of international life would be reclaimed at the price of extinguishing theory.

Neorealism breaks with realism in four major ways. The first and most important one I have examined at some length. The remaining three I shall treat more briefly. They follow from, and are made possible by, the first one. Neorealism departs from traditional realism in the following additional ways: Neorealism produces a shift in causal relations, offers a different interpretation of power, and treats the unit level differently.

THEORY AND REALITY

Causal Directions

Constructing theories according to different suppositions alters the appearance of whole fields of inquiry. A new theory draws attention to new objects of inquiry, interchanges causes and effects, and addresses different worlds. When John Hobson cast economics in macrotheoretical terms, he baffled his fellow economists. The London Extension Board would not allow him to offer courses on political economy because an economics professor who had read Hobson's book thought it "equivalent in rationality to an attempt to prove the flatness of the earth" (Keynes, 1951: 365–66). Hobson's figure was apt. Microtheory, the economic orthodoxy of the day, portrayed a world different from the one that Hobson's macrotheory revealed.

---

[5] See, for example, Joseph S. Nye Jr. (1988: 241–45), Keohane (1986: 184–200), and Buzan (1988: 28–34).

Similarly, the neorealist's world looks different from the one that earlier realists had portrayed. For realists, the world addressed is one of interacting states. For neorealists, interacting states can be adequately studied only by distinguishing between structural and unit-level causes and effects. Structure becomes a new object of inquiry, as well as an occasion for argument. In the light of neorealist theory, means and ends are differently viewed, as are causes and effects. Realists think of causes running in one direction, from interacting states to the outcomes their acts and interactions produce. This is clearly seen in Morgenthau's (1973: 4–14) "Six Principles of Political Realism," which form the substance of a chapter headed "A Realist Theory of International Politics." Strikingly, one finds much said about foreign policy and little about international politics. The principles develop as Morgenthau (1973: 5) searches for his well-known "rational outline, a map that suggests to us the possible meanings of foreign policy." The principles are about human nature, about interest and power, and about questions of morality. Political realism offers the perspective in which the actions of statesmen are to be understood and judged. Morgenthau's work was in harmony with the developing political science of his day, although at the time this was not seen. Methodological presuppositions shape the conduct of inquiry. The political-science paradigm was becoming deeply entrenched. Its logic is preeminently behavioral. The established paradigm of any field indicates what facts to scrutinize and how they are interconnected. Behavioral logic explains political outcomes through examining the constituent parts of political systems. When Aron and other traditionalists insist that theorists' categories be consonant with actors' motives and perceptions, they are affirming the preeminently behavioral logic that their inquiries follow (see Waltz, 1979: 44, 47, 62). The characteristics and the interactions of behavioral units are taken to be the direct causes of political events, whether in the study of national or of international politics. Aron, Morgenthau, and other realists tried to understand and explain international outcomes by examining the actions and interactions of the units, the states that populate the international arena and those who guide their policies. Realism's approach is primarily inductive. Neorealism is more heavily deductive.

Like classical economists before them, realists were unable to account for a major anomaly. Classical theory held that disequilibria would be righted by the working of market forces without need for governmental intervention. Hobson's, and later in fuller form John Maynard Keynes's, macroeconomic theory explained why in the natural course of events recovery from depressions was such a long time coming.[6] A similarly big anomaly in realist theory is seen in the attempt to explain alternations of war and peace. Like most students of international politics, realists infer outcomes from the salient attri-

[6] In his *General Theory*, Keynes (1951) gives Hobson full credit for setting forth the basic concepts of macroeconomic theory.

butes of the actors producing them. Governmental forms, economic systems, social institutions, political ideologies: These are but a few examples of where the causes of war and peace have been found. Yet, although causes are specifically assigned, we know that states with every imaginable variation of economic institution, social custom, and political ideology have fought wars. If an indicated condition seems to have caused a given war, one must wonder what accounts for the repetition of wars even as their causes vary. Variations in the quality of the units are not linked directly to the outcomes their behaviors produce, nor are variations in patterns of interaction. Many, for example, have claimed that World War I was caused by the interaction of two opposed and closely balanced coalitions. But then many have claimed that World War II was caused by the failure of some states to right an imbalance of power by combining to counter an existing alliance. Over the centuries, the texture of international life has remained impressively, or depressingly, uniform even while profound changes were taking place in the composition of states which, according to realists, account for national behavior and international outcomes. Realists cannot explain the disjunction between supposed causes and observed effects. Neorealists can.

Neorealism contends that international politics can be understood only if the effects of structure are added to traditional realism's unit-level explanations. More generally, neorealism reconceives the causal link between interacting units and international outcomes. Neorealist theory shows that causes run not in one direction, from interacting units to outcomes produced, but rather in two directions. One must believe that some causes of international outcomes are located at the level of the interacting units. Since variations in unit-level causes do not correspond to variations in observed outcomes, one has to believe that some causes are located at the structural level of international politics as well. Realists cannot handle causation at a level above states because they fail to conceive of structure as a force that shapes and shoves the units. Causes at the level of units interact with those at the level of the structure, and because they do so, explanation at the level of units alone is bound to mislead. If one's theory allows for the operation of both unit-level and structure-level causes, then it can cope with both the changes and the continuities that occur in a system.

Power as Means and End

For many realists, the desire for power is rooted in the nature of man. Morgenthau recognized that given competition for scarce goods with no one to serve as arbiter, a struggle for power will ensue among the competitors, and that consequently the struggle for power can be explained without reference to the evil born in men. The struggle for power arises because people want things and not necessarily because of the evil in their desires. This he labels one of the two roots of conflict, but even while discussing it he pulls toward the "other root of conflict and concomitant evil"—the *animus dominandi*, the desire for power. He often considers man's drive for power as a datum more basic than the chance conditions under which struggles for power occur (Morgenthau, 1946: 192).

The reasoning is faithful to Hobbes for whom the three causes of quarrels were competition, diffidence (i.e., distrust), and glory. Competition leads to fighting for gain, diffidence to fighting to keep what has been gained, glory to fighting for reputation. Because some hunger for power, as Thomas Hobbes argued in *Leviathan*, it behooves others to cultivate their appetites. For Morgenthau, as for Hobbes, even if one has plenty of power and is secure in its possession, more power is nevertheless wanted. As Morgenthau put it:

> Since the desire to attain a maximum of power is universal, all nations must always be afraid that their own miscalculations and the power increases of other nations might add up to an inferiority for themselves which they must at all costs try to avoid. (Morgenthau, 1973: 208)

Both Hobbes and Morgenthau saw that conflict is in part situationally explained, but both believed that even were it not so, pride, lust, and the quest for glory would cause the war of all against all to continue indefinitely. Ultimately, conflict and war are rooted in human nature.

The preoccupation with the qualities of man is understandable in view of the purposes Hobbes and Morgenthau entertain. Both are interested in understanding the state. Hobbes seeks a logical explanation of its emergence; Morgenthau seeks to explain how it behaves internationally. Morgenthau thought of the "rational" statesman as striving ever to accumulate more and more power. Power is seen as an end in itself. Nations at times may act aside from considerations of power. When they do, Morgenthau (1973: 27) insists, their actions are not "of a political nature." The claim that "the desire to attain a maximum of power is universal" among nations is one of Morgenthau's (1973: 27) "objective laws that have their roots in human nature." Yet much of the behavior of nations contradicts it. Morgenthau does not explain why other desires fail to moderate or outweigh the fear states may have about miscalculation of their relative power. His opinions about power are congenial to realism. They are easily slipped into because the effort to explain behavior and outcomes by the characteristics of units leads realists to assign to them attributes that seem to accord with behavior and outcomes observed. Unable to conceive of international politics as a self-sustaining system, realists concentrate on the behavior and outcomes that seem to follow from the characteristics they have attributed to men and states. Neorealists, rather than viewing power as an end in itself, see power as a possibly useful means, with states running risks if they have either too little or too much of it. Weakness may invite an attack that greater strength would dissuade an adversary from launching. Excessive strength may prompt other states to increase their arms and pool their efforts. Power is a possibly useful means, and sensible statesmen try to have an appropriate amount of it. In crucial situations, the ultimate concern of states is not for power but for security. This is an important revision of realist theory.

A still more important one is neorealism's use of the concept of power as a defining characteristic of structure. Power in neorealist theory is simply the combined capability of a state. Its distribution across states, and changes in that distribution, help to define structures and changes in them as explained above. Some complaints have been made about the absence of efforts on the part of neorealists to devise objective measures of power. Whatever the difficulties of measurement may be, they are not theoretical difficulties but practical ones encountered when moving from theory to its practical application.

Interacting Units

For realists, anarchy is a general condition rather than a distinct structure. Anarchy sets the problem that states have to cope with. Once this is understood, the emphasis of realists shifts to the interacting units. States are unlike one another in form of government, character of rulers, types of ideology, and in many other ways. For both realists and neorealists, differently constituted states behave differently and produce different outcomes. For neorealists, however, states are made functionally similar by the constraints of structure, with the principal differences among them defined according to capabilities. For neorealists, moreover, structure mediates the outcomes that states produce. As internal and external circumstances change, structures and states may bear more or less causal weight. The question of the relative importance of different levels cannot be abstractly or definitively answered. Ambiguity cannot be resolved since structures affect units even as units affect structures. Some have thought that this is a defect of neorealist theory. It is so, however, only if factors at the unit level or at the structural level determine, rather than merely affect, outcomes. Theories cannot remove the uncertainty of politics, but only help us to comprehend it.

Neorealists concentrate their attention on the central, previously unanswered question in the study of international politics: How can the structure of an international-political system be distinguished from its interacting parts? Once that question is answered, attention shifts to the effects of structure on interacting units. Theorists concerned with structural explanations need not ask how variations in units affect outcomes, even though outcomes find their causes at both structural and unit levels. Neorealists see states as like units; each state "is like all other states in being an autonomous political unit." Autonomy is the unit-level counterpart of anarchy at the structural level.[7] A

---

[7] On page 95 of *Theory of International Politics* (Waltz, 1979), I slipped into using "sovereignty" for "autonomy." Sovereignty, Ruggie (1986: 142–48) points out, is particular to the modern state.

theory of international politics can leave aside variation in the composition of states and in the resources and technology they command because the logic of anarchy does not vary with its content. Realists concentrate on the heterogeneity of states because they believe that differences of behavior and outcomes proceed directly from differences in the composition of units. Noticing that the proposition is faulty, neorealists offer a theory that explains how structures affect behavior and outcomes.

The logic of anarchy obtains whether the system is composed of tribes, nations, oligopolistic firms, or street gangs. Yet systems populated by units of different sorts in some ways perform differently, even though they share the same organizing principle. More needs to be said about the status and role of units in neorealist theory. More also needs to be said about changes in the background conditions against which states operate. Changes in the industrial and military technologies available to states, for example, may change the character of systems but do not change the theory by which their operation is explained. These are subjects for another essay. Here I have been concerned not to deny the many connections between the old and the new realism but to emphasize the most important theoretical changes that neorealism has wrought. I have been all the more concerned to do this since the influence of realist and behavioral logic lingers in the study of international politics, as in political science generally.

REFERENCES

Aron, Raymond. (1967) "What Is a Theory of International Relations?" *Journal of International Affairs* 21 (Winter): 185–206.
Boltzman, Ludwig. (1960) "Theories as Representations," excerpt, Rudolph Wiengartner, trans., in Arthur Danto and Sidney Morgenbesser, eds., *Philosophy of Science*. Cleveland: World.
Buchanan, James M. (1966) "An Individualistic Theory of Political Process," in David Easton, ed., *Varieties of Political Theory*. Englewood Cliffs, N.J.: Prentice-Hall.
Buzan, Barry. (1988) "Systems, Structures and Units: Reconstructing Waltz's Theory of International Politics," unpublished paper.
Child, Josiah. (1740) *A New Discourse of Trade*, 4th ed. London: J. Hodges.
Hobbes, Thomas. (1651) *Leviathan*. Edited by Michael Oakeshott. Oxford: Basil Blackwell.
Keohane, Robert O. (1986) "Theory of World Politics: Structural Realism and Beyond," pp. 158–203 in Robert O. Keohane, ed., *Neorealism and Its Critics*. New York: Columbia University Press.
Keynes, John Maynard. (1951) *The General Theory of Employment, Interest, and Money*. London: Macmillan.
Knight, Frank Hyneman. (1936) *The Ethics of Competition and Other Essays*. London: George Allen & Unwin.
Letwin, William. (1959) *Sir Josiah Child, Merchant Economist*. Cambridge, Mass.: Harvard University Press.

Morgenthau, Hans J. (1973) *Politics among Nations*, 5th ed. New York: Alfred A. Knopf.
_____. (1970a) "International Relations: Quantitative and Qualitative Approaches," in Norman Palmer, ed., *A Design for International Relations Research: Scope, Theory, Methods, and Relevance*. Philadelphia: American Academy of Political and Social Science.
_____. (1970b) *Truth and Power*. New York: Praeger.
_____. (1946) *Scientific Man vs. Power Politics*. Chicago: University of Chicago Press.
Nye, Joseph S., Jr. (1988) "Neorealism and Neoliberalism," *World Politics* 40 (January): 235–51.
Rapoport, Anatol. (1957) "Lewis F. Richardson's Mathematical Theory of War," *Journal of Conflict Resolution* 1 (September): 249–99.
Ruggie, John G. (1986) "Continuity and Transformation in the World Polity: Toward a Neorealist Synthesis," pp. 131–57 in Robert O. Keohane, ed., *Neorealism and Its Critics*. New York: Columbia University Press.
Schumpeter, Joseph. (1967) *Economic Doctrine and Method: An Historical Sketch*, R. Aris, trans. New York: Oxford University Press.
Waltz, Kenneth N. (1986) "Response to My Critics," pp. 322–45 in Robert O. Keohane, ed., *Neorealism and Its Critics*. New York: Columbia University Press.
_____. (1979) *Theory of International Politics*. Reading, Mass.: Addison-Wesley.

CHAPTER 4

Liberalism and World Politics Revisited[1]

MICHAEL W. DOYLE

Promoting freedom will produce peace, we have often been told. In a speech before the British Parliament in June 1982, President Reagan (1982) proclaimed that governments founded on a respect for individual liberty exercise "restraint" and "peaceful intentions" in their foreign policy. He then announced a "crusade for freedom" and a "campaign for democratic development."

In making these claims the president joined a long list of liberal theorists (and propagandists) and echoed an old argument: The aggressive instincts of authoritarian leaders and totalitarian ruling parties make for war. Liberal states, founded on such individual rights as equality before the law, free speech and other civil liberties, private property, and elected representation are fundamentally against war, this argument asserts. When the citizens who bear the burdens of war elect their governments, wars become impossible. Furthermore, citizens appreciate that the benefits of trade can be enjoyed only under conditions of peace. Thus the very existence of liberal states, such as the United States, Japan, and our European allies, makes for peace.

Building on a growing literature in international political science and events following the end of the Cold War that have lent additional credence to liberal theories, I re-examine the liberal claim that the president reiterated for us. I look at three distinct theoretical traditions of liberalism, attributable to three theorists: Schumpeter—a brilliant explicator of the liberal pacifism the president invoked; Machiavelli—a classical republican whose glory is an imperialism we often practice; and Kant.

Despite the contradictions of liberal pacifism and liberal imperialism, I find with Kant and other liberal republicans that liberalism does leave a

---

[1] This essay draws on "Liberalism and World Politics," *American Political Science Review* 80 (December 1986): 1151–69. It adds references to recent work, expands the inventory of liberal states that resulted from the recent wave of newly democratic governments, and tries to clarify a few arguments from the *APSR* essay which appear to have been obscure.

coherent legacy on foreign affairs that challenges in important ways the dominant realist paradigm. Liberal states are different. They are indeed peaceful. But they are also prone to make war. Liberal states, as Kant argued they would, have created a separate peace. They also, as he feared they might, have discovered liberal reasons for aggression. I conclude by arguing that the differences among liberal pacifism, liberal imperialism, and Kant's liberal internationalism are not arbitrary. They are rooted in differing conceptions of the citizen and the state, and hold different implications for the future of international politics in the post–Cold War system.

LIBERAL PACIFISM

There is no canonical description of liberalism. What we tend to call liberal resembles a family portrait of principles and institutions, recognizable by certain characteristics—for example, a commitment to individual freedom, government through democratic representation, rights of private property, and equality of opportunity—that most liberal states share, although none has perfected them all. Joseph Schumpeter clearly fits within this family when he considers the international effects of capitalism and democracy.

Schumpeter's "Sociology of Imperialisms," which was published in 1919, made a coherent and sustained argument concerning the pacifying (in the sense of nonaggressive) effects of liberal institutions and principles (Schumpeter, 1955; Doyle, 1986: 155–59). Unlike some of the earlier liberal theorists, who focused on a single feature, such as trade (Montesquieu, I, Bk. 20, chap. 1), or failed to examine critically the arguments they were advancing, Schumpeter saw the interaction of capitalism and democracy as the foundation of liberal pacifism and he tested his arguments in a sociology of historical imperialisms.

Schumpeter (1955: 6) defined "imperialism" as "an objectless disposition on the part of a state to unlimited forcible expansion." Excluding imperialisms that were mere "catchwords" and object-ful imperialisms (e.g., defensive), he traced the roots of objectless imperialism to three sources, each an atavism. Modern imperialism resulted from the combined impact of a "war machine," warlike instincts, and export monopolism.

Once necessary, the war machine later developed a life of its own and took control of a state's foreign policy. "Created by the wars that required it, the machine now created the wars it required." And so, Schumpeter (1955: 25) tells us, the army of ancient Egypt, created to drive the Hyksos out of Egypt, took over the state and pursued militaristic imperialism. Like the later armies of the courts of absolutist Europe, it fought wars for the sake of glory and booty, for the sake of warriors and monarchs—wars gratia warriors.

A warlike disposition, elsewhere called "instinctual elements of bloody primitivism," is the natural ideology of a war machine. It also exists independently; the Persians, Schumpeter (1955: 25–32) says, were a warrior nation from the outset.

Under modern capitalism, export monopolists, the third source of modern imperialism, push for imperialist expansion as a way to expand their closed markets. But the absolute monarchies were the last clear-cut imperialisms. Nineteenth-century imperialisms merely represent the vestiges of the imperialisms created by Louis XIV and Catherine the Great. Thus the export monopolists are an atavism of the absolute monarchies, for they depend completely on the tariffs imposed by the monarchs and their militaristic successors for revenue (Schumpeter, 1955: 82–83). Without tariffs, monopolies would be eliminated by foreign competition.

Modern (nineteenth-century) imperialism, therefore, rests on an atavistic war machine, militaristic attitudes left over from the days of monarchical wars, and export monopolism, which is nothing more than the economic residue of monarchical finance. In the modern era, imperialists gratify their private interests. From the national perspective, their imperialistic wars are objectless.

Schumpeter's theme now emerges. Capitalism and democracy are forces for peace. Indeed, they are antithetical to imperialism. And the further (to Schumpeter) development of capitalism and democracy means that imperialism will inevitably disappear.

Capitalism produces an unwarlike disposition; its populace is "democratized, individualized, rationalized" (Schumpeter, 1955: 68). The people's (daily) energies are daily absorbed in production. The disciplines of industry and the market train people in "economic rationalism"; the instability of industrial life necessitates calculation. Capitalism also "individualizes"; "subjective opportunities" replace the "immutable factors" of traditional, hierarchical society. Rational individuals demand democratic governance.

And democratic capitalism leads to peace. As evidence, Schumpeter (1955: 95–96) claims that (1) throughout the capitalist world an opposition has arisen to "war, expansion, cabinet diplomacy"; (2) contemporary capitalism is associated with peace parties; and (3) the industrial worker of capitalism is "vigorously anti-imperialist." In addition, (4) the capitalist world has developed the means of preventing war, such as the Hague Court; and (5) the least feudal, most capitalist society—the United States—has demonstrated the least imperialistic tendencies. (The United States left over half of Mexico unconquered in the war of 1846–1848.)

His explanation for liberal pacifism was quite simple. Only war profiteers and military aristocrats gain from wars. No democracy would pursue a minority interest and tolerate the high costs of imperialism. When free trade prevails, "no class" gains from forcible expansion: "Foreign raw materials and food stuffs are as accessible to each nation as though they were in its own territory. Where the cultural backwardness of a region makes normal economic intercourse dependent on colonization it does not matter, assuming free trade, which of the 'civilized' nations undertakes the task of colonization" (Schumpeter, 1955: 75–76).

Schumpeter's arguments are difficult to evaluate. In partial tests of quasi-Schumpeterian propositions, Michael Haas (1974: 464–65) discovered a cluster that associates democracy, development, and sustained modernization with peaceful conditions. But Melvin Small and J. David Singer (1976; also Wright, 1942: 841; Wilkenfeld, 1968) have discovered that there is no clearly negative correlation between democracy and war in the period from 1816 to 1965—the period that would be central to Schumpeter's argument.

Later in his career, in *Capitalism, Socialism, and Democracy*, Schumpeter (1950: 127–28) acknowledged that "almost purely bourgeois commonwealths were often aggressive when it seemed to pay—like the Athenian or the Venetian commonwealths." But he stuck to his (pacifistic) guns, restating the view that capitalist democracy "steadily tells . . . against the use of military force and for peaceful arrangements, even when the balance of pecuniary advantage is clearly on the side of war which, under modern circumstances, is not in general very likely" (Schumpeter, 1950: 128).[2] Recently, a study by Rudolph J. Rummel (1983) of "libertarianism" and international violence is the closest test that Schumpeterian pacifism has received. "Free" states (those enjoying political and economic freedom) have considerably less conflict at the level of economic sanctions or above (more violent) than "Nonfree" states. The Free, the Partly Free (including the democratic socialist countries such as Sweden), and the Nonfree accounted for .24, .26, and .61 of the violence, respectively.

These correlations are impressive, but not conclusive for the Schumpeterian thesis. The data set is limited, in this test, to the period from 1976 to 1980. It includes, for example, the Russian–Afghan War, the Vietnamese invasion of Cambodia, China's invasion of Vietnam, and Tanzania's invasion of Uganda, but just misses the U.S. quasi-covert intervention in Angola (1975) and the not-so-covert war against Nicaragua that the United States began to wage in 1981. More important, it excludes the Cold War period with its numerous interventions and the long history of colonial wars (the Boer War, the Spanish–American War, the Mexican intervention, etc.) that marked the history of liberal, including democratic capitalist, states.

The discrepancy between the warlike history of liberal states and Schumpeter's pacifistic expectations highlights three extreme assumptions. First, his "materialistic monism" leaves little room for noneconomic objectives, whether espoused by states or individuals. Neither glory, nor prestige, nor ideological justification, nor the pure power of ruling shapes policy. These nonmaterial goals leave little room for positive-sum gains, such as the comparative advantages of trade. Second and relatedly, his states are the same. The political life of individuals seems to have been homogenized at the same time as the individuals were "rationalized, individualized, and democratized." Citizens—capitalists and workers, rural and urban—seek material welfare. Schumpeter presumes that no one seems to want to rule. He also presumes that no one is prepared to take those measures (such as stirring up foreign

---

[2] He notes that testing this proposition is likely to be very difficult, requiring "detailed historical analysis." But the bourgeois attitude toward the military, the spirit and manner by which bourgeois societies wage war, and the readiness with which they submit to military rule during a prolonged war are "conclusive in themselves" (Schumpeter, 1950: 129).

quarrels to preserve a domestic ruling coalition) that enhance one's political power, despite detrimental effects on mass welfare. Third, just as domestic politics is homogenized, so world politics, too, is homogenized. Materially monistic and democratically capitalist, all states evolve toward free trade and liberty together. Countries differently constituted seem to disappear from Schumpeter's analysis. "Civilized nations" govern "culturally backward regions." These assumptions are not shared by Machiavelli's theory of liberalism.

LIBERAL IMPERIALISM

Machiavelli argues that not only are free republics not pacifistic, they are the best form of state for imperial expansion. Establishing a republic fit for imperial expansion is, moreover, the best way to guarantee the survival of a state.

Machiavelli's republic is a classical mixed republic. It is not a democracy, which he thought would quickly degenerate into a tyranny; nor is it founded on the modern liberal view of fundamental human rights. But it is characterized by popular liberty and political participation (Machiavelli, 1950, Bk. 1, chap. 2: 112; see also Mansfield, 1970; Skinner, 1981, chap. 3; and Huliung, 1983, chap. 2). The consuls serve as "kings," the senate as an aristocracy managing the state, the people in the assembly as the source of strength.

Liberty results from the "disunion"—the competition and necessity for compromise required by the division of powers among senate and consuls and tribunes (the last representing the common people). Liberty also results from the popular veto. The powerful few, Machiavelli says, threaten tyranny because they seek to dominate; the mass demands not to be dominated. Their veto thus preserves the liberties of the state (Machiavelli, 1950, Bk. I, chap. 5: 122). But since the people and the rulers have different social characters, the people need to be "managed" by the few to avoid having their recklessness overturn or their fecklessness undermine the ability of the state to expand (Machiavelli, 1950, Bk. I, chap. 53: 249–50). Thus the senate and the consuls plan expansion, consult oracles, and employ religion to manage the resources that the energy of the people supplies.

Strength, and then imperial expansion, result from the way liberty encourages increased population and property, which grow when the citizens know that their lives and goods are secure from arbitrary seizure. Free citizens equip large armies and provide soldiers who fight for public glory and the common good, because they are in fact their own (Machiavelli, 1950, Bk. II, chap. 2: 287–90). Thus, if you seek the honor of having your state expand, Machiavelli advises, you should organize it as a free and popular republic like Rome rather than as an aristocratic republic like Sparta or Venice. Expansion thus calls for a free republic.

"Necessity"—political survival—calls for expansion. If a stable aristocratic republic is forced by foreign conflict "to extend her territory, in such a case we shall see her foundations give way and herself quickly brought to ruin." If domestic security, on the other hand, prevails, "the continued tranquillity would enervate her, or provoke internal dissensions, which together, or either of them separately, will apt to prove her ruin" (Machiavelli, 1950, Bk. I, chap. 6: 129). Machiavelli therefore believes that it is necessary to take the constitution of Rome, rather than that of Sparta or Venice, as our model.

Hence liberal imperialism. We are lovers of glory, Machiavelli announces. We seek to rule, or at least to avoid being oppressed. In either case, we want more for ourselves and our states than just material welfare (materialistic monism). Because other states with similar aims thereby threaten us, we prepare ourselves for expansion. Because our fellow citizens threaten us if we do not allow them either to satisfy their ambition or to release their political energies through imperial expansion, we expand.

There is considerable historical evidence for liberal imperialism. Machiavelli's (Polybius's) Rome and Thucydides's Athens both were imperial republics in the Machiavellian sense (Thucydides, 1954, Bk. 6). The historical record of numerous U.S. interventions in the postwar period supports Machiavelli's argument (Aron, 1974, chaps. 3–4; Barnet, 1968, chap. 11). But the current record of liberal pacifism, weak as it is, calls some of Machiavelli's insights into question. To the extent that the modern populace actually controls (and thus unbalances) the mixed republic, their diffidence may outweigh elite ("senatorial") aggressiveness.

We can conclude either that (1) liberal pacifism has at last taken over with the further development of capitalist democracy, as Schumpeter predicted it would; or (2) the mixed record of liberalism—pacifism and imperialism—indicates that some liberal states are Schumpeterian democracies while others are Machiavellian republics. But before we accept either conclusion, we must consider a third apparent regularity of modern world politics.

LIBERAL INTERNATIONALISM

Modern liberalism carries with it two legacies. They affect liberal states, not separately, according to whether they are pacifistic or imperialistic, but simultaneously.

The first of these legacies is the pacification of foreign relations among liberal states.[3] During the nineteenth century, the United States and Great

---

[3] Clarence Streit (1938: 88, 90–92) seems to have been the first to point out (in contemporary foreign relations) the empirical tendency of democracies to maintain peace among themselves, and he made this the foundation of his proposal for a (non-Kantian) federal union of the fifteen leading democracies of the 1930s. In a very interesting book, Ferdinand Hermens (1944) explored some of the policy implications of Streit's analysis. D. V. Babst (1972: 55–58) performed a quantitative study of this phenomenon of "democratic peace," and Rudolph J. Rummell (1983) did a similar study of "libertarianism" (in the sense of laissez-faire) focusing on the postwar period, which drew on an unpublished study (Project No. 48) noted in Appendix 1 (Rummel, 1979: 386). I use "liberal" in a wider (Kantian) sense in my discussion of this issue in an earlier publication (Doyle, 1983a). In that essay, I survey the period from 1790 to the present and find no war among liberal states.

Britain engaged in nearly continual strife. But after the Reform Act of 1832 defined actual representation as the formal source of the sovereignty of the British Parliament, Britain and the United States negotiated their disputes despite, for example, British grievances against the Northern blockade of the South, with which Britain had close economic ties. Despite severe Anglo-French colonial rivalry, liberal France and liberal Britain formed an entente against illiberal Germany before World War I. And in 1914–1915, Italy, the liberal member of the Triple Alliance with Germany and Austria, chose not to fulfill its treaty obligations under the Triple Alliance to support its allies. Instead, Italy joined in an alliance with Britain and France, which prevented it from having to fight other liberal states, and then declared war on Germany and Austria. And despite generations of Anglo-American tension and Britain's wartime restrictions on American trade with Germany, the United States leaned toward Britain and France from 1914 to 1917, before entering World War I on their side.[4]

Beginning in the eighteenth century and slowly growing since then, a zone of peace, which Kant called the "pacific federation" or "pacific union," began to be established among liberal societies. (More than fifty liberal states currently make up the union. Most are in Europe and North America, but they can be found on every continent, as Table 4.1 indicates.)

Here the predictions of liberal pacifists (and President Reagan) are borne out: Liberal states do exercise peaceful restraint and a separate peace exists among them. This separate peace provides a solid foundation for the crucial alliances between the United States and the liberal powers (NATO, our Japanese alliance, and the bilateral ties with Australia and New Zealand that emanate from the components of the ANZUS pact).[5] This liberal alliance engendered the unbalanced preponderance of resources that the "West" enjoyed during the Cold War and appears to be impervious to economic competition and personal quarrels with liberal allies. It also offers the promise of a continuing peace among liberal states. And, as the number of liberal states

---

[4] Recently, a number of younger scholars have made important contributions to the diplomatic history of the liberal peace. I have found the following papers especially informative: "Fashoda" by Hongying Wang (1992), which shows that the liberal peace hung by a lucky thread in 1898; "Whose Tyranny? Constitutionalism, Democracy, and the War of 1812" by John Owen (1992), which demonstrates the political significance of liberal institutions and ideologies in nineteenth-century Anglo-American diplomacy; and Erik Yesson's (1993) critical comparison of Anglo-American liberal accommodation and Anglo-French realist balancing in his study of early twentieth-century "Power and Diplomacy in World Politics." Each of these papers independently develops and (of course) complicates the liberal claim. In the literature on international law, a striking contribution to an understanding of the impact of liberalism has been made by Anne-Marie Burley (1992) in "Law among Liberal States: Liberal Internationalism and the Act of State Doctrine." There she shows that liberal states treat each other differently; they assume that fellow liberal states, unlike nonliberal states, will obey the law, and they therefore hold fellow liberals to exacting standards in judicial proceedings.

[5] Generally and statistically speaking, democratic political systems have a higher than normal propensity to ally with each other (Siverson and Emmons, 1991; see also James Lee Ray, 1994).

The Liberal Community (by date "liberal")[a]

Period		Total Number
18th century	Swiss Cantons[b]	3
	French Republic 1790–1595	
	United States[b] 1776–	
1800–1850	Swiss Confederation,	8
	United States	
	France 1830–1849	
	Belgium 1830–	
	Great Britain 1832–	
	Netherlands 1848–	
	Piedmont 1848–	
	Denmark 1849–	
1850–1900	Switzerland	13
	United States	
	Belgium	
	Great Britain	
	Netherlands	
	Piedmont 1861, Italy 1861–	
	Denmark 1866	
	Sweden 1864–	
	Greece 1864–	
	Canada 1867–[c]	
	France 1871–	
	Argentina 1880–	
	Chile 1891–	
1900–1945	Switzerland,	29
	United States,	
	Great Britain,	
	Sweden, Canada	
	Greece 1911, 1928–1936	
	Italy 1922	
	Belgium 1940	
	Netherlands 1940	
	Argentina 1943	
	France 1940	
	Chile 1924, 1932	
	Australia 1901	
	Norway 1905–1940	
	New Zealand 1907–	
	Colombia 1910–1949	
	Denmark 1914–1940	
	Poland 1917–1935	
	Latvia 1922–1934	
	Germany 1918–1932	
	Austria 1918–1934	
	Estonia 1919–1934	
	Finland 1919–	
	Uruguay 1919–	
	Costa Rica 1919–	
	Czechoslovakia 1920–1939	
	Ireland 1920–	

TABLE 4.1 (*Continued*)

Period		Total Number
1900–1945	Mexico 1928–	
(*continued*)	Lebanon 1944–	
1945^d–1988	Switzerland	54
	United States	
	Great Britain	
	Sweden	
	Canada	
	Australia	
	New Zealand	
	Finland	
	Ireland	
	Mexico	
	Uruguay 1973, 1985–	
	Chile 1973	
	Lebanon 1975	
	Costa Rica 1948, 1953–	
	Iceland 1944–	
	France 1945–	
	Denmark 1945–	
	Norway 1945–	
	Austria 1945–	
	Brazil 1945–1954, 1955–1964, 1985–	
	Belgium 1946–	
	Luxembourg 1946–	
	Netherlands 1946–	
	Italy 1946–	
	Philippines 1946–1972, 1987–	
	India 1947–1975, 1977–	
	Sri Lanka 1948–1961, 1963–1971, 1978–1983	
	Ecuador 1948–1963, 1979–	
	Israel 1949–	
	West Germany 1949–	
	Greece 1950–1967, 1975–	
	Peru 1950–1962, 1963–1968, 1980–	
	El Salvador 1950–1961	
	Turkey 1950–1960, 1966–1971, 1984–	
	Japan 1951–	
	Bolivia 1956–1969, 1982–	
	Colombia 1958–	
	Venezuela 1959–	
	Nigeria 1961–1964, 1979–1984	
	Jamaica 1962–	
	Trinidad and Tobago 1962–	
	Senegal 1963–	
	Malaysia 1963–	
	Botswana 1966–	
	Singapore 1965–	
	Portugal 1976–	

(*Table continues on p. 92.*)

TABLE 4.1 (*Continued*)

Period		Total Number
1945^d–1988 (*continued*)	Spain 1978– Dominican Republic 1978– Honduras 1981– Papua New Guinea 1982– Argentina 1983– South Korea 1988– Taiwan 1988–	

[a] I have drawn up this approximate list of "liberal regimes" (through 1988) according to the four "Kantian" institutions described as essential: market and private property economies; polities that are externally sovereign; citizens who possess juridical rights; and "republican" (whether republican or parliamentary monarchy), representative government. This latter includes the requirement that the legislative branch have an effective role in public policy and be formally and competitively (either inter- or intraparty) elected. Furthermore, I have taken into account whether male suffrage is wide (that is, 30 percent) or, as Kant would have had it, open to "achievement" by inhabitants (for example, to poll tax payers or householders) of the national or metropolitan territory. (This list of liberal regimes is thus more inclusive than a list of democratic regimes, or polyarchies. Female suffrage is granted within a generation of its being demanded by an extensive female suffrage movement; and representative government is internally sovereign [for example, including and especially over military and foreign affairs] as well as stable [in existence for at least three years].) (Banks and Overstreet [1983]; U.K. Foreign and Commonwealth Office [1980]; *The Europa Yearbook, 1985*; Langer [1968]; U.S. Department of State [1981]; Gastil [1985]; Freedom House [1991].)
[b] There are domestic variations within these liberal regimes. For example, Switzerland was liberal only in certain cantons; the United States was liberal only north of the Mason–Dixon line until 1865, when it became liberal throughout. These lists also exclude ancient "republics," since none appear to fit Kant's criteria (Holmes [1979]).
[c] Canada, as a commonwealth within the British Empire, did not have formal control of its foreign policy during this period.
[d] Selected list, excludes liberal regimes with populations less than 1 million. These include all states categorized as "Free" by Freedom House and those "Partly Free" (45 or more free) states with a more pronounced capitalist orientation.

increases, it announces the possibility of global peace this side of the grave or world conquest.

Of course, the outbreak of war—in any given year, between any two given states—is a low probability event. But the occurrence of a war between any two adjacent states, considered over a long period of time, would be more probable. The apparent absence of war between liberal states, whether adjacent or not, for almost two hundred years thus may have significance. Similar claims cannot be made for feudal, "fascist," communist, authoritarian, or totalitarian forms of rule (Doyle, 1983a: 222), nor for pluralistic or merely similar societies. More significant, perhaps, is that when states are forced to decide on which side of an impending world war they will fight, liberal states wind up all on the same side, despite the complexity of the paths that take them there. These characteristics do not prove that the peace among liberals is statistically significant, nor that liberalism is the peace's sole valid explanation.[6] But they do suggest that we consider the possibility that liberals have indeed established a separate peace—but only among themselves.

Liberalism also carries with it a second legacy—international "imprudence" (Hume, 1963: 346–47). Peaceful restraint only seems to work in the liberals' relations with other liberals. Liberal states have fought numerous wars with nonliberal states (Small and Singer, 1976). Many of these wars have been defensive, and thus prudent by necessity. Liberal states have been attacked and threatened by nonliberal states that do not exercise any special restraint in their dealings with liberal states. Authoritarian rulers both stimulate and respond to an international political environment in which conflicts of prestige, of interest, and of pure fear of what other states might do all lead states toward war. War and conquest have thus characterized the careers of many authoritarian rulers and ruling parties—from Louis XIV and Napoleon to Mussolini's Fascists, Hitler's Nazis, and Stalin's Communists.

But we cannot blame warfare simply on the authoritarians or totalitarians, as many of our more enthusiastic politicians would have us do.[7] Most wars arise out of calculations and miscalculations of interest, misunderstandings, and mutual suspicions, such as those that characterized the origins of World War I. But aggression by the liberal state has also characterized a large number of wars. Both France and Britain fought expansionist colonial wars throughout the nineteenth century. The United States fought a similar war with Mexico in 1846–1848, waged a war of annihilation against the American Indians, and intervened militarily against sovereign states many times before and after World War II. Liberal states invade weak

---

[6] Babst (1972: 56) did make a preliminary test of the significance of the distribution of alliance partners in World War I. He found that the possibility that the actual distribution of alliance partners could have occurred by chance was less than 1 percent. But this assumes that there was an equal possibility that any two nations could have gone to war with each other, and this is a strong assumption. The most thorough statistical demonstration of the significance of the liberal peace, controlling for alliance patterns, proximity, economic interdependence, etc., can be found in Zeev Maoz and Bruce Russett (1992a).

[7] There are, however, serious studies that show that marxist regimes have higher military spending per capita than nonmarxist regimes (Payne, 1986). But this should not be interpreted as a sign of the inherent aggressiveness of authoritarian or totalitarian governments or—with even greater enthusiasm—the inherent and global peacefulness of liberal regimes. Marxist regimes, in particular, represent a minority in the current international system; they are strategically encircled, and, due to their lack of domestic legitimacy, they might be said to "suffer" the twin burden of needing defenses against both external and internal enemies. Stanislav Andreski (1980), moreover, argues that (purely) military dictatorships, due to their domestic fragility, have little incentive to engage in foreign military adventures. And according to Walter Clemens (1982: 117–18), the United States intervened in the Third World more than twice as often in the period from 1946 to 1976 as the Soviet Union did between 1946 and 1979. Relatedly, Barry Posen and Stephen Van Evera (1980: 105; 1983: 86–89) found that the United States devoted one quarter and the Soviet Union one tenth of their defense budgets to forces designed for Third World interventions (where responding to perceived threats would presumably have a less than purely defensive character).

nonliberal states and display striking distrust in dealings with powerful nonliberal states (Doyle, 1983b).

Neither realist (statist) nor marxist theory accounts well for these two legacies. They can account for aspects of certain periods of international stability (Aron, 1968: 151–54; Russett, 1985), but neither the logic of the balance of power nor of international hegemony explains the separate peace maintained for more than 150 years among states sharing one particular form of governance—liberal principles and institutions. Balance-of-power theory expects, indeed is premised on, flexible arrangements of geostrategic rivalry that include preventive war. Hegemonies wax and wane, but the liberal peace holds. Marxist "ultra-imperialists" expect a form of peaceful rivalry among capitalists, but only liberal capitalists maintain peace. Leninists expect liberal capitalists to be aggressive toward nonliberal states, but they also (and especially) expect them to be imperialistic toward fellow liberal capitalists.

Kantian Theory

Kant's theory of liberal internationalism helps us understand these two legacies. The importance of Immanuel Kant as a theorist of international ethics has been well appreciated (Armstrong, 1931; Friedrich, 1948; Waltz, 1962; Hoffmann, 1965; Hinsley, 1967, chap. 4; Hassner, 1972; Galston, 1975; Gallie, 1978, chap. 1; Williams, 1983). But Kant also has an important analytical theory of international politics. "Perpetual Peace," written in 1795, helps us understand the interactive nature of international relations. Methodologically, Kant tries to teach us that we cannot study either the systemic relations of states or the varieties of state behavior in isolation from each other. Substantively, he anticipates for us the ever-widening pacification of a liberal pacific union, explains that pacification, and at the same time suggests why liberal states are not pacific in their relations with nonliberal states. Kant argues that perpetual peace will be guaranteed by the ever-widening acceptance of three "definitive articles" of peace. When all nations have accepted the definitive articles in a metaphorical "treaty" of perpetual peace he asks them to sign, perpetual peace will have been established.

The *First Definitive Article* requires that the civil constitution of the state be republican. By republican Kant means the legal order that has solved, at least juridically, the problem of combining moral autonomy, individualism, and political order. A private property and market-oriented economy partially addressed that dilemma in the private sphere. The public, or political, sphere was more troubling. His answer was a republic that preserved juridical freedom—the legal equality of citizens as subjects—on the basis of a representative government with a separation of powers. Juridical freedom is preserved because the morally autonomous individual is by means of representation a self-legislator making laws that apply to all citizens equally, including himself.

And tyranny is avoided because the individual is subject to laws he does not also administer (PP: 99–102).[8]

Liberal republics will progressively establish peace among themselves by means of the pacific treaty, or union (*foedus pacificum*), described in his *Second Definitive Article*. The pacific union will establish peace within a federation of free states and securely maintain the rights of each state. The world will not have achieved the "perpetual peace" that provides the ultimate guarantor of republican freedom until "a late stage and after many unsuccessful attempts" (UH: 47). Then right conceptions of the appropriate constitution, great and sad experience, and goodwill will have taught all the nations the lessons of peace. Not until then will individuals enjoy perfect republican rights or the full guarantee of a global and just peace. But in the meantime, the "pacific federation" of liberal republics—"an enduring and gradually expanding federation likely to prevent war"—brings within it more and more republics (despite republican collapses, backsliding, and disastrous wars), creating an expanding separate peace (PP: 105).[9] And Kant emphasizes:

> It can be shown that this idea of federalism, extending gradually to encompass all states and thus leading to perpetual peace, is practicable and has objective reality. For if by good fortune one powerful and enlightened nation can form a republic (which is by nature inclined to seek peace), this will provide a focal point for federal association among other states. These will join up with the first one, thus securing the freedom of each state in accordance with the idea of international right, and the whole will gradually spread further and further by a series of alliances of this kind. (PP: 104)

The pacific union is neither a single peace treaty ending one war nor a world state or state of nations. Kant finds the first insufficient. The second and third are impossible or potentially tyrannical. National sovereignty precludes reliable subservience to a state of nations; a world state destroys the civic freedom on which the development of human capacities rests (UH: 50). Although Kant obliquely refers to various classical interstate confederations and modern diplomatic congresses, he develops no systematic organizational embodiment of this treaty, and presumably he does not find institutionalization necessary (Schwarz, 1962: 77; Riley, 1983, chap. 5). He appears to have

---

[8] The citations from Kant are from Kant (1970), the H. B. Nisbet translation edited by Hans Reiss. I cite "Perpetual Peace" (1795) as PP; "The Idea for a Universal History with a Cosmopolitan Purpose" (1784) as UH; "The Contest of Faculties" (1798) as CF; "The Metaphysics of Morals" (1797) as MM.

[9] I think Kant meant that the peace would be established among liberal regimes and would expand by ordinary political and legal means as new liberal regimes appeared. By a process of gradual extension the peace would become global and then perpetual; the occasion for wars with nonliberals would disappear as nonliberal regimes disappeared.

in mind a mutual nonaggression pact, perhaps a collective security agreement, and the cosmopolitan law set forth in the Third Definitive Article.[10]

The *Third Definitive Article* establishes a cosmopolitan law to operate in conjunction with the pacific union. The cosmopolitan law "shall be limited to conditions of universal hospitality." In this he calls for the recognition of the "right of a foreigner not to be treated with hostility when he arrives on someone else's territory." This "does not extend beyond those conditions which make it possible for them to attempt to enter into relations [commerce] with the native inhabitants" (PP: 106). Hospitality does not require extending either the right to citizenship to foreigners or the right to settlement, unless the foreign visitors would perish if they were expelled. Foreign conquest and plunder also find no justification under this right. Hospitality does appear to include the right of access and the obligation of maintaining the opportunity for citizens to exchange goods and ideas, without imposing the obligation to trade (a voluntary act in all cases under liberal constitutions).

Perpetual peace, for Kant, is an epistemology, a condition for ethical action, and (most important) an explanation of how the "mechanical process of nature visibly exhibits the purposive plan of producing concord among men, even against their will and indeed by means of their very discord" (PP: 108; UH: 44–45). Understanding history requires an epistemological foundation, for without a teleology, such as the promise of perpetual peace, the complexity of history would overwhelm human understanding (UH: 51–53). But perpetual peace is not merely a heuristic device with which to interpret history. It is guaranteed, Kant explains in the "First Addition" of "Perpetual Peace" ("On the Guarantee of Perpetual Peace"), to result from men fulfilling their ethical duty or, failing that, from a hidden plan.[11] Peace is an ethical duty because it is only under conditions of peace that all men

---

[10] Kant's *foedus pacificum* is thus neither a *pactum pacis* (a single peace treaty) nor a *civitas gentium* (a world state). He appears to have anticipated something like a less formally institutionalized League of Nations or United Nations. One could argue that these two institutions in practice worked for liberal states and only for liberal states. But no specifically liberal "pacific union" was institutionalized. Instead liberal states have behaved for the past almost 200 years as if such a Kantian pacific union and treaty of perpetual peace had been signed.

[11] In the "Metaphysics of Morals" (the *Rechtslehre*), Kant seems to write as if perpetual peace is only an epistemological device, and perpetual peace, while an ethical duty, is empirically merely a "pious hope" (MM: 164–75) (though even here Kant [MM: 171] finds that the pacific union is not "impracticable"). In the "Universal History," Kant writes as if the brute force of physical nature drives men toward inevitable peace. Yovel (1980: 168ff) argues that "Perpetual Peace" reconciles the two views of history, from a postcritical (post Critique of Judgment) perspective. "Nature" is human-created nature (culture or civilization). Perpetual peace is the "*a priori* of the *a posteriori*" (a critical perspective that then enables us to discern causal, probabilistic patterns in history). Law, and the "political technology" of republican constitutionalism, are separate from ethical development. But both interdependently lead to perpetual peace: the first through force, fear, and self-interest; the second through progressive enlightenment; and both together through the widening of the circumstances in which engaging in right conduct poses smaller and smaller burdens.

can treat each other as ends (UH: 50; Murphy, 1970, chap. 3). In order for this duty to be practical, Kant needs, of course, to show that peace is in fact possible. The widespread sentiment of approbation that he saw aroused by the early success of the French revolutionaries showed him that we can indeed be moved by ethical sentiments with a cosmopolitan reach (CF: 181–82; Yovel, 1980: 153–54). This does not mean, however, that perpetual peace is certain ("prophesyable"). Even the scientifically regular course of the planets could be changed by a wayward comet striking them out of orbit. Human freedom requires that we allow for much greater reversals in the course of history. We must, in fact, anticipate the possibility of backsliding, temporary declines in the numbers of liberal republics, and destructive wars (though these will serve to educate nations to the importance of peace) (UH: 47–48).

But, in the end, our guarantee of perpetual peace does not rest on ethical conduct, as Kant emphasizes:

> We now come to the essential question regarding the prospect of perpetual peace. What does nature do in relation to the end which man's own reason prescribes to him as a duty, i.e., how does nature help to promote his moral purpose? And how does nature guarantee that what man ought to do by the laws of his freedom (but does not do) will in fact be done through nature's compulsion, without prejudice to the free agency of man? . . . This does not mean that nature imposes on us a duty to do it, for duties can only be imposed by practical reason. On the contrary, nature does it herself, whether we are willing or not: *facta volentem ducunt, nolentem tradunt.* (PP: 112)

The guarantee thus rests, Kant (PP: 112) argues, on the probable behavior not of moral angels but of "devils, so long as they possess understanding." In explaining the sources of each of the three definitive articles of the perpetual peace, Kant then tells us how we (as free and intelligent devils) could be motivated by fear, force, and calculated advantage to undertake a course of actions whose outcome we can reasonably anticipate to be perpetual peace. But, while it is possible to conceive of the Kantian road to peace in these terms, Kant himself recognizes and argues that social evolution also makes the conditions of moral behavior less onerous and hence more likely (CF: 187–89; Kelly, 1969: 106–13). In tracing the effects of both political and moral development, he builds an account of why liberal states do maintain peace among themselves and of how it will (by implication, has) come about that the pacific union will expand. He also explains how these republics would engage in wars with nonrepublics and therefore suffer the "sad experience" of wars that an ethical policy might have avoided.

The first source derives from a political evolution, from a constitutional law. Nature (providence) has seen to it that human beings can live in all the regions where they have been driven to settle by wars. (Kant, who once taught geography, reports on the Lapps, the Samoyeds, the Pescheras.) "Asocial sociability" draws men together to fulfill needs for security and material welfare as it drives them into conflicts over the distribution and control of social products (UH: 44–45; PP: 110–11). This violent natural evolution tends toward the liberal peace because "asocial sociability" inevitably leads toward republican governments, and republican governments are a source of the liberal peace.

Republican representation and separation of powers are produced because they are the means by which the state is "organized well" to prepare for and meet foreign threats (by unity) and to tame the ambitions of selfish and aggressive individuals (by authority derived from representation, by general laws, and by nondespotic administration) (PP: 112–13). States that are not organized in this fashion tend to fail. Monarchs thus encourage commerce and private property in order to increase national wealth. They cede rights of representation to their subjects in order to strengthen their political support or to obtain willing grants of tax revenue (Hassner, 1972: 583–86).

Kant shows how republics, once established, lead to peaceful relations. He argues that once the aggressive interests of absolutist monarchies are tamed and once the habit of respect for individual rights is ingrained by republican government, wars would appear as the disaster to the people's welfare that he and the other liberals thought them to be. The fundamental reason is this:

> If, as is inevitably the case under this constitution, the consent of the citizens is required to decide whether or not war should be declared, it is very natural that they will have a great hesitation in embarking on so dangerous an enterprise. For this would mean calling down on themselves all the miseries of war, such as doing the fighting themselves, supplying the costs of the war from their own resources, painfully making good the ensuing devastation, and, as the crowning evil, having to take upon themselves a burden of debts which will embitter peace itself and which can never be paid off on account of the constant threat of new wars. But under a constitution where the subject is not a citizen, and which is therefore not republican, it is the simplest thing in the world to go to war. For the head of state is not a fellow citizen, but the owner of the state, and war will not force him to make the slightest sacrifice so far as his banquets, hunts, pleasure palaces and court festivals are concerned. He can thus decide on war, without any significant reason, as a kind of amusement, and unconcernedly leave it to the diplomatic corps (who are always ready for such purposes) to justify the war for the sake of propriety. (PP: 100)

Yet these domestic republican restraints do not end war. If they did, liberal states would not be warlike, which is far from the case. They do introduce republican caution, Kant's "hesitation," in place of monarchical caprice. Liberal wars are only fought for popular, liberal purposes. The historical liberal legacy is laden with popular wars fought to promote freedom, protect private property, or support liberal allies against nonliberal enemies. Kant's position is ambiguous. He regards these wars as unjust and warns liberals of their susceptibility to them (PP: 106). At the same time, Kant argues that each nation "can and ought to" demand that its neighboring nations enter into the pacific union of liberal states (PP: 102). Thus to see how the pacific union removes the occasion of wars among liberal states and not wars between liberal and nonliberal states, we need to shift our attention from constitutional law to international law, Kant's second source.

Complementing the constitutional guarantee of caution, international law adds a second source—a guarantee of respect. The separation of nations that asocial sociability encourages is reinforced by the development of separate languages and religions. These further guarantee a world of separate states—an essential condition needed to avoid a "global, soul-less despotism." Yet, at the same time, they also morally integrate liberal states. "As culture grows and men gradually move towards greater agreement over their principles, they lead to mutual understanding and peace" (PP: 114). As republics emerge (the first source) and as culture progresses, an understanding of the legitimate rights of all citizens and of all republics comes into play; and this, now that caution characterizes policy, sets up the moral foundations for the liberal peace.

Correspondingly, international law highlights the importance of Kantian publicity. Domestically, publicity helps ensure that the officials of republics act according to the principles they profess to hold just and according to the interests of the electors they claim to represent. Internationally, free speech and the effective communication of accurate conceptions of the political life of foreign peoples are essential to establish and preserve the understanding on which the guarantee of respect depends. Domestically just republics, which rest on consent, then presume foreign republics to be also consensual, just, and therefore deserving of accommodation. The experience of cooperation helps engender further cooperative behavior when the consequences of state policy are unclear but (potentially) mutually beneficial. At the same time, liberal states assume that nonliberal states, which do not rest on free consent, are not just. Because nonliberal governments are in a state of aggression with their own people, their foreign relations become for liberal governments deeply suspect. In short, fellow liberals benefit from a presumption of amity; nonliberals suffer from a presumption of enmity. Both presumptions may be accurate. Each, however, may also be self-confirming.

Last, cosmopolitan law adds material incentives to moral commitments. The cosmopolitan right to hospitality permits the "spirit of commerce" sooner or later to take hold of every nation, thus impelling states to promote peace and to try to avert war. Liberal economic theory holds that these cosmopolitan ties derive from a cooperative international division of labor and free trade according to comparative advantage. Each economy is said to be better off than it would have been under autarky; each thus acquires an incentive to avoid policies that would lead the other to break these economic ties. Since keeping open markets rests upon the assumption that the next set of transactions will also be determined by prices rather than coercion, a sense of mutual security is vital to avoid security-motivated searches for economic autarky. Thus avoiding a challenge to another liberal state's security or even enhancing each other's security by means of alliance naturally follows economic interdependence.

A further cosmopolitan source of liberal peace is that the international market removes difficult decisions of production and distribution from the direct sphere of state policy. A foreign state thus does not appear directly responsible for these outcomes; states can stand aside from, and to some degree above, these contentious market rivalries and be ready to step in to resolve crises. The interdependence of commerce and the international contacts of state officials help create crosscutting transnational ties that serve as lobbies for mutual accommodation. According to modern liberal scholars, international financiers and transnational and transgovernmental organizations create interests in favor of accommodation. Moreover, their variety has ensured that no single conflict sours an entire relationship by setting off a spiral of reciprocated retaliation (Polanyi, 1944, chaps. 1–2; Brzezinski and Huntington, 1963, chap. 9; Neustadt, 1970; Keohane and Nye, 1977, chap. 7). Conversely, a sense of suspicion, such as that characterizing relations between liberal and nonliberal governments, can lead to restrictions on the range of contacts between societies. And this can increase the prospect that a single conflict will determine an entire relationship.

No single constitutional, international, or cosmopolitan source is alone sufficient, but together (and only together) they plausibly connect the characteristics of liberal polities and economies with sustained liberal peace. Alliances founded on mutual strategic interest among liberal and nonliberal states have been broken, economic ties between liberal and nonliberal states have proven fragile, but the political bonds of liberal rights and interests have proven a remarkably firm foundation for mutual nonaggression. A separate peace exists among liberal states.

But in their relations with nonliberal states, liberal states have not escaped from the insecurity caused by anarchy in the world political system considered as a whole. Moreover, the very constitutional restraint, international respect for individual rights, and shared commercial interests that establish grounds for peace among liberal states establish grounds for additional conflict in relations between liberal and nonliberal societies.

COMPARISONS

Much of the debate on the democratic peace or liberal pacifism isolates one feature of democracy or liberalism and then tests it against the historical record. It is thus worth stressing that Kant's theory rejects that approach.[12]

---

[12] A useful survey of that literature can be found in Harvey Starr (1992).

He presents the three "definitive articles" as each necessary conditions and only together a sufficient condition of establishing a pacific union.

Representation or democracy (the so-called domestic "structural" cause of the democratic peace) only ensure that foreign policy reflects the preferences of the median voter, whatever they may be. If those preferences are rational and egoistic, then however rational or powerful the state may be, it will only be pacific to the extent that a particular bilateral peace produces greater material benefits than would aggression (discounting for but still counting all systemic and temporal effects). This is a very weak reed for a wealthy, resource-rich or strategically vital state but very weak for a democratic state to rely on in its relations with powerful and also democratic states.[13]

A related objection applies to purely "normative" explanations of the liberal peace. The norms, to the extent they are normative, apply to all statespersons as moral agents, as human beings, anywhere, whatever their state structure. Yet states other than liberal states, despite the presence of moral statespersons, do not maintain peace (and liberals maintain peace only with each other).[14] In short, Kant's argument stressing the combined effect of structures, norms, and interests warrants our attention.

In order to sort out the varied legacy of liberalism on international relations and to reconsider its implications for the construction of international theories in the post–Cold War international system, we should recall that Kant's liberal internationalism, Machiavelli's liberal imperialism, and Schumpeter's liberal pacifism rest on fundamentally different views of the nature of man, the state, and international relations.[15] Schumpeter's man is rationalized, individualized, and democratized. He is also homogenized, pursuing material interests "monistically." Since his material interests lie in peaceful trade, he and the democratic state that he and his fellow citizens control are pacifistic. Machiavelli's citizens are splendidly diverse in their goals, but they are fundamentally unequal in them as well, seeking to rule or fearing being dominated. Whether extending the rule of the dominant elite or avoiding the political collapse of their state, each call for imperial expansion.

Kant's citizens, too, are diverse in their goals, and they are individualized and rationalized. But most important, they are capable of appreciating the moral equality of all individuals and of treating other individuals as ends rather than as means. The Kantian state thus is governed publicly according to law, as a republic. Kant's is the state that solves the problem of governing individualized equals, whether they are the "rational devils" he says we often find ourselves to be or the ethical agents we can and should become. Republics tell us:

---

[13] David Lake (1992).

[14] Zeev Maoz and Bruce Russett (1992b).

[15] For a comparative discussion of the political foundations of Kant's ideas, see Judith Shklar (1984: 232–38).

> In order to organize a group of rational beings who together require universal
> laws for their survival, but of whom each separate individual is secretly
> inclined to exempt himself from them, the constitution must be so designed
> so that, although the citizens are opposed to one another in their private
> attitudes, these opposing views may inhibit one another in such a way that
> the public conduct of the citizens will be the same as if they did not have
> such evil attitudes. (PP: 113)

Unlike Machiavelli's republics, Kant's republics are capable of achieving
peace among themselves because they exercise democratic caution and because they are capable of appreciating the international rights of foreign republics. These international rights of republics derive from the representation of
foreign individuals, who are our moral equals. Unlike Schumpeter's capitalist
democracies, Kant's republics—including our own—remain in a state of war
with nonrepublics. Liberal republics see themselves as threatened by aggression from nonrepublics that are not constrained by representation. And even
though wars often cost more than the economic return they generate, liberal
republics, also are prepared to protect and promote—sometimes forcibly—
democracy, private property, and the rights of individuals overseas against
nonrepublics which, because they do not authentically represent the rights
of individuals, have no rights to noninterference. These wars may liberate
oppressed individuals overseas; they also can generate enormous suffering.

Preserving the legacy of the liberal peace without succumbing to the
legacy of liberal imprudence is both a moral and a strategic challenge. The
near certainty of mutual devastation resulting from a nuclear war between
the superpowers created a "crystal ball effect," which has helped to constrain
the tendency toward miscalculation that was present at the outbreak of so
many wars in the past (Carnesale et al., 1983: 44). But this "nuclear peace"
appears to have been limited to the superpowers. It did not curb military
interventions in the Third World. Moreover, it was subject to a desperate
technological race designed to overcome its constraints and to crises that
pushed even the superpowers to the brink of war (Kegley, 1992). We must
still reckon with the war fevers that have swept great powers into interventions. And, especially now (as in the 1920s), we should recognize the powerful
tug of priorities focused on domestic economic welfare that have led to short-
sighted neglect of mounting international crises.

Yet restraining liberal imprudence, whether aggressive or passive, may
not be possible without threatening liberal pacification. Improving the strategic acumen of leaders calls for introducing steadier strategic calculations of
the long-run national interest and more flexible responses to changes in the
international political environment. Constraining the indiscriminate meddling
of foreign interventions calls for a deeper appreciation of the "particularism
of history, culture, and membership" (Walzer, 1983: 5). But both the improvement in strategy and the constraint on intervention, in turn, seem to require
an executive freed from the restraints of a representative legislature in the

management of foreign policy and a political culture indifferent to the universal rights of individuals. And these, in their turn, could break the chain of constitutional guarantees, the respect for representative government, and the web of transnational contact that have sustained the pacific union of liberal states.

Perpetual peace, Kant says, is the endpoint of the hard journey his republics will take. The promise of perpetual peace, the violent lessons of war, and the experience of a partial peace are proof of the need for and the possibility of world peace. They provide the premises for an alternative view of the dynamics of world politics. They are also the grounds for moral citizens and statesmen to assume the duty of striving for peace.

REFERENCES

Andreski, Stanislav. (1980) "On the Peaceful Disposition of Military Dictatorships," *Journal of Strategic Studies* 3: 3–10.

Armstrong, A. C. (1931) "Kant's Philosophy of Peace and War," *The Journal of Philosophy* 28: 197–204.

Aron, Raymond. (1974) *The Imperial Republic.* Frank Jellinek, trans. Englewood Cliffs, N.J.: Prentice-Hall.

———. (1966) *Peace and War: A Theory of International Relations.* Richard Howard and Annette Baker Fox, trans. Garden City, N.Y.: Doubleday.

Babst, Dean V. (1972) "A Force for Peace," *Industrial Research* 14 (April): 55–58.

Banks, Arthur, and William Overstreet, eds. (1983) *A Political Handbook of the World: 1982–1983.* New York: McGraw-Hill.

Barnet, Richard. (1968) *Intervention and Revolution.* Cleveland: World.

Brzezinski, Zbigniew, and Samuel Huntington. (1963) *Political Power: USA/USSR.* New York: Viking Press.

Burley, Anne-Marie. (1992) "Law among Liberal States: Liberal Internationalism and the Act of State Doctrine," *Columbia Law Review* 92: 1907–96.

Carnesale, Albert, Paul Doty, Stanley Hoffmann, Samuel Huntington, Joseph Nye, and Scott Sagan. (1983) *Living with Nuclear Weapons.* New York: Bantam.

Chan, Steve. (1984) "Mirror, Mirror on the Wall . . .: Are Freer Countries More Pacific?" *Journal of Conflict Resolution* 28: 617–48.

Clemens, Walter C. (1982) "The Superpowers and the Third World," pp. 111–35 in Charles Kegley Jr. and Pat McGowan, eds., *Foreign Policy: USA/USSR.* Beverly Hills: Sage Publications.

Doyle, Michael W. (1986) *Empires.* Ithaca, N.Y.: Cornell University Press.

———. (1983a) "Kant, Liberal Legacies, and Foreign Affairs: Part 1," *Philosophy and Public Affairs* 12: 205–35.

———. (1983b) "Kant, Liberal Legacies, and Foreign Affairs: Part 2," *Philosophy and Public Affairs* 12: 323–53.

The Europa Yearbook for 1985. (1985) 2 vols. London: Europa Publications.

Friedrich, Karl. (1948) *Inevitable Peace.* Cambridge, Mass.: Harvard University Press.

Gallie, W. B. (1978) *Philosophers of Peace and War.* Cambridge: Cambridge University Press.

Galston, William. (1975) *Kant and the Problem of History*. Chicago: University of Chicago Press.

Gastil, Raymond (1985) "The Comparative Survey of Freedom 1985," *Freedom at Issue* 82: 3–16.

Haas, Michael. (1974) *International Conflict*. New York: Bobbs-Merrill.

Hassner, Pierre. (1972) "Immanuel Kant," pp. 554–93 in Leo Strauss and Joseph Cropsey, eds., *History of Political Philosophy*. Chicago: Rand McNally.

Hermens, Ferdinand A. (1944) *The Tyrants' War and the People's Peace*. Chicago: University of Chicago Press.

Hinsley, F. H. (1967) *Power and the Pursuit of Peace*. Cambridge: Cambridge University Press.

Hoffmann, Stanley. (1965) "Rousseau on War and Peace," pp. 45–87 in Stanley Hoffmann, ed., *The State of War*. New York: Praeger.

Holmes, Stephen. (1979) "Aristippus in and out of Athens," *American Political Science Review* 73: 113–28.

Huliung, Mark. (1983) *Citizen Machiavelli*. Princeton, N.J.: Princeton University Press.

Hume, David. (1963) "Of the Balance of Power," in *Essays: Moral, Political, and Literary*. Oxford: Oxford University Press.

Kant, Immanuel. (1970) *Kant's Political Writings*. Hans Reiss, ed., H. B. Nisbet, trans. Cambridge: Cambridge University Press.

Kegley, Charles W., Jr. (1992) "The Long Postwar Peace during the Cold War: Some New Conventional Wisdoms Reconsidered," *Jerusalem Journal of International Relations* 14 (December): 1–18.

Kelly, George A. (1969) *Idealism, Politics, and History*. Cambridge: Cambridge University Press.

Keohane, Robert, and Joseph Nye. (1977) *Power and Interdependence*. Boston: Little Brown.

Lake, David. (1992) "Powerful Pacifists: Democratic States and War," *American Political Science Review* 86 (March): 24–37.

Langer, William L., ed. (1968) *The Encyclopedia of World History*. Boston: Houghton Mifflin.

Machiavelli, Niccoló. (1950) *The Prince and the Discourses*. Max Lerner, ed. Luigi Ricci and Christian Detmold, trans. New York: Modern Library.

Mansfield, Harvey C. (1970) "Machiavelli's New Regime," *Italian Quarterly* 13: 63–95.

Maoz, Zeev, and Bruce Russett. (1992a) "Alliance, Contiguity, Wealth and Political Stability: Is the Lack of Conflict among Democracies a Statistical Artifact?" *International Interactions* 17 (No. 3): 245–67.

———. (1992b) "Structural and Normative Causes of Peace between Democracies." Paper presented at the Annual Meeting of the International Studies Association, March 30–April 2, Atlanta.

Montesquieu, Charles de. (1949 [1748]) *Spirit of the Laws*. New York: Hafner.

Murphy, Jeffrie. (1970) *Kant: The Philosophy of Right*. New York: St. Martin's.

Neustadt, Richard. (1970) *Alliance Politics*. New York: Columbia University Press.

Owen, John. (1992) "Whose Tyranny? Constitutionalism, Democracy, and the War of 1812." Paper presented at the Annual Meeting of the American Political Science Association, September 2–5, Chicago.

Payne, James L. (1986) "Marxism and Militarism," *Polity* 19 (Winter): 270–89.

Pocock, J. G. A. (1975) *The Machiavellian Moment*. Princeton, N.J.: Princeton University Press.

Polanyi, Karl. (1944) *The Great Transformation*. Boston: Beacon Press.

Posen, Barry, and Stephen Van Evera. (1983) "Reagan Administration Defense Policy," pp. 67–104 in Kenneth Oye, Robert Lieber, and Donald Rothchild, eds., *Eagle Defiant*. Boston: Little Brown.

————. (1980) "Overarming and Underwhelming," *Foreign Policy* 40 (Fall): 99–118.

Powell, G. Bingham. (1982) *Contemporary Democracies*. Cambridge, Mass.: Harvard University Press.

Ray, James Lee. (1994) *Democracies and International Conflict*. Columbia: University of South Carolina Press.

Reagan, Ronald. (1982) "Address to Parliament," *New York Times* (June 9).

Riley, Patrick. (1983) *Kant's Political Philosophy*. Totowa, N.J.: Rowman and Littlefield.

Rummel, Rudolph J. (1983) "Libertarianism and International Violence," *Journal of Conflict Resolution* 27 (June): 27–71.

————. (1979) *Understanding Conflict and War*, 5 vols. Beverly Hills: Sage Publications.

Russett, Bruce. (1985) "The Mysterious Case of Vanishing Hegemony," *International Organization* 39 (Spring): 207–31.

Schumpeter, Joseph. (1955 [1919]) "The Sociology of Imperialisms," in *Imperialism and Social Classes*. Cleveland: World.

————. (1950) *Capitalism, Socialism, and Democracy*. New York: Harper Torchbooks.

Schwarz, Wolfgang. (1962) "Kant's Philosophy of Law and International Peace," *Philosophy and Phenomenonological Research* 23: 71–80.

Shell, Susan. (1980) *The Rights of Reason*. Toronto: University of Toronto Press.

Shklar, Judith. (1984) *Ordinary Vices*. Cambridge, Mass.: Harvard University Press.

Siverson, Randolph M., and Julian Emmons. (1991) "Birds of a Feather: Democratic Political Systems and Alliances Choices," *Journal of Conflict Resolution* 35 (June): 285–306.

Skinner, Quentin. (1981) *Machiavelli*. New York: Hill and Wang.

Small, Melvin, and J. David Singer. (1982) *Resort to Arms*. Beverly Hills: Sage Publications.

————. (1976) "The War-Proneness of Democratic Regimes," *Jerusalem Journal of International Relations* 1 (December): 50–69.

Starr, Harvey. (1992) "Why Don't Democracies Fight One Another? Evaluating the Theory-Findings Research Loop," *Jerusalem Journal of International Relations* 14 (December): 41–57.

Streit, Clarence. (1938) *Union Now: A Proposal for a Federal Union of the Leading Democracies*. New York: Harpers.

Thucydides. (1954) *The Peloponnesian War*. Rex Warner, ed. and trans. Baltimore: Penguin.

U.K. Foreign and Commonwealth Office. (1980) *A Yearbook of the Commonwealth 1980*. London: HMSO.

U.S. Congress. Senate. Select Committee to Study Governmental Operations with Respect to Intelligence Activities. (1975) *Covert Action in Chile, 1963–74*. 94th Cong., 1st sess., Washington, D.C.: U.S. Government Printing Office.

U.S. Department of State. (1981) *Country Reports on Human Rights Practices*. Washington, D.C.: U.S. Government Printing Office.

Waltz, Kenneth. (1964) "The Stability of a Bipolar World," *Daedalus* 93 (Summer): 881–909.

———. (1962) "Kant, Liberalism, and War," *American Political Science Review* 56 (June): 331–40.

Walzer, Michael. (1983) *Spheres of Justice*. New York: Basic Books.

Wang, Hongying. (1992) "Fashoda." Paper presented at the Annual Meeting of the American Political Science Association, September 2–5, Chicago.

Weede, Erich. (1984) "Democracy and War Involvement," *Journal of Conflict Resolution* 28 (December): 649–64.

Wilkenfeld, Jonathan. (1968) "Domestic and Foreign Conflict Behavior of Nations," *Journal of Peace Research* 1: 56–69.

Williams, Howard. (1983) *Kant's Political Philosophy*. Oxford: Basil Blackwell.

Wright, Quincy. (1942) *A Study of History*. Chicago: University of Chicago Press.

Yesson, Erik. (1993) "Power and Diplomacy in World Politics," unpublished Ph.D. dissertation, Princeton University.

Yovel, Yirmiahu. (1980) *Kant and the Philosophy of History*. Princeton, N.J.: Princeton University Press.

CHAPTER 5

Liberal International Theory: Common Threads, Divergent Strands[1]

MARK W. ZACHER AND RICHARD A. MATTHEW

In typologies of international relations theory, liberalism, realism, and marxism are often presented as the three dominant traditions of the twentieth century. Each of these traditions includes many variants which frequently overlap in complicated ways such that indentifying their key features is a difficult and controversial task. This chapter analyzes the development of liberal international theory until World War II, reviews and organizes the multifaceted scholarship it has engendered in recent years, evaluates its potential for guiding international relations scholarship, and suggests avenues for future research.

There are good reasons for embarking on such a project. While contemporary marxist international theories reflect canons articulated in the writings of Marx, Engels, and Lenin and modern realist theories are rooted in the expositions of Hans Morgenthau (1967) and Kenneth Waltz (1979), a systematic presentation of liberal international theory is not offered in any well-known texts. Michael Doyle (1986: 1152) notes that "there is no canonical description

[1] A previous draft of this chapter was discussed at the American Political Science Association meeting in September 1992 and in seminars at the University of British Columbia, University of California (Berkeley), Cambridge University, Keele University, and Stanford University. We are most appreciative to the participants for their comments. We would also like to thank the following for written comments: David Armstrong, Barry Buzan, Max Cameron, James Caporaso, Joseph Grieco, Ernst Haas, Kal Holsti, Robert Jackson, Masaru Kohno, David Long, Francine Mackenzie, Sheldon Simon, Sasson Sofer, Michael Webb, and Robert Wolfe. We also greatly benefited from the assistance and insights of a number of students who participated in a discussion group on the subject of the paper: Tim Carter, Ian Cooper, Ron Deibert, and Michael Merlingen.

of liberalism." And Arthur Stein (1990: 7, fn. 6) suggests that "liberalism is multifaceted, and what is or is not at its core can be disputed."

While these observations are certainly accurate, they do not mean that a clear and relatively comprehensive theory cannot be articulated. There is a rich literature, which spans three centuries, that most scholars associate with liberal international theory. Also, it is very important at this time that attention be given to this theoretical enterprise. Intense debates, accelerated by the end of the Cold War, suggest widespread dissatisfaction with realism and marxism and a growing belief that various trends may be affecting profoundly the nature of international relations. A number of the challengers have explicitly identified themselves with liberalism or neoliberalism, and they do, in fact, highlight theses that have their roots in liberal international theory as it evolved from the seventeenth to the early twentieth century (Morse, 1976; Beitz, 1979; Hoffmann, 1981, 1987; Doyle, 1983, 1986, 1992; Keohane, 1989a, 1989b; Moravcsik, 1992). In order to judge whether liberal international theory offers a viable alternative to the dominant variants of realism and marxism, it is important to explore its theoretical components and its coherence.

In establishing the distinctiveness of the core of liberal international theory it is valuable to recall the central features of realism and marxism. Realism contends that the international political system is composed of political entities (states in the contemporary world) that are concerned first and foremost with their own survival and/or the maximization of power. While the strategies that states employ can change in certain ways, the underlying concerns for survival under threatening conditions and for relative power positions do not. For example, Robert Gilpin (1981: 211) argues "that the nature of international relations has not changed fundamentally over the millennia" (see also Gilpin, 1986; Holsti, 1985; Donnelly, 1992; Forde, 1992). For realists, international relations are repetitive or cyclical.

Central to marxism is the claim that the mode of production determines the nature of social and political relations within political entities and among them. When a new mode of production develops, new classes arise, and a new class becomes dominant. Domestic and international politics are fundamentally about the struggle for wealth among economic classes. Marxism does, however, envisage that a final end state will emerge with the progress of industrial modernization and the advent of communism (Lenin, 1939; Baran, 1957; Wallerstein, 1974; variants discussed in Holsti, 1985, chap. 4; Gilpin, 1987, chaps. 1–2; Brown, 1992).

Liberal international theory has its roots in the development of liberal political theory in the seventeenth century. The major contributors until the mid-twentieth century were not international relations scholars, but political philosophers, political economists, and people generally interested in international affairs. While the theory was not set forth in a systematic fashion, a study of writers associated with the liberal international tradition indicates that it has several central theses.

The first thesis is that international relations are gradually being transformed such that they promote greater human freedom by establishing conditions of peace, prosperity, and justice. This attitude toward progress reflects a general liberal stance because, as John Gray (1986: x) writes, liberalism, apart from being individualist, egalitarian, and universalist, is "*meliorist* in its affirmation of the corrigibility and improvability of all social institutions and political arrangements." Pertinent specifically to international liberals, Michael Howard (1978: 11) observes that they "have faith in the power of human reason and human action so to change [the world] that the inner potential of all human beings can be more fully realized."

An aspect of the progressive outlook of most international liberals that deserves stressing is that it is not teleological; that is to say, it does not project the emergence of a particular historical end state in which humankind will realize perfect freedom. Liberals see progress occurring gradually and along different paths at different times, and they do not foresee a world of perfect freedom in which all have what they want without any serious conflicts with others. Gray (1986: 91) writes concerning the classical liberal tradition that its "conception of man as a rational and moral being is not associated with the doctrine of human perfectibility and it does not issue in any expectation that men will converge upon a single, shared view of the ends of life." He goes on to argue that

> the classical liberals believed we will benefit from a continuing antagonism of ideas and proposals. Even when they harbored dark doubts as to the ultimate stability of free societies, the classical liberal remained convinced that our best hope of progress lies in releasing the spontaneous forces of society to develop in new, unthought of and sometimes conflicting directions. For them, progress consisted not in the imposition on society of any rational plan, but rather in the many unpredictable forms of growth and advance which occur when human efforts are not bound by prevailing conceptions to follow a common direction. (Gray, 1986: 91)

Gray (1986: 90–93) accepts that there is a teleological strand of thought in some "liberals" that projects the evolution of humankind toward a very specific rational plan (based on a perfect harmony of interests), but he thinks that this actually violates the liberal notion of liberty. In other words, one part of the classical liberal understanding of progress is that attempts to define it in rigid terms should be regarded with skepticism—especially in an era such as our own when conditions are changing so rapidly.

Related to the above comments, *most* international liberals are not "idealists" in the sense that they believe that a perfect harmony of interests waits to be discovered, that the social and political obstacles to the rational and/or morally right are minimal, and that what obstacles exist are malleable or changeable. E. H. Carr (1946, especially parts 1 and 2) identifies some liberals as idealists. However, he exaggerates the mutuality of interests they portray, and in any case such idealist liberals are not common in the late twentieth century. Along the lines of the comments of Gray quoted above, we would judge that true liberals focus on how states are able to harmonize their different conceptions of interests and not on perfect concord among nations. They also accept that discord and coercion have been and always will be parts of international life, but they believe as a part of their evolutionary perspective that mutualities of interests and noncoercive bargaining will become more prominent features of international life. The key for the empirical liberal theorist is to understand the balances between conflicting and mutual interests, coercive and noncoercive bargaining, and moral and self-interested concerns that can exist in particular stages of international history.

The second and third central theses of liberal international theory are analyzed in depth in subsequent sections and are presented very briefly here. The second thesis is that central to the realization of greater human freedom is the growth of international cooperation. Cooperation is needed to maximize the possible benefits and minimize the possible damages of interactions and interdependencies and to capture opportunities for realizing greater peace, welfare, and justice. The nature and strength of international cooperation that liberal theorists envisage in a particular era or over time vary, but they all see cooperation as central to progress in human freedom.

The third and last thesis is that international relations are being transformed by a process of modernization that was unleashed by the scientific revolution and reinforced by the intellectual revolution of liberalism; and it is promoting cooperation among nations and greater peace, welfare, and justice for humankind. This modernization process has at least five interactive and evolving components and should not be confused with the now widely discredited model of political development based on the European experience of democratization and industrialization, which was developed by comparative politics scholars in the 1960s. These core components are liberal democracy or republican government; international interdependence; cognitive progress; international sociological integration; and international institutions. Liberals suggest that the period since the late seventeenth century has constituted a historical watershed, a period during which a multifaceted process of modernization has introduced or enhanced the possibility of a dramatic improvement in the moral character and material welfare of humankind.

The following analysis of liberal international theory is divided into several sections. The first section provides a historical overview of the evolution of liberal international theory from the late seventeenth through the early twentieth century by focusing on the most important writers. Differences among the writers relate largely to the importance of different facets of the modernization process for international political change. There is a subsection at the end of this section that draws together the major themes of liberal international theory as it evolved over three centuries. The second section discusses recent writings that fall within the scope of liberal international theory. It is organized around those dimensions of the modernization process that promote greater international exchanges and cooperation—and consequently greater human freedom. Both of these two sections seek to synthesize and summarize large bodies of literature, and therefore the writing is often quite detailed in its discussions. The concluding section reflects on some of the strengths and weaknesses of liberal international theory and future research directions.

THE HISTORICAL DEVELOPMENT OF LIBERAL INTERNATIONAL THEORY THROUGH WORLD WAR II

The late Middle Ages (1200–1500) witnessed the demise of the feudal system, the rise of a middle class, the failure of papal Christendom to exert political control throughout Europe, the beginnings of the Reformation, a renaissance of the republican and cultural traditions of antiquity, and the early approximations of the modern state (Strayer, 1970; Poggi, 1978). This tumultuous period was followed in the sixteenth and seventeenth centuries by the scientific revolution and the gradual reconstruction of Europe into a system ordered on the basis of the sovereign state. It was during this era of important intellectual, economic, and political change that liberalism emerged to become the dominant political theory of modernity. Child of the Enlightenment, liberal theory expressed a deep, if at times guarded, optimism in the capacity of people to improve the moral and material conditions of their existence.

In general terms, liberalism is committed to the steady, if uneven, expansion of human freedom through various political and economic strategies, such as democratization and market capitalism, ascertained through reason and, in many cases, enhanced by technology. Although progress and freedom are rather abstract concepts, liberals have focused on pursuing these ends in very specific and concrete ways. The earliest liberal intellectuals sought to use an empiricist methodology developed in the natural sciences to determine a political theory that would organize and defend the aspirations of the emergent middle class for a defense of private property, a rationalized system of laws, and a voice in lawmaking, while still providing a basis for moral and ethical life consistent with deep-seated Christian values and beliefs. The history of its efforts could fill several volumes. For our purposes it is sufficient to identify two variants of liberalism which together significantly shaped its evolution.

The first variant, laissez-faire liberalism, conceptualized government, or the state, as a necessary evil that had to be sharply constrained in order to allow the private sector to flourish. Introduced by John Locke (1960) in the seventeenth century, it was later endorsed by Voltaire and Benjamin Constant (1988) in France and von Humboldt in Germany, among others. Their desire was for a rational government based on consent and limited to enforcing a minimal set of laws, adjudicating disputes, and defending property and individual rights, especially against foreign aggression. In this variant, moral and ethical principles were seen as independent of political processes, as in Locke's notion of an objective natural law against which positive law might be assessed.

All of these thinkers believed that under liberal regimes, the material and moral condition of people would improve steadily, principally due to the unconstrained economic and other activities of the private sector.

The second variant, democratic or interventionist liberalism, had less confidence in the progressive potential of the private sector and regarded the state more favorably, often characterizing it as a vehicle for education and the redistribution of wealth and power. Further, it tended to depict moral and ethical principles as properly determined by democratic practices. Its early advocates included Jean-Jacques Rousseau in France and later Matthew Arnold and T. H. Green in England and Friedrich Wilhem in Germany. In contrast to their laissez-faire counterparts, supporters of this approach usually related progress explicitly to the level of democratization.

The proponents of these two variants of liberalism in the seventeenth and eighteenth centuries focused mainly on domestic politics. On the matter of international politics, the views of Locke and Rousseau dovetailed, recognizing that liberal values had very limited roles and that self-interest and power would reign. The qualifications are perhaps clearest in Locke (1960: 431–44) who, in his famous chapter "Of Conquest," for example, affirmed the relevance of natural law to limited spheres of international relations, arguing for strong moral and ethical obligations on the part of wealthy states to poor ones and victors in war to losers. In general, however, Locke (1960: 412) advocated "Prudence" in foreign policy and acting "for the advantage of the Commonwealth."

If one accepts Locke's fusion of empirical and normative claims, the prudent application of natural law to international relations makes sense. Rousseau (1962, 1978), however, was skeptical about natural law, choosing instead to relate moral and ethical principles to democratic practices, a strategy that clearly limits their applicability to the international realm. He argued, however, that a world of democratic states would be a peaceful world because its units would value self-sufficiency and adopt isolationist foreign policies. Rousseau (1962: 297) acknowledged that such a world did not exist and that consequently a state's "security . . . requires that it make itself more powerful than its neighbors." To overcome this, Rousseau considered the possibility of creating a security community, or "confederative republic," but he was not optimistic about such an outcome. As Christine Jane Carter (1987: 210) has argued, Rousseau concluded that "power rather than reason will continue to be the major determinant in international relations."

In spite of their brevity, Locke's and Rousseau's reflections on international relations identified salient themes that became central to liberal international theory: the relationship between democracy and peace, the possibility of achieving security through international organization, the salience of international moral and ethical principles, and the diminishing but ineradicable relevance of power relations and self-interest among both democratic and nondemocratic states. These themes were clarified, enhanced, and added to by later generations of liberal thinkers.

Late-eighteenth- and nineteenth-century liberals were more optimistic than their predecessors about progress in international relations. They often argued that war and aggression were maintained by aristocratic regimes and mercantilist economic policies and that peace and wealth could be promoted by democratization and free trade. The most comprehensive statement was prepared by Immanuel Kant (1957). He foresaw the possibility of world peace attained through the gradual emergence of republican states whose citizens would oppose wars because of the cost in lives and financial resources; "the spirit of commerce," which would promote cooperation and interdependence; and the growth of international or cosmopolitan law, which would give further support to peaceful and cooperative relations. Unifying these forces were an increasing sense of moral duty among humankind and a growing recognition of the progressive direction of historical change or "nature's mechanical course" (Hoffmann, 1987: 402). While Kant's commitment to progress in international relations is indisputable, his image of the ultimate form that universal peace would assume has been the subject of disagreement (Hurrell, 1990). Whether one reads in Kant a future world of cooperative states or some form of world government, it is clear that, like earlier liberals, he accepted a strong, but gradually diminishing, role for power relations and the use of force. He did, however, regard the balance of power as important to the maintenance of international order in the short term (Hinsley, 1963, chap. 4; Doyle, 1983, 1986; Gray, 1986, chap. 3; Hurrell, 1990: 189–90). Another late-eighteenth-century writer whose views are very close to those of Kant is the American Thomas Paine. He emphasized both the nature of governments (aristocratic or democratic) and the virtues of free trade in promoting international peace and welfare (Howard, 1978: 29–31; Wolfers and Martin, 1956, chap. 10).

While regime type, international law and organization, and commerce are integral and interactive components of liberal international theory, it was the concept of free trade that sparked the imagination of most liberal thinkers of this period. Adam Smith (1937; Gray, 1986: 24–25) laid the groundwork for this attitude in *The Wealth of Nations*, his famous defense of international commerce as the inevitable—and generally desirable—outcome of human history. In his *Plan for Universal and Perpetual Peace*, the British Utilitarian Jeremy Bentham (1937) argued that free trade would bring the greatest economic benefits to the greatest number of people and asserted that active trade relations would discourage war. Like Kant and Paine, however, Bentham believed that an energetic, commerce-oriented private sector presupposed some form of democracy.

In terms of the development of liberal international theory, Bentham and other Utilitarian thinkers are important for their appreciation of its robustness. This notion has been well expressed by Vittorio de Caprariis (1957: 305–6) who, writing in an otherwise unrelated context, warned against "the danger of making liberalism an immobile philosophy" and argued that liberalism must be regarded as the "progressive outlook of any age, as a perennial method for solving concretely the problems of the century" (see also Wolfers and Martin, 1956, chap. 14; Hinsley, 1963, chap. 5; Howard, 1978: 34–35; Holsti, 1985: 27–29).

Following Smith and Bentham, liberal international theory in the nineteenth century contended that modern liberty, an outcome of democratization and reason, encouraged private citizens to focus on the accumulation of wealth. Through trade, humankind would be woven together by material interdependencies that would raise the costs of war and conflict, while rewarding fair cooperation and competition and indirectly generating macrolevel goods such as peace, prosperity, and, potentially, justice. For example, in *The Principles of Political Economy and Taxation*, David Ricardo (1911: 114) claimed that free trade "binds together, by one common tie of interest and intercourse, the universal society of nations throughout the civilized world." Similarly, James Mill, John Stuart Mill, Richard Cobden, Benjamin Constant, and Herbert Spencer all agreed that (1) international prosperity, peace, and cooperation would be products of free trade; (2) because trade was conducted outside the public realm, a vital private sector was the site of the engine of human progress; and (3) this vitality depended in turn on the type of freedom enabled by modern democratic or republican government. Among these thinkers, Spencer (1969) adopted a rather unique position in that he viewed free trade in terms of Social Darwinism, a process that weeded out the weak, resulting in the general improvement of humankind (Hinsley, 1963, chaps. 5–7; Wolfers and Martin, 1956, chaps. 15–17; Howard, 1978, chap. 2).

In the early (prewar) twentieth century, liberal international theory received considerable attention from a variety of thinkers, most notably J. A. Hobson and Norman Angell. Hobson (1938) is well known for his book *Imperialism*, which identified commercial competition among European states in the non-European world as the major cause of international conflict. In making his argument, Hobson combined traditional liberal opposition to aristocratic regimes with socialist critiques of financial elites. He regarded national imperialist elites as alliances of aristocratic and business groups. Overcoming these alliances, and creating the conditions for progress in realizing broad crossnational interests, required the thorough democratization of states. In view of this, Hobson prescribed political reforms that would be conducive to peace. In keeping with the spirit of his age, he was also a supporter of free trade insofar as it created economic ties that deterred countries from going to war.

In *The Great Illusion*, Angell (1910) argued that dramatic transformations in production, transportation, and communication technologies had made national economies so interdependent that war could only be disruptive and costly to all. Although he appreciated that political ignorance and the political influence of special interests could lead states into war, he was persuaded that they could not gain from it, pointing, for example, to the burgeoning international network of national financial elites whose welfare depended on cooperation. Angell further contended that states could not achieve security by seeking military superiority over other countries. But unlike earlier liberals, Angell did not imply that desirable macrolevel outcomes would emerge spontaneously with an increase in trade. Publics and politicians had to be educated, and peace required active international cooperation. Angell's concern for education recalls a theme of liberalism that earlier had received careful consideration by Locke and Rousseau, both of whom wrote treatises on education. His emphasis on interstate cooperation, an idea endorsed in principle by both Rousseau and Kant, presaged a shift in the agenda of liberal international theory that would become decisive after World War I (Baldwin, 1980; Miller, 1986; Navari, 1989; de Wilde, 1991, chap. 3).

During the interwar period, liberal international theory continued to stress the familiar themes of democratization, trade, and the high costs of war (Howard, 1978: 75; Wolfers and Martin, 1956, chap. 20). There was, however, a movement from Locke to Rousseau, from unflinching confidence in the private sector to a renewed sense of the need for strong international organizations to promote and guarantee peace. Hidemi Suganami (1989: 93, 79), in reviewing the views of the reformist writers of this era, remarks that they thought that "it was the absence of the machinery which could ensure the peaceful settlement of international disputes that had caused the catastrophe [of World War I]." He adds that "One of the consequences of this shattering experience was a tendency among the writers on world order to converge on one central theme: the introduction of the element of coercion into the international system'" (on the prewar–postwar differences, see also Hinsley, 1963: 116; Hoffmann, 1987: 403–5).

Key interwar liberals who were strong advocates of international organization include Woodrow Wilson (Link, 1957; Schulte Nordholt, 1991), Hobson, Ramsay Muir (1971; de Wilde, 1991, chap. 4), Alfred Zimmern (1936; Markwell, 1986), Francis Delaisi (1925; de Wilde, 1991, chap. 5), and David Mitrany (1948, 1966). Of these Wilson is perhaps the best known, and this period frequently is referred to as "the Wilson era." Arthur Link (1957: 12–15) argues that Wilson's world view was shaped by his early commitments to Christian moral and ethical beliefs and democracy, and his sense that the United States had a moral mission in international relations. After World War I, he also became a strong advocate of international organization, especially in the form of a collective security mechanism that would make the "world safe for democracy." These various beliefs were aggregated in his famous Fourteen Points address, delivered to the U.S. Congress in 1918. Central to this address were Wilson's call to establish the League of Nations, remove barriers to free trade, and promote national self-determination. The belief that national self-determination would promote international peace is a variant of democratic liberalism and has its roots in Rousseau and later in nineteenth-century writers such as John Stuart Mill and Guiseppi Mazzini. On the basis of his liberal tenets, Wilson hoped to lay the foundations for a peaceful, prosperous, and just world order (Link, 1957: 102–3; on the U.S. liberal tradition, see Armstrong, 1993, chap. 2).

Although after World War I Hobson continued to believe that it was trade and democracy that created the conditions for peace, he also began to argue that strong international institutions were necessary (Wolfers and Martin,

1956, chap. 19; Long, 1991). Similarly, Muir believed that growing international interdependence was inevitable and would have to be managed through international organization. Additionally, he identified the spread of Western culture as an important force in promoting peace, prosperity, and justice. He regarded "European civilization as the best conceivable," and he defined "progress . . . in terms of liberalism" (de Wilde, 1991: 99–101).

While today this may appear parochial, it signals a more general liberal commitment to some form of international culture. Zimmern stressed the centrality of democracy and public education in the evolution of a more humane world and regarded the League of Nations as an important step toward world peace and prosperity. D. J. Markwell (1986: 283) captures a key feature of the attitude of these thinkers in his comment, "What is most striking about [Alfred Zimmern's] *The League of Nations and the Rule of Law* is the underlying belief that progress is possible in international relations and might already be far advanced."

Francis Delaisi's thought prefigured Mitrany's well-known theory of functionalism, which he developed largely during World War II (de Wilde, 1991: 138). Both regarded nationalism and sovereignty as the fertile soil of international conflict and war. Both argued for an initial separation of high and low politics, believing that the unhampered pursuit of economic welfare would knit states together in peaceful relations. And both endorsed the creation of specialized international economic organizations to guide and manage this process. In his work, Mitrany further developed the implications of these positions in his theory of functionalism. He argued that cooperation was easier to achieve in technical areas, and once successful, it would spill over into other areas, gradually embedding states in a network of cooperative mechanisms that would make war highly unlikely, if not impossible. Over time, Mitrany believed there would also be an adjustment in loyalties, such that international values would vie successfully with national ones. Mitrany's functionalism was extremely influential in the 1950s and 1960s, inspiring many of the international integration theorists.

The emergence of "welfare internationalism" among writers such as Mitrany and Delaisi together with the general advocacy of stronger international organizations marks an important change in the outlook of international liberalism. Whereas in the nineteenth century there was a widespread belief that laissez-faire economic practices and the spread of democracy would on their own produce public goods such as peace, prosperity, and justice, post–World War I liberals argued that this process also required substantial and focused intergovernmental cooperation. Some writers, such as Mitrany, regarded intergovernmental cooperation as a step toward full global integration; others were less willing to make such dramatic predictions. (One sees a similar tension in the writings of Kant [Hurrell, 1990]). In any case, a belief in the immediate need for, and extensive potential benefits of, strong international institutions has become increasingly central to the liberal world view (Suganami, 1989, chap. 6).

The evolution of liberal international theory in its first three hundred years reveals a set of themes that have proven robust, continually adapting to new circumstances to offer new insights into international relations. Although the relative importance of these themes has shifted over time, their interrelationships have been recognized by each new generation of thinkers.

An Overview of Liberal International Theory

Having reviewed some of the major writers associated with liberal international theory from the seventeenth century through World War II, it is valuable to summarize the central theses of the theory before moving on to look at postwar scholarship in the next section.

(1) Since the late eighteenth century, liberals have believed that international relations are evolving (or probably will evolve) gradually and irregularly along lines that will promote *greater human freedom* conceived in terms of increases in physical security, material welfare, and opportunities for free expression and political influence (i.e., human rights). Reflecting on the evolution of liberal scholarship, Robert Keohane (1989a: 174) writes that "liberalism believes in at least the possibility of cumulative progress, whereas realism assumes that history is not progressive."

(2) International liberals believe that peace, welfare, and justice are realized significantly through *international cooperation*, although they differ on the nature and strength of the cooperation that is likely to occur. Cooperation can include an acceptance of moral norms, adherence to international law, or collaboration through international organizations. While Kant was an important early exponent of this position, it did not become a central thesis in the thinking of the great majority of all liberals until after World War I.

(3) Liberals believe that peace, welfare, justice, and cooperation are being driven by a number of interdependent forces that we view as aspects of *the process of modernization*. Beginning in the late eighteenth century, liberals were aware that the scientific revolution and the liberal intellectual revolution were promoting a profound transformation in international relations. Liberals would agree with Karl Deutsch (1969: 190) that "The whole thrust of the technological development of our time pushes beyond wars and beyond the economic fences of nation-states" (on the modernization process and its impacts, see Morse, 1976; Fukuyama, 1992; Zacher, 1992). The key components of the process are liberal democracy, interdependencies (commercial and military), cognitive progress, international sociological integration, and international institutions. These components of the process of modernization are not stressed by all pre–World War II liberal writers. In fact, military interdependence and sociological integration only began to emerge as important in the twentieth century. Also, many of the early writers, particularly the Utilitarians, did not highlight international institutions beyond a general acceptance of the norm of economic openness and some minimal laws to facilitate

commerce. The elements that existed in the thought of almost all international liberals from the eighteenth through the mid-twentieth century are liberal democracy, a growth in economic transactions and interdependence, and the expansion in humankind's knowledge and reasoning capacities.

In addition to the three general theses of liberal international theory, it is valuable to draw out from the writings of liberal theorists the underlying assumptions on issues such as the nature of international actors, actors' interests, the determinants of interests, and the determinants of international outcomes. It is important to try to define them in order to better understand the rationales for the previously stated assertions, to assist in identifying liberal theorists, to allow comparisons with other theories such as realism and marxism, and to facilitate the development of liberal international theory. This last issue is very important: In order to make projections and offer theoretical explanations of specific phenomena it is necessary to define actors, interests, the forces shaping interests, and the forces shaping outcomes. The assumptions are, in fact, very general—in part because liberal theory must accommodate a historical evolutionary process. They are presented below with some corroborative citations to contemporary literature (for good general analyses, see Doyle, 1983, 1986; Keohane, 1989a; Moravcsik, 1992; Smith, 1992).

(1) Liberal international theory's conceptualization of progress in terms of human freedom and the importance attributed to liberal democracy, free trade, cognitive changes, communications, and moral norms all indicate that liberals regard *individual human beings as the primary international actors*. Liberals view *states* as the most important collective actors in our present era, but they are seen as *pluralistic actors* whose interests and policies are determined by bargaining among groups and elections. A propos of this point Robert Keohane (1989a: 172) comments that "liberalism is an approach to the analysis of social reality that begins with individuals as the relevant actors" and "seeks to understand how organizations composed of aggregations of individuals interact."

(2) Liberals view the *interests of states as multiple and changing and both self-interested and other-regarding* (Hoffmann, 1960: 31, 185; Grieco, 1988; Stein, 1990, chap. 1; Smith, 1992). The interests of states (or priorities among interests) are viewed as changing because liberals see individuals' values and the power relations among interest groups evolving over time. Also, most liberals regard states' policies as other-regarding to some extent since they believe that the growth of liberal democracy increases people's concern for other humans. These ideas can be traced back to Locke, Rousseau, and Kant. With regard to specific interests, liberals accept that state survival and autonomy are important—at least in our contemporary era—but they are viewed as secondary interests to the primary interests of individuals (on the importance of state autonomy to realists, see Gilpin, 1987: 34; Grieco, 1988 and 1991: 14). Certainly over the long run, liberals see states as increasingly supportive of peace, welfare, and justice, but exploitative interests (including power over others as an end in itself) are unlikely ever to disappear.

(3) Liberals believe that *human and state interests are shaped by a wide variety of domestic and international conditions*. Ultimately they are determined by bargaining power among interest groups, but these groups' definitions of their interests are affected by a host of factors. At the domestic level they include the nature of the economic and political systems, economic interactions, and personal values; at the international level there are technological capabilities that allow states to affect each other in different ways, patterns of interactions and interdependencies, transnational sociological patterns, knowledge, and international institutions. The predominant collective actors—states—are embedded in both their own societies and the international system, and their interests and policies are affected by conditions in both arenas. Such a complex perspective flows from the writings of most of the major liberal writers (for a recent synthetic view of international factors, see Buzan, Jones, and Little, 1993). Specifically on the matter of institutions and political hierarchy in the international system, liberals have not been and are not comfortable with a simple conception of the system as anarchical. While explicit analyses of this issue are recent, the growth of international institutions was, in fact, very important to Kant's image of the international system's evolution. Contrary to realists, contemporary liberals think that the network of international institutions is too pervasive and influential not to integrate it into an overall conception of the international system (Waltz, 1979: 88–92, 102–28; Grieco, 1988; Keohane, 1989b: 1, 6; Miller and Vincent, 1990; Milner, 1991).

(4) *The relative influence of patterns of interests and coercion on international outcomes evolves over time—with the impact of patterns of interests growing*. In the early stages of modernization, coercion based on power relations has an important influence, but as liberal democracies, interdependencies, knowledge, international social ties, and international institutions grow, noncoercive bargaining and international patterns of interests have an increasing impact. (Moravcsik [1992] posits that for liberals patterns of interest always predominate; we believe that for liberals their impact is dependent on the state of modernization.)

Specifically on the matter of *cooperation*, liberals do not think that the existence of a hegemonic power is necessary for cooperation; rather, *mutual interests can sustain* international regimes. Pertinent to this, Oran Young (1989: 200) writes

> There is nothing in theories of bargaining or negotiation as such to justify the conclusion that a hegemony is needed to produce agreement, so long as a contract zone or a zone of agreement exists. On the contrary, the usual assumption embedded in such theories is that rational actors will find a way to realize feasible joint gains. (See also Keohane, 1984)

The main reasons for liberals' expectations of increased cooperation based on mutual interests are that mutualities of interests will grow with increased interdependencies and the spread of democratic values; states and other actors will be better able to understand their common interests with improved knowledge and communications; states are less worried about the prospect that cooperating partners will cheat because of improvements in monitoring (international organizations, technological advances); and states are less worried that relative gains can be turned into coercive power because of the increasing reluctance to use coercion (Lipson, 1984; Grieco, 1988; Keohane, 1989b; Stein, 1990, chap. 1; Snidal, 1991; Powell, 1991; Cornett and Caporaso, 1992; Baldwin, 1993).

Pre–World War II international liberals did not analyze when states seek relative as opposed to absolute gains in their international bargaining in the same way that realist international relations scholars have explored the issue over the past decade (Baldwin, 1993). However, it would have been logical for the early liberals to argue that states are concerned with relative gains only in those conditions where the relative gains are likely to be turned against them in future bargaining situations. Also, since the proclivity of states to use coercion decreases with the growth of democracy, interdependencies, and international institutions, states should become less worried with relative gains over time.

It should, however, be stressed that liberals are very interested in tracking over time where, how, and why coercive power, especially military power, is important. Liberals are not, or should not be, ostriches when it comes to the study of power. To quote Judith Shklar: "No liberal ever forgets that governments are coercive" (quoted in Keohane, 1989a: 194). On the other hand, international liberals are prone to see the situations that will mitigate against the use of coercive diplomacy as emerging faster and more strongly than is, in fact, often the case. This is, more often than not, the source of the accusation that liberals are idealists (Carr, 1946).

THE STRANDS OF CONTEMPORARY LIBERAL INTERNATIONAL THEORY

As is clear from the preceding section, the common threads of liberal international theory (apart from several assumptions) include beliefs in progress conceived in terms of greater human freedom, the importance of cooperation to progress, and a process of scientific and intellectual modernization as the driving force behind cooperation and human progress. The key strands of the theory refer to the components of the modernization process. While this section focuses on these strands, it is desirable to discuss briefly postwar liberals' thinking about progress because it differs from that of most prewar writers.

The most striking change in attitude is that confidence in progress has been more qualified in the postwar period. Prior to World War II most liberal writers had a reasonably strong belief in the growing, albeit gradual, realization of human freedom. In the postwar period the reluctance of most nonrealist and nonmarxist scholars to commit themselves to the liberal notion of progress has been grounded in a number of considerations. Liberals have not wanted to be branded as idealists as were many interwar liberals; the international events of this century (including two world wars and the Cold War) have made them wary about being too optimistic, and, in keeping with the ethos of contemporary social science, many have felt more comfortable explaining than predicting.

With the exception of David Mitrany (1966), who was largely a product of the interwar period, most scholars who have predicted "progress" have confined their claims to specific issue-areas. For example, John Mueller (1989) has predicted the end of major wars, and a variety of other scholars have been optimistic about international economic cooperation or European integration. With regard to the overall evolution of international politics, even Francis Fukuyama (1992) questions whether liberal democracy and hence international comity will be able to survive without coexisting "irrational" belief systems and with the constant challenge of reconciling people's competitive urges with the egalitarian norms of a democratic society. While a high level of optimism concerning the evolution of world politics has been rare, a growing number of scholars think that it is *possible* that international relations are evolving so as to improve the condition of humankind. A very good statement of this perspective was voiced by Stanley Hoffmann (1981: 8):

> To be liberal does not mean necessarily to believe in progress, it means only to believe in a (limited and reversible) perfectibility of man and society, and particularly in the possibility of devising institutions based on consent, that will make society more humane and more just, and the citizens' lot better.

A comparable point was made by Robert Keohane (1989b: 11), who wrote that liberalism "rests on a belief in at least the possibility of cumulative progress in human affairs." He went on to remark, "For me, politics is open-ended and potentially progressive, rather than bleakly cyclical." For liberals, the possibility of progress is constant but its realization (and hence their level of optimism) vary over time and space.

The rest of this chapter focuses on postwar writings on the six well-developed strands of liberal international theory. Some of our labels are taken from existing literature (Nye, 1988; Keohane, 1989a), and some are new. They are:

- Republican liberalism
- Interdependence liberalism
  1. Commercial liberalism
  2. Military liberalism
- Cognitive liberalism
- Sociological liberalism
- Institutional liberalism

A new component of the modernization process that is generating mutual interests in international cooperation has emerged in recent decades—ecological interdependence. Future studies of liberal international theory should include *ecological liberalism* as a distinctive strand.

Before discussing the literature relevant to each strand, it is important to make several points.

- The strands of liberalism are not competing. They are all facets of a larger dynamic of international change and are often closely interrelated. Individual researchers focus on certain factors, but, if asked, they would probably view other aspects of modernization as having some influence on international progress.
- The different components of modernization both generate mutual interests and facilitate cooperation. However, certain factors tend to be *generators* or *facilitators*. In particular, republican and interdependence liberalism are basically generators of mutual interests, whereas cognitive, sociological, and institutional liberalism tend to be facilitators of cooperation.
- It is inappropriate to label all contributors to the explanation of international cooperation as supporters of liberal theory. It is likely that they are at least implicit adherents, but often they have not committed themselves to a particular stance.

Republican Liberalism

During most of the postwar era there was little academic interest in the thesis that democracies promote international peace and cooperation, although it was a common theme of Western politicians. This changed decidedly in the 1980s largely due to two articles by Michael Doyle (1983, 1986). According to Doyle, while democratic states do go to war, they rarely, if ever, go to war with each other, a claim well-supported by the record of the past two centuries. Doyle (1986: 1156) concludes that "liberal states have indeed established a separate peace—but only among themselves," a claim that has received wide support in the field (see also Maoz and Abdoladli, 1989; Ember, Ember, and Russett, 1992; Lake, 1992; Maoz and Russett, 1992; for a criticism, see Cohen, 1992). This liberal peace is grounded in the existence of an international moral community in which governments accept the standards of mutual respect and peaceful resolution of differences that exist among individuals within their societies (Doyle, 1986: 1160; Schweller, 1992: 245–46; Gilbert, 1992: 10). In the words of Zeev Maoz and Bruce Russett (1992: 5), "The norms of regulated political competition, compromise solutions to political conflicts, and peaceful transfer of power are externalized by democracies in their dealing with other national actors in world politics."

In addition to the above ethics-based explanation, scholars have identified various nonethical considerations that might underlie the peaceful and cooperative proclivities of democratic states:

- The majority of the population who bear the brunt of the costs of war is unlikely to support parties and leaders who are interested in launching wars (Doyle, 1986: 1160; Gilbert, 1992; Schweller, 1992). Related to this, political parties in a democracy are prone to appeal to middle-of-the-road voters who are likely to be risk-averse (Snyder, 1990: 18–19; and 1991: 49–52), and the fragmentation of interest groups makes it very difficult to put together a coalition supportive of imperialism and war (Schweller, 1992: 244–45; Maoz and Russett, 1992: 7).
- The openness or transparency of democratic states reduces possibilities of misjudging the activities and intentions of such states (reducing the fear of cheating and enhancing a willingness to cooperate), and it prevents "war-causing national misperceptions—militarist myths, hyper-nationalist myths, or elite arguments for 'social imperial' wars" (Van Evera, 1990–1991: 27; Kupchan and Kupchan, 1991: 148).
- Democratic states have a lower capability than authoritarian states to extract rents from their citizens for ventures such as imperial expansion. Consequently, they regard peaceful trade as a more reliable route to the accumulation of wealth than war (Lake, 1992).
- Echoing Adam Smith, democratic states are oriented to economic welfare and international commerce rather than military glory. Modern democratic states focus on maximizing wealth, and economic success is vital for the legitimation of their governments. This leads to foreign policies supportive of collective security and mutually beneficial commerce (Doyle, 1986; Schweller, 1992: Kupchan and Kupchan, 1991; Morse, 1976; Rosecrance, 1986).

A recent addition to republican liberalism is the argument that liberal democracies not only form a "zone of peace" but also constitute a "zone of law." They allow more private transnational economic interactions than do groupings that include nondemocratic states; they permit myriad agreements involving bureaucratic units and private actors; and they charge their courts with the responsibility for deciding on the law that should be applicable to private disputes. Anne-Marie Burley (1992: 7) states that "relations among liberal states include a *type* of legal relations much less likely to be found in relations between liberal and nonliberal states: *transnational legal relations monitored and enforced by domestic courts.*"

The growing support for republican liberalism is the most striking development in liberal international theory in the postwar period. While the thesis concerning the prospects for greater international peace and comity rests on the growth of liberal democratic governments, it is still a very important empirical finding. The relevant studies that have been published since the early 1980s have breathed more life into liberal international theory than any other body of scholarly writings. A logical next step for liberals is to explore the impact of the process of democratization on the international relations of non-Western countries.

Commercial Liberalism

Following the scientific revolution, a variety of technological innovations significantly increased the opportunities for mutual gains through economic exchanges. Unlike realists, liberals have regarded the consequences of trade—interdependence and autonomy-limiting cooperation—in positive terms. According to Edward Morse (1976: 116): "In liberal thought, interdependence became a goal of foreign policy that should be implemented with global industrialization and that should result in a framework in which natural harmony of interests among nations could unfold" (see also Gilpin, 1987, chap. 1). What liberals envisage transforming the international system and promoting greater peace, welfare, and justice is what Barry Buzan calls "interaction capacity" or the physical ability of states to affect each other in military, economic, and other ways. Buzan (Buzan, Little, and Jones, 1993: 78) states that "The proponents of interdependence and world society are essentially supporting the systemic hypothesis that high interaction capacity profoundly conditions the logic of political structure. . . . In other words, when the volume, speed, range and reliability of interaction become sufficiently high, they might begin systematically (and systemically) to override the deep structural effects of anarchy." Buzan's position is consistent with a set of causal relationships central to liberal thought: Scientific/technological progress produces increased international exchanges because of people's desire for greater economic welfare; growing exchanges produce growing interdependence; and greater interdependence pressures states into international cooperation to enhance the gains and minimize the losses from new economic relationships.

In the postwar period the belief that international economic interdependence would grow and would assure international peace has not been as pronounced as in the nineteenth and early twentieth centuries. One reason for this cautious attitude is that there were very modest economic relations between East and West during the Cold War. The end of the Cold War has opened up the possibility for closer economic ties, but whether a highly integrated global trading system will develop is problematic.

There have been important examples of increasing economic interdependence and a more pervasive and stable peace, but they have generally been limited to regions. Both the growing integration of the European Union and the long-standing economic ties within the Western alliance system have been regarded as important deterrents to political and military conflict in the West. However, these developments have not been widely regarded as promising an end to international wars. A recent statement representative of this position is that "the current interdependent international political economy may have inhibited—or at least has not encouraged—widespread resort to force" (Keohane, 1989a: 189; for negative, positive, and noncommittal views, see Herz, 1950: 172–76; Morse, 1976; Buzan, 1984; Ferguson and Mansbach, 1988: 208). On the other hand, there are some positive trends concerning the relationship between economic interdependence and peace. Robert Jervis

(1991–1992: 56) has recently commented on the potentially stabilizing international impact of the European Union, which is likely to demand peaceful behavior as a price for access to its market.

While few contemporary commercial liberals focus on the relationship between economic interdependence and the incidence of wars, many focus on economic interdependence as the basis for prosperity and cooperation. One argument put forward by many scholars is that international cooperation to maintain openness and control the adverse effects of greater liberalization is important to assure global economic welfare (Cooper, 1968, 1972; Morse, 1976; Ruggie, 1983; Rosecrance, 1986; Keohane and Nye, 1989; Webb, 1991). To quote Richard Cooper (1972: 179), "The growing interdependence of the world economy creates pressures for common policies, and hence for procedures whereby countries discuss and coordinate actions that hitherto were regarded as being of domestic concern exclusively." On the same issue, John Ruggie (1983) argues that modern states have accepted international regimes based on "embedded liberalism," which seeks to balance the benefits of liberalization with the right of states to take "safeguard" actions to protect domestic welfare goals. Some commercial liberals concentrate on regional economic integration. A significant aspect of their analysis concerns how modern economies of scale pressure states to coordinate their policies in creating larger markets. Without being part of a larger market, it is difficult for states to provide their populations with the same level of welfare that other industrialized states are giving their citizens. While there was a lull in academic theorizing in this field in the 1970s and 1980s, movements in the expansion of the European Union and elsewhere have provoked latent scholarly optimism (Lindberg and Scheingold, 1971; Haas, 1970, 1975b, 1976; Wallace, 1990; Moravcsik, 1991; Tranholm-Mikkelsen, 1991).

An important argument of some economic liberals is that states are losing a degree of control over their economies because of growing interdependence, strong international regimes, and the activities of multinational firms. They project a world in which there are both stronger formal intergovernmental institutions and an informal sharing of governance between state and private commercial organizations. On the ability of modern industrial states to develop economic policies free of international constraints, Morse (1976: 97) writes that "No amount of political will can recreate a world where independence and autonomy can be obtained, except perhaps at costs that no governments are willing to incur because losses in wealth that would accompany increased autonomy would handicap the legitimacy of those governments in the eyes of their citizens." A particular twist to this loss-of-control or sovereignty-at-bay argument is that multinational corporations are increasingly managing international economic relations and possibly creating the basis for a more politically integrated international community (Vernon, 1971; Rosenau, 1980; Ohmae; 1990).

A particular analytical approach within contemporary commercial liberalism has been labeled a "functional" or a "contractual approach" to international cooperation. But a more appropriate title might be a market correction approach (Keohane, 1984, chaps. 5–6, and 1990: 744–53; Haggard and Simmons, 1987: 506–9; Zacher, 1990). It affirms the neoclassical assertion that under certain market conditions (generally referred to as "market failures"), states have mutual interests in creating regimes because collaboration and regulation can enhance the global welfare pie. In the words of James Caporaso (1993: 452), "Market failure provides a major theoretical entry point between economics and politics." Market failures include imperfect information, transaction costs, barriers to the flow of goods and services, collusion, natural monopoly, public goods, scarce common property resources, and externalities.

While scholars who focus on market failures in the study of international political economy do not have to be international liberals, most of them are since they tend to posit important mutualities of interest and the likelihood of cooperation. They do not think that distributional problems will usually undermine cooperation when the regimes in question will yield absolute gains for all or the great majority of states (for debate, see Baldwin, 1993). It is true, as Stephan Haggard and Beth Simmons (1987: 506) comment, that a functional or market correction approach is better at identifying when regimes will be demanded than when they will be supplied. However, any insights into those conditions that lead a large majority of states to anticipate absolute gains from cooperation provide insights that other theoretical approaches have not been able to offer.

In a discussion of theories of international economic relations, Peter Gourevitch (1978: 911) comments that international relations scholars have to recognize that "Interdependence is an old reality, as is anarchy. The argument ought to be about how interdependent-anarchic situations differ, not whether they are new." Commercial liberals, who Gourevitch divides into the liberal development school and the transnational relations/modernization/interdependence school, would not object to this general judgment. However, they would assert that the long-term historical trend is toward greater interdependence and stronger regimes to manage these interdependencies for the good of national populations.

Military Liberalism

A dramatic innovation in liberal scholarship in recent decades, and especially the last decade, is the emergence of military liberalism as one of the most important strands in liberal international theory. It makes two general arguments: (1) military technology and interdependencies are creating greater mutualities of interest in peace and cooperation, and (2) a reduction in the threat of military violence facilitates international economic cooperation.

The costs of war in terms of death and destruction have been an incentive for forms of international security cooperation for millennia. However, such cooperation has been infrequent, and when it has occurred, it has usually

broken down. Perhaps the most successful example of great-power collaboration until the nuclear revolution was the Concert of Europe during the half
century after the Napoleonic Wars (Jervis, 1983: 178–87; Holsti, 1992). There
was, however, no sense that collaboration was required because warfare had
become intolerably destructive. It took the carnage of World War I to bring
forth declarations that the destructiveness of armed conflict had made war
unthinkable for rational statespersons (Carr, 1946; Fussell, 1975; Howard,
1978: 52–84; for pretwentieth century, see Bloch, 1991). Although John Mueller (1988, 1989) contends that the nineteenth century and the twentieth century through World War II saw an increasing revulsion toward "conventional"
war that would have prevented a major war after 1945, his argument is not
widely supported (Dupuy, 1980; Jervis, 1988a: 84–87).

The revolution in nuclear weapons technology, coupled with the stability
in superpower relations and then the end of the Cold War, has given military
liberalism a major surge in popularity among security analysts, although many
so-called liberal theorists would shy away from the "liberal" label. Numerous
writers have noted the irrationality and moral depravity inherent in the use
of nuclear weapons and have called for either their abolition or non-use. But,
more important, there have also been a growing number of scholars who have
commented on the evolution of a nuclear war-prevention regime, which has
become a de facto great-power war-prevention regime. The underlying theme
of these writers is captured by the title of Mueller's (1989) book *Retreat from
Doomsday: The Obsolescence of Major War.*

The beginnings of postwar military liberalism can be traced to Bernard
Brodie's (1946) book *The Absolute Weapon* in which he argues that the only
real purpose of nuclear weapons is deterrence. Another landmark was John
Herz's (1959) *International Politics in the Atomic Age* in which he declares,
"Now that power can destroy power from center to center everything is
different." Herz thought that the territorial state was doomed by its new
permeability although he did not predict specific changes in global political
regimes. In an article published in the late 1950s, he wrote that the nation-
state

> is giving way to a permeability which tends to obliterate the very meaning
> of unit and unity, power and power relations, sovereignty and independence.
> The possibility of "hydrogenization" merely rendered the traditional defense
> structure of nations obsolete through the power to by-pass the shell protecting
> a two-dimensional territory and thus to destroy—vertically, as it were—even
> the most powerful ones. Paradoxically, utmost strength now coincides in the
> same unit with utmost vulnerability, absolute power with utter impotence.
> (1957: 476)

In the 1960s, Herz (1976, chap. 8) modified his position on the survivability
of the nation-state in the nuclear era precisely because of the emergent stability in nuclear deterrence, which was grounded in a desire to prevent horren-

dous losses of life and an explicit and tacit cooperation between the super-powers.

While many international relations scholars in the 1960s observed various specific forms of cooperation to stabilize security relations, it was not until the 1980s (especially after the dramatic changes in the Soviet Union) that scholarly consensus began to evolve from one optimistic about the stability of deterrence to one that posited the existence of a nuclear war/great-power war-prevention regime. In the late 1970s and early 1980s there was a recognition of elements of stability in strategic relations, but these relations were generally not seen as based on a long-term acceptance of norms and rules. However, by the late eighties and early nineties there were assertions that at least the developed world had become an area committed to the prevention of major warfare. One of the best statements concerning such a regime came from the diplomatic historian John Lewis Gaddis (1986), who identified various rules of the game for war avoidance (see also George, Farley, and Dallin, 1988; Weber, 1990, 1992; Rittberger, 1990; Breslauer and Tetlock, 1991; and Adler, 1991b).

Perhaps the best example of the evolution in thinking toward what we have called military liberalism is found in the writings of Robert Jervis (1978, 1983, 1988, 1989, 1991–1992) between 1978 and 1992. For Jervis there have been a number of factors that have contributed to mutual interests in war prevention in the industrialized world and the evolution of a great-power regime, but unquestionably the cornerstone of the new security regime is the existence of nuclear weaponry. He noted:

> What is new about this world with nuclear weapons (or, to be more precise, mutual second-strike that is successful enough to prevent retaliation from the other) is not overkill, but mutual kill—the side that is "losing" the war as judged by various measures of military capability can inflict as much damage on the "winner" as the "winner" can on the "loser."(1989: 5)

On this issue Kal Holsti (1991: 287, 333) wrote, "An actor cannot use such weapons in the Clausewitzian instrumental sense of war. . . . To say that any political value is worth national self-immolation and probably the destruction of modern civilization makes no sense." He goes on to comment: "The greatest threat to the security of the modern industrial state is not a particular adversary but nuclear war and perhaps even some forms of conventional war" (see also Booth, 1991).

It is instructive to consider briefly what leading proponents of realism and neorealism say about these military developments. Hans J. Morgenthau (1966: 9, 11) remarked, "Modern technology has rendered the nation state obsolete as a principle of political organization; for the nation state is no longer able to perform what is the elementary function of any political organization: to protect the lives of its members and their way of life." He added that "nationalism as a principle of political organization is not only obsolete; but in the nuclear age it is also self-destructive." Kenneth Waltz (1990: 733) wrote that "Although the possibility of war remains, nuclear weapons have drastically reduced the probability of its being fought by the states that have them. . . . Waging war has more and more become the privilege of poor and weak states." Increasingly, the position of realist writers overlaps with liberal thought: Military interdependence leads to cooperation designed to assure peace and protect human life.

The claim that military developments affect international economic cooperation is familiar throughout international relations scholarship. A central thrust of hegemonic stability theory (whether in its realist version or its collective-goods liberal version) is that a military hegemon promotes economic cooperation through the use of carrots and sticks (Gilpin, 1975; Keohane, 1984; Snidal, 1985; Gowa, 1989; Webb and Krasner, 1989). In the future the influence of the nuclear stalemate and great-power security cooperation on economic relations could be similar to the impact of a military hegemon in that they will greatly reduce concerns about relative gains from economic cooperation. But the cooperation is likely to be more durable and to reflect liberal concerns to protect human life and welfare. These perspectives are reflected in a comment by Jervis (1991–1992: 51) that "Both the fear of dependence and concern about relative gains are less when states expect to remain at peace with each other" (see also Powell, 1991). Contrary to past trends in thinking about international relations, a primary generator of mutual interests and cooperation among nations may now be military interdependencies. Further, these increased interdependencies are probably a significant facilitator of economic, as well as security, regimes.

Cognitive Liberalism

An interest in education, reason, and knowledge is not the preserve of either modern or liberal thinkers. Thucydides (1954: 48) intended his study of the Peloponnesian War to serve a didactic purpose, noting that "It will be enough for me . . . if these words of mine are judged useful by those who want to understand clearly the events which happened in the past and which (human nature being what it is) will . . . be repeated in the future." During the Renaissance numerous writers wrote how-to books for rulers that explained the international political world, the most famous of which is Machiavelli's *The Prince*.

Enlightenment liberalism, however, went considerably further in its claims, suggesting that cognitive factors could have a decisive effect on the very nature of international relations. Locke and Rousseau wrote treatises on education aimed at improving the state from below by producing virtuous citizens, a strategy that would ultimately affect the nature of the international system. Kant argued that "the ultimate end of education . . . [is] to promote the realization of the peaceful international state as the embodiment of human perfection" (Price, 1967: 237). By the late nineteenth and early twentieth centuries, many thinkers afforded education, reasoning, and knowledge a central role in their discussions of progress in international relations, including John Stuart Mill (1947), Hobson (1938; see Long, 1991), Zimmern (1936; see Markwell, 1986) and Arnold Toynbee (see Brewin, 1992).

In large measure, the above scholars were concerned with the relationship between democracy and education. From an international perspective, democracy was good; to succeed, citizens of democracies required a high level of education. But in practice foreign policy is often made without significant public participation (Henkin, 1990; Nincic, 1992). In our era scholars have begun to explore cognitive factors as important influences on policymakers' perceptions of common interests, strategies for realizing these interests, and values. One variant of this scholarship concerns how states are socialized into the norms and rules of the interstate system—an issue of particular concern to the international society school (Armstrong, 1993, especially chap. 1 and the conclusion). Pertinent to this general issue, Nye (1988: 238) has commented that "One of the most thought-provoking questions in international relations is how states learn." One might restate the question in more general terms: How do actors in international relations reason, learn, and utilize knowledge?

Answering this question has not proven easy. An early postwar effort was mounted by the functionalist and neofunctionalist schools. David Mitrany (1948, 1966) suggested that scientific and technical experts could understand mutualities of interests among countries in "technical" issue-areas and that if they assumed important decision-making roles within international organizations, there would soon develop an expanding web of international cooperation that would transform the international system. His theory rested on the ability to differentiate between technical and political issues and on the existence of common interests among peoples in the vast range of technical issues. These assumptions were viewed skeptically by many political observers (Haas, 1958; 1964: 1–50; Claude, 1964, chap. 17), but others sought to incorporate some of Mitrany's insights into a more pragmatic theory, now referred to as *neofunctionalism*. Focusing on regional patterns of integration, its proponents argued that technical experts, especially if linked to important interest groups, were a moderately influential force in furthering international integration (Haas, 1958; Lindberg and Scheingold, 1971). The neoclassical assertion that regulation can benefit all or most parties in situations of "market failure" can be seen as compatible with the functionalist tradition.

Recently, Ernst Haas (1990: 3) has investigated how international organizations respond to new knowledge by changing—or failing to change—"the definition of the problem to be solved." He concludes that over the past four centuries, scientific knowledge and the scientific method have led to a better understanding of the complex and interdependent nature of the human condition that is reflected in the policies of international organizations. Because of this, "the successful reform of international organization is a step in the moral evolution of the human species" (Haas, 1990: 193). Although Haas rejects the label "liberal," his position is compatible with a longstanding liberal belief in the possibility of material and moral progress through the accumulation of knowledge and improvements in learning.

In a book dedicated to Haas, Emanuel Adler, Beverly Crawford, and Jack Donnelly (1991: 28) state that "For Haas, the real test of progress is whether disagreement among actors (over goals or means) is bridged with the help of more new knowledge and shared meanings and whether actors come to a more complex understanding of the issues as a result" (see Haas, 1975a, 1980, 1983, 1990; and Haas, Williams, and Babai, 1977). Their analyses stress the importance of the knowledge generated by modern science in compelling international actors to identify problems in the same way, to appreciate their interdependent and complex nature, and to recognize the desirability of collaborative solutions. They conclude that

> Perceptions of interdependence can change decision makers' calculations about the usefulness of unilateral action in states' international relations. It can trigger the creation of shared values, meanings, rights, and obligations. And it can modify the calculations by which states choose to exercise their power. Within the anarchic condition, then, interdependence can pave the way for a redefinition of states' interests in ways that can embrace human interests. (1991: 38)

This trend has received cautious support from Peter Haas (1990, 1992) in his work on the role of epistemic communities in bringing specialized knowledge into the policy-making process to promote cooperative outcomes. He and his collaborators have produced very focused studies on the success of epistemic communities in furthering international collaboration in specific issue-areas. Both competing explanations and the extent to which epistemic communities may be limited to influencing certain issue-areas are questions that require further research. Haas himself has been cautious in making generalizations about this process.

How reason, learning, and knowledge may shape the values and interests of actors, change priorities, conduce toward cooperative solutions, and ultimately affect the nature of international relations is an area that is intuitively persuasive but highly elusive as a scholarly enterprise. Work has ranged from the very general, but poorly substantiated, claims of scholars such as Mitrany to the far more narrowly focused assertions of people such as Haas. In light of the rapid escalation of information technologies, debates on our reliance on scientific knowledge, and the massive transfer of knowledge from North to South, liberal investigations into the postmodern problematic of knowledge–power relations are likely to be an increasingly fruitful area for future research.

Sociological Liberalism

A diverse group of liberal international theorists are concerned with the impact of nongovernmental aspects of international society—communications, organizational linkages, and patterns of cultural homogeneity—on states' abilities to discern mutual interests and to cooperate with regard to them. We will call these writers "sociological liberals," a term coined by Joseph Nye (1988: 246), although he focused on transnational relations. Two bodies of literature that have been particularly concerned with these sociological factors in recent years are those on political integration and transnational relations.

The scholar who has focused most on the influence of communications flows and cultural patterns is Karl Deutsch (1953, 1957, 1964, 1966). In his 1953 study Deutsch highlighted how communications flows influence cultures, people's sense of political identity, and international political integration. He defined a political community as one that "consists of people who have learned to communicate with each other and to understand each other well beyond the mere interchange of goods and services" (1953: 65). For Deutsch, the organization of the world into nation-states reflects the "uneven distribution of overlapping clusters of communications facilities" (1953: 50). However, evolving patterns of communication hold out hope that people may come to better understand "the essential unity of their fate on this planet" and consequently that "the age of nationalism and of the growth of nations may recede into its proper historical perspective" (1953: 166).

In a 1957 coauthored study on security integration, Deutsch distinguishes between pluralistic and amalgamated security communities—the latter possessing governmental structures. He relates their development to communication patterns and cultural homogeneity (especially the compatibility of main values). Not only does cultural homogeneity lead to a "we-feeling," but it creates a "mutual predictability of behavior" that eliminates "the characteristic fears of all the alleged treacherousness, secretiveness, or unpredictability of 'foreigners'" (1957: 56–57). Deutsch further acknowledges the impact of transnational and intergovernmental organizations, noting that their main value in the integration process may be that they encourage habits of communication (Deutsch, 1957: 189). Finally, in his discussion of the emergence of a pluralistic community in the contemporary North Atlantic area, where he stresses societal consensuses on constitutionalism, democracy, and a modified capitalist economy, Deutsch (1957: 179) also mentions a "new political attitude which may mean a decisive break with the past: the new realization that *wars* are almost certain to be totally destructive for all parties to a conflict."

Neofunctionalist scholars of regional integration have focused on somewhat different sociological factors, particularly the emergence of transnational organizations and patterns of homogeneity. They have not been as concerned with communications patterns as was Deutsch, and they have tended to focus on interactions among elites whereas Deutsch was concerned with entire societies. Also, neofunctionalists have placed considerable importance on the roles of intergovernmental institutions in facilitating the influence of transnational groups. Still, their focus on transnational societal characteristics and transnational groups makes them important contributors to sociological liberalism (Haas, 1958, 1970, 1976; Lindberg and Scheingold, 1971).

A strand of the sociological liberal literature that has received considerable attention since the 1970s concerns transnational relations (Keohane and Nye, 1971, 1974; Burton, 1972; Rosenau, 1980; Willets, 1982; Taylor, 1984). This concern is in part an offshoot of integration theory and also overlaps the writings on multinational corporations discussed in the section on commercial liberalism. One of its central claims is that states are losing ground in international relations to nonstate actors, but more important for the purposes of this chapter is that it posits that nongovernmental actors are able to cooperate across state lines. Democratic states find it difficult to control cooperation among nongovernmental groups, which, in fact, often pressure governments to accept cooperative ventures.

The growth in international communications and transnational actors, the rising interest in the impact of cultural patterns, and the globalization of business and industry are trends that are likely to make the concerns of sociological liberals important areas for future research. However, since changes in these factors tend to be gradual and their influence difficult to discern, research on sociological integration is not likely to have the dramatic impact on academic thinking that research on some of the other strands will.

Institutional Liberalism

While the body of international institutions that promotes liberal values is a central dependent variable of liberal scholarship, it is also seen by liberals as an important independent variable that affects the likelihood of further cooperation. Such institutions take a variety of forms ranging from transnational values or belief systems to substantive regimes to international organizations.

The relevance of transnational moral values for liberal theorists goes back to Locke and Kant, and concern with their importance has been increasing in the present era (Nardin and Mapel, 1992; Matthew, forthcoming). In a recent review of theories of multilateralism, James Caporaso (1992: 630) comments that neorealism "underestimates the extent to which cooperation depends on a prior set of unacknowledged claims about the embeddedness of cooperation habits, shared values, and taken-for-granted rules."

One approach that combines the importance of both societal values and general regulatory regimes is what has been called Grotianism, the international society school, or the English school. It contends that there is an international society of states held together by at least a minimal set of rules and formal institutions that are based on common interests and values. Within the international society school there is a "pluralist" position—states accept certain norms and laws for the mutual protection of sovereignty and the facilitation of commerce—and a "solidarist" position—states accept norms and rules to realize common values that go beyond self-preservation and sovereignty. According to Grotius, these values are derived from natural law.

Today a more widely accepted position is Martin Wight's claim that these propositions flow from the dominant Western civilization. Of the two major British proponents of the international society school, Hedley Bull is generally regarded as representing the pluralist position while, at least in some of his writings, Martin Wight's views suggest a solidarist outlook (Bull, 1966a, 1966b, 1976, 1977a; Wight, 1966, 1977; Bull, Kingsbury, and Roberts, 1990; Miller and Vincent, 1990; Cutler, 1991; Jackson, 1991; Armstrong, 1993). Barry Buzan (1993) suggests that this distinction may be misleading for some purposes, pointing out that it is impossible for there to be a significant expansion of "international society" without some commensurate growth in "global society." In other words, the development of international institutions or regimes requires a commensurate increase in shared values and beliefs.

Given the bifurcation that exists within the English school, one might question how well it falls within international liberalism. While a minimal pluralist stance would probably best be defined as a form of realism, the general evolution of this approach has closely followed liberal themes. Arguments set out by one of its foremost contemporary proponents, Adam Watson, are telling in this regard. Watson's (1992) recent book, *The Evolution of International Society*, documents the global expansion of the European state system and the development of important international norms and rules. He grounds these developments in familiar liberal territory: technological innovation, the growth of international economic and security interdependencies, shared ethical values, and the spillover effects of preexisting international institutions. Watson's work confirms James Mayall's (1990: 148) comment that "The modifications and additions to the original conception of international society stem from the acceptance of new principles. They are all derived, in the first instance, from liberal theory."

The impact of transnational moral values on the evolution of cooperative regimes is addressed in a variety of specific studies. An interesting analysis by Ethan Nadelman concerns the emergence of international prohibition regimes with regard to piracy, slavery, treatment of fugitives, drug trafficking, and the killing of certain animals, which he attributes to the moral sensibilities (and power) of the European nations and the United States. He writes that

> Moral and emotional factors related to neither political nor economic advantage but instead involving religious beliefs, humanitarian sentiments, faith in universalism, compassion, conscience, paternalism, fear, prejudice, and the compulsion to proselytize can and do play important roles in the creation and the evolution of international regimes. (Nadelman 1990: 480)

The most substantial literature examines the transnational moral and ethical basis of human rights regimes (Vincent, 1986; Donnelly, 1981, 1986; Forsythe,

1991; for a general discussion, see Jones, 1991). A potentially supportive literature is emerging on the impact of moral and ethical value systems on the decline of war and the rise of war-prevention regimes (Mueller, 1989; Ray, 1989). Shared values have also been viewed as undergirding the growth of the European Union—a point that is observed by neofunctionalists as well as by more historically oriented scholars (Hay, 1968; Lindberg and Scheingold, 1971). It should also not be overlooked that many international legal scholars regard international law as having its own inherent morality: Adherence to law is a good in and of itself. Its relevance to human freedom and progress is implicit in Terry Nardin's (1992: 27) comment that "States that repudiate the authority of international law remove themselves from international society, which is the closest that the international system can approach to a civil order, and withdraw into barbarism."

Writers have tended to see the impact of transnational values on regimes as growing with the increase of interdependence and communications as well as with the growth of a global civilization. Beverly Crawford (1991: 447, 449) divides international relations theories between those that do and those that do not predict human progress, and central to the former is the strengthening of common values through the growth of interdependence. She observes that "interdependence . . . can create shared values, meanings, rights, and obligations" and that "*within* the anarchic condition, interdependence can pave the way for a redefinition of states' interests in ways that can embrace human interests." This point was previously considered in the writings of Karl Deutsch (Puchala, 1981). In a similar vein, a theme of James Rosenau's *Turbulence in World Politics* (1990) is that the rise of the "global citizen" possessing cosmopolitan values and new patterns of cooperation is related to the complex and growing pattern of transactions among states (see also Linklater, 1982).

An interesting and important strand of thinking related to the impact of belief systems and general regimes has been called "reflectivism" or "constructivism." It posits that there is a mutually causal relationship between general values or regimes, on the one hand, and the nature of actors and their interests, on the other (Ruggie and Kratochwil, 1986; Wendt, 1987, 1992; Keohane, 1988; Kratochwil, 1989). In discussing the reflectivist school, Haggard (1991: 404, 413–15) states that it seeks "to identify *common* norms, principles, and knowledge that orient action across states" and that "*the norms that shape actor preferences themselves constitute an investigable structure.*" John Ruggie (1986) makes the point in his critique of neorealism that it ignores changes in the values or intersubjective understandings that distinguish international systems. He supports his stance by analyzing the transition from the medieval to the modern international system.

While the importance of norms and belief systems has been stressed by many scholars, the aspect of international institutionalism that has attracted the most attention among liberal scholars has been the roles of international organizations and the prescriptive regimes in which they are embedded. As a recent study observes: "The liberal tradition is replete with schemes to

bolster international law [and] to create new international organizations"
(Smith, 1992: 215). The faith in the ability of international organizations to
reshape international politics has not been as great as it was in the interwar
period, but there has been a very rich scholarship in the area (Krasner, 1983;
Keohane, 1984, 1989b, 1993; Ruggie and Kratochwil, 1986; Karns and Mingst,
1990; Zacher, 1993; Ruggie, 1990). There are a number of theses in what has
been called the institutionalist approach. Institutions enhance cooperation by
improving the quality of information, reducing transactions costs, facilitating
tradeoffs among issue-areas, facilitating enforcement of accords, and enhancing
states' ethical concerns. On this latter issue Keohane (1984: 257) notes:

> Empathy by the advantaged [for the disadvantaged] may be more likely to
> develop in the context of well-functioning international institutions than in
> an international state of nature that approximates Hobbes' "war of all against
> all." Closer approximation to the ideals of cosmopolitan morality is therefore
> more likely to be promoted by modifying current international regimes than
> by abandoning them and attempting to start all over.

Other roles of international institutions noted by some liberals are that
they can promote new political loyalties (a broadening and strengthening of
a community "we-feeling") and a growth in international governance. David
Mitrany (1948, 1966) argued that within the context of regular international
meetings, participants better understand common interests, learn the benefits
of international cooperation, and gradually develop new political loyalties.
These developments then spark additional cooperation. When Ernst Haas
and others used Mitrany's spillover thesis as a backdrop for their studies on
regional integration, the limits and possibilities of institutional impacts on
political loyalties and integration became refined—and claims became more
modest (Haas, 1970, 1976; Lindberg and Scheingold, 1971). Along these lines,
Alexander Wendt (1992: 417), in a discussion of the European Community,
argues that "A strong liberal or constructivist analysis of this problem would
suggest four decades of cooperation may have transformed a positive interdependence of outcomes into a collective 'European identity' in terms of which
states increasingly define their 'self'-interests." It is likely that both developments within the European Community and the growth of global regimes
will promote a continued expansion of scholarship on institutional liberalism.

In reflecting on postwar writings on the six strands of liberal theory (and
the emergence of a seventh—ecological interdependence), it is noteworthy
that there was little important liberal scholarship during the post-1945 decade
when the Cold War was developing. Then, from the mid-1950s through the
1970s, most liberal writings were concerned with sociological, cognitive, institutional, and economic questions, and even then the analyses tended to be
limited to regional groupings or the Western alliance system. It was at this
time that the United States, in cooperation with its European allies, was
putting a clearly liberal normative stamp on the international institutions,
nongovernmental networks, and national political systems of the noncommu-

nist world (Ruggie, 1992), and academic analyses were influenced by these trends. On the other hand, while within the Western world there was a growing image of liberal interdependence, outside of that sphere there was an acceptance of realpolitik. Almost no international relations specialists identified themselves as liberals. The resolution of the Cuban missile crisis and the détente of the late 1960s and the early 1970s led to some interest in global security cooperation, but it was very limited. (One liberal globalist of the 1950s and 1960s was Dag Hammarskjold [Zacher, 1970].)

Liberal scholarship experienced two dramatic shifts in emphasis in the 1980s. First, there was the recrudescence of republican liberalism in the form of the "democracies do not fight each other" school. Second, beginning in the mid-1980s and exploding during and after the disintegration of the socialist bloc in the late 1980s, military interdependence became a central strand of international liberalism in terms of its projected impact on international relations. The increasing skepticism of realists' claims concerning the prevalance of relative gains in international bargaining is one manifestation of this intellectual shift (Baldwin, 1993). If the nuclear revolution abetted by the end of the Cold War leads to a great-power war-prevention regime (and possibly a mitigation of war in the Third World), we are witnessing a true transformation in both international relations and the credibility of liberal international theory. Of course, technological and political changes could always undermine the favorable trends and intellectual reorientation of recent years.

A final point that deserves highlighting is that all of these strands of liberal international theory are ultimately about enhancing the security, prosperity, and human rights of individuals. While analyses often focus on state interests and interstate interactions, the lens through which they are evaluated by liberals is how they affect the material and moral conditions of people.

CONCLUSION

This study originated with the recognition that there is no article or book that describes liberal international theory in a systematic way, provides an overview of its evolution, and links current scholarship with the theoretical core of the older literature. The preceding analysis has sought to accomplish these tasks, although it is still possible to agree with Arthur Stein (1990: 7, fn. 6) that the core elements of liberalism are disputable. Still, many international theorists would probably agree with our conceptualization of liberalism's common threads and divergent strands. Sharp differences are likely to emerge on the questions of how people and states define and redefine progress, the relative importance of the components of modernization, and the extent to which these components or strands engender or facilitate forms of cooperation conducive to progress. This concluding section provides brief comments on the major aspects of the theory and suggests future research directions relating to these aspects. It then addresses several major issues or criticisms that are relevant to the theory as a whole.

One aspect of the theory that has not been discussed at length in this chapter concerns the *assumptions*. Indeed, compared to realists and marxists, liberals spend little time clarifying assumptions. However, the future development of the theory rests on clearly describing actors, interests, and the factors that shape actors, interests, and outcomes. For liberals the nature of these phenomena are historically contingent, and therefore conceptualizations of them must be revised constantly according to the era and issue-area under study. For example, pluralistic states can vary in important ways, and their characteristics can influence how and why they cooperate (Milner, 1992). At times liberal international theory looks like "thick description" because of the richness of the world that liberals see, but well-organized analysis and generalizations are possible. To stress the point made above, liberal scholars should try to clarify their assumptions on key matters at the beginning of their studies and should reflect on them at the end.

In very general terms, liberals argue that, by applying reason to its moral and material problems, humankind can gradually increase the freedom each individual has to pursue his or her conception of the good life. At the level of international relations, liberals have linked this general aspiration to the promotion of peace, prosperity, and justice through various forms of cooperation. *Progress* occurs when international cooperation increases. Liberals, however, rarely have been utopian—they regard progress as a gradual and uneven process. Some liberals were victims of heady optimism in the nineteenth and early twentieth centuries, but this has become muted in the postwar era. While it would be misleading to suggest that contemporary liberals have returned to the restrained and even negative outlooks of Locke and Rousseau, today they tend to see progress in terms of possibility rather than certainty. There is even some musing that the steady erosion of the Christian mythology on which liberalism was constructed could seriously undermine it in the long run (Fukuyama, 1992, chaps. 28 and 31).

There is, however, an embryonic reevaluation of progress taking shape within the liberal camp that can be labeled post-Enlightenment liberalism. It has been stimulated by ecological crises, new trends in gender relations, and even the weakening of religion. It is concerned in particular with controlling the effects of technological innovation, rethinking the nature of competitive and hierarchical relations in society, and revalorizing the need for spiritual roots. This reevaluation may provide an excellent case study of how and why people's and states' interests change. In any case, people's redefinition of progress should be at the center of the liberal research agenda as it was in the late nineteenth and early twentieth centuries when advocates of laissez-faire and state intervention engaged in fervent debates. It is, of course, closely tied to understandings of people's interests and the factors that influence their transformation.

This chapter has argued that the various strands of liberal international theory represent distinct but interrelated aspects of an evolving *process of modernization.* Three of these strands can be regarded as the backbone of a traditional liberal understanding of progress in international relations: republican liberalism, commercial liberalism, and institutional liberalism. The other three—military liberalism, cognitive liberalism, and sociological liberalism—are largely products of the twentieth century. As noted above, a seventh strand is emerging and likely to have a major impact on liberal international theory in the decades ahead—ecological liberalism. As scholars and policymakers seek to unravel the many implications for international relations of a multitude of ecological interdependencies in order to identify viable strategies for progress, many of the values and assumptions vested in other aspects of the modernization process are likely to be challenged and gradually revised.

All of the strands of liberal international theory deserve considerable attention by academic researchers. However, liberal democracy and military interdependence are likely to be the crucial generators of mutual interests in cooperation, and therefore they should be at the center of the research agenda. The implications of economic interdependence for peace, welfare, and justice have been problematic in the past, but on the whole commercial ties seem to have had positive effects. A great deal of research should be conducted on contemporary international economic interactions, given questions about their past effects, especially at the level of global distribution, and their current and future impact on the world environment. Of the three strands that are mainly facilitators of cooperation (cognitive development, sociological integration, and institutional growth), research on the former two is less developed than it is on the other strands, and a significant increase in research is called for. Of central importance are the influence of increasing knowledge on changes in values and the influence of communications and patterns of cultural homogeneity on the process of international cooperation. International institutions have been and will rightfully continue to be at the center of liberal scholarship. Analyzing the impacts of institutions on the growth in cooperation is very difficult, and intellectually inventive studies are needed.

Having discussed theoretical assumptions, progress, and the driving forces of modernization, it is important to consider two interrelated criticisms that are sometimes leveled at liberal international theory: It is too general and complex to provide a good understanding of international relations or a clear research agenda, and it cannot stand on its own and must be amalgamated with other theories to achieve a complete understanding of international politics. On the matter of the *generality* of its assumptions, the main riposte is that any evolutionary theory must leave room for changes in actors, interests, and underlying causal forces in international relations. Researchers working on certain problems in particular time periods must supply the specific content. At the same time, a recognition that collective actors such as states must be understood in terms of their constituent groups does orient researchers in ways that other theories do not. Likewise, an understanding that actor interests and international outcomes are shaped by a particular set of variables does structure theoretical investigations. The *complexity* of the causal processes does, of course, undermine theoretical parsimony, but if the world is not simple, thinking it is simple does not enhance intellectual understanding. In fact, both realist and marxist theoretical writings have generally become much more complex because the scholars have found that their initial parsimonious outlooks could not account for certain developments. Jack Donnelly (1992) notes the many qualifications or "hedges" that realist writers introduce into their analyses; in so doing they take into consideration those factors that liberals say should be included in the basic theoretical structure. (Of relevance is the "structural realism" of Buzan, Jones, and Little [1993].) Liberals believe that international relations scholars have to accept complexity but should try to structure it as clearly as they can.

A final issue is, *Can liberal international theory stand on its own* as a comprehensive theoretical framework, or must it be integrated with other theories to develop such a framework? Relevant to this point Keohane (1989a: 175) remarks that "Liberalism does not purport to provide a complete account of international relations. On the contrary, most contemporary liberals seem to accept large portions of both marxist and realist explanations." This comment assumes that liberal international theory is only concerned with what promotes "progress" and not what sustains coercion, exploitation, and injustice. Of course, the two cannot and should not be separated. Locke and Rousseau were pessimistic about realizing liberal principles on the international scene in their era and discussed why this was the case. And Kant saw the balance of power as the central mechanism of international order in the late eighteenth century while believing that the forces of modernization would create a much more cooperative and just world over the long run. For international liberals, world politics is about evolution, and they should be concerned with all dimensions of that evolution. If liberals integrate insights from other theories into their analyses, their theoretical positions do not become less liberal as long as they adhere to the central assumptions of liberal international theory. At the core what makes international relations scholars liberals is that they think that international politics is about the changing interests of the inhabitants of states (or other entities) and that the underlying forces of change are creating opportunities for increased cooperation and a greater realization of peace, welfare, and justice. The historian Michael Howard (1978: 11) has written that such a definition would encompass most political thinkers in Britain and the United States. Perhaps international relations scholars have not recognized the central theoretical paradigm that guides scholarship in their field.

REFERENCES

Adler, Emanuel. (1991a) "Cognitive Evolution: A Dynamic Approach for the Study of International Relations and Their Progress," pp. 43–88 in Emanuel Adler and Beverly Crawford, eds., *Progress in Postwar International Relations*. New York: Columbia University Press.

———. (1991b) "Seasons of Peace: Progress in Postwar International Security," pp. 128–73 in Emanuel Adler and Beverly Crawford, eds., *Progress in Postwar International Relations*. New York: Columbia University Press.

Adler Emanuel, Beverly Crawford, and Jack Donnelly. (1991) "Defining and Conceptualizing Progress in International Relations," pp. 1–42 in Emanuel Adler and Beverly Crawford, eds., *Progress in Postwar International Relations*. New York: Columbia University Press.

Angell, Norman. (1912) *The Great Illusion*. London: G. P. Putnam.

Armstrong, David, ed. (1993) *Revolution and World Order: The Revolutionary State in International Society*. Oxford: Clarendon.

Baldwin, David A. (1993) *Neorealism and Neoliberalism: The Contemporary Debate*. New York: Columbia University Press.

———. (1980) "Interdependence and Power: A Conceptual Analysis," *International Organization* 34 (Autumn): 471–506.

Bloch, J. S. (1991 [1899]) *Is War Now Impossible? Being an Abridgement of "The War of the Future in Its Technical, Economic, and Political Dimensions."* Aldershot, U.K.: Gregg Revivals.

Baran, Paul. (1957) *The Political Economy of Growth*. New York: Monthly Review Press.

Beitz, Charles. (1979) *Political Theory and International Relations*. Princeton, N.J.: Princeton University Press.

Bentham, Jeremy. (1927) *Plan for Universal and Perpetual Peace*. Cambridge: Grotius Society Publications.

Booth, Ken. (1991) "Security in Anarchy: Utopian Realism in Theory and Practice," *International Affairs* 67: 527–45.

Breslauer, George W., and Philip E. Tetlock, eds. (1991) *Learning in the U.S. and Soviet Foreign Policy*. Boulder, Colo.: Westview.

Brewin, Christopher. (1992) "Research in a Global Context: A Discussion of Toynbee's Legacy," *Review of International Studies* 18 (April): 115–30.

Brodie, Bernard, ed. (1946) *The Absolute Weapon*. New York: Harcourt and Brace.

Brown, Chris. (1992) "Marxism and International Ethics," pp. 225–49 in Terry Nardin and David R. Mapel, eds., *Traditions of International Ethics*. Cambridge: Cambridge University Press.

Bull, Hedley. (1977a) *The Anarchical Society: A Study of Order in World Politics*. New York: Columbia University Press.

———. (1977b) "Introduction: Martin Wight and the Study of International Relations," pp. 1–20 in Martin Wight, *Systems of States*. Leicester: Leicester University Press.

———. (1976) "Martin Wight and the Theory of International Relations," *British Journal of International Studies* 2: 101–16.

———. (1966a) "Society and Anarchy in International Relations," pp. 35–50 in Herbert Butterfield and Martin Wight, eds., *Diplomatic Investigations: Essays in the Theory of International Relations*. London: George Allen and Unwin.

———. (1966b) "The Grotian Conception of International Society," pp. 51–73 in Herbert Butterfield and Martin Wight, eds., *Diplomatic Investigations: Essays in the Theory of International Relations*. London: George Allen and Unwin.

Bull, Hedley, Benedict Kingsbury, and Adam Roberts, eds. (1990) *Hugo Grotius and International Relations*. Oxford: Clarendon.

Burley, Anne-Marie. (1992) "Liberal States: A Zone of Law." Paper presented to the Annual Meeting of the American Political Science Association, September 3–6, Chicago.

Burton, John. (1972) World Society. Cambridge: Cambridge University Press.

Buzan, Barry. (1993) "From International System to International Society: Structural Realism and Regime Theory Meet the English School," International Organization 47: 327–52.

——. (1984) "Economic Structure and International Security: The Limits of the Liberal Case," International Organization 38: 597–624.

Buzan, Barry, Charles Jones, and Richard Little. (1993) The Logic of Anarchy: Rethinking Neorealism to Structural Realism. New York: Columbia University Press.

Caporaso, James A. (1993) "Global Political Economy," pp. 451–81 in Ada W. Finifter, ed., Political Science: The State of the Discipline II. Washington, D.C.: American Political Science Association.

——. (1992) "International Relations Theory and Multilateralism: The Search for Foundations," International Organization 46: 599–632.

Carr, E. H. (1946) The Twenty Years' Crisis, 1919–39. New York: Macmillan.

Carter, Christine Jane. (1987) Rousseau and the Problem of War. New York: Garland.

Claude, Inis L. (1964) Swords into Plowshares. New York: Random House.

Cobden, Richard. (1870) Speeches on Questions on Public Policy by Richard Cobden, M.P. London: Macmillan.

Cohen, Raymond. (1992) "Premature Celebration: A Reappraisal of the Democracy-Peace Theory." Paper presented to the Annual Meeting of the International Studies Association, April 1–4, Atlanta, Georgia.

Constant, Benjamin. (1988) Political Writings. Biancamaria Fontana, trans. and ed., Cambridge: Cambridge University Press.

Cooper, Richard. (1972) "Economic Interdependencies and Foreign Policy in the Seventies," World Politics 24: 158–81.

——. (1968) The Politics of Interdependence. New York: McGraw-Hill.

Cornett, Linda, and James Caporaso. (1992) "'And It Still Moves!': State Interests and Social Forces in the European Community," pp. 219–49 in James N. Rosenau and Ernst-Otto Czempiel, eds., Governance without Government: Order and Change in World Politics. Cambridge: Cambridge University Press.

Crawford, Beverly. (1991) "Toward a Theory of Progress in International Relations," pp. 438–68 in Emanuel Adler and Beverly Crawford, eds., Progress in Postwar International Relations. New York: Columbia University Press.

Cutler, A. Claire. (1991) "The 'Grotian Tradition' in International Relations," Review of International Studies 17: 41–65.

de Caprariis, Vittorio. (1957) "The Crisis of Contemporary Political Philosophy," Confluence: An International Forum 5: 291–306.

Delaisi, Francis. (1925) Political Myths and Economic Realities. New York: Viking.

Deutsch, Karl W. (1969) Nationalism and Its Alternatives. New York: Knopf.

——. (1966) Nerves of Government. New York: Free Press.

——. (1953) Nationalism and Social Communication. Cambridge, Mass.: MIT Press.

Deutsch, Karl W., et al. (1964) The Integration of Political Communities. Philadelphia: Lippincott.

——. (1957) Political Community and the North Atlantic Area. Princeton, N.J.: Princeton University Press.

de Wilde, Jaap. (1991) Saved from Oblivion: Interdependence Theory in the First Half of the Twentieth Century. Aldershot, U.K.: Dartmouth.

Donnelly, Jack. (1992) "Twentieth-Century Realism," pp. 85–111 in Terry Nardin and David A. Mapel, eds., *Traditions in International Ethics*. Cambridge: Cambridge University Press.

———. (1986) "Human Rights: A Regime Analysis," *International Organization* 40: 599–642.

———. (1981) "Recent Trends in UN Human Rights Activity: Description and Polemic," *International Organization* 35: 633–56.

Doyle, Michael W. (1992) "An International Liberal Community," pp. 307–33 in Graham Allison and Gregory Treverton, eds., *Rethinking America's Security*. New York: W.W. Norton.

———. (1986) "Liberalism and World Politics," *American Political Science Review* 80: 1151–69.

———. (1983) "Kant, Liberal Legacies, and Foreign Affairs," *Philosophy and Public Affairs* 12: 205–35, 323–53.

Dupuy, Trevor N. (1980) *The Evolution of Weapons and Warfare*. Indianapolis, Ind.: Bobbs-Merrill.

Ember, Carol R., Melvin Ember, and Bruce Russett. (1992) "Peace between Participatory Polities: A Cross-National Test of the 'Democracies Rarely Fight Each Other' Hypothesis," *World Politics* 44: 573–99.

Ferguson, Yale H., and Richard W. Mansbach. (1988) *The Elusive Quest: Theory and International Politics*. Columbia: University of South Carolina Press.

Forde, Steven. (1992) "Classical Realism," pp. 62–84 in Terry Nardin and David A. Mapel, eds., *Traditions in International Ethics*. Cambridge: Cambridge University Press.

Forsythe, David P. (1991) *The Internationalization of Human Rights*. Lexington, Mass.: Lexington Books.

Fukuyama, Francis. (1992) *The End of History and the Last Man*. New York. Free Press.

Fussell, Paul. (1975) *The Great War and Modern Memory*. London: Oxford University Press.

Gaddis, John Lewis. (1986) "The Long Peace: Elements of Stability in the Postwar International System," *International Security* 10: 99–142.

George, Alexander L., Philip J. Farley, and Alexander Dallin, eds. (1988) *U.S.–Soviet Security Cooperation: Achievements, Failures, Lessons*. Oxford: Oxford University Press.

Gilbert, Alan. (1992) "Must Global Politics Constrain Democracy? Realism, Regimes, and Democratic Internationalism," *Political Theory* 20: 8–37.

Gilpin, Robert G. (1987) *The Political Economy of International Relations*. Princeton, N.J.: Princeton University Press.

———. (1986) "The Richness of the Tradition of Political Realism," pp. 301–21 in Robert O. Keohane, ed., *Neorealism and Its Critics*. New York: Columbia University Press.

———. (1981) *War and Change in World Politics*. Cambridge: Cambridge University Press.

———. (1975) *US Power and the Multinational Corporation: The Political Economy of Foreign Direct Investment*. New York: Basic Books.

Gourevitch, Peter. (1978) "The Second Image Reversed: The International Sources of Domestic Politics," *International Organization* 32: 881–912.

Gowa, Joanne. (1989) "Rational Hegemons, Excludable Goods, and Small Groups: An Epitaph for Hegemonic Stability Theory," *World Politics* 41: 307–24.

Gray, John. (1986) *Liberalism*. Minneapolis: University of Minnesota Press.

Grieco, Joseph M. (1991) "Realist Theory and the Study of International Relations." (mimeo)

———. (1988) "Anarchy and the Limits of International Cooperation: A Realist Critique of the Newest Liberal Institutionalism," *International Organization* 42: 485–507.

Haas, Ernst B. (1990) *When Knowledge Is Power: Three Models of Change in International Organizations*. Berkeley: University of California Press.

———. (1983) "Words Can Hurt You; or, Who Said What to Whom About Regimes," pp. 23–59 in Stephen D. Krasner, ed., *International Regimes*. Ithaca, N.Y.: Cornell University Press.

———. (1980) "Why Collaborate? Issue-Linkage and International Regimes," *World Politics* 32: 357–405.

———. (1976) "Turbulent Fields and the Study of Regional Integration," *International Organization* 30: 173–212.

———. (1975a) "Is There a Hole in the Whole? Knowledge, Technology, Interdependence and the Construction of International Regimes," *International Organization* 29: 827–76.

———. (1975b) *The Obsolescence of Regional Integration Theory*. Berkeley: Institute of International Studies, University of California.

———. (1970) "The Study of Regional Integration: Reflections on the Joys and Anguish of Pretheorizing," *International Organization* 24: 607–46.

———. (1964) *Beyond the Nation-State: Functionalism and International Organization*. Stanford, Calif.: Stanford University Press.

———. (1958) *The Uniting of Europe*. Stanford, Calif.: Stanford University Press.

Haas, Ernst B., Mary Pat Williams, and Don Babai. (1977) *Scientists and World Order: The Uses of Technical Knowledge in International Organizations*. Berkeley: University of California Press.

Hass, Peter, ed. (1992) "Knowledge, Power, and International Policy Coordination." Special issue of *International Organization* 46: 1–390.

———. (1990) *Saving the Mediterranean: The Politics of International Environmental Protection*. New York: Columbia University Press.

Haggard, Stephan. (1991) "Structuralism and Its Critics: Recent Progress in International Relations Theory," pp. 403–37 in Emanuel Adler and Beverly Crawford, eds., *Progress in Postwar International Relations*. New York: Columbia University Press.

Haggard, Stephan, and Beth A. Simmons. (1987) "Theories of International Regimes," *International Organization* 41: 491–517.

Hay, Denys. (1968) *Europe: The Emergence of an Idea*. Edinburgh: Edinburgh University Press.

Henkin, Louis. (1990) *Constitutionalism, Democracy, and Foreign Affairs*. New York: Columbia University Press.

Herz, John H. (1976) *The Nation-State and the Crisis of World Politics*. New York: David McKay.

———. (1959) *International Politics in the Atomic Age*. New York: Columbia University Press.

———. (1957) "The Rise and Demise of the Territorial State," *World Politics* 9: 473–93.

———. (1950) "Idealist Internationalism and the Security Dilemma," *World Politics* 2: 157–80.

Hinsley, F. H. (1963) *Power and the Pursuit of Peace*. Cambridge: Cambridge University Press.

Hobbes, Thomas. (1968) *Leviathan*. Edited by C. B. MacPherson. Harmondsworth, U.K.: Penguin Books.

Hobson, John. (1938) *Imperialism: A Study*, rev. ed. London: George Allen and Unwin.

Hoffmann, Stanley H. (1987) *Janus and Minerva: Essays in the Theory and Practice of International Politics*. Boulder, Colo.: Westview Press.

————. (1981) *Duties Beyond Borders: On the Limits and Possibilities of Ethical International Politics*. Syracuse, N.Y.: Syracuse University Press.

————. (1960) *Contemporary Theory in International Relations*. Englewood Cliffs, N.J.: Prentice-Hall.

Holsti, Kalevi J. (1992) "Governance without Government: Polyarchy in Nineteenth-Century European International Politics," pp. 30–57 in James N. Rosenau and Ernst-Otto Czempiel, eds., *Governance without Government*. Cambridge: Cambridge University Press.

————. (1991) *Peace and War: Armed Conflicts and International Order, 1648–1989*. Cambridge: Cambridge University Press.

————. (1985) *The Dividing Discipline: Hegemony and Diversity in International Theory*. Boston: Unwin Hyman.

Howard, Michael. (1978) *War and the Liberal Conscience*. London: Temple Smith.

Hurrell, Andrew. (1990) "Kant and the Kantian Paradigm in International Relations," *Review of International Studies* 16: 183–205.

Jackson, Robert H. (1991) *Quasi-States: Sovereignty, International Relations and the Third World*. Cambridge: Cambridge University Press.

Jervis, Robert. (1991–1992) "The Future of World Politics: Will It Resemble the Past?" *International Security* 16: 39–73.

————. (1989) *The Meaning of the Nuclear Revolution*. Ithaca, N.Y.: Cornell University Press.

————. (1988a) "The Political Effects of Nuclear Weapons," *International Security* 13: 80–90.

————. (1988b) "Realism, Game Theory, and Cooperation," *World Politics* 40: 317–49.

————. (1983) "Security Regimes," pp. 173–94 in Stephen D. Krasner, ed., *International Regimes*. Ithaca, N.Y.: Cornell University Press.

————. (1978) "Cooperation under the Security Dilemma," *World Politics* 30: 167–214.

————. (1976) *Perception and Misperception in International Politics*. Princeton: N.J.: Princeton University Press.

Jones, Dorothy V. (1991) *Code of Peace: Ethics and Security in the Warlord States*. Chicago: University of Chicago Press.

Kant, Immanuel. (1957) *Perpetual Peace*. Translated by Lewis W. Beck. Indianapolis, Ind.: Bobbs-Merrill.

Karns, Margaret P., and Karen A. Mingst, eds. (1990) *The United States and Multilateral Institutions*. Boston: Unwin Hyman.

Keohane, Robert O. (1993) "Institutionalist Theory and the Realist Challenge after the Cold War," pp. 269–300 in David Baldwin, ed., *Neorealism and Neoliberalism: The Contemporary Debate*. New York: Columbia University Press.

————. (1990) "Multilateralism: An Agenda for Research," *International Journal* 45: 744–53.

————. (1989a) "International Liberalism Reconsidered," pp. 165–94 in John Dunn, ed., *The Economic Limits of Politics*. Cambridge: Cambridge University Press.

————. (1989b) "Neoliberal Institutionalism," pp. 1–22 in Robert O. Keohane, ed., *International Institutions and State Power: Essays in International Relations Theory*. Boulder, Colo.: Westview.

————. (1988) "International Institutions: Two Perspectives," *International Studies Quarterly* 32: 379–96.

————. (1986) "Reciprocity in International Relations," *International Organization* 40: 1–27.

————. (1984) *After Hegemony: Cooperation and Discord in the World Political Economy*. Princeton: N.J.: Princeton University Press.

Keohane, Robert O., and Joseph S. Nye. (1989) *Power and Interdependence: World Politics in Transition*, 2nd ed. Glenview, Ill.: Scott, Foresman.

————. (1974) "Transgovernmental Relations and International Organizations," *World Politics* 27: 39–62.

————, eds. (1971) *Transnational Relations and World Politics*. Cambridge, Mass.: Harvard University Press.

Kingsbury, Benedict, and Adam Roberts, eds. (1990) *Hugo Grotius and International Relations*. Oxford: Clarendon.

Krasner, Stephen D., ed. (1983) *International Regimes*. Ithaca, N.Y.: Cornell University Press.

Kratochwil, Friedrich. (1989) *Norms, Rules and Decisions*. New York: Cambridge University Press.

Kupchan, Charles A., and Clifford A. Kupchan. (1991) "Concerts, Collective Security, and the Future of Europe," *International Security* 16: 114–61.

Lake, David. (1992) "Powerful Pacifists: Democratic States and War," *American Political Science Review* 86: 24–37.

Lenin, Vladimir. (1939) *Imperialism: The Highest Stage of Capitalism*. New York: International Publishers.

Lindberg, Leon N., and Stuart A. Scheingold, eds. (1971) *Regional Integration: Theory and Research*. Cambridge, Mass.: Harvard University Press.

Link, Arthur S. (1957) *Wilson the Diplomatist: A Look at His Major Foreign Policies*. Baltimore: Johns Hopkins University Press.

Linklater, Andrew. (1982) *Men and Citizens in the Theory of International Relations*. London: Macmillan.

Lipson, Charles. (1984) "International Cooperation in Economic and Security Affairs," *World Politics* 37: 1–23.

Locke, John. (1960) *Two Treatises of Government*. Cambridge: Cambridge University Press.

Long, David. (1991) "J. A. Hobson and Idealism in International Relations," *Review of International Studies* 17: 285–304.

Machiavelli, Niccoló. (1988) *The Prince*. Translated by Quentin Skinner and Russell Price. Cambridge: Cambridge University Press.

Maoz, Zeev, and Nasrin Abdoladli. (1989) "Regime Types and International Conflict, 1816–1976," *Journal of Conflict Resolution* 29: 3–35.

Maoz, Zeev, and Bruce Russett. (1992) "Normative and Structural Causes of Democratic Peace, 1946–1986." Paper presented to the Annual Meeting of the International Studies Association, April 1–4, Atlanta, Georgia.

Markwell, D. J. (1986) "Sir Alfred Zimmern Revisited: Fifty Years On," *Review of International Studies* 12: 279–92.

Matthew, Richard A. (forthcoming) *Politics Divided: Justice, Interest and World Political Order*. Mimeo.

Mayall, James. (1990) *Nationalism and International Society*. Cambridge: Cambridge University Press.

Mill, John Stuart. (1947) *On Liberty*. New York: Crofts.

Miller, J. D. B. (1986) *Norman Angell and the Futility of War*. London: Macmillan.

Miller, J. D. B., and R. J. Vincent, eds. (1990) *Order and Violence: Hedley Bull and International Relations*. Oxford: Clarendon.

Milner, Helen. (1992) "International Theories of Cooperation among Nations," *World Politics* 44: 466–96.

———. (1991) "The Assumption of Anarchy in International Relations Theory: A Critique," *Review of International Studies* 17: 67–85.

Mitrany, David. (1966) *A Working Peace System*, reprinted with an introduction by Hans J. Morgenthau. Chicago: Quadrangle.

———. (1948) "The Functional Approach to World Organization," *International Affairs* 24: 350–63.

Moravcsik, Andrew. (1992) "Liberalism and International Relations Theory," Working Paper, Center of International Affairs, Harvard University.

———. (1991) "Negotiating the Single European Act: National Interests and Conventional Statecraft in the European Community," *International Organization* 45: 19–56.

Morgenthau, Hans J. (1967) *Politics among Nations*, 4th ed. New York: Knopf.

———. (1966) "Introduction," pp. 7–11 in David Mitrany, *A Working Peace System*. Chicago: Quadrangle.

Morse, Edward. (1976) *Modernization and the Transformation of International Relations*. New York: Basic Books.

Mueller, John. (1989) *Retreat from Doomsday: The Obsolescence of Major War*. New York: Basic Books.

———. (1988) "The Essential Irrevelance of Nuclear Weapons: Stability in the Postwar World," *International Security* 13: 55–79.

Muir, Ramsay. (1971) *The Interdependent World and Its Problems*. Washington, D.C.: Kennikat.

Nadelman, Ethan A. (1990) "Global Prohibition Regimes: The Evolution of Norms in International Society," *International Organization* 44: 479–526.

Nardin, Terry. (1992) "International Ethics and International Law," *Review of International Studies* 18: 19–30.

———. (1983) *Law, Morality, and the Relations of States*. Princeton, N.J.: Princeton University Press.

Nardin, Terry, and David A. Mapel, eds. (1992) *Traditions in International Ethics*. Cambridge: Cambridge University Press.

Navari, Cornelia. (1989) "The Great Illusion Revisited: The International Political Theory of Norman Angell," *Review of International Studies* 15: 341–58.

Nincic, Miroslav. (1992) *Democracy and Foreign Policy: The Fallacy of Political Realism*. New York: Columbia University Press.

Nye, Joseph S. (1988) "Neorealism and Neoliberalism," *World Politics* 40: 235–51.

Ohmae, Kenichi. (1990) *The Borderless World: Power and Strategy in the Interlinked Economy*. New York: Harper Business.

Poggi, Gianfranco. (1978) *The Development of the Modern State: A Sociological Introduction*. Stanford, Calif.: Stanford University Press.

Powell, Robert. (1991) "Absolute and Relative Gains in International Relations Theory," *American Political Science Review* 85: 1303–20.

Price, Kingsley. (1967) "History of Philosophy of Education," in *The Encyclopedia of Philosophy, Volume 6.* New York: Macmillan.

Puchala, Donald. (1981) "Integration Theory and the Study of International Relations,"
pp. 145–64 in Richard Merritt and Bruce Russett, eds., *From Development to Global Community.* London: George Allen and Unwin.

Ray, James Lee. (1989) "The Abolition of Slavery and the End of International War,"
International Organization 43: 405–40.

Ricardo, David. (1911) *The Principles of Political Economy and Taxation.* London:
G. Bell.

Rittberger, Volker. (1990) *International Regimes in East–West Politics.* London:
Pinter.

Rosecrance, Richard. (1986) *The Rise of the Trading State: Commerce and Conquest in the Modern World.* New York: Basic Books.

Rosenau, James N. (1990) *Turbulence in World Politics: A Theory of Change and Continuity.* Princeton, N.J.: Princeton University Press.

———. (1980) *The Study of Global Interdependence: Essays on the Transnationaliza-
tion of World Affairs.* New York: Nichols.

Rousseau, Jean-Jacques. (1990) "State of War" and "Summary and Critique of Abbe
Saint-Pierre's Project for Perpetual Peace," pp. 185–229 in Grace G. Roosevelt,
Reading Rousseau in the Nuclear Age. Philadelphia: Temple University Press.

———. (1978) *On the Social Contract* with *Geneva Manuscript* and *Political Economy.*
Edited by Roger D. Masters and translated by Judith R. Masters. New York:
St. Martin's.

———. (1962) *The Political Writings of Jean-Jacques Rousseau, Vol. I.* Edited by C. E.
Vaughan. Oxford: Basil Blackwell.

Ruggie, John Gerard, ed. (1993) *Multilateralism Matters: The Theory and Praxis of an Institutional Form.* New York: Columbia University Press.

———. (1992) "Multilateralism: The Anatomy of an Institution," *International Organization* 46: 561–98.

———. (1986) "Continuity and Transformation in the World Polity: Toward a Neorealist Synthesis," pp. 131–57 in Robert O. Keohane, ed., *Neorealism and Its Critics.*
New York: Columbia University Press.

———. (1983) "International Regimes, Transactions, and Change: Embedded Liberalism in the Postwar Economic Order," pp. 195–232 in Stephen D. Krasner, ed.,
International Regimes. Ithaca, N.Y.: Cornell University Press.

Ruggie, John Gerard, and Friedrich Kratochwil. (1986) "International Organization:
The State of the Art on an Art of the State," *International Organization* 40:
753–76.

Schulte, Nordholt J. W. (1991) *Woodrow Wilson: A Life for World Peace.* Translated
by Herbert H. Rowen. Berkeley: University of California Press.

Schweller, Randall L. (1992) "Domestic Structure and Preventive War: Are Democracies More Pacific?" *World Politics* 44: 235–69.

Smith, Adam. (1937) *An Inquiry into the Nature and Causes of the Wealth of Nations.*
Edited by Edward Canaan. New York: Modern Library.

Smith, Michael Joseph. (1992) "Liberalism and International Reform," pp. 201–24 in
Terry Nardin and David A. Mapel, eds., *Traditions of International Ethics.*
Cambridge: Cambridge University Press.

Snidal, Duncan. (1991) "Relative Gains and the Pattern of International Cooperation," *American Political Science Review* 85: 701–26.

Snyder, Jack. (1991) *Myths of Empire: Domestic Politics and International Ambition.* Ithaca, N.Y.: Cornell University Press.

———. (1990) "Averting Anarchy in the New Europe," *International Security* 14: 5–41.

Spencer, Herbert. (1969) *Social Statics; or, the Conditions Essential to Human Happiness Specified, and the First of Them Developed.* New York: A. M. Kelley.

Stein, Arthur. (1990) *Why Nations Cooperate: Circumstance and Choice in International Relations.* Ithaca, N.Y.: Cornell University Press.

Strayer, Joseph. (1970) *On the Medieval Origins of the Modern State.* Princeton, N.J.: Princeton University Press.

Suganami, Hidemi. (1989) *The Domestic Analogy and World Order Proposals.* Cambridge: Cambridge University Press.

Taylor, Paul. (1978) "Functionalism: The Theory of David Mitrany," pp. 236–52 in Paul Taylor and A. J. R. Groom, eds., *International Organisation.* London: Frances Pinter.

Taylor, Philip. (1984) *Nonstate Actors in International Politics.* Boulder, Colo.: Westview.

Thucydides. (1954) *The Peloponnesian War.* Translated by Rex Warner. Harmondsworth, U.K.: Penguin Books.

Tranholm-Mikkelsen, Jeppe. (1991) "Neofunctionalism: Obstinate or Obsolete? A Reappraisal in Light of the New Dynamism of the EC," *Millennium* 20: 1–22.

Van Evera, Stephen. (1990–1991) "Primed for Peace: Europe after the Cold War," *International Security* 15: 7–57.

Vernon, Raymond. (1971) *Sovereignty at Bay: The Multinational Spread of U.S. Enterprises.* New York: Basic Books.

Vincent, R. J. (1986) *Human Rights and International Relations.* Cambridge: Cambridge University Press.

Wallace, William, ed. (1990) *The Dynamics of European Integration.* New York: Pinter.

Wallerstein, Immanuel. (1974) *The Modern World System: Capitalist Agriculture and the Origins of the European World Economy in the Sixteenth Century.* London: Academic Press.

Waltz, Kenneth N. (1990) "Nuclear Myths and Political Realities," *American Political Science Review* 84: 731–46.

———. (1979) *Theory of International Politics.* Reading, Mass.: Addison-Wesley.

Watson, Adam. (1992) *The Evolution of International Society: A Comparative Historical Analysis.* London: Routledge.

Webb, Michael C. (1991) "International Economic Structures, Government Interests, and International Coordination of Macroeconomic Adjustment," *International Organization* 45: 309–42.

Webb, Michael C., and Stephen D. Krasner. (1989) "Hegemonic Stability Theory: An Empirical Assessment," *Review of International Studies* 15: 183–98.

Weber, Steve. (1992) "Security after the Revolutions of 1989: The Future with Nuclear Weapons," in Patrick J. Garrity and Steven A. Maaranen, eds., *Nuclear Weapons and the Changing World.* New York: Plenum.

———. (1990) "Realism, Detente and Nuclear Weapons," *International Organization* 44 (Winter): 55–82.

Wendt, Alexander. (1992) "Anarchy Is What States Make of It: The Social Construction of Power Politics," *International Organization* 46: 391–426.

_____. (1987) "The Agent-Structure Problem in International Relations Theory," *International Organization* 41: 335–70.

Wight, Martin. (1977). *Systems of States*. Leicester, U.K.: Leicester University Press.

_____. (1966) "Western Values in International Theory," pp. 89–131 in Herbert Butterfield and Martin Wight, eds., *Diplomatic Investigations*. London: George Allen and Unwin.

Willets, Peter, ed. (1982) *Pressure Groups in the Global System*. London: St. Martin's.

Wolfers, Arnold, and Laurence W. Martin, eds. (1956) *The Anglo-American Tradition in Foreign Affairs*. New Haven, Conn.: Yale University Press.

Young, Oran. (1989) *International Cooperation: Building Resources for Natural Resources and the Environment*. Ithaca, N.Y.: Cornell University Press.

Zacher, Mark W. (1993) "Multilateral Organizations and the Institution of Multilateralism: The Development of Regimes for Nonterrestrial Spaces," pp. 399–439 in John Gerard Ruggie, ed., *Multilateralism Matters*. New York: Columbia University Press.

_____. (1992) "The Decaying Pillars of the Westphalian Temple: Implications for International Order and Governance," pp. 58–101 in James N. Rosenau and Ernst-Otto Czempiel, eds., *Governance without Government*. Cambridge: Cambridge University Press.

_____. (1990) "Toward a Theory of International Regimes," *Journal of International Affairs* 44: 139–57.

_____. (1970) *Dag Hammarskjold's United Nations*. New York: Columbia University Press.

Zimmern, Alfred. (1936) *The League of Nations and the Rule of Law, 1918–1935*. London: Macmillan.

CHAPTER 6

Anarchy and the Limits of Cooperation: A Realist Critique of the Newest Liberal Institutionalism

JOSEPH M. GRIECO

Realism has dominated international relations theory at least since World War II.[1] For realists, international anarchy fosters competition and conflict among states and inhibits their willingness to cooperate even when they share common interests. Realist theory also argues that international institutions are unable to mitigate anarchy's constraining effects on interstate cooperation. Realism, then, presents a pessimistic analysis of the prospects for international cooperation and of the capabilities of international institutions.

The major challenger to realism has been what I shall call liberal institutionalism. Prior to the current decade, it appeared in three successive presentations: functionalist integration theory in the 1940s and early 1950s, neofunctionalist regional integration theory in the 1950s and 1960s, and interdependence theory in the 1970s.[2] All three versions rejected realism's propositions about states and its gloomy understanding of world politics. Most significantly, they argued that international institutions can help states cooperate. Thus, compared to realism, these earlier versions of liberal institutionalism offered a more hopeful prognosis for international cooperation and a more optimistic assessment of the capacity of institutions to help states achieve it.

[1] Major realist works include E. H. Carr (1964), Hans J. Morgenthau (1973), Raymond Aron (1966), Kenneth N. Waltz (1959, 1979), and Robert Gilpin (1975, 1981).

[2] On functionalism, see David Mitrany (1966) and Ernst B. Haas (1964). On neofunctionalism, see Haas (1958, 1968: 149–76) and Joseph S. Nye Jr. (1971: 192–231). On interdependence theory, see Richard C. Cooper (1972), Edward S. Morse (1970), and Robert O. Keohane and Joseph S. Nye Jr. (1977).

International tensions and conflicts during the 1970s undermined liberal institutionalism and reconfirmed realism in large measure. Yet that difficult decade did not witness a collapse of the international system, and, in the light of continuing modest levels of interstate cooperation, a new liberal institutionalist challenge to realism came forward during the early 1980s (Axelrod, 1984; Axelrod and Keohane, 1985; Keohane, 1984; Lipson, 1984; and Stein, 1983: 115–40). What is distinctive about the newest liberal institutionalism is its claim that it accepts a number of core realist propositions, including, apparently, the realist argument that anarchy impedes the achievement of international cooperation. However, the core liberal arguments—that realism overemphasizes conflict and underestimates the capacities of international institutions to promote cooperation—remain firmly intact. The new liberal institutionalists basically argue that even if the realists are correct in believing that anarchy constrains the willingness of states to cooperate, states nevertheless can work together and can do so especially with the assistance of international institutions.

This point is crucial for students of international relations. If neoliberal institutionalists are correct, then they have dealt realism a major blow while providing the intellectual justification for treating their own approach, and the tradition from which it emerges, as the most effective for understanding world politics.

This essay's principal argument is that, in fact, neoliberal institutionalism misconstrues the realist analysis of international anarchy and therefore it misunderstands the realist analysis of the impact of anarchy on the preferences and actions of states. Indeed, the new liberal institutionalism fails to address a major constraint on the willingness of states to cooperate which is generated by international anarchy and which is identified by realism. As a result, the new theory's optimism about international cooperation is likely to be proven wrong.

Neoliberalism's claims about cooperation are based on its belief that states are atomistic actors. It argues that states seek to maximize their individual *absolute* gains and are indifferent to the gains achieved by others. Cheating, the new theory suggests, is the greatest impediment to cooperation among rationally egoistic states, but international institutions, the new theory also suggests, can help states overcome this barrier to joint action. Realists understand that states seek absolute gains and worry about compliance. However, realists find that states are *positional*, not atomistic, in character, and therefore realists argue that, in addition to concerns about cheating, states in cooperative arrangements also worry that their partners might gain more from cooperation than they do. For realists, a state will focus both on its absolute and relative gains from cooperation, and a state that is satisfied with a partner's compliance in a joint arrangement might nevertheless exit from it because the partner is achieving relatively greater gains. Realism, then, finds that there are at least two major barriers to international cooperation: state concerns about cheating and state concerns about relative achievements of gains. Neoliberal institutionalism pays attention exclusively to the former, and is unable to identify, analyze, or account for the latter.

Realism's identification of the relative gains problem for cooperation is based on its insight that states in anarchy fear for their survival as independent actors. According to realists, states worry that today's friend may be tomorrow's enemy in war, and fear that achievements of joint gains that advantage a friend in the present might produce a more dangerous *potential* foe in the future. As a result, states must give serious attention to the gains of partners. Neoliberals fail to consider the threat of war arising from international anarchy, and this allows them to ignore the matter of relative gains and to assume that states only desire absolute gains. Yet, in doing so, they fail to identify a major source of state inhibitions about international cooperation.

In sum, I suggest that realism, its emphasis on conflict and competition notwithstanding, offers a more complete understanding of the problem of international cooperation than does its latest liberal challenger. If that is true, then realism is still the most powerful theory of international politics.

REALISM AND LIBERAL INSTITUTIONALISM

Realism encompasses five propositions. First, states are the major actors in world affairs (Morgenthau, 1973: 10; Waltz, 1979: 95). Second, the international environment severely penalizes states if they fail to protect their vital interests or if they pursue objectives beyond their means; hence, states are "sensitive to costs" and behave as unitary-rational agents (Waltz, 1986: 331). Third, international anarchy is the principal force shaping the motives and actions of states (Waltz, 1959: 224–38; 1979: 79–128; Hoffmann, 1965: 27, 54–87, 129; Aron, 1966: 6–10). Fourth, states in anarchy are preoccupied with power and security, are predisposed toward conflict and competition, and often fail to cooperate even in the face of common interests (Aron, 1966: 5; Gilpin, 1986: 304). Fifth, international institutions affect the prospects for cooperation only marginally (Waltz, 1979: 115–16; Morgenthau, 1973: 512; Hoffmann, 1973: 50).

Liberal institutionalists sought to refute this realist understanding of world politics. First, they rejected realism's proposition about the centrality of states. For functionalists, the key new actors in world politics appeared to be specialized international agencies and their technical experts; for neofunctionalists, they were labor unions, political parties, trade associations, and supranational bureaucracies; and for the interdependence school, they were multinational corporations and transnational and transgovernmental coalitions (Mitrany, 1966: 17, 85–87, 133–34; Haas, 1964: 32–40; 1958: 16–31, 113–239, 283–340; Nye, 1971: 195–206; Keohane and Nye, 1972: ix–xxix, 371–98).

Second, liberal institutionalists attacked the realist view that states are unitary or rational agents. Authority was already decentralized within modern states, functionalists argued, and it was undergoing a similar process internationally (Mitrany, 1966: 54–55, 63, 69–73, 88, 134–38). Modern states, according to interdependence theorists, were increasingly characterized by "multiple channels of access," which, in turn, progressively enfeebled the grip on foreign policy previously held by central decision makers (Mitrany, 1966: 20, 32–38; Haas, 1968: 152, 155–56; Keohane and Nye, 1972: xxv, 375–78; Morse, 1970: 387–89; Cooper, 1972: 177, 179; Keohane and Nye, 1977: 33–35, 226–29).

Third, liberals argued that states were becoming less concerned about power and security. Internationally, nuclear weapons and mobilized national populations were rendering war prohibitively costly (Mitrany, 1966: 13; Morse, 1970: 380–81; Keohane and Nye, 1977: 27–29, 228). Moreover, increases in inter-nation economic contacts left states increasingly dependent on one another for the attainment of such national goals as growth, full employment, and price stability (Mitrany, 1966: 131–37; Haas, 1968: 161–62; Cooper, 1972: 161–68, 173–74; Keohane and Nye, 1977: 26, 228). Domestically, industrialization had created the present "social century": The advanced democracies (and, more slowly, socialist and developing countries) were becoming welfare states less oriented toward power and prestige and more toward economic growth and social security (Mitrany, 1966: 41–42, 95–96, 136–37, 144–45; Haas, 1968: 155–58; Morse, 1970: 383–85; Keohane and Nye, 1977: 227). Thus, liberals rejected realism's fourth proposition that states are fundamentally disinclined to cooperate, finding instead that states increasingly viewed one another not as enemies, but instead as partners needed to secure greater comfort and well-being for their home publics.[3]

Finally, liberal institutionalists rejected realism's pessimism about international institutions. For functionalist theory, specialized agencies like the International Labor Organization could promote cooperation because they performed valuable tasks without frontally challenging state sovereignty (Mitrany, 1966: 133–37, 198–211; Haas, 1968). For neofunctionalist theory, supranational bodies like the European Economic Community were "the appropriate regional counterpart to the national state which no longer feels capable of realizing welfare goals within its own narrow borders" (Haas, 1968: 159). Finally, interdependence theory suggested that "in a world of multiple issues imperfectly linked, in which coalitions are formed transnationally and transgovernmentally, the potential role of international institutions in political bargaining is greatly increased" (Keohane and Nye, 1977: 35; see also 36, 232–34, 240–42).

Postwar events, and especially those of the 1970s, appeared to support realist theory and to invalidate liberal institutionalism. States remained autonomous in setting foreign policy goals; they retained the loyalty of government

---

[3] See Haas (1968: 158, 160–62, 166–67); see also Mitrany (1966: 92–93); Morse (1970: 383–85); and Cooper (1972: 164–67, 170–72, 179).

officials active in "transgovernmental networks"; and they recast the terms of their relationships with such seemingly powerful transnational actors as high-technology multinational corporations (Krasner, 1978; Russell, 1973; Grieco, 1984). Industrialized states varied in their economic performance during the 1970s in the face of similar challenges (oil shortages, recession, and inflation). Scholars linked these differences in performance to divergences, and not convergence, in their domestic political–economic structures (Katzenstein, 1978 and 1985; Gourevitch, 1986: 181–217). A number of events during the 1970s and early 1980s also demonstrated that the use of force continued to be a pervasive future of world politics: increases in East–West tensions and the continuation of the Soviet–American arms competition; direct and indirect military intervention and counterintervention by the superpowers in Africa, Central America, and Southwest Asia; and the Yom Kippur and Iran–Iraq wars.[4] International institutions appeared to be unable to reshape state interests; instead, they were often embroiled in and paralyzed by East–West and North–South disputes.[5] Finally, supranationalism in Western Europe was replaced by old-fashioned intergovernmental bargaining, and the advanced democracies frequently experienced serious trade and monetary conflicts and sharp discord over economic relations with the Soviet Union.[6]

And yet, international cooperation did not collapse during the 1970s as it had during the 1930s (Krasner, 1983: viii). In finance, private banks and governments in developed countries worked with the International Monetary Fund to contain the international debt crisis (Lipson, 1985; Kahler, 1986). In trade, the advanced states completed the Tokyo Round negotiations under the General Agreement on Tariffs and Trade (Winham, 1986; Lipson, 1983: 233–72; Finlayson and Zacher, 1983: 273–314). In energy, the advanced states failed to coordinate responses to the oil crises of 1973–1974 and 1979, but cooperated effectively—through the International Energy Agency—following the outbreak of the Iran–Iraq war in 1980 (Lieber, 1983; Badger and Belgrave, 1982; Keohane, 1984: 217–40). Finally, in high technology, the European states initiated and pursued during the 1970s a host of joint projects such as Airbus Industrie, the ARIANE rocket program, and the ESPRIT information technology effort (Smith, 1986; McDougall, 1985). Governments had not transformed their foreign policies, and world politics was not in transition, but *states* achieved cooperation through *international institutions*

[4] See Alexander L. George and Richard Smoke (1974), Barry M. Blechman and Stephen S. Kaplan (1978), Stephen S. Kaplan (1981), and Richard Betts (1987).

[5] East–West disputes in a specialized international agency are examined in Walter Galenson (1981). North–South struggles within international institutions are discussed in Stephen D. Krasner (1985).

[6] On the problem of European integration, see Donald J. Puchala (1975) and Paul Taylor (1983). On trade conflicts during the 1970s, see John H. Jackson (1978), Bela and Carol Balassa (1984), and Miles Kahler (1985). On monetary disputes, see Susan Strange (1976: 320–53) and Benjamin J. Cohen (1979). On disputes over economic ties with the Soviet Union, see Stephen Woolcock (1982) and Bruce W. Jentleson (1986).

even in the harsh 1970s. This set the stage for a renewed, albeit truncated, liberal challenge to realism in the 1980s.

THE NEW LIBERAL INSTITUTIONALISM

In contrast to earlier presentations of liberal institutionalism, the newest liberalism accepts realist arguments that states are the major actors in world affairs and are unitary-rational agents. It also claims to accept realism's emphasis on anarchy to explain state motives and actions. Robert Axelrod (1984: 3; see also 4, 6), for example, seeks to address this question: "Under what conditions will cooperation emerge in a world of egoists without central authority?" Similarly, Axelrod and Robert Keohane (1985: 226) observe of world politics that "there is no common government to enforce rules, and by the standards of domestic society, international institutions are weak."

Yet neoliberals argue that realism is wrong to discount the possibilities for international cooperation and the capacities of international institutions. Neoliberals claim that, contrary to realism and in accordance with traditional liberal views, institutions can help states work together (Keohane, 1984: 9, 26). Thus, neoliberals argue, the prospects for international cooperation are better than realism allows (Keohane, 1984: 14, 16, 29, 67, 84). These points of convergence and divergence among the three perspectives are summarized in Table 6.1.

Neoliberals begin with assertions of acceptance of several key realist propositions; however, they end with a rejection of realism and with claims of affirmation of the central tenets of the liberal institutionalist tradition. To develop this argument, neoliberals first observe that states in anarchy often face mixed interests and, in particular, situations that can be depicted by Prisoner's Dilemma (see Axelrod, 1984: 7; Keohane, 1984: 66–69; Axelrod and Keohane, 1985: 231; Lipson, 1984: 2; Stein, 1983: 120–24). In the game, each state prefers mutual cooperation to mutual noncooperation (CC > DD), but also successful cheating to mutual cooperation (DC > CC) and mutual defection to victimization by another's cheating (DD > CD); overall, then, DC > CC > DD > CD. In these circumstances, and the absence of a centralized authority or some other countervailing force to bind states to their promises, each defects regardless of what it expects the other to do.

However, neoliberals stress that countervailing forces often do exist—forces that cause states to keep their promises and thus to resolve the Prisoner's Dilemma. They argue that states may pursue a strategy of tit-for-tat and cooperate on a conditional basis—that is, each adheres to its promises so long as partners do so. They also suggest that conditional cooperation is more likely to occur in Prisoner's Dilemma if the game is highly iterated, since states that interact repeatedly in either a mutually beneficial or harmful manner are likely to find that mutual cooperation is their best long-term

TABLE 6.1
Liberal Institutionalism, Neoliberal Institutionalism, and Realism: Summary of Major Propositions

Proposition	Liberal Institutionalism	Neoliberal Institutionalism	Realism
States are the only major actors in world politics	No; other actors include: specialized international agencies supranational authorities interest groups transgovernmental policy networks transnational actors (multinational corporations, etc.)	Yes (but international institutions play a major role)	Yes
States are unitary-rational actors	No; state is fragmented	Yes	Yes
Anarchy is a major shaping force for state preferences and actions	No; forces such as technology, knowledge, welfare orientation of domestic interests are also salient	Yes (apparently)	Yes
International institutions are independent forces facilitating cooperation	Yes	Yes	No
Optimistic/pessimistic about prospects for cooperation	Optimistic	Optimistic	Pessimistic

strategy. Finally, conditional cooperation is more attractive to states if the costs of verifying one another's compliance, and of sanctioning cheaters, are low compared to the benefits of joint action. Thus, conditional cooperation among states may evolve in the face of international anarchy and mixed interests through strategies of reciprocity, extended time horizons, and reduced verification and sanctioning costs.

Neoliberals find that one way states manage verification and sanctioning problems is to restrict the number of partners in a cooperative arrangement (Keohane, 1984: 77; Axelrod and Keohane, 1985: 234–38; Lipson, 1985). However, neoliberals place much greater emphasis on a second factor—international institutions. In particular, neoliberals argue that institutions reduce verification costs, create iterativeness, and make it easier to punish cheaters. As Keohane (1984: 97) suggests, "in general, regimes make it more sensible to cooperate by lowering the likelihood of being double-crossed." Similarly, Axelrod and Keohane (1985: 250) assert that "international regimes do not substitute for reciprocity; rather, they reinforce and institutionalize it. Regimes incorporating the norm of reciprocity delegitimize defection and thereby make it more costly." In addition, finding that "coordination conventions" are often an element of conditional cooperation in Prisoner's Dilemma, Charles Lipson (1984: 6) suggests that "in international relations, such conventions, which are typically grounded in ongoing reciprocal exchange, range from international law to regime rules." Finally, Arthur Stein (1983: 123) argues that just as societies "create" states to resolve collective action problems among individuals, so too "regimes in the international arena are also created to deal with the collective suboptimality that can emerge from individual [state] behavior." Hegemonic power may be necessary to establish cooperation among states, neoliberals argue, but it may endure after hegemony with the aid of institutions. As Keohane (1984: 246) concludes, "When we think about cooperation after hegemony, we need to think about institutions."

REALISM AND THE FAILURE OF THE NEW
LIBERAL INSTITUTIONALISM

The new liberals assert that they can accept key realist views about states and anarchy and still sustain classic liberal arguments about institutions and international cooperation. Yet, in fact, realist and neoliberal perspectives on states and anarchy differ profoundly, and the former provides a more complete understanding of the problem of cooperation than the latter.

Neoliberals assume that states have only one goal in mixed-interest interactions: to achieve the greatest possible individual gain. For example, Axelrod (1984: 6; see also 14) suggests that the key issue in selecting a "best strategy" in Prisoner's Dilemma—offered by neoliberals as a powerful model of the problem of state cooperation in the face of anarchy and mixed interests—is to determine "what strategy will yield a player the highest possible score." Similarly, Lipson (1984: 2, 5) observes that cheating is attractive in a single play of Prisoner's Dilemma because each player believes that defecting "can maximize his own reward," and, in turning to iterated plays, Lipson retains the assumption that players seek to maximize individual payoffs over the long run. Indeed, reliance on conventional Prisoner's Dilemma to depict international relationships and on iteration to solve the dilemma unambiguously requires neoliberalism to adhere to an individualistic payoff maximization assumption, because a player responds to an integrated conventional Prisoner's Dilemma with conditional cooperation *solely out of a desire to maximize its individual long-term total payoffs.*

Moreover, neoliberal institutionalists assume that states define their interests in strictly individualistic terms. Axelrod (1984: 9), for example, indicates that his objective is to show how actors "who pursue their own interests" may nevertheless work together. He (1984: 22) also notes that Prisoner's Dilemma is useful to study states in anarchy because it is assumed in the game that "the object is to do as well as possible, regardless of how well the other player does." Similarly, Lipson (1984: 2) suggests that Prisoner's Dilemma "clearly parallels the Realist conception of sovereign states in world politics" because each player in the game "is assumed to be a self-interested, self-reliant maximizer of his own utility."

Finally, Keohane (1984: 27) bases his analysis of international cooperation on the assumption that states are basically atomistic actors. He suggests that states in an anarchical context are, as microeconomic theory assumes with respect to business firms, "rational egoists." Rationality means that states possess "consistent, ordered preferences, and . . . calculate costs and benefits of alternative courses of action in order to maximize their utility in view of these preferences." In turn, he defines utility maximization atomistically; egoism, according to Keohane, "means that their [i.e., state] utility functions are independent of one another: they do not gain or lose utility simply because of the gains or losses of others."

Neoliberalism finds that states attain greater utility—that is, a higher level of satisfaction—as they achieve higher individual payoffs. Also, in keeping with the concept of rational egoism, a utility function specified by the new theory for one state would not be "linked" to the utility functions of others. Hence, if a state enjoys utility, U, in direct proportion to its payoff, V, then the neoliberal institutionalist specification of that state's utility function would be $U = V$.[7]

Overall, "rational egoist" states care only about their own gains. They do not care whether partners achieve or do not achieve gains, or whether those gains are large or small, or whether such gains are greater or less than the

---

[7] On payoffs and utility functions, see Anatol Rapoport (1960: 121) and Michael Taylor (1976: 70–74).

gains they themselves achieve. The major constraint on the cooperation in mixed-interest international situations is the problem of cheating.

And yet, realist theory rejects neoliberalism's exclusive focus on cheating. Differences in the realist and neoliberal understanding of the problem of cooperation result from a fundamental divergence in their interpretations of the basic meaning of international anarchy. Neoliberal institutionalism offers a well-established definition of anarchy, specifying that it means "the lack of common government in world politics" (Axelrod and Keohane, 1985: 226; see also Keohane, 1984: 7; Lipson, 1984: 1–2; Axelrod, 1984: 3–4; Stein, 1983: 116). Neoliberalism then proceeds to identify one major effect of international anarchy. Because of anarchy, according to neoliberals, individuals or states believe that no agency is available to "enforce rules," or to "enact or enforce rules of behavior," or to "force them to cooperate with each other" (Axelrod and Keohane, 1985: 226; Keohane, 1984: 7; Axelrod, 1984: 6). As a result, according to neoliberal theory, "cheating and deception are endemic" in international relations (Axelrod and Keohane, 1985: 226).[8] Anarchy, then, means that states may wish to cooperate, but, aware that cheating is both possible and profitable, *lack a central agency to enforce promises.* Given this understanding of anarchy, neoliberal institutional theory correctly identifies the problem of cheating and then proceeds to investigate how institutions can ameliorate that particular problem.

For realists, as for neoliberals, international anarchy means the absence of a common interstate government. Yet, according to realists, states do not believe that the lack of a common government means only that no agency can reliably enforce promises. Instead, realists stress, states recognize that, in anarchy, *there is no overarching authority to prevent others from using violence, or the threat of violence, to destroy or enslave them.* As Kenneth Waltz suggests, in anarchy, wars can occur "because there is nothing to prevent them," and therefore "in international politics force serves, not only as the *ultima ratio,* but indeed as the first and constant one" (Waltz, 1959: 232; Waltz, 1979: 113). Thus, some states may sometimes be driven by greed or ambition, but anarchy and the danger of war cause all states always to be motivated in some measure by fear and distrust (Gilpin, 1986: 87–88).

Given its understanding of anarchy, realism argues that individual well-being is not the key interest of states; instead, it finds that *survival* is their core interest. Raymond Aron (1966: 7, 64–65), for example, suggested that "politics, insofar as it concerns relations among states, seems to signify—in both ideal and objective terms—simply the survival of states confronting the potential threat created by the existence of other states." Similarly, Robert Gilpin (1986: 305) observes that individuals and groups may seek truth, beauty, and justice, but he emphasizes that "all these more noble goals will be lost unless one makes provision for one's security in the power struggle among groups."[9]

---

[8] In addition, see Lipson (1984: 4), Keohane (1984: 93), and Stein (1983: 116).

[9] In addition, see Waltz (1979: 126, 91–92, and 1986: 334).

Driven by an interest in survival, states are acutely sensitive to any erosion of their relative capabilities, which are the ultimate basis for their security and independence in an anarchical, self-help international context. Thus, realists find that the major goal of states in any relationship is not to attain the highest possible individual gain or payoff. Instead, *the fundamental goal of states in any relationship is to prevent others from achieving advances in their relative capabilities*. For example, E. H. Carr (1964: 111, emphasis added) suggested that "the most serious wars are fought in order to make one's own country militarily stronger, or, *more often*, to prevent another from becoming militarily stronger." Along the same lines, Gilpin (1981: 87–88) finds that the international system "stimulates, and may compel, a state to increase its power; at the least, it necessitates that the prudent state prevent relative increases in the power of competitor states." Indeed, states may even forego increases in their absolute capabilities if doing so prevents others from achieving even greater gains. This is because, as Waltz (1979: 126; see also Waltz, 1986: 334) suggests, "the first concern of the states is not to maximize power but to maintain their position in the system."

States seek to prevent increases in others' relative capabilities. As a result, states always assess their performance in any relationship in terms of the performance of others. Thus, I suggest that the states are positional, not atomistic, in character. Most significant, *state positionality may constrain the willingness of states to cooperate*. States fear that their partners will achieve relatively greater gains; that, as a result, the partners will surge ahead of them in relative capabilities; and, finally, that their increasingly powerful partners in the present could become all the more formidable foes at some point in the future.[10]

State positionality, then, engenders a "relative gains problem" for cooperation. That is, a state will decline to join, will leave, or will sharply limit its commitment to a cooperative arrangement if it believes that partners are achieving, or are likely to achieve, relatively greater gains. It will eschew cooperation even though participation in the arrangement was providing it, or would have provided it, with large absolute gains. Moreover, a state concerned about relative gains may decline to cooperate even if it is confident that partners will keep their commitments to a joint arrangement. Indeed, if a state believed that a proposed arrangement would provide all parties absolute gains, but would also generate gains favoring partners, then greater certainty that partners would adhere to the terms of the arrangement would only accentuate its relative gains concerns. Thus, a state worried about relative gains might respond to greater certainty that partners would keep their promises with a lower, rather than higher, willingness to cooperate.

---

[10] As Waltz (1979: 105) suggests, "When faced with the possibility of cooperating for mutual gains, states that feel insecure must ask how the gain will be divided. They are compelled to ask not 'Will both of us gain?' but 'Who will gain more?' If an expected gain is to be divided, say, in the ratio of two to one, one state may use its disproportionate gain to implement a policy intended to damage or destroy the other."

I must stress that realists do not argue that positionality causes all states to possess an offensively oriented desire to maximize the difference in gains arising from cooperation to their own advantage. They do not, in other words, attribute to states what Stein (1983: 134) correctly calls a mercantilist definition of self-interest. Instead, realists argue that states are more likely to concentrate on the danger that relative gains may advantage partners and thus may foster the emergence of a more powerful potential adversary. Realism, then, finds that states are positional, but it also finds that state positionality is more defensive than offensive in nature.

In addition, realists find that defensive state positionality and the relative gains problems for cooperation essentially reflect the persistence of uncertainty in international relations. States are uncertain about one another's future *intentions*; thus, they pay close attention to how cooperation might affect relative *capabilities* in the future.[11] This uncertainty results from the inability of states to predict or readily to control the future leadership or interests of partners. As Robert Jervis (1978: 168) notes, "Minds can be changed, new leaders can come to power, values can shift, new opportunities and dangers can arise."

Thus, realism expects a state's utility function to incorporate two distinct terms. It needs to include the state's individual payoff, V, reflecting the realist view that states are motivated by absolute gains. Yet it must also include a term integrating both the state's individual payoff and the partner's payoff, W, in such a way that gaps favoring the state add to its utility while, more important, gaps favoring the partner detract from it. One function that depicts this realist understanding of state utility is $U = V - k (W - V)$, with k representing the state's coefficient of sensitivity to gaps in payoffs either to its advantage or disadvantage.

This realist specification of state utility can be contrasted with that inferred from neoliberal theory, namely $U = V$. In both cases, the state obtains utility from the receipt of absolute payoffs. However, while neoliberal institutional theory assumes that state utility functions are independent of one another and that states are indifferent to the payoffs of others, realist theory argues that state utility functions are at least partially interdependent and that one state's utility can affect another's.[12] We may also observe that this realist-specified function does not suggest that any payoff achieved by a partner detracts from the state's utility. Rather, *only gaps in payoffs to the advantage of a partner do so.*

[11] Waltz (1979: 105) observes that "the impediments to collaboration may not lie in the character and the immediate intention of either party. Instead, the condition of insecurity—at the least, the uncertainty of each about the other's future intentions and actions—works against their cooperation."

[12] Robert Jervis (1988: 334–36) also argues that realist theory posits at least partially interdependent state utility functions.

The coefficient for a state's sensitivity to gaps in payoffs—k—will vary, but it will always be greater than zero. In general, k will increase as a state transits from relationships in what Karl Deutsch and his associates (1957: 5–7) termed a "pluralistic security community" to those approximating a state of war. The level of k will be greater (1) if a state's partner is a long-term adversary rather than a long-term ally; (2) if the issue involves security rather than economic well-being; (3) if the state's relative power has been on the decline rather than on the rise; (4) if payoffs in the particular issue-area are more rather than less easily converted into capabilities within that issue-area; or (5) if these capabilities and the influence associated with them are more rather than less readily transferred to other issue-areas.[13] Yet, given the uncertainties of international politics, a state's level of k will be greater than zero even in interactions with allies because gaps in payoffs favoring partners will always detract from a state's utility to some degree.[14]

Faced with both problems—cheating and relative gains—states seek to ensure that partners in common endeavors comply with their promises and that their collaboration produces "balanced" or "equitable" achievements of gains. According to realists, states define balance and equity as distributions of gains that roughly maintain precooperation balances of capabilities. To attain this balanced relative achievement of gains, according to Hans Morgenthau, states offer their partners "concessions"; in exchange, they expect to receive approximately equal "compensations." As an example of this balancing tendency, Morgenthau (1973: 179) offers the particular case of "cooperation" among Prussia, Austria, and Russia in their partitions of Poland in 1772, 1793, and 1795. He indicates that in each case, "the three nations agreed to divide Polish territory in such a way that the distribution of power among themselves would be approximately the same after the partitions as it had been before." For Morgenthau (1973: 180, emphasis added), state balancing of joint gains is a universal characteristic of the diplomacy of cooperation. He attributes this to the firmly grounded practice of states to balance power, arguing that "given such a system, no nation will agree to concede political advantages to another nation without the expectation, which may or may not be well founded, of receiving *proportionate* advantages in return."

In sum, neoliberals find that anarchy impedes cooperation through its generation of uncertainty in states about the compliance of partners. For neoliberals, the outcome a state most fears in mixed-interest situations is to be cheated. Yet, successful unilateral cheating is highly unlikely, and the more probable neoliberal "worst case" is for all states to defect and find themselves less well off than if they had all cooperated. For neoliberal institu-

---

[13] Contextual influences on state sensitivities to gaps in gains are explored in Joseph M. Grieco (1988: 600–24).

[14] In contrast, Keohane (1984: 54) finds that relative gains concerns may impede cooperation only in cases in which states pursue "positional goods" such as "status." Similarly, Lipson (1984: 14–16) expects that states will be sensitive to relative gains only in security relationships.

tionalists, then, anarchy and mixed interests often cause states to suffer the opportunity costs of not achieving an outcome that is mutually more beneficial. Keohane and Axelrod argue that games like Prisoner's Dilemma, Stag Hunt, Chicken, and Deadlock illustrate how many international relationships offer both the danger that "the myopic pursuit of self-interest can be disastrous" and the prospect that "both sides can potentially benefit from cooperation—if they can only achieve it" (Axelrod and Keohane, 1985: 231; see also Stein 1983: 123–24).

Realists identify even greater uncertainties for states considering cooperation: Which among them could achieve the greatest gains, and would imbalanced achievements of gains affect relative capabilities? In addition, a state that knows it will not be cheated still confronts another risk that is at least as formidable: Perhaps a partner will achieve disproportionate gains and, thus strengthened, might someday be a more dangerous enemy than if they had never worked together. For neoliberal theory, the problem of cooperation in anarchy is that states may fail to achieve it; in the final analysis, the worst possible outcome is a lost opportunity. For realist theory, state efforts to cooperate entail these dangers plus the much greater risk, for some states, that cooperation might someday result in lost independence or security.

Realism and neoliberal institutionalism offer markedly different views concerning the effects of international anarchy on states. These differences are summarized in Table 6.2. Compared to realist theory, neoliberal institutionalism understates the range of uncertainties and risks states believe they must overcome to cooperate with others. Hence, realism provides a more comprehensive theory of the problem of cooperation than does neoliberal institutionalism.

CONCLUSION

Neoliberal institutionalism is not based on realist theory; in fact, realism specifies a wider range of systemic-level constraints on cooperation than does neoliberalism. Thus, the next scholarly task is to conduct empirical tests of the two approaches. It is widely accepted—even by neoliberals—that realism has great explanatory power in national security affairs. However, international political economy would appear to be neoliberalism's preserve. Indeed, economic relationships among the advanced democracies would provide opportunities to design "crucial experiments" for the two theories.[15] That is, they would provide the opportunity to observe behavior confirming realist expectations in circumstances least likely to have generated such observations

[15] On the methodology of crucial experiments, see Arthur L. Stinchcombe (1968: 20–28) and Harry Eckstein (1975: 118–20).

TABLE 6.2
**Anarchy, State Properties, and State Inhibitions about Cooperation:
Summary of Neoliberal and Realist Views**

Basis of Comparison	Neoliberal Institutionalism	Political Realism
Meaning of anarchy	No central agency is available to enforce promises	No central agency is available to enforce promises *or* to provide protection
State properties		
Core interest	To advance in utility defined individualistically	To enhance prospects for survival
Main goal	To achieve greatest possible absolute gains	To achieve greatest gains *and* smallest gap in gains favoring partners
Basic character	Atomistic ("rational egoist")	Defensively positional
Utility function	Independent: $U = V$	Partially interdependent: $U = V - k(W - V)$
State inhibitions concerning cooperation		
Range of uncertainties associated with cooperation	Partners' compliance	Compliance *and* relative achievement of gains *and* uses to which gaps favoring partners may be employed
Range of risks associated with cooperation	To be cheated and to receive a low payoff	To be cheated *or* to experience decline in relative power if others achieve greater gains
Barriers to cooperation	State concerns about partners' compliance	State concerns about partners' compliance *and* partners' relative gains

unless realism is truly potent, while at the same time they might disconfirm neoliberal claims in circumstances most likely to have produced observations validating neoliberal theory.

According to neoliberal theory, two factors enhance prospects for the achievement and maintenance of political–economic cooperation among the advanced democracies. First, these states have the broadest range of common political, military, and economic interests (Keohane, 1984: 6–7). Thus, they have the greatest hopes for large absolute gains through joint action. This should work against realism and its specification of the relative gains problem for cooperation. That is, states that have many common interests should have the fewest worries that they might become embroiled in extreme conflicts in the future and, as a result, they should have the fewest concerns about relative achievements of gains arising from their common endeavors.

Neoliberal theory emphasizes another background condition: The economic arrangements of advanced democracies are "nested" in larger political–strategic alliances. Nesting, according to the theory, accentuates itera-tiveness and so promotes compliance (Keohane, 1984: 90–91; Aggarwal, 1985). This condition should also place realist theory at a disadvantage. If states are allies, they should be unconcerned that possible gaps in economic gains might advantage partners. Indeed, they should take comfort in the latter's success, for in attaining greater economic gains these partners become stronger mili-tary allies.

We can identify a number of efforts by advanced democracies to cooperate in economic issue-areas that were characterized by high common interests and nesting. In the trade field, such efforts would include the Tokyo Round codes on nontariff barriers and efforts by the Nordic states to construct region-al free-trade arrangements. In the monetary field, there are the experiences of the European Community with exchange-rate coordination—the Economic and Monetary Union and the European Monetary System. In the field of high technology, one might examine European collaboration in commercial aviation (Airbus Industrie) or data processing (the Unidata computer consortium). If these cooperative arrangements varied in terms of their success (and indeed such variance can be observed), and the less successful or failed arrangements were characterized not by a higher incidence of cheating but by a greater severity of gains problems, then one could conclude that realist theory explains variation in the success or failure of international cooperation more effectively than neoliberal institutional theory. Moreover, one could have great confi-dence in this assessment because it would be based on cases that were most hospitable to neoliberalism and most hostile to realism.

However, additional tests of the two theories can and should be under-taken. For example, one might investigate realist and neoliberal expectations as to the *durability* of arrangements states prefer when they engage in joint action. Neoliberal theory argues that cheating is less likely to occur in a mixed-interest situation that is iterated; hence, it suggests that "the most direct way to encourage cooperation is to make the relationship more durable."[16] If, then, two states that are interested in cooperation could choose between two institutional arrangements that offered comparable absolute gains but that differed in their expected durability—one arrangement might, for example, have higher exit costs than the other—neoliberalism would expect the states to prefer the former over the latter because each state could then be more confident that the other would remain in the arrangement. Realism generates a markedly different hypothesis. If two states are worried or uncertain about relative achievements of gains, then each will prefer a less durable cooperative arrangement because each would want to be more readily able to exit from the arrangement if gaps in gains did come to favor the other.

A second pair of competing hypotheses concerns the *number of partners* states prefer to include in a cooperative arrangement. Advocates of neoliberal-

[16] Axelrod (1984: 129); see also Keohane (1984: 257–59) and Axelrod and Keohane (1985: 234).

ism find that a small number of participants facilitates verification of compliance and sanctioning of cheaters. Hence, they would predict that states with a choice would tend to prefer a smaller number of partners. Realism would offer a very different hypothesis. A state may believe that it might do better than some partners in a proposed arrangement but not as well as others. If it is uncertain about which partners would do relatively better, the state will prefer more partners because larger numbers would enhance the likelihood that the relative achievements of gains advantaging (what turn out to be) better-positioned partners could be offset by more favorable sharings arising from interactions with (as matters develop) weaker partners.

A third pair of competing empirical statements concerns the effects of *issue linkages* on cooperation. Neoliberalism's proponents find that tightly knit linkages within and across issue-areas accentuate iterativeness and thus facilitate cooperation (Keohane, 1984: 91–92, 103–6; Axelrod and Keohane, 1985: 239–43). Realism, again, offers a very different proposition. Assume that a state believes that two issue-areas are linked and that it believes that one element of this linkage is that changes in relative capabilities in one domain affect relative capabilities in the other. Assume also that the state believes that relative achievements of jointly produced gains in one issue-area would advantage the partner. This state would then believe that cooperation would provide additional capabilities to the partner not only in the domain in which joint action is undertaken, but also in the linked issue-area. Cooperation would therefore be unattractive to this state in direct proportion to its belief that the two issue-areas were interrelated. Thus, issue linkages may impede rather than facilitate cooperation.

These tests are likely to demonstrate that realism offers the most effective understanding of the problem of international cooperation.[17] In addition, further analysis of defensive state positionality may help pinpoint policy strategies that facilitate cooperation. If relative gains concerns do act as a constraint on cooperation, then we should identify methods by which states have been able to address such concerns through unilateral bargaining strategies or through the mechanisms and operations of international institutions. For example, we might investigate states' use of side-payments to mitigate the relative gains concerns of disadvantaged partners.[18] Thus, with its understanding of defen-

---

[17] Still, there remain at least two related clusters of modern literature that are firmly rooted in the liberal institutionalist tradition, that attempt no compromise with realism, and that present an understanding of world politics markedly at odds with realist theory. The first cluster argues that international institutions embody jointly held norms that facilitate and guide states in their cooperative endeavors (see Ruggie [1975; 1983a: 195–231; 1983b], Kratochwil [1984], Ruggie and Kratochwil [1986], and Puchala and Hopkins [1983: 61–92]). The second cluster suggests that international institutions help states develop consensual knowledge leading to cooperation (see Haas [1964: 12–13, 47–48, 79–85; 1975; 1980; 1983], Haas, Williams, and Babai [1977], and Crawford and Lenway [1985]).

[18] On the general concept of side-payments, see R. Duncan Luce and Howard Raiffa (1957: 168–69) and William H. Riker (1962: 34, 108–23).

sive state positionality and the relative gains problem for collaboration, realism may provide guidance to states as they seek security, independence, and mutually beneficial forms of international cooperation.

REFERENCES

Aggarwal, Vinod K. (1985) *Liberal Protection: The International Politics of Organized Textile Trade.* Berkeley: University of California Press.

Aron, Raymond. (1966) *Peace and War: A Theory of Peace and War.* Translated by Richard Howard and Annette Baker Fox. Garden City, N.Y.: Doubleday.

Axelrod, Robert. (1984) *The Evolution of Cooperation.* New York: Basic Books.

Axelrod, Robert, and Robert O. Keohane. (1985) "Achieving Cooperation Under Anarchy: Strategies and Institutions," *World Politics* 38 (October): 226–54.

Badger, Daniel, and Robert Belgrave. (1982) *Oil Supply and Price: What Went Right in 1980?* Paris: Atlantic Institute for International Affairs.

Balassa, Bela, and Carola Balassa. (1984) "Industrial Protection in the Developed Countries," *World Economy* 7 (June): 179–86.

Betts, Richard. (1987) *Nuclear Blackmail and Nuclear Balance.* Washington, D.C.: Brookings Institution.

Blechman, Barry M., and Stephen S. Kaplan. (1978) *Force without War: U.S. Armed Forces as a Political Instrument.* Washington, D.C.: Brookings Institution.

Carr, E. H. (1964) *The Twenty Years' Crisis, 1919–1939: An Introduction to the Study of International Relations.* London: Macmillan.

Cohen, Benjamin J. (1979) "Europe's Money, America's Problems," *Foreign Policy* 35 (Summer): 31–47.

Cooper, Richard N. (1972) "Economic Interdependence and Foreign Policies in the 1970s," *World Politics* 24 (January): 158–81.

Crawford, Beverly, and Stefanie Lenway. (1985) "Decision Modes and International Regime Change: Western Collaboration on East–West Trade," *World Politics* 37 (April): 375–402.

Deutsch, Karl, et al. (1957) *Political Community and the North Atlantic Area.* Princeton, N.J.: Princeton University Press.

Eckstein, Harry. (1975) "Case Study and Theory in Political Science," in Fred I. Greenstein and Nelson W. Polsby, eds., *Strategies of Inquiry.* Vol. 7 of the *Handbook of Political Science.* Reading, Mass.: Addison-Wesley.

Finlayson, Jock A., and Mark W. Zacher. (1983) "The GATT and the Regulation of Trade Barriers: Regime Dynamics and Functions," in Stephen D. Krasner, ed., *International Regimes.* Ithaca, N.Y.: Cornell University Press.

Galenson, Walter. (1981) *The International Labor Organization: An American View.* Madison: University of Wisconsin Press.

George, Alexander L., and Richard Smoke. (1974) *Deterrence in American Foreign Policy: Theory and Practice.* New York: Columbia University Press.

Gilpin, Robert. (1986) "The Richness of the Tradition of Political Realism," in Robert O. Keohane, ed., *Neorealism and Its Critics.* New York: Columbia University Press.

———. (1981) *War and Change in World Politics.* Cambridge: Cambridge University Press.

———. (1975) *U.S. Power and the Multinational Corporation: The Political Economy of Foreign Direct Investment*. New York: Basic Books.

Gourevitch, Peter A. (1986) *Politics in Hard Times: Comparative Responses to International Economic Crises*. Ithaca, N.Y.: Cornell University Press.

Grieco, Joseph M. (1988). "Realist Theory and the Problem of International Cooperation," *Journal of Politics* 50 (August): 600–624.

———. (1984) *Between Dependency and Autonomy: India's Experience with the International Computer Industry*. Berkeley: University of California Press.

Haas, Ernst B. (1983) "Words Can Hurt You; Or, Who Said What to Whom About Regimes," in Stephen D. Krasner, ed., *International Regimes*. Ithaca, N.Y.: Cornell University Press.

———. (1980) "Why Collaborate: Issue-Linkage and International Regimes," *World Politics* 32 (April): 357–405.

———. (1975) "Is There a Hole in the Whole? Knowledge, Technology, Interdependence and the Construction of International Regimes," *International Organization* 29 (Summer): 827–76.

———. (1968) "Technology, Pluralism, and the New Europe," in Joseph S. Nye Jr., ed., *International Regionalism*. Boston: Little, Brown.

———. (1964) *Beyond the Nation-State: Functionalism and International Organization*. Stanford, Calif.: Stanford University Press.

———. (1958) *The Uniting of Europe: Political, Economic, and Social Forces, 1950–1957*. Stanford, Calif.: Stanford University Press.

Haas, Ernst B., Mary Pat Williams, and Don Babai. (1977) *Scientists and World Order: The Uses of Technical Information in International Organizations*. Berkeley: University of California Press.

Hoffmann, Stanley. (1973) "International Organization and the International System," in Leland M. Goodrich and David A. Kay, eds., *International Organization: Politics and Process*. Madison: University of Wisconsin Press.

———. (1965) *The State of War: Essays in the Theory and Practice of International Politics*. New York: Praeger.

Jackson, John H. (1978) "The Crumbling Institutions of the Liberal Trade System," *Journal of World Trade Law* 12 (March–April): 93–106.

Jentleson, Bruce W. (1986) *Pipeline Politics: The Complex Political Economy of East–West Energy Trade*. Ithaca, N.Y.: Cornell University Press.

Jervis, Robert. (1988) "Realism, Game Theory, and Cooperation," *World Politics* 40 (April): 317–49.

———. (1978) "Cooperation under the Security Dilemma," *World Politics* 30 (January): 167–214.

Kahler, Miles, ed. (1986) *The Politics of International Debt*. Ithaca, N.Y.: Cornell University Press.

———. (1985) "European Protectionism in Theory and Practice," *World Politics* 37 (July): 475–502.

Kaplan, Stephen S. (1981) *Diplomacy of Power: Soviet Armed Forces as a Political Instrument*. Washington, D.C.: Brookings Institution.

Katzenstein, Peter J. (1985) *Small States in World Markets: Industrial Policy in Europe*. Ithaca, N.Y.: Cornell University Press.

———, ed. (1978) *Between Power and Plenty: Foreign Economic Policies of Advanced Industrialized States*. Madison: University of Wisconsin Press.

Keohane, Robert O. (1984) *After Hegemony: Cooperation and Discord in the World Political Economy*. Princeton, N.J.: Princeton University Press.

Keohane, Robert O., and Joseph S. Nye Jr. (1977) *Power and Interdependence: World Politics in Transition*. Boston: Little, Brown.

——. (1972) "Introduction and Conclusion," in Keohane and Nye, eds., *Transnational Relations and World Politics*. Cambridge, Mass.: Harvard University Press.

Krasner, Stephen D. (1985) *Structural Conflict: The Third World against Global Liberalism*. Berkeley: University of California Press.

——. (1983) "Preface," in Stephen D. Krasner, ed., *International Regimes*. Ithaca, N.Y.: Cornell University Press.

——. (1978) *Defending the National Interest: Raw Materials Investments and U.S. Foreign Policy*. Princeton, N.J.: Princeton University Press.

——. (1976) "State Power and the Structure of International Trade," *World Politics* 28 (April): 317–345.

Kratochwil, Friedrich. (1984) "The Force of Prescriptions," *International Organization* 38 (Autumn): 685–708.

Lieber, Robert J. (1983) *The Oil Decade: Conflict and Cooperation in the West*. New York: Praeger.

Lipson, Charles. (1985) "Banker's Dilemmas: Private Cooperation in Rescheduling Sovereign Debts," *World Politics* 38 (October): 200–25.

——. (1984) "International Cooperation in Economic and Security Affairs," *World Politics* 37 (October): 1–23.

——. (1983) "The Transformation of Trade: The Sources and Effects of Regime Change," in Stephen D. Krasner, ed., *International Regimes*. Ithaca, N.Y.: Cornell University Press.

Luce, R. Duncan, and Howard Raiffa. (1957) *Games and Decisions: Introduction and Critical Survey*. New York: Wiley.

McDougall, Walter A. (1985) "Space-Age Europe: Gaullism, Euro-Gaullism, and the American Dilemma," *Technology and Culture* 26 (April): 179–203.

Mitrany, David. (1966) *A Working Peace System*. Chicago: Quadrangle Press.

Morgenthau, Hans. (1973) *Politics among Nations: The Struggle for Power and Peace*. New York: Knopf.

Morse, Edward S. (1970) "The Transformation of Foreign Policies: Modernization, Interdependence and Externalization," *World Politics* 22 (April): 371–92.

Nye, Joseph S., Jr. (1971) "Comparing Common Markets: A Revised Neo-Functional Model," in Leon N. Lindberg and Stuart A. Scheingold, eds., *Regional Integration: Theory and Research*. Cambridge, Mass.: Harvard University Press.

Puchala, Donald J. (1975) "Domestic Politics and Regional Harmonization in the European Communities," *World Politics* 27 (July): 496–520.

Puchala, Donald J., and Raymond F. Hopkins. (1983) "International Regimes: Lessons from Inductive Analysis," in Stephen D. Krasner, ed., *International Regimes*. Ithaca, N.Y.: Cornell University Press.

Rapoport, Anatol. (1960) *Fights, Games and Debates*. Ann Arbor: University of Michigan Press.

Riker, William H. (1962) *The Theory of Political Coalitions*. New Haven, Conn.: Yale University Press.

Ruggie, John Gerard. (1983a) "International Regimes, Transactions, and Change: Embedded Liberalism in the Postwar Economic Order," in Stephen D. Krasner, ed., *International Regimes*. Ithaca, N.Y.: Cornell University Press.

_____. (1983b) "Continuity and Transformation in the World Polity: Toward a Neorealist Synthesis," *World Politics* 35 (January): 261–85.

_____. (1975) "International Responses to Technology: Concepts and Trends," *International Organization* 29 (Summer): 557–83.

Ruggie, John Gerard, and Friedrich Kratochwil. (1986) "International Organization: The State of the Art on an Art of the State," *International Organization* 40 (Autumn): 753–76.

Russell, Robert W. (1973) "Transgovernmental Interaction in the International Monetary System, 1960–1972," *International Organization* 27 (Autumn): 431–64.

Smith, Bruce L. (1986) "A New Technology Gap in Europe?" *SAIS Review* 6 (Winter–Spring): 219–36.

Stein, Arthur. (1983) "Coordination and Collaboration: Regimes in an Anarchic World," in Stephen D. Krasner, ed., *International Regimes*. Ithaca, N.Y.: Cornell University Press.

Stinchcombe, Arthur L. (1968) *Constructing Social Theories*. New York: Harcourt, Brace.

Strange, Susan. (1976) "International Monetary Relations of the Western World, 1959–1971," in Andrew Schonfield, ed., *International Economic Relations of the Western World, 1959–1971*. Oxford: Oxford University Press.

Taylor, Michael. (1976) *Anarchy and Cooperation*. London: Wiley.

Taylor, Paul. (1983) *The Limits of European Integration*. New York: Columbia University Press.

Waltz, Kenneth N. (1986) "Reflections on *Theory of International Politics*: A Response to My Critics," in Robert O. Keohane, ed., *Neorealism and Its Critics*. New York: Columbia University Press.

_____. (1979) *Theory of International Politics*. Reading, Mass.: Addison-Wesley.

_____. (1959) *Man, the State, and War: A Theoretical Analysis*. New York: Columbia University Press.

Winham, Gilbert. (1986) *International Trade and the Tokyo Round Negotiation*. Princeton, N.J.: Princeton University Press.

Woolcock, Stephen. (1982) *Western Policies on East–West Trade*. Chatham House Papers No. 15. London: Routledge & Kegan Paul for the Royal Institute of International Affairs.

PART II

Reevaluating Institutions in the Post–Cold War World

In the remaining portions of *Controversies in International Relations Theory: Realism and the Neoliberal Challenge,* original essays will explore the core aspects of world affairs from the realist and liberal perspectives. These essays address the central dimensions of world politics.

What are those core aspects? Since humans first began to reflect on the character of international relations, their reflections have focused on many of the same factors. Thus it is not surprising that with the end of the Cold War, attention in theoretical inquiry has returned to consideration of enduring fundamentals. A comparative reading of textbooks on world politics will reveal that today, as in the past, analysts are required, almost imperatively, to consider contending ideas about such issues as

- What are, and should be, the primary units of analysis in world politics, and what are the consequences when authority passes from one type of actor to others (for example, from nation-states to international organizations)?
- What difference (if any) does it make if the types of governments of the units change (for example, from dictatorships to democracies)?
- To what extent is it feasible for the units to act collaboratively to promote their mutual interests in survival and stability? Is it advantageous for them to share their power with or to sacrifice sovereign authority to international or regional organizations in order to advance their common interests?
- What armaments should the units seek to acquire in order to preserve peace, and what are the consequences for the shifts in the global distribution of military capabilities when the units act in accordance with different objectives?
- What effects do *economic* influences (for example, market versus planned economies, free versus protective barriers to international trade) exert on the *political* relations of these various units?
- What rules (if any) does or should international law embrace to foster orderly relations among the units?

- What rules (if any) does or should international law embrace to foster orderly relations among the units?
- Which ethical principles or norms (if any) should guide the choices of decision makers acting on behalf of the units they lead?
- To what degree is it reasonable to expect institutional reforms to engineer improvements in world affairs, so that ingrained but dysfunctional practices once regarded as inexorable laws might give way to new patterns of behavior—to historical progress?

The arena in which international politics occurs invites many more issues and concerns than this elementary list suggests. Still, this list helps to organize thinking about the questions on which theoretical inquiry remains directed and, as such, provides a rudimentary framework that classifies the main cleavages in inquiry.

The essays that follow in *Controversies in International Relations Theory* direct attention to the diverging and converging perspectives on these questions. Each author addresses the neoliberal reaction to the realist (and/or neorealist) posture in order to describe the ways in which revived liberal theories have arisen in the post–Cold War era to challenge the realist position on each discrete issue under examination, as well as to trace the origins and evolution of liberal thinking on the controversy. Thus, each contribution will summarize the realist perspective and the neoliberal perspectives that are emerging in response to it.

At the risk of being selective (or even arbitrary), we can classify the central debates in international relations theory by arguing that they customarily revolve around (1) the impact of different types of institutions on international conduct, (2) the means to peace, and (3) the moral and legal issues raised by the preceding. We shall introduce these clusters of inquiry in sequence, looking first (Part II) at realist and neoliberal theories of the role of institutions, then (Part III) at the factors that those theories most presume can constrain the use of force, and next (Part IV) at views about the place of law and morality in world affairs. All of this serves as a prelude, in the absence of a firm conclusion, to a consideration (Part V) of the future of international relations and of realism and neoliberalism as interpretations of that future. We begin here in Part II with the first basket of controversies.

At least since Aristotle, theorists have suspected that the extent to which the leader of a political unit is accountable to his other followers correlates with the probability that the unit would make war on its neighbors. The assumption here is that an accountable leader will have a harder time declaring war because the population of a country tends to resist the high costs of war. As several of the chapters described above discuss, this hypothesis is central to the liberal tradition. To liberals, it matters whether a government is a democracy or one of its closed political system alternatives—dictatorships, monarchies, tyrannies, or totalitarian and/or authoritarian systems under centralized rule. Indeed, it matters a great deal.

This proposition is deeply antagonistic to both realist and neorealist theory. Realism presents a model of international politics in which how a unit organizes itself to make foreign policy decisions does not potently influence the kinds of choices it reaches (recall the chapters by Holsti and Waltz). Against this view that changes in the internal character of states will not modify the character of international politics is the liberal vision, expressed by Francis Fukuyama in *The End of History and the Last Man* (1992: 28), in which today's

> neo-Wilsonians . . . believe instead that the advent of modern liberal democracy makes a break with the past because developed democracies are much less inclined to fight one another than authoritarian regimes—though democracies can certainly fight non-democracies. The nature of the regime, in other words, makes an enormous difference in the type of foreign policy a nation will choose; those that disregard the rights of their own citizens are much more likely to disregard the rights of neighboring countries as well.

Hence, this controversy, at the vortex of the realist–liberal debate, is one on which the two traditions are almost diametrically opposed. These find themselves expressed in inquiries addressed at both the *national* level of analysis, which considers the impact of regime type, and at the international or *systemic* level, which evaluates the impact of international and regional organizations.

REGIME TYPE AND INTERNATIONAL BEHAVIOR

In "Peace in the Liberal World: Does Democracy Matter?," Nicholas G. Onuf and Thomas J. Johnson provide a panoramic review of the controversy, centering their focus on this question: What is it about democracies and their circumstances that explains their pacific relations? In order to explore the reasons why the pacificity of democracies toward one another has practically achieved the status of a law, Onuf and Johnson revisit the complex intellectual strands in both the liberal tradition and in realist thought, the unacceptably loose way in which both schools use the term "democracy," and their consequent inability to achieve greater definitional precision in the effort to trace the relationship between democracy and peace. In order to promote conceptual clarity, Onuf and Johnson demonstrate not only the problems to valid inference posed by the failure of theorists to draw a distinction between domestic and international affairs, but also how a vocabulary informed by the properties of democracies in liberal theory can contribute to greater understanding of the controversy.

The problem with realism, Onuf and Johnson observe, is that in its quest for parsimony and rigor, realism treats the state as a constant and, as a result, eliminates the state from consideration. Yet, they show that liberal scholars do not do much better since they have not been able to break out of theory as defined by the realists and thus "were reduced to providing the realist camp with logistical support." The authors advance some proposals that, if followed, would allow liberal theory to free itself from realist precepts.

To refine theories regarding "republicanism" and its foreign policy consequences, Onuf and Johnson disentangle the intellectual roots of thinking about the domestic sources of international behavior. Drawing on the writings of Aristotle, Kant, Montesquieu, Hume, Madison, and Hamilton, they examine the characteristics of republics believed most conducive to peace, with particular attention given to representative government, constitutional arrangements, confederation, and the promotion of commerce. Their illuminating summary incisively unravels the logic that has led quite diverse liberal thinkers to the conclusion that representative governance *is* a viable solution to the chronic problem of recurrent warfare in international society, despite the resistance of realism to this old idea. By showing how peace can be explained by reference to the liberal proposition that prosperity through commerce fosters the growth of representative governance and peace, Onuf and Johnson advance a convincing argument on behalf of the thesis that through the power of public opinion, "a cosmopolitan, politically active elite constitutes the *liberal* world as a peaceful place in which democracy . . . has an opportunity to flourish."

INTERNATIONAL ORGANIZATION AND ORGANIZED INTERNATIONAL SOCIETY: GLOBAL INSTITUTIONS AND REGIONAL GOVERNANCE

To realists, domestic institutions do not matter greatly. Moreover, realists believe that the interests of the nation-state also supersede the collective interests of the international community and therefore of supranational institutions like the United Nations, which serve primarily as arenas for the pursuit and exercise of national power and should never be allowed to become a substitute for national units or to compromise national sovereignty. By making national interests sacrosanct and global interests subservient, realism eschews supranational institutions that limit the freedom and independence of national competitors.

In "The United Nations in a New World Order: Reviving the Theory and Practice of International Organization," J. Martin Rochester explores global trends affecting the contemporary international system's ability to move to the next stage of global institution building, as represented by the system's most ambitious supranational organization, the United Nations. In particular, Rochester examines how the twentieth-century "move to institutions" of a broadly multilateral, formal character was until recently accompanied by the concomitant move away from attention to such institutions and the liberal theories that prescribe that attention. He also examines whether developments since the early 1990s, and the general milieu surrounding them, now warrant revived scholarly attention to global organization and the liberal assumptions associated with advocacy of such institution building. This sets the stage for Rochester's consideration of the prospects for UN reform, wherein he inspects institutional changes of a legal-formal nature, which are relevant not only to the war/peace arena, including collective security, but to global problem solving in general. In so doing, Rochester places into context the theoretical discourse between and among realists and neoliberals about the prospects for these changes and the implications that they suggest for theoretical redirections.

The need and prospects for this potential theoretical reorientation are explored at another level by Barry B. Hughes in "Evolving Patterns of European Integration and Governance: Implications for Theories of World Politics." Hughes directly confronts the question of whether humanity has reached a point in its history "at which it is possible to envision the emergence of liberal ideals as serious challengers to the global organizing principles described by realism." His analysis thus proceeds from the reasonable assumption that the escalating complexity of global interdependence may require, as almost an imperative, that nongovernmental organizations (NGOs) and other supranational organizations play an increasing role in preserving world order.

To test this hypothesis and explore its implications for the liberal rejoinder to realism, Hughes concentrates on the premier example of successful regional integration: twentieth-century Europe, where an overall trend toward larger units claiming sovereignty is most visible. The inquiry is broken into three parts. The first sketches traditional institution-building images embedded in liberal understandings of global governance as advanced in integration theory, functionalism, and neofunctionalism, and suggests why an alternative image, termed complex governance—"a world of overlapping, multi-tiered, dynamic governance structures in which the state continues to play a critical role, but in which many other institutions become increasingly important—better accounts for the trends observable in the European Union (EU) experience. The second part reviews the theoretically eclectic roots of complex governance and advances some propositions about the sources of shared European sovereignty and the underpinnings on which they depend. The third examines the degree to which the processes and structures of European integration appear consistent with the expectations generated by these propositions. Specifically, to extract conclusions about the degree to which a pattern of governance based on liberalism is emerging, this chapter looks at the role of what is now officially dubbed the European Union and other regional institutions in providing five types of goods: respect for human rights, preservation of national and ethnic autonomy, economic welfare, military security, and environmental quality.

The chapter concludes that the EU can and often does take a leadership role in extending governance in these issue-areas, but that it does not appear to have the ideal scope for governance in any of them. Thus the EU, Hughes predicts, is likely to assist the development of alternative forms of governance in processes that are embedding it in considerably more extensive and variegated structures. The implications of this prediction for neoliberal theories are then examined in an insightful conclusion, which warns that the time has *not* yet arrived "to throw out realism and embrace liberalism with its alternative explanations of and expectations for world politics." Although European integration "provides considerable support for the argument that the process underway is consistent with an emergence of governance based on liberal ideals," Hughes submits that "it will probably be a very long time before governance based on liberalism prevails globally." Accordingly, "the anarchic state system of realists still better describes most of the global system" despite the fact that "the complex governance evolving in large and powerful pockets of the global system demonstrate the growing strength of the liberal vision."

CHAPTER 7

Peace in the Liberal World: Does Democracy Matter?

NICHOLAS G. ONUF
AND THOMAS J. JOHNSON

Democracies do not fight one another. In recent years no proposition about relations among states has garnered more attention or empirical support. Most scholars in the field of international relations seem to believe that democracies do not fight one another *because* they are democracies. If this hypothesis seems obvious, appearances are deceiving. What is it about democracies and their circumstances that explains their pacific relations? The term "democracy" is used too freely and inclusively to make most answers plausible (cf. Starr, 1992: 55–56).

No doubt scholars in the field find the term unproblematic because it has no place in their conceptual vocabulary. Democracy is a key term in liberal political discourse. A different tradition of discourse dominates the field of international relations under the banner of realism. In this tradition, the way states—their agents and their publics—generally behave warrants talk of self-interest, power, insecurity, and war. States are alike, lasting peace an anomaly. Democracies at peace are an anomaly to be ignored or explained in the narrowest possible terms (Lake, 1992).

The liberal tradition reaches back to a time when no one drew a firm distinction between domestic and international affairs. Realism depends on this distinction; liberals who accept it accept realism's hold on the field of international relations. Earlier liberal thought made lasting peace a central concern and sought to identify conditions that would make it possible. Today this concern is conventionally associated with Immanuel Kant, who is ritually invoked, rarely discussed, and always ripped from his late-eighteenth-century Enlightenment context.

In this chapter we return to Kant and his time to broaden the discussion of lasting peace and achieve some conceptual clarity in the process. We start by showing how realism and the effort to make realism more rigorous eliminate the state from theoretical consideration. We then show how recent attempts to develop a liberal perspective on international relations implicitly concede the field's theoretical space to realists by accepting the way they define that space.

Moving to Kant and the Enlightenment context, we focus on republicanism as it goes back to Aristotle. We draw on the writings of Montesquieu, Hume, Madison, and Hamilton as well as Kant to examine those properties of republics that are conducive to peace: representative government, constitutional arrangements, confederation, and encouragement of commerce. The last of these relates republicanism to liberalism, which explains peace by reference to the prosperity brought on by commerce.

Enlightenment writers more generally associated commerce and prosperity with cosmopolitan attitudes, including a penchant for peace. We conclude by relating the growth of these attitudes to another important liberal theme—the power of public opinion. A cosmopolitan, politically active elite constitutes the *liberal world* as a peaceful place in which democracy, loosely defined, has an opportunity to flourish.

REALISM AND THE QUEST FOR RIGOR

International relations emerged as an organized field of study after World War II. Before that time, international thought, at least among speakers of English, tended to reflect developments in the liberal world. Self-styled "realists" organized the field in conscious rejection of liberal ideas. Since then realism has dominated the field (see Vasquez, 1983, for evidence, and Walker, 1993, for a different interpretation).

In 1979, Kenneth Waltz's *Theory of International Politics* gave realism a theoretical rigor it had long promised in the name of science (Hoffmann, 1987: 5–9) but never delivered. As counted in the *Social Sciences Citation Index*, more than 350 scholarly articles have cited this volume in the last decade (1983–1992). No other single work in the field has enjoyed this much success. Even though Hans Morgenthau's *Scientific Man* vs. *Power Politics* (1946) and *Politics among Nations* (1948 through 1985) were together cited 276 times during this interval, Waltz clearly has succeeded Morgenthau as realism's most influential exponent, and *Theory of International Politics* is not its canonical text.

Waltz had developed over a number of years a framework for a properly rigorous theory of international politics. In *Man, the State and War* (1959) he identified three "images," or long-standing autonomous traditions, to account for the causes of war. The first tradition focused on human nature and behavior, the second on political and economic arrangements within states, and the third on the system of states. Waltz presented each tradition in its own terms and evaluated each on its implicit claim to provide a sufficient explanation for interstate war. Although the third image fares best in Waltz's evaluation, all three images have a place. "The third image describes the framework of world politics, but without the first and second images there can be no knowledge of the forces that determine policy; the first and second images describe the forces in world politics, but without the third image it is impossible to assess their importance or predict their results" (Waltz, 1959: 238).

Man, the State and War was an enormous success. Yet scholars immediately abandoned the soft, unfocused idea of "images" in favor of the hard, evidently precise typology of spatially differentiated and hierarchically organized "levels." J. David Singer's review of *Man, the State and War* led the way by equating Waltz's "images" with "levels of social organization which the observer selects as his point of entry into any study of the subject"—the subject broadly understood as "international political relations" and not just war (Singer, 1960: 453). Singer's (1961) influential discussion of the "level of analysis problem" soon followed.

Singer identified two levels: system and actor. Because the two levels share a hard boundary, propositions appropriate to each level "defy theoretical integration; one may well be a corollary of the other, but they are not immediately combinable" (Singer, 1961: 91). Analysts must choose one level or the other and define terms accordingly. Levels are discrete theoretical domains, their choice dictated by a preference for explanatory power (the system) or descriptive richness (its actors). Either choice eliminates the political and economic arrangements of state and society.

Waltz himself switched from "images" to "levels." In the process, three became two.

> Theories of international politics can be sorted out a number of ways. Elsewhere I have distinguished explanations of international politics, and especially efforts to locate the causes of war and to define the conditions of peace, according to the *level* at which causes are located. . . . A still simpler division may be made, one that separates theories according to whether they are reductionist or systemic. Theories of international politics that concentrate causes at the individual or national level are reductionist; theories that conceive of causes operating at the international level as well are systemic. (Waltz, 1979: 18, emphasis added)

In Singer's scheme, two levels commend themselves on procedural grounds. In Waltz's, an ontological judgment requires that two levels fold into one (behavior, whether *in* or *of* the state) and opposes that level to the level of the system of states. Behavioral analysis seeks to explain international politics additively: "the whole is understood by knowing the attributes and the interactions of its parts" (Waltz, 1979: 18). If, however, the whole is greater than its summed parts, "outcomes are affected not only by the properties and interconnections of variables but also by the way in which they are organized. . . . In international politics, systems-level forces seem to be at work" (Waltz, 1979: 39); only systems-level theory will work.

Waltz (1979: 90–91) argued that an international system functions like a market. "The market is a cause interposed between the economic actors and the results they produce. It conditions their calculations, their behaviors, and their interactions." Markets and systems "are formed by the coaction of self-regarding units," all seeking to fulfill "their own internally defined interests by whatever means they can muster." In the international system, these actors are states and, as Waltz clearly implied, they respond rationally to the circumstances in which they find themselves.

Not all contemporary realists accept Waltz's position on the international system as analogous to a market. Many treat the system as a frame of reference. Specifying the relevant system is a descriptive task; its specification points to the particular actors and interactions on which to focus attention. Nonetheless, all realists join Waltz in making states the primary actors in the system, however specified. The assumption that states are "rational unitary actors" is central to the realist tradition (Keohane, 1986: 165). Such an assumption does not depend on the market or system except insofar as these terms indicate the existence of two or more autonomous and interacting entities.

Today's realists start with rational decision makers acting on behalf of states, or with a system defined in terms of states. The state as such does not function as an independent variable or even an intervening variable. Instead the state functions as a constant—a partition between unrelated levels of analysis. For unit-level theorists, the system of states provides a frame of reference; for systems-level theorists, rational decision makers act on behalf of states. Without the state as a constant, neither can define its theoretical domain sufficiently against the claims of the other. Both define their domains by excluding the state from active consideration; even if a few realists are still able to work on both sides of the fence, they keep the fence in place.

In the quest for theoretical rigor, realism consolidated its hold over the field. Realists had earlier discredited the long-dominant liberal tradition by ridiculing its idealistic and utopian tendencies (Walker, 1993: 22). The failure of the League of Nations and the horrors of World War II assured realism its first success. The perilous and seemingly permanent character of the Cold War assured realism's continuing dominance and fostered the quest for rigor. Waltz himself (1964, 1979: 170–76) had long and strenuously argued that a bipolar system, and thus the Cold War, had the advantage of stability. Many scholars saw the need for increased rigor to assess Waltz's claim. Even today theoretical discussion of polarity and stability animates the field (see Hopf, 1991, 1993; Kegley and Raymond, 1992; Midlarsky, 1993).

With the ascendance of realism, liberal concerns for law, institutions, and societal influences within and among states were pushed to the margins of the field. Liberalism offered no theory by which to organize the field, much less to promote rigor. British scholarship epitomized by John Burton (1972) and Hedley Bull (1977) pursued liberal concerns broadly but less rigorously than Waltz demanded. Nevertheless, liberal scholars in the United States identified a series of significant targets for theoretical development: transnational relations (Keohane and Nye, 1972), interdependence (Keohane and Nye, 1977), issue-areas and agenda politics (Mansbach and Vasquez, 1981), international regimes (Krasner, 1982), and international cooperation (Keohane, 1984).

Retrospectively it is at least somewhat surprising that these initiatives did so little to dislodge realism from its commanding position in the field. After all, Robert Keohane and Joseph Nye's *Power and Interdependence* (1977) was second only to Waltz's *Theory of International Politics* as the decade's most cited book. For Keohane and Nye (1977: 24–37), "realist assumptions define an ideal type of world politics." They proposed an alternative idealization defined by reference to the "complex interdependence" of states and societies. An emphasis on complexity suggests a gain in descriptive richness at a cost to explanatory power.

Richard Mansbach and John Vasquez (1981) pursued Keohane and Nye's initiative with a commendable emphasis on conceptual development. Proclaiming the advent of a new paradigm, they found few followers (thirty-five citations in the *Social Sciences Citation Index*, 1983–1992). When Stephen Krasner (1982) distinguished "Grotian" and "structural" perspectives on international regimes, he diminished the liberal perspective by naming it after an early-seventeenth-century natural lawyer whose work is archaic, unread, and hardly liberal. Krasner's liberal collaborators seem not to have objected. When Robert Keohane (1984: 9) turned to the persistent phenomenon of international cooperation, he called it "puzzling," as indeed it is for any realist. Not only did Keohane locate his inquiry in the realist tradition, he started with a systems-level theory "based on traditional egoist assumptions" (Keohane, 1984: 27). In choosing this level, Keohane (1984: 25–27) specifically drew on Waltz's *Theory of International Politics*. Keohane's care in positioning his work was duly rewarded. By 1992, *After Hegemony* had appeared 289 times in the *Social Sciences Citation Index*.

In short, liberal scholars with theoretical interests were reduced to providing the realist camp with logistical support. Keohane (1986: 160–61, following Lakatos, 1970) presented a rationale for this role by styling realism a "scientific research programme" and not the "descriptive ideal type" he and Nye had earlier posited.

> Consider a research program, with a set of observational hypotheses, a "hard core" of irrefutable assumptions, and a set of scope conditions. In the course of research, anomalies are bound to appear. . . . For Lakatos, the reaction of scientists developing the research plan is to protect the hard core by developing auxiliary hypotheses that will explain the anomalies. (Keohane, 1986: 160, 161)

In Waltz's hands, realism provides the hard core of assumptions, scope conditions, and a related set of hypotheses, or theory. Liberal theorists, like Keohane, offer additional hypotheses that, if substantiated, enrich rather than replace realist theory. "Progressive research programs display 'continuous growth': their auxiliary hypotheses increase our capacity to understand reality" (Keohane, 1986: 161). Progressively improved (such a liberal idea!), realist theory of international politics permanently reigns.

Keohane has lately retreated from this position. Despite "affinities" with the realist research program, his recent essays "take us to the threshold of an institutionalist research program" (Keohane, 1989: 8, 13). To make this claim credible, Keohane must state core assumptions, define scope conditions, and specify hypotheses. Only the last of these activities has he even begun, without knowing if they follow from (as yet unstated) core assumptions or fall within the program's (as yet undefined) scope.

This is not the place to propose core assumptions (see instead Onuf, 1989). We do suggest that such assumptions must reverse the practice of constantly invoking the state, but only as a given. In other words, the scope of the new program must put the political and economic arrangements of state and society *back* at the center. Space must be made for the missing second level. Even better, abandoning the language of levels would permit the second image to regain its place as the fulcrum in international thought. In such a realignment, flanking images of rational conduct and system structure would then become sources of auxiliary hypotheses with which to enrich the new program's initial set of "observational hypotheses."

Much observed is the phenomenon of peace in the liberal world. In *Power and Interdependence*, Keohane and Nye (1977: 27) noted that industrial, democratic states do not fight wars with each other. In sketching a new research program, Keohane (1989: 11) subsumed this subject to the realist puzzle of cooperation. Liberal theorists have generally neglected it (Doyle [1983, 1986] is the major exception). Instead, empirically inclined scholars deserve most of the credit for focusing attention on the relationship between peace and political organization (see Levy, 1989: 269–70; Russett, 1990: 122–24; Ember et al., 1992: 573–78; and Starr, 1992, for discussion and citations).

While most theorists cling to their preferred levels of analysis, empirical researchers must specify *units* of analysis. The state is impossible to ignore as a unit of analysis, and many attributes of states lend themselves to measurement and statistical manipulation. What empirical researchers established is "as close as anything we have to an empirical law in international relations" (Levy, 1989: 270; see also Russett, 1990: 123). With the end of the Cold War, this one empirical law, and not a tradition of thought or even a theory, holds the field in its grip.

If democratic states do not fight each other, is it *because* they have democratic governments? This is the working hypothesis guiding most of the empirical work. It begs for inclusion in a theoretically driven research program such as Keohane has proposed. Nevertheless, it should be only one of an ensemble of hypotheses. We need to ask: What in the liberal world makes it peaceful? Many hypotheses may be offered. Waltz's second-image theorists of an earlier time already offered a number of them.

LIBERALISM AND REPUBLICANISM

"Bad states lead to war" (Waltz, 1959: 122). Conversely, good (read open, liberal, democratic, republican) states make for a peaceful world. Given the disposition to ransack history for evidence, one might question whether a transhistorical, not to mention transcultural (Ember et al., 1992), category of "good" states is defensible on conceptual grounds. In particular, republicanism and liberalism have had a problematic historical relation to each other and to "democracy"—the one term now used more than any other to describe good states.

What we commonly refer to as the liberal tradition (when not dismissing it as idealist or utopian) emerged with as much coherence as it ever possessed in the late eighteenth century. A product of the Enlightenment, this tradition's great voice belonged to Kant. In his famous essay "Perpetual Peace" ([1795] 1991), Kant held that republics alone could hope for peace. Kant also claimed, as did many liberal writers after him, that commercial activity and material prosperity inhibit war (Kant, 1991: 100–102, 114). When Waltz joined these claims in his exposition of the second image, he simultaneously fixed a narrow meaning for the term "republic" and subordinated it to liberalism, which deflects attention from the polity, its purpose and form to individuals, their concerns and rights. In Waltz's (1962) reading, Kant was a liberal.

More recently, Michael Doyle subjected Kant's position to a fuller and more sympathetic treatment. In Doyle's judgment, the very conditions Kant found contributing to peace among "liberal societies" exacerbate relations between liberal and other societies. Liberal societies exhibit "constitutional restraint, shared commercial interests, and international respect for individual rights," and their constitutions are republican because they successfully combine "moral autonomy, individualism, and social order" (Doyle, 1983: 225–26, 324–25; 1986: 1157–58; see also chap. 4 in this book). Evidently, liberal republics are nothing more than liberal societies ruling themselves, through representative institutions, only to the extent they need to be ruled. Liberal republics are thus democratic republics or liberal democracies or, simply, open societies.

A republican form of government is but one feature of good states in a liberal world. Yet republicanism is a tradition of thought that antedates the state as the primary political entity by which the world is organized. The republican tradition offers a capacious view of politics. The locus of political activity, wherever found, is the polity, of which the state is but one example. With the rise of the state, and thus a world of states, other polities either disappeared or were subsumed. Republicanism survived only because its view of politics radically narrowed. The language of republicanism no longer describes polities in general, or even states in general. Reserved for states with a republican form of government, it has lost conceptual and expressive power.

Aristotle's *Politics*, written in the fourth century B.C.E., is the paradigmatic source of the republican tradition. Aristotle ([1252a-b] 1958: 1–8) defined the polity as an association of people that exists for their common good. Ordained by nature, the polity is a *condition* of rule logically anterior to the *conditions* of rule, that is, the relation between ruler and ruled. Some such relation is necessary to secure the common good, but the particulars vary with material conditions and the play of contingency. Nevertheless, in Aristotle's system, the purpose, nature, and conditions of rule are all aspects of the same pervasive phenomenon and their separation an analytic contrivance. That phenomenon is human association, which is never merely contingent.

The *Politics* necessarily begins with the purpose and general properties of the polity. It then proceeds to the conditions of rule, treated at a lesser but still high level of generality and at necessarily greater length. Aristotle ordered the many particulars of rule by reference to a simple, logically complete set of formal categories. Rule may rest in the hands of one person, or a few people, or many people. In whosoever hands, rule may realize the common good; or it may betray the common good in favor of the one, few, or many who happen to rule. Each of these six possibilities constitutes a form of rule—*politeia* in Greek, *status* in Latin. Of the six, rule by a few, who (evidently as an empirical generalization) are also the best, results in an aristocracy. Any polity in this form is a republic.

Forms of rule categorize contingent relations of rule, each recognizable as an arrangement of offices—government in English. With the rise of the state, "republic" disappeared both as a summary term for rule itself and as one of the formal categories of rule. The word remained as a description of contingent arrangements, now informally cast as one type of government. Machiavelli ([1513] 1985: 61) would seem to have initiated this shift; recall the opening words of *The Prince*: "All states, all dominions that have held and do hold empire over men have been and are either republics or principalities." Machiavelli can hardly have meant the term "state" in the fully modern sense of an impersonal apparatus of rule (Hexter, 1957: 150–72; Skinner, 1978: 353–54; Mansfield, 1983: 849–57). Nor did his use of the term in place of "republic" become standard practice for another two centuries. Only in the eighteenth century were political thinkers able to move from a formal conception of republican rule—rule by the few—to an informal summary description, or typing, of contingent arrangements.

The historic problem for the formal conception of a republic is the inference that no republican polity can efficiently exceed a relatively small size. The likelihood that the few who rule will, as an empirical matter, be the best suited for the role decreases with the credibility of Aristotle's assumption that all citizens have direct knowledge of each other's character. Furthermore, rulers increasingly lack direct knowledge of all the activities that affect the common good. Unless a polity remains small, rule by one (effectively, rule by delegation) is the better part of virtue. Yet to be well ruled encourages expansion (as in the case of Rome) and of course larger polities are less vulnerable to predatory neighbors. Republics give way to principalities when Aristotle's normative concerns are superimposed on social and material conditions more heterogeneous than any Aristotle had in mind.

Hume and Montesquieu are respectively and paradigmatically identified with two solutions to the size problem. For Hume ([1741–1742: II, xvi] 1963: 511), "A small commonwealth is the happiest government in the world within itself, because everything lies within the eyes of the rulers: but it may be subdued by great force from without." Hume's solution is a system of representation in which citizens of small jurisdictions would elect representatives who would themselves elect representatives of yet larger jurisdictions who would then have the responsibility of rule. Such a system would "refine" democracy on a local scale, take advantage of the evident fact that "aristocracies are better adapted for peace and order," and provide the security of "an extensive country" (Hume, 1963: 514).

For Montesquieu ([1748: IX, i–v] 1989: 131–34), "the spirit of republics is peace and moderation," but monarchies have the advantage of size. The only possible substitute is an association of republics with limited or (in Locke's sense, 1963: 382–84) "federative" powers. The Constitution of the United States combines these solutions to form, in Madison's words, "a compound republic," the rationale for which Hamilton and Madison propounded in *The Federalist Papers* (Nos. 9 and 10, Hamilton et al. [1788] 1961: 71–84). Thereafter, size ceases to matter; Kant ignored it (Riley, 1983: 131). However large states are republics if their constitutions specify arrangements involving representative institutions and/or a division of governmental powers and responsibilities between the state and its constituent "states."

Any such arrangement is presumptively republican because, formally speaking, those who rule are few in number. Nevertheless, the form of *rule* matters little because it explains little or nothing by itself. The form of *government* does matter because it is held to explain the pacific disposition of states in that form. The difficulty is that the explanation is undiscriminating. The republican form of government is a type, loosely defined at that. To which of the several properties that a republican state may, but need not, possess do we assign explanatory significance? This difficulty is clearly present in Kant's "Perpetual Peace" and, we believe, has never been addressed by anyone friendly to Kant's position (which, we must remember, was an eighteenth-century commonplace, and not Kant's in particular). On the contrary, Hamilton's devastating critique of this position in Federalist No. 6, which precedes "Perpetual Peace" by several years, has never had an answer of comparable power (Hamilton et al. [1788] 1961: 53–60; see also Stourzh, 1970, chap. 4).

There are two properties of republics taken as a form of rule and four properties of republican governments, variably present and variously combined, that might be seen as conducive to peace. As to the properties of republics: First, they are peaceful because they are small. In such circumstances, rule by a few is efficient and benign, and, as Hume suggested, everyone is happy with the way things are. Two objections immediately come to mind, both of which challenge the implicit assumption that the world outside the republic does not matter. As Machiavelli understood, republics may be efficiently organized for aggressive purposes in an environment of small polities competing for scarce values. Or, as Hume and Montesquieu concluded, small polities with large neighbors are forced to extend themselves through a variety of strategies, not all of them peaceful, with the result that they are no longer small and vulnerable. Either way, relative size overwhelms absolute size and affects conduct accordingly; Waltz's third image prevails.

Second, and even less plausibly, republics are peaceful because the few who rule are the best, in the Aristotelian sense of being competent and committed to the common good. Aristotle himself drew no such conclusion. Peace is a common good, but cannot be assumed to result from peaceful policies. "Training for war should not be pursued with a view to enslaving men who do not deserve such a fate. Its objects should be these—first, to prevent men from ever becoming enslaved themselves; secondly to put men in a position to exercise leadership" (Aristotle [1332b], 1958: 319). As Aristotle intimated, competence in ruling is often enough associated with warriors for whom internal pacification and external engagement are practically inseparable.

A more general objection is Hamilton's. "Have republics in practice been less addicted to war than monarchies? Are not the former administered by *men* as well as the latter? Are there not predilections, rivalships, and desires of unjust acquisitions that affect nations as well as kings?" (*Federalist* No. 6, Hamilton et al. [1788] 1961: 56). One, few, or many, rulers are prone to war because human beings are. Kant ([1784] 1991: 42) agreed: "Despite the wisdom of individual actions here and there, everything as a whole is made up of folly and childish vanity, and often of childish malice and destructiveness." Some few who rule may be disposed to peace, but this is dumb luck at best. Unless there is some principle or bias in the selection of the few that favors a preference for peace, the odds favor the bellicose. History suggests as much; Waltz's first image prevails.

Associating one form of rule with a proclivity for peace was no more persuasive in the eighteenth century than it is today. By contrast, associating a loosely defined type of government with such a proclivity was popular then and has become so today. Four properties of republican governments call for comment, all of them discernible in Kant's "Perpetual Peace." First is "the great principle of representation," as Madison called it: The few who rule represent the interests of the citizenry, who have elected the few for this purpose (*Federalist* No. 14, Hamilton et al. [1788] 1961: 100).

The ancients lacked a clear idea of representation (Pitkin, 1989: 133). Hamilton thought the discovery of representation a great advance in the science of politics; Madison defined the term "republic" exclusively by reference to this principle (*Federalist* Nos. 9 and 10, Hamilton et al. [1788] 1961: 72, 81). Kant ([1795] 1991: 102) also held that a system of representation "alone makes possible a republican state" and added, "without it, despotism and violence will result, no matter what kind of constitution is in force." In

Kant's opinion, this was precisely the experience of "the so-called 'republics' of antiquity."

How does representation overcome the objection that rulers are people and people are bad? One possibility is that it introduces a selection bias favoring pacific leaders. Chosen for their wisdom, leaders return the favor by displaying a Burkean independence of mind. Madison (*Federalist* No. 10, Hamilton et al. [1788] 1961: 82–83) argued that a large republic based on representation enables the selection of rulers "who possess the most attractive merit and the most diffused and established characters" and who do not indulge in the factionalism to which democratic governments are vulnerable.

The evidence for this assertion is hardly compelling. No more compelling are the twin assumptions that people will select rulers to represent them because the latter are wise and rulers once selected will detach themselves from partisan interests and rule wisely. Nor, finally, is the assumption behind those assumptions beyond challenge: The wise policy is the one more conducive to peace. As president, Madison chose war in 1812 for a republic he participated in designing (for complicated and much-debated reasons; see Stagg, 1983).

The second property of republican government that may incline states toward peace is, as Doyle put it, "constitutional restraint." Kant ([1795] 1991: 102) related representation to the separation of powers: "*Republicanism* is that political principle whereby the executive power (the government) is separated from the legislative power." Different functions require institutional separation to avoid conflicts of interest. Yet institutional separation does not require a system of representation, except perhaps in a virtual sense. Kings and chiefs no less than elected presidents may "represent" the country; the legislature may "represent" the people, or constituencies or an "estate," whether and by whom elected; judges are appointed, or elected, to "represent" justice. Kant ([1795] 1991: 101) himself said rule by a hereditary prince or nobility could accord with "the *spirit* of a representative system" (on "virtual representation" as a matter much debated in late-eighteenth-century England and America, see Wood, 1972: 173–81; Reid, 1989: 52–62). Kant was on stronger footing to suggest that representation and the separation of powers depend on a "lawful" constitution, without which no state can properly claim to have a republican form of government.

Does a constitution minimally providing for rule by law and separation of powers incline a government toward peace? This possibility cannot be so easily dismissed. The separation of powers necessitates a degree of consultation or corroboration in making important choices, which militates against rash or single-minded choices favoring war. More generally, constitutions foster sensitivity to the requirements of law. Furthermore, constitutions may impose specific limitations on government choices, for example, by abolishing standing armies or prohibiting borrowing to pay for military activities, as Kant ([1795] 1991: 94–95) proposed. Madison ([1792] 1983: 208; but see Madison [1790] 1981: 19) also proposed the latter expedient: "Each generation should be made to bear the burden of its own wars, instead of carrying them on, at the expense of other generations." In this view, the constitutional separation of generations would foster peace.

Proposals this drastic rarely find their way into constitutions. Conversely constitutions *can* make war easier by making government more efficient and legitimating access to societal resources. They may even delay the choice of war but promote its righteous prosecution once the choice is made (Osgood, 1953). Obviously constitutions differ so much in content and effect that any generalization about their impact on war is risky.

A third property of at least some republican governments that may contribute to peace is the creation of two levels of political organization and division of governmental powers between them (the language of levels long precedes Singer; see Onuf and Onuf, 1993, chaps. 2, 3). Republics may ally with other republics for security from both internal and external threat. So may polities of any form, in whatever degree of institutionalization they choose. When republics permanently surrender powers over such matters to a "higher" government, they necessarily create a constitutional republic that divides governmental powers even before separating them.

In "Perpetual Peace," Kant ([1795] 1991: 104) wrote in favor of what "we might call a *pacific federation*," which, he claimed, "does not seek to acquire any power like that of a state" or require its members "to submit to public laws and to a coercive power which enforces them." It would have been more accurate (or less ingenuous) for Kant to have said that the government of any such federation need not hold all the powers to which unitary governments are accustomed, but that it minimally must have the power to maintain security among its members. No other arrangement rules out dissolution or internal war. At least a universal federation—Kant ([1795] 1991: 104) saw his "extending gradually to encompass all states"—would not require the power to defend members from other states. Kant could hardly have advocated local or regional federation as the road to peace because any effectively ruled federation is, by that fact, a threat to its smaller or less well organized neighbors. Nor did he.

Many eighteenth-century republicans linked commerce and peace. Kant ([1795] 1991: 114) wrote: "The *spirit of commerce* sooner or later takes hold of every people, and it cannot exist side by side with war." Notice that republican government is not expressly factored into this relationship. Instead, republican government is assumed to foster commerce, with peace following. Or something else favors commerce and republican arrangements at the same time. Kant ([1795] 1991: 99) argued that a republican constitution is "founded" on principles of liberty, legality, and equality, all of which protect individuals and their various enterprises. Such a position would seem to make "natural rights" the common source of a largely self-regulating society and constitutionally limited government. It may even imply that rights-conscious members of liberal society, wanting the least government consistent with their peaceful pursuits, will ordinarily choose a government specifically of the republican type.

Kant's ([1785] 1959) constitutional principles bring to mind his ethical system, which is predicated on the moral autonomy of the individual. Kant ([1795] 1991: 96) also imputed autonomy to the state and inferred from this a duty of nonintervention. "No state shall forcibly interfere in the constitution and government of another state." No wonder contemporary writers like Waltz and Doyle take Kant to have been a liberal. Certainly nothing is more liberal than the belief that commerce leads to peace if governments stay out of everyone's affairs, including those of other governments. Nor is there any belief more characteristic of nineteenth-century liberal internationalism. Richard Cobden (quoted in Bull, 1977: 251) reduced it to a simple formula: "as little intercourse as possible betwixt the governments, as much connection as possible between the nations of the world."

Not everyone in the eighteenth century believed that commerce would bring peace in its wake. Rousseau ([1772] 1991: 176) held otherwise. So did Hamilton:

> Has commerce hitherto done anything more than change the objects of war? Is not the love of wealth as domineering and enterprising a passion as that of power and glory? Have there not been as many wars founded upon commercial motives since that has become the prevailing system of nations, as were before occasioned by the cupidity of territory or dominion? Has not the spirit of commerce, in many instances, administered new incentives to the appetite, both for the one and the other? Let experience, the least fallible of human opinions, be appealed to for an answer to these inquiries. (*Federalist* No. 6, Hamilton et al., 1961: 57)

Hamilton doubted that commerce and government could be kept apart. Later experience with the complexities of capitalism as well as the persistence of mercantilism only strengthen Hamilton's position.

THE LIBERAL WORLD

Enlightenment thinkers thought that commerce would bring many benefits beyond peace (Hirschman, 1977: 48–66; Schlereth, 1977: 97–103; Neff, 1990: 28–37). For example, Hume ([1741–2: I, xiv] 1963: 120, emphasis deleted) averred that "nothing is more favourable to the rise of politeness and learning, than a number of neighbouring and independent states, connected together by commerce and policy." Montesquieu ([1748: XX, i] 1989: 338) concurred: "Commerce cures destructive prejudices, and it is an almost general rule that everywhere there are gentle mores, there is commerce and that everywhere there is commerce, there are general mores."

Manners and learning connote a peaceful disposition. They depend on prosperity, which demonstrably results from commerce. Nineteenth-century liberals made a direct connection between peace and prosperity—no one benefiting from commerce would rationally give up prosperity for war. Enlightenment writers drew attention not to prosperity as such, but to its uses. These are leisure well and agreeably spent, education, arts, and sciences. All of these activities point to a cosmopolitan world view.

Kant shared in this world view (Schlereth, 1977). A number of scholars in the field of international relations (Bull, 1977: 24–27; Beitz, 1979: 179–83; Linklater, 1982: 114–17; Hurrell, 1990) have made much of Kant's cosmopolitanism—perhaps too much. Kant's ([1795] 1991: 105) cosmopolitan law, consisting solely of "the right of a stranger not to be treated with hostility when he arrives on someone else's territory," can hardly be the basis of a pacific federation or have much to do with peace at all. Instead, it is a self-serving privilege for cosmopolitans who, unlike Kant himself, are generally disposed to travel.

The cosmopolitan world view embodies a series of assumptions that are never fully stated: people will become cosmopolitans as they become prosperous; cosmopolitan pursuits require peace; cosmopolitans affirm universal values but appreciate diversity (within bounds); cosmopolitans have learned that war is childish or parochial and that it can be outgrown; government officials, themselves cosmopolitan, will follow the lead of enlightened public opinion. Later liberals were also frequently cosmopolitan, their simpler equation of peace and commerce gaining unacknowledged weight from cosmopolitan assumptions. Indeed, later liberals made the last assumption central to their vision of a world ruled by law. In the absence of enforcement machinery, world public opinion gave international law its bite (Hinsley, 1963: 92–113).

Realists (for example, Carr, 1946: 31–38) treated this claim with particular scorn. Nevertheless, all of these assumptions are plausible and indeed are supported by history, *within the liberal world*. While people do not automatically become cosmopolitan because they are prosperous, in our own time a quite substantial number of people have become cosmopolitan in outlook after experiencing a degree of prosperity unimaginable in the eighteenth century. Wars threaten increasingly sophisticated networks of activities on which cosmopolitan privilege depends. The liberal preoccupation with human rights comports with the value that cosmopolitans place on tolerance and diversity. In the nineteenth century, cosmopolitans condemned dueling and slavery; these institutions disappeared (Mueller, 1989; Ray, 1989, and chap. 14 in this book). Cosmopolitan ambivalence delayed and impaired the abolition of war except within the liberal world. Even then it took war in the United States to end slavery. While a growing aversion to war has gained normative weight (Kegley, 1982: 189–92), support for rules limiting the use of force is not the most important way in which public opinion fosters peace in the liberal world.

In the eighteenth century, cosmopolitan opinion constituted public opinion for most purposes. Popular opinion achieved political significance early in the nineteenth century, just as dueling and slavery lost favor (Johnson, 1991: 321–27, 462–72, 530–37). Realists tend to fear popular opinion because they believe it disrupts efficient governance or encourages pandering to a fickle public (Nincic, 1992: 5–45). At least in the United States, recent evidence provides little support for these fears. "Perhaps the change . . . wrought by World War II was the last big policy shift attributable to a clear shift in elite and mass opinion" (Russett, 1990: 117). Realists leave elite opinion out of the equation. Yet cosmopolitan views often prevail among elite opinion leaders, filter down to the public at large, and percolate back to the top where public officers are already likely to hold those same views.

Today stunning advances in communications technology simultaneously promote the downward movement of cosmopolitan opinion and make governments more responsive to the upward movement of popular opinion. This is democracy at work in unforeseen conditions. Democracy remains as it has always been in the liberal world—a cosmopolitan call for peace *within* societies to be achieved without oppression. The success of this and the related call for peace *among* those same societies has, in John Mueller's provocative formulation, benefited from successful marketing.

> The idea that war is undesirable and inefficacious and the idea that democracy is a good form of government have largely followed the same market trajectory. . . . In the view, war aversion not only is associated with the rise of democracy, but also with the decline of slavery, religion, capital punishment, and cigarette smoking and with the growing acceptance of capitalism, scientific methodology, environmentalism, and abortion. (Mueller, 1991: 58; see also 1992)

In short, cosmopolitan attitudes make a difference on a variety of fronts, and these attitudes are learned, just as Hume and Montesquieu suggested. What eighteenth-century cosmopolitans could not have imagined is the extent to which the transformation of communications technology and the capitalist mode of consumption would contribute to such developments.

As we have already emphasized, these are developments in the *liberal* world. Indeed they are measures of its development. Realists insist on a single world of international relations—a world of states, a world of war. Recently some liberal-minded scholars have identified "two worlds" (Rosecrance, 1986: 16–43; Rosenau, 1990: 243–96). These worlds are not just divisions within a single world based on the distribution of power and geographical circumstances. These worlds "reflect fundamentally different modes of organizing international relations" (Rosecrance, 1986: 16). One is the realists' world of territory, sovereignty, insecurity, and war. The other is the liberals' world of trade, interdependence, prosperity, and peace. Both worlds exist on the same planet at the same time.

Yet beholden to realism, Richard Rosecrance (1986: 43) defined the liberal world as one in which states choose to trade for "national advancement"; they choose to participate in the other world for the same reason. While acknowledging social learning, Rosecrance gave states' leaders more discretion than their situations permit them. However instrumental their motives, they become trapped by the conditions their choices help to create. In the liberal world these conditions foster complex arrangements from which it is impossible to extricate the state, practically or conceptually. Cosmopolitan attitudes legitimize these arrangements even as they capture states' leaders.

James Rosenau's characterization of the liberal world owes nothing to realism. Hundreds of thousands of actors pursue diverse goals with limited means (Rosenau, 1990: 250, 266–68). In such a world, it is barely intelligible to speak of international relations as if they constitute a system with its own mode of organization. Despite the number of actors and their inability to control outcomes, their relations in general do not reflect a market mode of organization. The liberal world lacks the coherence that such structure would provide. Instead it exhibits an extraordinary constellation of intersecting social and economic arrangements.

Complex economic and social arrangements depend on analytic skills to make them work (Lasswell, 1935; Rosenau, 1990). With such skills come cosmopolitan attitudes, all needed to render these arrangements complementary and bind them together. As the site of material prosperity, enduring peace, and unabated change, the liberal world is a cosmopolitan social construction two centuries in the making. Cosmopolitan attitudes mark its limits. Where, or when, those attitudes end, so too does that world.

REFERENCES

Aristotle. (1958) *The Politics of Aristotle*. Edited and translated by Ernest Barker. New York: Oxford University Press.

Beitz, Charles R. (1979) *Political Theory and International Relations*. Princeton, N.J.: Princeton University Press.

Bull, Hedley. (1977) *The Anarchical Society: A Study of Order in World Politics*. New York: Columbia University Press.

Burton, John W. (1972) *World Society*. Cambridge: Cambridge University Press.

Carr, Edward Hallett. (1946) *The Twenty Years' Crisis, 1919–1939: An Introduction to the Study of International Relations*, 2nd ed. New York: St. Martin's Press.

Doyle, Michael W. (1986) "Liberalism and World Politics," *American Political Science Review* 80 (December): 1151–69.

———. (1983) "Kant, Liberal Legacies, and Foreign Affairs," *Philosophy and Public Affairs* 12 (Summer and Fall): 205–35, 323–53.

Ember, Carol R., Melvin Ember, and Bruce M. Russett. (1992) "Peace between Participatory Democracies: A Cross-Cultural Test of the 'Democracies Rarely Fight Each Other' Hypothesis," *World Politics* 44 (July): 573–99.

Hamilton, Alexander, John Jay, and James Madison. ([1788] 1961) *The Federalist Papers*. Edited by Clinton Rossiter. New York: New American Library.

Hexter, J. H. (1957) *The Vision of Politics on the Eve of the Reformation*. New York: Basic Books.

Hinsley, F. H. (1963) *Power and the Pursuit of Peace: Theory and Practice in the History of Relations between States.* Cambridge: Cambridge University Press.

Hirschman, Albert O. (1977) *The Passions and the Interests: Political Arguments for Capitalism before Its Triumph.* Princeton, N.J.: Princeton University Press.

Hoffmann, Stanley. (1987) *Janus and Minerva: Essays in the Theory and Practice of International Politics.* Boulder, Colo.: Westview.

Hopf, Ted. (1993) "Polarity and International Stability: Response," *American Political Science Review* 87 (March): 177–80.

———. (1991) "Polarity, the Offense–Defense Balance, and War," *American Political Science Review* 85 (June): 475–93.

Hume, David. ([1741–1742] 1963) *Essays: Moral, Political and Literary.* Oxford: Oxford University Press.

Hurrell, Andrew. (1990) "Kant and the Kantian Paradigm in International Relations," *Review of International Studies* 16 (July): 183–205.

Johnson, Paul. (1991) *The Birth of the Modern World Society: 1815–1830.* New York: HarperCollins.

Kant, Immanuel. ([1795] 1991) "Perpetual Peace: A Philosophical Sketch," pp. 93–130 in Hans Reiss, ed., *Kant: Political Writings*, 2nd ed., H. B. Nisbet, trans. Cambridge: Cambridge University Press.

———. ([1784] 1991) "Idea for a Universal History with a Cosmopolitan Purpose," pp. 41–53 in Hans Reiss, ed., *Kant: Political Writings*, 2nd ed., H. B. Nisbet, trans. Cambridge: Cambridge University Press.

———. ([1785] 1959) *Foundations of the Metaphysics of Morals.* Translated by Lewis W. Beck. New York: Liberal Arts Press.

Kegley, Charles W., Jr. (1982) "Measuring Transformation in the Global Legal System," pp. 173–209 in Nicholas Greenwood Onuf, ed., *Law-Making in the Global Community.* Durham, N.C.: Carolina Academic Press.

Kegley, Charles W., Jr., and Gregory A. Raymond. (1992) "Must We Fear a Post–Cold War Multipolar System?" *Journal of Conflict Resolution* 36 (September): 573–85.

Keohane, Robert O. (1989) *International Institutions and State Power: Essays in International Relations Theory.* Boulder, Colo.: Westview.

———. (1986) "Theory of World Politics: Structural Realism and Beyond," pp. 158–203 in Robert O. Keohane, ed., *Neorealism and Its Critics.* New York: Columbia University Press.

———. (1984) *After Hegemony: Cooperation and Discord in the Modern World Economy.* Princeton, N.J.: Princeton University Press.

Keohane, Robert O., and Joseph S. Nye. (1989) *Power and Interdependence: World Politics in Transition*, 2nd ed. Glenview, Ill.: Scott, Foresman.

———. (1977) *Power and Interdependence: World Politics in Transition.* Boston: Little, Brown.

———, eds. (1972) *Transnational Relations and World Politics.* Cambridge, Mass.: Harvard University Press.

Krasner, Stephen D. (1982) "International Regimes," *International Organization* 36 (Spring): 185–510.

Lakatos, Imre. (1970) "Falsification and the Methodology of Scientific Research Programmes," pp. 91–196 in Imre Lakatos and Alan Musgrave, eds., *Criticism and the Growth of Knowledge.* Cambridge: Cambridge University Press.

Lake, David A. (1992) "Powerful Pacifists: Democratic States and War," *American Political Science Review* 86 (March): 24–37.

Lasswell, Harold D. (1935) *World Politics and Personal Insecurity.* New York: The Free Press.

Levy, Jack S. (1989) "The Causes of War: A Review of Theories and Evidence," pp. 209–333 in Philip E. Tetlock et al., eds., *Behavior, Society, and Nuclear War* 1. New York: Oxford University Press.

Linklater, Andrew. (1982) *Men and Citizens in the Theory of International Relations.* New York: St. Martin's Press.

Locke, John. ([1690] 1963) *Two Treatises on Government.* Edited by Peter Laslett. Cambridge: Cambridge University Press.

Machiavelli, Niccoló. ([1513] 1985) *The Prince.* Translated by Harvey C. Mansfield Jr. Chicago: University of Chicago Press.

Madison, James ([1792] 1983) "Universal Peace," *National Gazette*, Philadelphia (31 January), pp. 206–9 in Robert A. Rutland et al., eds., *The Papers of James Madison* 14. Charlottesville, Va.: University Press of Virginia.

———. ([1790] 1981) Letter to Thomas Jefferson (4 February), pp. 18–21 in Charles F. Hobson and Robert A. Rutland, eds., *The Papers of James Madison* 13. Charlottesville, Va.: University Press of Virginia.

Mansbach, Richard W., and John A. Vasquez. (1981) *In Search of Theory: A New Paradigm for Global Politics.* New York: Columbia University Press.

Mansfield, Harvey C., Jr. (1983) "On the Impersonality of the Modern State: A Comment on Machiavelli's Use of *Stato*," *American Political Science Review* 77 (December): 849–57.

Midlarsky, Manus I. (1993) "Polarity and International Stability," *American Political Science Review* 87 (March): 173–77.

Montesquieu, Baron De. ([1748] 1989) *The Spirit of the Laws.* Edited and translated by Anne M. Cohler et al. Cambridge: Cambridge University Press.

Morgenthau, Hans J. (1948–1985) *Politics among Nations: The Struggle for Power and Peace*, 1st–5th eds. Kenneth W. Thompson, ed., 6th ed. New York: Alfred A. Knopf.

———. (1946) *Scientific Man versus Power Politics.* Chicago: University of Chicago Press.

Mueller, John. (1992) "The Obsolescence of Major War," pp. 41–50 in Charles W. Kegley Jr. and Eugene R. Wittkopf, *The Global Agenda: Issues and Perspectives*, 3rd ed. New York: McGraw-Hill.

———. (1991) "Is War Still Becoming Obsolete?" Paper presented at the 1991 Annual Meeting of the American Political Science Association, August 29–September 1, Washington, D.C.

———. (1989) *Retreat from Doomsday: The Obsolescence of Major War.* New York: Basic Books.

Neff, Stephen C. (1990) *Friends but No Allies: Economic Liberalism and the Law of Nations.* New York: Columbia University Press.

Nincic, Miroslav. (1992) *Democracy and Foreign Policy: The Fallacy of Political Realism.* New York: Columbia University Press.

Onuf, Nicholas Greenwood. (1989) *World of Our Making: Rules and Rule in Social Theory and International Relations.* Columbia: University of South Carolina Press.

Onuf, Peter, and Nicholas Onuf. (1993) *Federal Union, Modern World: The Law of Nations in an Age of Revolutions, 1776–1814.* Madison, Wisc.: Madison House.

Osgood, Robert Endicott. (1953) *Ideals and Self-Interest in America's Foreign Relations: The Great Transformation of the Twentieth Century.* Chicago: University of Chicago Press.

Pitkin, Hanna Fenichel. (1989) "Representation," pp. 132–54 in Terence Ball, James Farr, and Russell L. Hanson, eds., *Political Innovation and Conceptual Change*. Cambridge: Cambridge University Press.

Ray, James Lee. (1989) "The Abolition of Slavery and the End of International War," *International Organization* 43 (Summer): 405–39.

Reid, John P. (1989) *The Concept of Representation in the Age of the American Revolution*. Chicago: University of Chicago Press.

Riley, Patrick. (1983) *Kant's Political Philosophy*. Totowa, N.J.: Rowman and Littlefield.

Rosecrance, Richard. (1986) *The Rise of the Trading State: Commerce and Conquest in the Modern World*. New York: Basic Books.

Rosenau, James N. (1990) *Turbulence in World Politics: A Theory of Change and Continuity*. Princeton, N.J.: Princeton University Press.

Rousseau, Jean-Jacques. ([1772] 1991) "Considerations on the Government of Poland," pp. 162–96 in Stanley Hoffmann and David P. Fidler, eds., *Rousseau on International Relations*. Oxford: Oxford University Press.

Russett, Bruce. (1990) *Controlling the Sword: The Democratic Governance of National Security*. Cambridge, Mass.: Harvard University Press.

Schlereth, Thomas J. (1977) *The Cosmopolitan Ideal in Enlightenment Thought: Its Form and Function in the Ideas of Franklin, Hume, and Voltaire, 1694–1790*. Notre Dame, Ind.: Notre Dame University Press.

Singer, J. David. (1961) "The Level of Analysis Problem in International Relations," *World Politics* 14 (October): 77–92.

————. (1960) "International Conflict: Three Levels of Analysis," *World Politics* 12 (April): 453–61.

Skinner, Quentin. (1978) *The Foundations of Modern Political Thought*, Vol. 2, *The Age of the Reformation*. Cambridge: Cambridge University Press.

Social Sciences Citation Index, Annuals 1983–1992 (1984–1992). Philadelphia: Institute for Scientific Information.

Stagg, J. C. A. (1983) *Mr. Madison's War: Politics, Diplomacy, and Warfare in the Early American Republic, 1783–1830*. Princeton, N.J.: Princeton University Press.

Starr, Harvey. (1992) "Why Don't Democracies Fight One Another? Evaluating the Theory-Findings Feedback Loop," *Jerusalem Journal of International Relations* 14 (December): 41–59.

Stourzh, Gerald. (1970) *Alexander Hamilton and the Idea of Republican Government*. Stanford, Calif.: Stanford University Press.

Vasquez, John A. (1983) *The Power of Power Politics*. New Brunswick, N.J.: Rutgers University Press.

Walker, R. B. J. (1993) *Inside/Outside: International Relations as Political Theory*. Cambridge: Cambridge University Press.

Waltz, Kenneth N. (1979) *Theory of International Politics*. Reading, Mass.: Addison-Wesley.

————. (1964) "The Stability of a Bipolar World," *Daedalus* 93 (Summer): 881–909.

————. (1962) "Kant, Liberalism, and War," *American Political Science Review* 56 (June): 331–40.

————. (1959) *Man, the State and War: A Theoretical Analysis*. New York: Columbia University Press.

Wood, Gordon. (1972) *The Creation of the American Republic, 1776–1787*. New York: Norton.

CHAPTER 8

The United Nations in a New World Order: Reviving the Theory and Practice of International Organization

J. MARTIN ROCHESTER[1]

In an article in *International Organization* (Rochester, 1986) that was published shortly after the observance of the fortieth anniversary of the United Nations, I lamented what I argued was the passing of international organization (IO) as a distinct field of study in the international relations discipline. I took as my definition of international organization the traditional notion of "a formal arrangement transcending national boundaries that provides for the establishment of institutional machinery to facilitate cooperation among members in the security, economic, social, or related fields" (Plano and Olton, 1979: 288). As Friedrich Kratochwil and John Ruggie (1986: 753) also noted in the same volume, although with more approval than lament, the theory and practice of international organization were becoming increasingly divorced from each other: "The leading doctors have become biochemists and have stopped treating and in most cases even seeing patients." To the extent the IO field could still be said to exist, it was focused on the analysis of "recognized patterns . . . around which expectations converge," which "may or may not be accompanied by explicit organizational arrangements" (Young, 1980: 332–33), that is, regimes.

[1] This research has been supported by the United States Institute of Peace, the Weldon Spring Fund and the Center for International Studies of the University of Missouri-St. Louis, and the Lentz Peace Research Laboratory. The opinions, findings, and conclusions expressed in this work are those of the author and do not reflect the views of the U.S. Institute of Peace or other funding agencies. This article is a condensed treatment of a number of ideas discussed in *Waiting for the Millennium: The United Nations and the Future of World Order* (Columbia: University of South Carolina Press, 1993).

Kratochwil, Ruggie, and others could be forgiven for their skepticism about the worthiness of formal intergovernmental organizations (IGOs) as a subject of scholarly inquiry, particularly those operating at the global level. After all, the history of the UN system could be read as the steady erosion of the initial euphoria that accompanied its creation out of the ashes of World War II, with periods of decline punctuated by short-term revival and bursts of renewed hope only to be succeeded by another round of failure and ever-compounding cynicism.[2] In the mid-1980s especially—at a time when another grayish-looking Soviet *apparatchik* (Mikhail Gorbachev) had just come to power in the "evil empire" and when a U.S. secretary of defense (Caspar Weinberger) found it reasonable to declare that "we are no longer in the postwar era but a prewar era"—it was easy to dismiss world order, whether pursued through international organization or any other vehicle, as a rather hollow concept. Nonetheless, I ended my 1986 piece with the following words:

> There is every reason to believe that eventually, at some point in the future, international organization as traditionally conceived will be among the dominant subjects of political inquiry on the planet. One can only hope that we make it through the interim. (Rochester, 1986: 813)

Were these words prophetic, or hopelessly naive? Have we made it through "the interim," at least partially through, sooner than anyone expected? Is a UN-centered "new world order" ready to dawn in the wake of the demise of the Soviet Union, the Cold War, and the bipolar era, as was suggested in a *New York Times* editorial (1990: 23) trumpeting the UN's comeback?

> In a wondrous sea-change, the United Nations has silenced most of its detractors. A body once scorned as a dithering talk-shop has now mobilized impressively to punish Iraq's aggressions in the Persian Gulf. Elsewhere, from Afghanistan to Namibia, from Cambodia to Central America, the UN has also offered a glimpse of . . . hopes for a new world order to resolve conflicts by multilateral diplomacy and collective security.

Or, as suggested by the UN's subsequent failure in Afghanistan and more recent stumbling in the Balkans and elsewhere, is this merely yet another

---

[2] For example, compare President Truman's bombastic statement (1945b: 789) opening the San Francisco Conference expressing the expectation that the delegates were about to create "machinery which will make future peace not only possible, but certain" with Carlos Romulo's statement less than a decade later (1954: 32) that "the UN is in a state of coma, and there isn't much time left to revive it." Compare realist Henry Kissinger's lavish praise of the UN following the 1973 Arab–Israeli conflict ("I must say that the United Nations played a more effective role in this crisis than could have been deduced from my theoretical statements as a professor") with the despair evidenced a decade later by a UN secretary-general ("The UN goes through its paces in a workaday routine that is increasingly ignored or condemned and that threatens to become increasingly irrelevant in the real world") (Kissinger, 1973: 708; Waldheim, 1984: 106).

and perhaps potentially even more dangerous turn in the roller-coaster life of the world body? Is the emergent new world order—to paraphrase Voltaire's remark about the Holy Roman Empire—likely to be neither terribly new nor worldly nor orderly? Whether the UN will be able to move beyond the past cycle of ups and downs and chart a more steady course in the future is a question answerable not by looking for empirical indicators of unusual UN revival (for example, the authorization of more peacekeeping operations between 1988 and 1993 than in the previous forty-three years, with a fivefold increase in UN-mandated troops dispatched worldwide over the past year alone) or by following the latest news headlines reporting UN slippage, but by inquiring into much deeper phenomena having to do with the fundamental requirements for effective global organization.

In this essay I wish to examine, first, how the twentieth-century "move to institutions" (Kennedy, 1987) of a broadly multilateral, formal character on the part of states has been accompanied by a continued move away from such institutions on the part of students of interstate relations and, secondly, whether developments since the late 1980s and the general milieu surrounding them now warrant revived scholarly attention to global organization and the Wilsonian assumptions associated with that phenomenon. I will conclude with a consideration of UN reform, suggesting some connections between theory and practice.

THE ROAD FROM BAD IDEALISM TO BAD REALISM

The major problem of the international relations field since its beginnings as an identifiable academic discipline following World War I has been how to minimize conflict and maximize cooperation, thereby maintaining a semblance of order, in a decentralized system of sovereign states. Those working in both the idealist and realist traditions have tended to share a common view of the world (state-centrism) and a common research agenda (the world order *problematique*). In Inis Claude's words (1981: 199), "The major difference between realism and idealism pertains not to what is or should be but to what is possible." Realists have stressed world order approaches grounded in the enlightened management of power (hegemony, balance, or concert), while idealists have focused on the development of formal rules (international law) and formal machinery (international organization). Among idealists, Woodrow Wilson was closer to Immanuel Kant than Hugo Grotius in his view that international governance required not just a body of rules but some sort of ruling body. Although not to be equated with world federalism, the Wilsonian idealist paradigm proceeded from *institutionalist* and *globalist* assumptions that (1) the development of formal intergovernmental organization was at least as relevant to concerns about international order (and justice) as the development of less formal or demanding modes of interstate cooperation and

(2) any efforts at international institution building had to focus significantly on the global level.

These ideas, once part of the orthodoxy of the international relations field, have sounded almost heretical in recent times. If international relations scholarship in the interwar period suffered from "bad idealism," it seemed in the post–World War II years to become more and more characterized by an opposite tendency, "bad realism."[3] By the 1980s, not only had neoliberals (liberal institutionalists) and neorealists converged around a deprecation of IGOs in general and global IGOs in particular,[4] but the world order *problematique* commonly found in the scholarly literature had been reduced to the most elemental, primitive, and truly cynical of all questions: How is *any* interstate cooperation possible? How else can one interpret the disarmingly understated conclusion reached at the end of a widely cited 1985 symposium on "Cooperation Under Anarchy," acknowledging that "[despite anarchy] as the articles in this symposium have shown, cooperation is sometimes attained" (Axelrod and Keohane, 1985: 226)?

Just how far international relationists had traveled in distancing themselves from the Wilsonian paradigm can be seen in a few examples. In the aforementioned symposium, in their article focusing on the role of "institutions" in achieving cooperation under anarchy, Robert Axelrod and Robert Keohane (1985) managed never once to use the term "international organization." In the same volume, Duncan Snidal (1985: 57) equated the term "international organization" with an extreme idealist view of the world, stating that "the metaphors of 'Hobbesian anarchy' and 'international organization' have divided and obscured our understanding of international politics." To the extent Keohane associated himself with formal organizations, it was not notably of the global variety. In arguing against global unilateralism, Keohane and Joseph Nye (1985: 155–59) advocated subglobal multilateralism and minilateralism, noting that "only rarely are universal international organizations likely to provide the world with instruments for collective action."[5] By the end of the 1980s, despite their heavily guarded analyses of the prospects for global institution building, liberal institutionalists such as Keohane and Nye were being characterized as unduly optimistic about human and national behavior (Grieco, 1988).

Even as the practitioners in the 1990s have returned to the "world of actual international organizations" (Kratochwil and Ruggie, 1986: 753)—which they, of course, never entirely left—the theoreticians for the most part remain

---

[3] The terms "bad idealism" and "bad realism" are taken from Sartori (1965: 51).

[4] Kratochwil and Ruggie (1986: 760) found in their survey of all articles published in *International Organization* that "the formal institutional focus has declined steadily from the very beginning and now accounts for fewer than 5% of the total."

[5] Keohane's ideas are more fully developed in *After Hegemony* (1984). In the revised edition of *Power and Interdependence* (1989: xi), Keohane and Nye continue to be somewhat defensive about being labeled "liberals."

disengaged from the study of those organizations. The clarion call for a new world order reverberating at the outset of the decade masked a deep-seated incredulity that had taken hold in the scholarly community.[6] Despite some recent stirrings of renewed interest in IGOs such as the UN, formal, systemwide approaches to international governance are still being either studiously avoided or only sparingly treated by neorealists and neoliberals alike.[7] Witness:

- As recently as 1989, Oran Young (1989: 76) was writing: "I have . . . found it hard to become unduly alarmed by the apparent decline of the United Nations and certain other international organizations in recent years. . . . If one looks at institutions rather than at international organizations, I believe, there is less cause for alarm regarding the pursuit of international order and justice."
- In a later symposium on "Multilateralism," John Ruggie (1992: 567–84) still hedges on the subject of global organization. Although he speaks of "generalized organizing principles," he states that "the generic institutional form of multilateralism must not be confused with formal multilateral organizations, a relatively recent arrival, and still of only relatively modest importance." Of the "move to institutions" (IGO growth in the twentieth century), Ruggie expresses bewilderment: "I know of no good explanation in the literature of why states should have wanted to complicate their lives in this manner."[8]
- In the wake of the Persian Gulf War, Richard Rosecrance (1992) has speculated about "a new concert of powers," mentioning the UN only once in passing in his entire analysis; he points to the strains in maintaining cohesion among a concert of powers, suggesting that the common "threat of global economic breakdown" might serve to hold a somewhat expanded G-7 concert together. In the same vein, Charles Kupchan and Clifford Kupchan (1992) completely ignore the UN in speaking of "a new concert

---

[6] As a follow-up to the Kratochwil and Ruggie survey, an informal analysis I conducted of *International Organization* articles published between 1985 and 1991 showed that 17 percent of the total focused on formal institutions, and only 3 percent on the UN, even though by the late 1980s there was evidence of a major transformation of the international system.

[7] Clearly, there are many scholars who have had a sustained research focus on the UN and other international organizations, examining either the structures themselves or their performance. See, for example, Jacobson (1984), with a third edition forthcoming. Other scholars have rediscovered the UN of late, exemplified by Russett and Sutterlin (1991). There is a newly created Academic Council on the United Nations System, which has issued a report on "Strengthening the Study of International Organizations" (1987) and publishes annual reviews of the UN, such as those by Puchala and Coate (1989). One can also note a new Ford Foundation program on International Organizations and Law, as well as Harvard's pre- and postdoctoral fellowship program in the area of international institutions, including the UN. The point is that there has been a distinct overall decline in this brand of scholarship in the "IO field" in favor of investigating more general phenomena that are relatively indistinguishable from the rest of the international relations academic enterprise.

[8] See also Gallorotti (1991).

for Europe," expressing a degree of optimism about "collective security" but only in a regional context.

■ One can discern a highly guarded, almost anti-globalist and anti-institutionalist posture even on the part of scholars who focus their research on the UN. This was reflected in a study published under the auspices of the Academic Council on the UN System (Puchala and Coate, 1989: 102, 108), which concluded that "the fact [is] that globalist approaches to world order may have run their course, at least for the present" and that there are "limits to both globalism and intergovernmentalism."

FROM BAD REALISM TO NEOIDEALISM: CAN WILSONIANISM BE RESURRECTED?

"Faith," as Mark Twain once put it, "is believin' in what you know ain't true." Is belief in the Wilsonian vision merely an article of faith, or does it have an empirical basis? What is the likelihood that a UN-centered new world order might be constructed? I am particularly interested here in conscious, deliberate international institution building, what Young (1982: 282–85) has called "negotiated orders" as opposed to unplanned "spontaneous orders"; and within the category of negotiated orders, I am interested in what Young (1991: 282) terms "framework agreements encompassing the basic order or ordering principles of an entire social system." He cites "San Francisco in 1945" as belonging to "this class of comprehensive or framework agreements," which he recognizes to be a rare development. To speak of a "neoidealist" moment (Kegley, 1993) today is to ask whether the occasion now exists for forging the next framework agreement in the life of the interstate system, or at least reworking if not rethinking the one entered into in San Francisco.

The persistent skepticism surrounding the UN is odd in some respects. When one looks beyond present epiphenomena and takes a longer-term perspective, the following simple observations can be made: (1) the trend is unmistakably in the direction of international organizational growth, with one study documenting the proliferation of IGOs and counting over one thousand such entities in the contemporary global system (Jacobson, Reisinger, and Mathers, 1986: 141);[9] (2) the "expectation of international organization, the habit of organizing, the taking-for-granted of international bodies . . . are

[9] The authors note that regional IGO growth has exceeded global IGO growth since World War II, although "the absolute number [of IGOs with potentially universal membership] for the post–World War II era is impressively high" (1986: 145). Even skeptics acknowledge that "quantitatively, . . . IGOs are still an expanding force in international affairs" despite the fact that "qualitatively . . . the world of IGOs is not in good shape" (Ruggie, 1985: 343). Statistics on IGO growth are reported in Union of International Associations, *Yearbook of International Organizations 1988/89*, 25th ed. (1988), vol. 1, Appendix 7, and subsequent editions.

permanent results of the movement" that began almost from scratch a century or so ago (Claude, 1986: 25);[10] and (3) the United Nations—primitive, flawed, and fragile as it is—represents the latest, most ambitious stage in the historic process of global institution building. While this process is not completely linear—setbacks occur—there does seem to be a process at work.

If one is not impressed with these trends and is more inclined to look at current conditions and their ripeness for global institution building, consider the following:

> The constant presence of change that is pervasive but somewhat indetermi-
> nate with respect to overall pattern or direction constitutes a fundamental
> aspect of the international milieu in which the United Nations operates at
> the present time. The resultant fluidity of the international system shapes
> the activities of the Organization in a number of significant ways. Under
> these circumstances the problems of regulating relationships of power, for
> example, are highly complex. . . . The role of the United Nations as a creator
> of norms and a source of collective legitimization tends to be sharply empha-
> sized in a rapidly changing system in contrast to one that is more stable and
> slowly changing. And the opportunities thrown up by the pervasiveness of
> change constitute an invitation to various actors in the system to make an
> effort to harness the influence of the organization as an instrument for the
> accomplishment of political change. (Young, 1968: 906)

These observations were made in an article appearing in *International Organiza-tion* over twenty-five years ago, when such theorizing about the UN in scholarly journals was more commonplace than today, even though such remarks would seem far more germane to the 1990s.[11] As revolutionary as the international environment might have appeared in the 1960s, few would equate that decade with the present one as a period of ferment in international relations.

While there is a possibility that we will overreact to the upheavals from Moscow to Maastrich which have ushered in the post-postwar era and attribute larger importance to them than they deserve, especially coming as they have at a time when cosmic visions are being stirred by the impending arrival of a new century and millennium, there is also a chance we will underestimate them and fail to grasp their significance as evidence of a watershed period in the life of the international system. If it is much too premature to declare the epoch we are passing through in the late twentieth century as marking "the

---

[10] Claude adds that "we cannot ignore the successful implantation of the ideal of international organization. International organization may not have taken over the system, but it has certainly taken hold in the system. The twentieth century has seen the establishment of the prescription that multilateral agencies are essential to the conduct of international affairs" (1986: 25). Claude's classic *Swords into Plowshares* (1956) marked him as a scholar who defied either the realist or idealist label.

[11] These thoughts are in obvious contrast to those expressed more recently by the same author under the guise of "the new institutionalism" (see Young, 1989).

end of history" (Fukuyama, 1989) or to equate it historically with the Reformation (Will, 1989), it may be just as wrong to dismiss it as merely a *déjà vu* return to world politics as it looked prior to 1945 or 1914.

The convulsions in world politics since the late 1980s can be viewed in retrospect as the culmination of a process of ongoing erosion of the bipolar postwar international order traceable back to its beginnings. Long observable trends in the direction of a more complex international system are becoming more pronounced and accelerated. This complexity has four main aspects: (1) *the growing diffusion and ambiguity of power,* including not only the decline of the superpowers but also the proliferation of ministates capable at times of frustrating the will of major actors, as well as shifting relationships generally among military, economic, and technological bases of power; (2) *the growing fluidity of alignments,* including the depolarization of the East–West conflict as erstwhile East bloc states seek to find their way ideologically toward the West and West–West economic competition heats up as an axis of conflict, the North–South conflict losing its defining character also as increasing diversity among newly industrializing countries, OPEC states, Third World countries, and other less developed countries makes Southern solidarity harder to sustain, and greater localization of politics related to ethnicity and other issues beneath the global level; (3) *ever more intricate patterns of interdependence,* associated with an expanding agenda of concerns and a broadening conception of national security beyond traditional military considerations; and (4) *the growing role of nonstate actors along with increasing linkages among subnational, transnational, and intergovernmental levels of activity* even as the size of national governmental budgets and state apparatuses resists shrinkage.

The question remains whether we are witnessing merely the end of the postwar era and the transformation of the international system back to the more normal historical pattern of full-blown multipolarity, or whether we are on the brink of a more fundamental and epic transformation, namely the unraveling of the very fabric of the Westphalian state system itself that has been the primary basis of human political organization for the past three centuries. Some seize upon the first two systemic characteristics cited above (the fragmentation of postwar power and alignment structure) and suggest the *déjà vu* scenario is the correct one (Mearsheimer, 1990). Others seize upon the other two systemic characteristics (relating to interdependence, transnationalism, and intergovernmentalism) and suggest differently, that is, that the international system is experiencing unprecedented "turbulence"—a "bifurcated global politics" torn between state-centrism and multicentrism, calling for a wholly new "post-international politics" paradigm (Rosenau, 1990).[12]

----

[12] Rosenau's analysis is in the tradition of earlier writings in the 1970s that posed a "cobweb" paradigm as an alternative to the standard billiard-ball paradigm, such as that of Burton et al. (1974). Also, see Zacher (1991), although he does not see the state as much under siege as Rosenau. John Ruggie, whose writings have been clearly state-centric oriented, examines, in the manner of John Herz, the changing nature of the territorial state in a recent article. Ruggie (1993: 144) urges "addressing the question of whether the modern system of states may be yielding in some instances to postmodern forms of configuring political space."

It bears repeating that the metamorphosis that is the subject of this chapter is not a change *of* the Westphalian system (toward world government or some more hierarchical order) but a change *in* the Westphalian system. The United Nations can be understood as the resultant of large-scale, long-term technological and other forces contributing to the establishment of the "habit of international organization" in the nineteenth century and the creation of global organization in the twentieth century. Whether this historical pattern of growing formalization and universalization of international politics continues, and at what pace, will depend on several factors.

Granted the small number of cases to base conclusions on, the past dynamics of international institution building suggest that major innovation in the political development of the international system—in terms of new macro-level governance arrangements ("framework agreements") resulting from human design—tends to be associated with a *systemwide crisis* (systemic war) combined with the existence of *an actor or set of actors disposed toward and capable of moving the system.* In other words, significant institutional development in the international system may well materialize as part of a gradual, unfolding process, but acceleration requires a push from specific actors responding to a specific crisis. Assuming we are now living in a posthegemonic world in the nuclear age (Keohane, 1984: 244), it follows that any attempt to promote the development of the contemporary international system toward a more "mature" anarchy[13] or still higher political order, through UN reform, will require the imprimatur of a critical mass of states that have sufficiently compatible issue-positions, shared salience levels, and joint power capabilities (including hard and soft power) as to constitute a dominant coalition willing and able to lead the other members to act in accordance with the new principles.

To what extent do these conditions exist at present? The ecopolitics school argues that "the forces of ecological and technological change . . . are driving potentially revolutionary shifts in the structure of relations among nations and in the values that guide human behavior" (Pirages, 1989: 202). However, even if there is a compelling logic dictating a reformation in international governance arrangements, the question must be asked, as Stanley Hoffmann (1978: 193) has phrased it, "Will the need forge a way?" The biggest puzzle of our time is how it is that the need for coordinated problem solving on a global scale—in matters of security, economics, and ecology—is arguably greater than ever before, at the same moment when central guidance mechanisms seem less feasible in some respects than in previous historical periods due to the fourfold trends cited above. One might well argue that if comprehensive approaches to world order such as the League of Nations and its successor have failed or worked only marginally in the past, they are even less likely to succeed in the present environment. Compared with 1945, when in Harry Truman's (1945a: 4) words "there were many who doubted that

[13] Buzan (1983: 97) argues that the international system as of the 1980s was midway between high ("immature") and low ("mature") anarchy.

agreement could ever be reached by these 50 countries differing so much in race and religion, in language and culture," the challenge of global institution building appears all the more formidable today in a world body politic consisting of well over three times as many state members representing considerably greater diversity who are clamoring to be at the global bargaining table, not to mention the complications posed by nonstate actors. [14]

While it is true that "necessities [in themselves] do not create possibilities" (Waltz, 1979: 109), the starker the choices, the more likely that innovative actions will follow. Crisis provides the best opportunity for the inertia of existing arrangements to be overcome and for the learning of new behaviors to occur. Kenneth Boulding (1977) once remarked in this regard that "man is a strange creature who is incapable of seeing the handwriting on the wall until his back is up against it." As Kant expressed it earlier, "the very evils which thus arise compel men to find out means against them" (cited in Clark, 1989: 56). [15]

Whether individuals and societies in the contemporary international system are prepared to find their way toward a new world order, and what distance they are willing to go, will in part be contingent on just how urgent the need for change is perceived and whether problems are approaching crisis proportions and are being experienced at the systemic level. Is this a time of sufficient adversity as to provide adequate impetus to the next stage of global institution building? A "world in crisis" is not a new theme and in fact has been part of our vernacular for so long in the postwar period that it has become an almost banal notion. The litany of sermons sounding the alarm about Armageddon has desensitized many to the existence of any crisis, especially since there has been no concrete, palpable manifestation to galvanize concern—no single event or series of events equivalent to the Great Depression sandwiched between two World Wars experienced in successive decades by an older generation. Instead, what appear to be geographically and temporally isolated disasters have occurred—Chernobyl, the Sahel famine, the oil embargo and subsequent gas lines, the savings and loan debacle in the United States, and other episodes—which produced at most some rumblings of discontent and anxiety and an ill-defined malaise. Carl Kaysen (1990: 63) has stated that "to seek a different system with a more secure and a more humane basis for order is no longer the pursuit of an illusion but a necessary effort toward a necessary goal," yet in some respects the very thought of the "obsolescence of war" (at least among relatively highly developed societies) at a time

---

[14] On the problem of achieving cooperation among large numbers of actors in the international arena, see Oye (1986). On the possibilities for cooperation even among large numbers, see Kahler (1992).

[15] Clark (1989: 59) also quotes Robert Hutchins's musing in the 1940s about world government: The slogan of our faith today must be, world government is necessary and therefore possible." Clark is highly critical of what he calls "the twentieth-century neo-Kantians."

when "the long peace" has eventuated in the end of the Cold War may translate into a sense of relief and complacency rather than any reformist imperative.

Still, even if the national security state has seemingly bought itself some time, humanity's sense of satisfaction may well prove short-lived given the evolving specter of a nuclear-based unit-veto system in East Asia and other weapons proliferation nightmares on the horizon. Moreover, there is the growing dysfunctionality of the national welfare state, a condition which lies at the core of the "turbulence" that James Rosenau (1990) sees in contemporary world politics. He comments at length on the "declining effectiveness" of governments. Although he confesses this is largely an "assertion" in need of verification "with systematic data" (1990: 398), such data are being gathered in many quarters (Snyder, Hermann, and Lasswell, 1976; Jacobson, 1984, with an updated edition forthcoming; Sullivan, 1991; and Rochester, 1992).

As adversity arises, people and societies become increasingly disposed toward change. Today there would seem to be a general bias in the direction of change in the international system at large, given the fact that all categories of states are witnessing evidence of growing malfunctioning of their economic–social–ecological systems.[16] Small changes are ordinarily preferred to big changes, so that one's first inclination is to look for correctives closest to home, internally within one's borders rather than externally in the international realm and regionally rather than globally. Even if the international system is primed for change, as seems to be the case, states will have to be convinced that the failing of international governance structures are at the root of current problems—or that, whatever the explanation, the overhauling of these structures offers a way out—before the kind of innovative macro-level institution building I have alluded to can materialize. Assuming one values international institution building, things may have to get still worse before they can get better. Considering the nature of the high-case and base-case scenarios presented by the World Bank and other bodies in projecting trends in the 1990s, the future prognosis for most countries is at best guarded (World Bank, 1989: 20–21; UN DIESA, 1992; IMF, 1991).

As matters worsen, the paradox is that there is the opportunity not only for increased international institution building but also massive conflagration. If it is true that "history does not move forward without catastrophe" (Pollard, 1971: 81), a point can be reached at which crisis becomes immobilizing and destructive

---

[16] Obvious exceptions on some indicators can be cited. For example, China's real gross national product in 1992 grew 7 percent and industrial output 14 percent. At the same time, as one intelligence analysis (U.S. CIA, 1992: iii–iv) indicated, "these positive trends masked some fundamental weaknesses," such as a state budget deficit "which increased at a 22 percent average annual rate since 1987 to reach a record $12.2 billion (in 1992)." According to the UN *World Economic Survey, 1992*, the global economy's growth rate in 1991 fell to zero from 1 percent in 1990, 3 percent in 1989, and 4.3 percent in 1988. There was no improvement in 1992, with neither the United States nor the European Community nor Japan exceeding 2 percent growth, Eastern Europe and the former Soviet Union seeing output drop by 10 percent, and most Third World economies remaining stagnant.

rather than releasing creative energies. To quote Reinhold Niebuhr (1949: 97), "Undoubtedly, fear may be a creative force. . . . But the creative power of fear does not increase in proportion to its intensity." Whether the institution-building path is followed will depend not merely on the degree of stimulation furnished by crisis but on other variables as well. Power and will need to be added as additional elements in the equation of system change.

The contemporary international system that forms the organizational environment of the UN is like a great double-edged sword having various properties that pose constraints as well as opportunities for enhanced institution building at the global level. The very problems that recently have afflicted the United States and other states and that ostensibly have created in the system a stronger inclination to countenance change have at the same time sapped the power of many actors who might be candidates for a custodial role. However, despite the end of the superpower era and a trend toward diffusion of power, there has hardly been a leveling of capabilities in the system; just eight states constitute a virtual proprietorship over the "policing" instruments in the world body politic (as measured by their share of global arms expenditures and manpower levels), while also accounting for seventy percent of the planetary economic product and—relevant to legitimacy considerations and the use of soft power—well over a majority of the world's population.[17] What has been lost in power concentration has been more than offset by the reduced ridigity of alignments allowing more creative possibilities for an enlightened concert-of-power approach to international governance.[18] While "loss of control" has thrown into question the continued capacity of sovereign governments to engage in purposive, goal-directed behavior, including international institution building, it has also raised the salience of governance issues and perhaps the willingness of national governments to reexamine existing arrangements. One could argue based on a realist analysis that, insofar as IGOs represent not so much precursors to world government but rather adaptations of the Westphalian state system designed to make world government unnecessary, as international organizations go, so goes the state system in which the major states have the largest stake; as Lynn Miller notes (1990: 29), "it is *their* system" for the most part. Even though the stakes have become diffused, and no one actor may have a singularly vested interest in promoting global order as much as in the past, there would appear to be

[17] An analysis of current military, economic, and demographic power is undertaken in Rochester (1993). Among recent writings that have cautioned against exaggerating the extent to which power has become diffused in the international system, particularly the loss of American power, see Nye (1990) and Russett (1985).

[18] The GLOBUS project, which created a "political world model" out of twenty-five states "representing examples of industrialized and developing countries, western and non-western, noncommunist and communist-ruled" and accounting for "75 percent of the world's population, 80 percent of its income, and 85 percent of its armaments" is suggestive of the kind of critical mass of power that might be mobilizable. See Bremer (1987).

enough at stake for some subset of states to invest the necessary resources and provide the collective good represented by international institution building.[19]

IMPLICATIONS FOR UN REFORM

In the United Nations itself, the impetus for change provided by the collapse of the postwar order (along with the familiar categories and assumptions that colored world politics for the past half-century) contends with "restructuring fatigue" (Kaufmann and Schrijver, 1990: 55) fostered by years of reform failure. While there are persuasive arguments to be made against Charter revision of any kind, particularly given the historical record of aversion to constitutional change in the UN and the cumbersome nature of the amendment process, it seems rather dogmatic to assume that the Charter is completely off the bargaining table. If anything, the prospect of close to 200 states (including numerous "ministates" or "statelets") crowding the global bargaining table has created growing pressures against the kind of rigid state-centric egalitarianism embodied in one-state-one-vote formulas as in the General Assembly, so that associate or consultative membership status, weighted voting formulas, and other such devices are likely to be the wave of the future as long as states continue to feel a need for global IGOs.

George Bush, in his address to the 46th General Assembly, called for a "Pax Universalis" in place of a "Pax Americana" or any other such narrowly grounded peace—a new order "built upon shared responsibilities and aspiration" (*New York Times*, 1991: A14). While a Pax Universalis may be a "quixotic crusade" (Carpenter, 1991: 39), the prospects for peace and peaceful change can be enhanced greatly by the collective leadership provided by a dominant coalition of states able and willing to steer the system in a manner that offers incentives for others to follow. The coalition must be broad enough to possess sufficient material resources to support the demand load and, at the symbolic level, to make a reasonable claim to the aura of legitimacy, but not so broad as to be incapable of action and susceptible to breaking down.[20]

Economic resource transfers will be especially critical. Coalition members will not only have to pay their full assessments as currently calculated but

---

[19] For an analysis of "will," see Rochester (1993). On American will in particular, Hedley Bull once wrote: "The problem America presents for us is not, as so many Americans appear to think, the relative decline of its power, but the decline of its capacity for sound judgment and leadership" (cited in Strange, 1985). Kissinger (1993: 45) has pointed out that American willingness to lead will be severely tested in a wholly strange environment in which for the first time the United States today finds itself in a world that it can neither dominate nor withdraw from.

[20] Cox and Jacobson (1973: 435–36) stated in their pioneering work on IGO decision making that although "any significant future growth or task expansion of international organization is likely to be through [an] oligarchic model," in time "there is no reason to believe that the oligarchic model cannot be transformed in new ways toward a broader diffusion of influence."

must be prepared to accept a bigger burden, both to provide necessary side-payments to the bulk of the UN membership (in the form of debt relief or some other quid pro quo) to attract initial support for reforms as well as to maintain a reformed system once it is in place. Given the magnitude of the financial requirements and the weakened state of many economies, notably that of the United States and Russia, only a conglomerate of several states can hope to do the job. Major donor states might be willing to overcome the pattern of delinquency in paying their assessed dues—the United States, which is over $1 billion in arrears, remains the largest culprit responsible for the UN's current financial crisis—and might be willing to convert more voluntary funding into assessed funding, thereby putting UN budgets on much more solid footing, if they could be assured of greater control over the budget process. Such assurances are close to being realized through the recent budget reforms produced by the Group of 18 exercise. The UN financial crisis remains at bottom a political crisis. While the sums of money consumed by the UN system appear staggering, they are still miniscule as a percentage of the gross national product of any one lead donor, much less the aggregate GNPs of the ten largest benefactors. Consequently it is hardly the case that the international system has reached its limit in terms of its capacity to generate additional resources to support global organization.

Some states are better positioned than others as candidates to participate in a dominant coalition in support of UN reform, owing not just to economic clout but to other attributes. It is unthinkable not to make every effort to include China, for example, in such a coalition, even if China currently pays less than one percent of the UN budget. Different states will bring different assets and different responsibilities to a leadership coalition. There may also be different expectations. Some will settle for a role in power steering by virtue of being accorded proper standing on the Committee for Program and Coordination and/or a truncated Economic and Social Council (ECOSOC), while others may insist on the ultimate leadership trophy, that is, permanent membership on the Security Council. I hesitate to bring Security Council reform into the discussion since mere mention of it puts one immediately on the most treacherous constitutional terrain. However, the postwar order has now been so thoroughly changed that the concert of five permanent council members has an inherent impermanence about it. It seems a foregone conclusion that an institutional arrangement which was increasingly a glaring anomaly in world politics as the postwar era progressed and has become even more so in the post-postwar era cannot survive much longer into the future. It may or may not be worth at this time inviting the kind of wrenching Charter debate that would ensue over Security Council reform. One can at least think out loud what the Security Council of the future might look like.

The conventional wisdom presumes that any attempt to make additions to the roster of permanent members on the Security Council is doomed to defeat or, if successful, could tear the organization apart in the process, owing to two basic facts of life. One is the difficulty of getting the present Big Five to forego their use of the veto and permit the admission of new entrants into the permanent membership club when the effect is to diminish the elite status of the charter members. The second is the difficulty of formally including certain specified countries in an expanded council permanent membership club without alienating those who are excluded.

Regarding the first point, given their own strained global organizational support capabilities, the United States and other members of the Big Five might well welcome others into the fold who would be willing to share the leadership burden, as long as they could screen potential applicants. From the perspective of the Big Five, Security Council enlargement might have to be the price paid to co-opt both some wealthy states to assume a bigger donor role and some Third World states whose collaboration is critical to dealing with environmental or other issues. (For example, Brazil and India would be attractive candidates not only because of their demographic weight but also because of their strategic relevance to the forging of workable global regimes to combat greenhouse warming and to regulate arms exports.)

In reference to the second point, the cost of membership in the club can be expected to be high enough that not every state would clamor to join. There have been greater acts of self-abnegation performed by states than passing up opportunities for membership on the Security Council, notably the willingness—at least up to now—on the part of over 100 non-nuclear countries (including several with nuclear weapons potential) to do without what is seemingly an unmatched badge of security and status. The same cost–benefit calculations that have led many states to avoid joining the nuclear club also figure to shape their interest or disinterest in joining other elite clubs.

An expansion of the Security Council to accommodate new permanent members will have to provide for balanced representation of nonpermanent members as well. No matter the size or composition of the council, it is unlikely the UN membership-at-large will consent to grant the body any more competence than it already has to involve the organization in peace and security matters. An enlarged council might in fact serve as a brake against excessive sovereignty-threatening intervention by the UN, while providing enhanced legitimacy where action is approved. In the immediate term there might be a transition period allowing for different categories of Security Council membership, perhaps along the lines of the Japanese proposal to add six new permanent seats without veto power.

Collective security will remain a difficult concept to operationalize, for the same reasons that have always obtained, namely the problematical assumptions that (1) it is easy to define aggression and assign culpability, (2) alignments will remain sufficiently fluid and flexible and alliance commitments unencumbering so as to permit the mobilization of grand coalitions against aggressors, and (3) a grand coalition can be formed that will invariably be at least equal to or superior to any aggressors' forces. It continues to be hard to envision legally-formally or otherwise how the UN might be used to counter aggression committed by, say, the United States. Aside from these constraints, one must add that "the doctrine of collective security enshrined in the UN charter is state-centric, applicable when borders are crossed [as in the case of the Gulf war] but not when force is used against peoples within a state [as in Bosnia]" (Nye, 1992: 90). Notwithstanding the impressive demonstration of collective security possibilities in cases of interstate aggression provided by the Gulf war experience, the latter may not be easily replicable if only because the victors were the beneficiaries of an unusually propitious combination of circumstances (ranging from easily negotiable terrain to almost universal condemnation of the aggressor for violating the most elemental norm of international conduct that had been religiously observed since World War II). While collective security (under Chapter VII of the Charter) is likely to fall short of Wilsonian expectations, there is greater hope for peaceful settlement in intrastate and interstate conflicts—either preventive diplomacy prior to the onset of hostilities or peacemaking in the midst of hostilities (under Chapter VI)—as well as peacekeeping (Boutros-Ghali, 1992; Urquhart and Childers, 1990; Blechman and Durch, 1992; Peck, 1993).[21]

Even if the world is not quite ready for Security Council reform, what about ECOSOC and other parts of the UN system? There have been shifting views in recent years as to whether the organization should be (and can be) primarily looked to and relied on to address "war–peace" concerns as opposed to "other" concerns.[22] Although, as Harold Jacobson (1984: 212) notes, "historically, the first goal of early IGOs was to promote economic growth," Claude (1986: 2) has noted that "the organizing movement of the twentieth century can be interpreted as a reaction to the increasingly terrible consequences of armed conflict." How high-politics, peace and security concerns relate to low-politics, functional, welfare concerns, and what might be the proper place of the UN in these respective areas, have become somewhat muddled as the conceptual distinctions themselves have become blurred.

Lip service continues to be paid to the need for international organizations such as the UN to address both sets of issues, based on the link between physical and structural violence (alternatively phrased as "peacekeeping" and "peace-building" and the like). However, where once it was a given that the second set of issues offered the greater growth potential for the UN—based on the assumption shared by functionalists and nonfunctionalists alike that an international organization's ease and effectiveness in forging collaboration was likely to be inversely related to its degree of involvement in matters touching the core interests of states—this bit of conventional wisdom has now been turned on its head. In a stunning role reversal at odds with both the theory

[21] Nye (1992: 93), in contemplating "a UN rapid deployment force of 60,000 troops formed from earmarked brigades from a dozen countries" that could be used for both peacekeeping and peace enforcement purposes, acknowledges that "an idea that would have been silly or utopian during the Cold War suddenly becomes worth detailed practical examination in the aftermath of the Cold War and Gulf War."

[22] The reference to the "other UN" is found in Gregg (1972: 221).

of international organization and the practice of the UN historically (especially throughout much of the 1980s), the tractability of problems, the utility of the UN, and the prospects for institutional reform in the 1990s are being deemed greater in the war–peace area than in other areas, notably in the field of economic development. Two observers have summed up this situation in commenting that "the UN has become a Janus-like system of two faces—the UN of peace and security, relatively purposeful and effective, to which influential governments pay active and growing attention; and the UN of economic and social affairs, halting, hortatory, and often ignored by powers great and small" (Whitehead and Laurenti, 1991: 18).[23]

Again, one must be mindful of the pitfalls of overreacting to the latest developments, either exaggerating the promise of the UN in the war–peace area or dismissing it in the economic, social, and technical realm. If it was premature to write off the UN in the former domain at the start of the 1980s, it seems premature as well to do so in the latter domain at the end of the 1990s.[24] It may be true that more than ever there is no "sheltered area of concordant interests [in which] we are vouchsafed the privilege of warming up the motors of international collaboration . . ., getting off to an easy start and building up momentum for crashing the barriers of conflicting interests that interpose between us and the ideal of world order" (Claude, 1986: 399). Yet the basic logic of functionalism still would appear to have considerable validity.

One might envision the UN as a regime-processing center or, more ambitiously, as a fulcrum for "global policy" (Soroos, 1986; Rochester, 1990). As realists and neorealists are quick to point out, not all concerns are global in scope or require organizational solutions. One might reason that it is precisely the task of global policy to sort these matters out. The UN proper, as distinct from the specialized agencies, is uniquely situated to furnish the necessary filtering apparatus for engaging the international system in policy-relevant political–intellectual routines at the system-wide level, permitting a determination of how much globalism and institutionalism is optimal for the system. In other words, rather than starting with a priori anti-institutionalist and antiglobalist presumptions regarding the parameters of international problem solving, the UN might be viewed as a general facilitator of decisions by the international community as to what type of regime instrument is possible and

---

[23] Puchala and Coate in their interviews have found that "the [recent] enthusiasm and optimism of the peacekeepers differ markedly from the frustration and pessimism of the international developers" (1989: 45).

[24] Consider the unfortunate timing of the major UN study project undertaken by the United Nations Association-USA in the mid-1980s, at a time when the UN was experiencing a nadir in terms of its performance in the war–peace area. The UNA study *Successor Vision*, published in 1987 just prior to the end of the Cold War, assumed that "where UN peace and security mechanisms are concerned, major structural changes will not yield the sort of results anticipated in the realm of social, economic, and humanitarian affairs" (UNA-USA, 1987: 94).

desirable in a given problem-area (in terms of norms, rules, organizations, programs, or other outputs) as well as what the regime scope might be (global or subglobal). Present references to the "nuclear proliferation regime" or "the monetary regime" have the air of impressive accomplishments engineered by the international system in response to common problems. They would be all the more impressive if they could more rightly claim to be the fruits of policy—conscious, deliberate acts of creation and remaking that stretch the bounds of intelligent collaboration to the fullest extent imaginable. Such an image of the UN is consistent with current calls for "practical internationalism" (Gardner, 1988), yet at the same time offers a more expansive vision as a basis for framing the debate over institutional reform. In this way the UN might furnish an element of central guidance compatible with the systemic environment in which it is likely to operate into the next century, providing a single framework whereby parochialism (ranging from unilateralism to subglobal multilateralism) and pragmatism (including informal as well as formal modes of cooperation) can safely flourish.

CONCLUSION

The future of the UN can be captured in three possible scenarios. One scenario is that the organization will miss the current window of opportunity, will decline further, and maybe disappear as the League of Nations did. A second is that it will be supported enough by the membership to at least muddle through. The third is that it will experience organizational growth and be an engine for the political development of the international system, contributing to "the development of long-term viability for the states . . . in the system" (Young, 1968: 903). The second scenario seems more realistic than the first. Short of a systemwide, great-power war, which in the nuclear age would almost surely be the *last* crisis, the UN is not likely to suffer the fate of the League. As for the third scenario, it will depend on whether the "crisis of multilateralism" becomes perceived and felt more deeply—sufficiently to energize the major actors' willingness to have the UN do more than muddle through, but not so much as to render them incapable of action.[25]

International organization scholars may even be able to play at least a modest role here. The main raison d'être of the international organization

---

[25] Rosenau (1992), in an offshoot of his *Turbulence* book that examines the implications of present trends for the UN, sees relatively few changes in store for the UN. The few UN reform proposals he offers do not touch the basic political arrangements. For example, he suggests that it may be possible in the future to establish a UN mission (an embassy of sorts) in every nation-state, although it is hard to see how this differs much from the already extant reality of a UN resident representative present in virtually every country. He also suggests the possibility of UN ambassadors-at-large.

field over the years has been to provide a base of scholarship that can help inform and guide the practice of international collaboration. The problem with much contemporary "IO" scholarship is that as the field has sought to distance itself from its idealist past and to become more firmly grounded in science and reality testing, it has become further removed from the real-world institutions in which practitioners operate. The gap between international organizational phenomena studied by academics and those experienced by policymakers continues to widen as few explicit connections are made between theory and practice.

No greater challenge exists for students of international organization than that posed by the search for world order through global institution building, which finds its most concrete expression today in the form of the United Nations. Serious scholarship is normally defined by the degree of intellectual ferment and hard-nosed sobriety one brings to a subject. The subject of the UN in recent times has inspired widespread indifference and ridicule, with scholars tending to steer clear lest they be branded guilty of indulging in "institutionalist approaches of yesteryear" (Kratochwil and Ruggie, 1986: 772) or utopian futurism and risk pariah status in the international relations fraternity akin to some states in the international community. Excessive use of the terms "earth" and "planet" can damage one's credibility. There is the caveat that global international organization has become too large and unwieldy to be subjected to either serious scientific inquiry or social engineering. It is true that the world does not revolve around governments making "great global choices among grand alternatives" (Dahl, 1955: 46). Policymakers, Ruggie notes (1989: 32), "do not get to choose on the future of the state system; they confront choices on exchange rates, . . . terrorist attacks on airport lobbies and embassy compounds, and garbage that floats down a river or is transported through the air. If change comes it will be the product of micro practices. Hence, if we want to understand change or help to shape it, it is to these micro practices that we should look." Was the creation of the UN in 1945, like the League before it, a "micro practice"? If so, are there other such practices we should look to?

Nobody planned the national welfare state, which has been the dominant political structure of the twentieth century. It was the resultant of historical forces pushed along by myriad individual decisions and accumulated learning. If a global security-community comes to pass, it will not be planned but will emerge also as a product of historical forces that likewise can be nudged along in small ways if we have the knowledge and will to do so. There will always be an element of faith in our quest, although as John Herz (1959: 305) said in his requiem for the territorial-state, "It is not wishful thinking that leads us on, but an ever so faint ray of hope that that which is not entirely impossible will emerge as real." One can take heart in the old saw that most revolutions on their eve seem unimaginable and on the morning after seem to have been inevitable.[26] Just five years after the Red Army Band and Chorus was heard belting out "God Bless America" in Washington, D.C., the light is still flickering, however faintly.

REFERENCES

Academic Council on the United Nations System. (1987) *Strengthening the Study of International Organizations.* Hanover, N.H.: Academic Council of the United Nations System.

Axelrod, Robert, and Robert O. Keohane. (1985) "Achieving Cooperation under Anarchy: Strategies and Institutions," *World Politics* 38 (October): 226–54.

Blechman, Barry M., and William J. Durch. (1992) *Keeping the Peace: The United Nations in the Emerging World Order.* Washington, D.C.: The Henry L. Stimson Center.

Boulding, Kenneth. (1977) Remarks at Annual Meeting of International Studies Association, March 16, St. Louis.

Boutros-Ghali, Boutros. (1992) "An Agenda for Peace," report of the UN Secretary-General submitted to the UN Security Council, June 17 (S/24111).

Bremer, Stuart. (1987) *The Globus Model.* Boulder, Colo.: Westview Press.

Burton, John W., et al. (1974) *The Study of World Society.* Pittsburgh: International Studies Association.

Buzan, Barry. (1983) *People, States, and Fear.* Chapel Hill: University of North Carolina Press.

Carpenter, Ted Galen. (1991) "The New World Disorder," *Foreign Policy* 84 (Fall): 24–39.

Carr, E. H. (1939) *The Twenty Years' Crisis, 1919–1939.* London: Macmillan.

Clark, Ian. (1989) *The Hierarchy of States: Reform and Resistance in the International Order.* Cambridge: Cambridge University Press.

Claude, Inis L., Jr. (1986) "The Record of International Organizations in the Twentieth Century," Tamkang Chair Lecture Series, No. 64, Tamkang University, Taiwan.

————. (1981) "Comment," *International Studies Quarterly* 25 (June): 198–200.

————. (1956) *Swords into Plowshares.* New York: Random House.

Cox, Robert, and Harold K. Jacobson. (1983) *The Anatomy of Influence: Decisionmaking in International Organizations.* New Haven, Conn.: Yale University Press.

Dahl, Robert A. (1955) *Research Frontiers in Politics and Government.* Washington, D.C.: Brookings Institution.

Fukuyama, Francis. (1989) "The End of History," *The National Interest* 16 (Summer): 3–16.

Gallorotti, Guillo. (1991) "The Limits of International Organization: Systematic Failure in the Management of International Relations," *International Organization* 45 (Spring): 183–220.

Gardner, Richard. (1988) "Practical Internationalism," *Foreign Affairs* 66 (Spring): 827–45.

---

[26] One is also reminded of Winston Churchill's 1936 comments regarding the "spacious conception" of the League of Nations: "You must not underrate the force which these ideas exert. . . . One does not know how these seeds are planted by the winds of the centuries in the hearts of the working people" (cited in Hazzard, 1989: 76).

Gregg, Robert W. (1972) "UN Economic, Social, and Technical Activities," pp. 218–69 in James Barros, ed., *The United Nations: Past, Present, and Future*. New York: Free Press.

Grieco, Joseph. (1988) "Anarchy and the Limits of Cooperation," *International Organization* 42 (Summer): 486–507.

Hazzard, Shirley. (1989) "Breaking Faith," *The New Yorker* (September 25): 63–99.

Herz, John H. (1959) *International Politics in the Atomic Age*. New York: Columbia University Press.

Hoffmann, Stanley. (1978) *Primacy or World Order*. New York: McGraw-Hill.

International Monetary Fund (IMF). (1991) *World Economic Outlook*. Washington, D.C.: IMF.

Jacobson, Harold K. (1984) *Networks of Interdependence*, 2nd ed. New York: Knopf.

Jacobson, Harold K., William M. Reisinger, and Todd Mathers. (1986) "National Entanglements in International Governmental Organizations," *American Political Science Review* 80 (March): 141–59.

Kahler, Miles. (1992) "Multilateralism with Small and Large Numbers," *International Organization* 46 (Summer): 681–708.

Kaufmann, Johan, and Nico Schrijver. (1990) *Changing Global Needs: Expanding Roles for the United Nations System*. Hanover, N.H.: Academic Council of the United Nations System.

Kaysen, Carl. (1990) "Is War Obsolete?" *International Security* 14 (Spring): 42–64.

Kegley, Charles W., Jr. (1993) "The Neoidealist Moment in International Studies? Realist Myths and New International Realities," presidential address presented at the Annual Meeting of International Studies Association, March 26, Acapulco.

Kennedy, David. (1987) "The Move to Institutions," *Cardozo Law Review* 8 (April): 841–988.

Keohane, Robert O. (1984) *After Hegemony: Cooperation and Discord in the World Political Economy*. Princeton, N.J.: Princeton University Press.

Keohane, Robert O., and Joseph S. Nye. (1989) *Power and Interdependence*, 2nd ed. Boston: Scott, Foresman.

———. (1985) "Two Cheers for Multilateralism," *Foreign Policy* 60 (Fall): 148–67.

Kissinger, Henry. (1993) "Clinton and the World," *Newsweek* (February 1): 45–47.

———. (1973) "News Conference of November 21," *U.S. Department of State Bulletin* 69 (December 10): 701–11.

Kratochwil, Friedrich, and John G. Ruggie. (1986) "International Organization: A State of the Art on an Art of the State," *International Organization* 40 (Autumn): 754–75.

Kupchan, Charles A., and Clifford A. Kupchan. (1992) "A New Concert for Europe," pp. 249–67 in Graham Allison and Gregory F. Treverton, eds., *Rethinking America's Security*. New York: Norton.

Mearsheimer, John J. (1990) "Why We Will Soon Miss the Cold War," *The Atlantic* 266 (August): 35–50.

Miller, Lynn. (1990) *Global Order*. Boulder, Colo.: Westview Press.

New York Times. (1991) "Excerpts from Bush's Address to General Assembly: For a 'Pax Universalis'" (September 24): A14.

New York Times. (1990) Editorial (September 24): 23.

Niebuhr, Reinhold. (1949) "The Myth of World Government," *The Nation* (March 16): 97–101.

Nye, Joseph S. Jr. (1992) "What New World Order?" *Foreign Affairs* (Spring): 83–96.

———. (1990) *Bound to Lead: The Changing Nature of American Power*. New York: Basic Books.

Oye, Kenneth A., ed. (1986) *Cooperation under Anarchy*. Princeton, N.J.: Princeton University Press.

Peck, Connie. (1993) "Preventive Diplomacy: A Perspective for the 1990s," Occasional Paper XIII in the series published by the Ralph Bunche Institute on the United Nations, New York City.

Pirages, Dennis. (1989) *Global Technopolitics*. Pacific Grove, Calif.: Brooks/Cole.

Plano, Jack C., and Roy Olton. (1979) *The International Relations Dictionary*, 2nd ed. Kalamazoo, Mich.: New Issues.

Pollard, S. (1971) *The Idea of Progress*. Harmondsworth, U.K.: Penguin.

Puchala, Donald J., and Roger A. Coate. (1989) *The Challenge of Relevance: The United Nations in a Changing World Environment*. Hanover, N.H.: Academic Council on the United Nations System.

Rochester, J. Martin. (1993) *Waiting for the Millennium: The United Nations and the Future of World Order*. Columbia: University of South Carolina Press.

———. (1992) "The Contemporary International System: Is There a Growing Crisis?" Center for International Studies, Occasional Paper Series, University of Missouri-St. Louis.

———. (1990) "Global Policy and the Future of the UN," *Journal of Peace Research* 27 (May): 141–54.

———. (1986) "The Rise and Fall of International Organization as a Field of Study," *International Organization* 40 (Autumn): 777–813.

Romulo, Carlos. (1954) "The UN Is Dying," *Colliers* (July 23): 32–40.

Rosecrance, Richard. (1992) "A New Concert of Powers," *Foreign Affairs* 71 (Spring): 64–82.

Rosenau, James N. (1992) *The United Nations in a Turbulent World*. Boulder, Colo.: Lynne Rienner.

———. (1990) *Turbulence in World Politics*. Princeton, N.J.: Princeton University Press.

Ruggie, John G. (1993) "Territoriality and Beyond: Problematizing Modernity in International Relations," *International Organization* 47 (Winter): 139–74.

———. (1992) "Multilateralism: The Anatomy of an Institution," *International Organization* 46 (Summer): 567–84.

———. (1989) "International Structure and International Transformation: Space, Time and Method," pp. 21–36 in Ernst-Otto Czempiel and James N. Rosenau, eds., *Global Changes and Theoretical Challenges*. Lexington, Mass.: Lexington Books.

———. (1985) "The United States and the United Nations: Toward a New Realism," *International Organization* 39 (Spring): 343–56.

Russett, Bruce M. (1985) "The Mysterious Case of Vanishing Hegemony; Or Is Mark Twain Really Dead?" *International Organization* 39 (Spring): 207–32.

Russett, Bruce, and James Sutterlin. (1991) "The UN in a New World Order," *Foreign Affairs* 70 (Spring): 69–83.

Sartori, Giovanni. (1965) *Democratic Theory*. New York: Praeger.

Snidal, Duncan. (1985) "The Game Theory of International Politics," *World Politics* 38 (October): 25–57.

Snyder, Richard C., Charles F. Hermann, and Harold D. Lasswell. (1976) "A Global Monitoring System: Appraising the Effects of Government on Human Dignity," *International Studies Quarterly* 20 (June): 221–260.

Soroos, Marvin. (1986) *Beyond Sovereignty: The Challenge of Global Policy*. Columbia: University of South Carolina Press.

Strange, Susan. (1985) "Protectionism and World Politics," *International Organization* 39 (Spring): 233–60.

Sullivan, Michael J., III. (1991) *Measuring Global Values: The Ranking of 162 Countries*. Westport, Conn.: Greenwood Press.

Truman, Harry S. (1945a) Address to the Final Plenary Session of the UN Conference on International Organization, *U.S. Department of State Bulletin* 13 (July 1): 3–4.

———. (1945b) Address to the Opening Session of the UN Conference on International Organization, *U.S. Department of State Bulletin* 12 (April 29): 789–90.

United Nations Association-USA. (1987) *A Successor Vision: The United Nations of Tomorrow*. New York: UNA-USA.

United Nations Department of International Economic and Social Affairs (UN DIESA). (1992) *World Economic Survey, 1992*. New York: UN.

Urquhart, Brian, and Erskine Childers. (1990) "A World in Need of Leadership: Tomorrow's United Nations," *Development Dialogue*: 1–2.

U.S. Central Intelligence Agency. (1992) *The Chinese Economy in 1991 and 1992: Pressure to Revisit Reform Mounts*. Washington, D.C.: U.S. Central Intelligence Agency.

Waldheim, Kurt. (1984) "The United Nations: The Tarnished Image," *Foreign Affairs* 63 (Fall): 93–107.

Waltz, Kenneth W. (1979) *Theory of International Politics*. Reading, Mass.: Addison-Wesley.

Whitehead, John C., and Jeffrey Laurenti. (1991) "The Hydra-Headed UN," *Christian Science Monitor* (May 29): 18.

Will, George F. (1989) "Europe's Second Reformation," *Newsweek* (November 20): 90.

World Bank. (1989) *World Development Report, 1989*. New York: Oxford University Press.

Young, Oran R. (1991) "Political Leadership and Regime Formation: On the Development of Institutions in International Society," *International Organization* 45 (Summer): 281–308.

———. (1989) "Odysseus Twenty-five Years On: Reflections on the Study of International Relations," pp. 69–82 in Joseph R. Kruzel and James N. Rosenau, eds., *Journeys through World Politics*. Lexington, Mass.: Lexington Books.

———. (1982) "Regime Dynamics: The Rise and Fall of International Regimes," *International Organization* 36 (Spring): 277–98.

———. (1980) "International Regimes: Problems of Concept Formation," *World Politics* 32 (April): 331–56.

———. (1968) "The United Nations and the International System," *International Organization* 20 (Autumn): 902–22.

Zacher, Mark. (1991) "The Decaying Pillars of the Westphalian Temple: Implications for International Order and Governance," paper delivered at Annual Meeting of International Studies Association, March 22, Vancouver.

CHAPTER 9

Evolving Patterns of European Integration and Governance: Implications for Theories of World Politics

BARRY B. HUGHES[1]

This volume begins with the premise that humanity may have reached a remarkable point in its history: a defining moment, a time at which it is possible to envision the emergence of liberal ideals as serious challengers to the global organizing principles described by realism. This chapter argues that it is indeed necessary to give very considerable weight to liberalism in attempts to understand a particular phenomenon, that of European integration. It draws heavily on liberalism in interpreting ongoing developments within Europe regarding the evolution of what we here call "complex governance," an emerging pattern of human governance in which the state continues to play a critical role, but in which many other institutions become increasingly important.

In understanding the developing patterns of governance in Europe it is impossible to rely on either simple realist models or simple idealist/liberal ones. A simple realist explanation of European integration would begin with the reaction of the United States and Western Europe to the threat posed by the Soviet Union after World War II. The North Atlantic Treaty Organization (NATO) countries formed their alliance against that superior land power and in the process temporarily brought traditional adversaries France and Germany into the same grouping of countries. Although the main external threat to those Western European countries was the USSR, they also worried about

[1] My thanks to Jack Donnelly for reactions to an earlier draft and to Ritu Vij for research assistance.

U.S. political and economic power. They therefore began to build institutions for Western Europe into a credible "second pillar" within NATO and within the Western economic system.

Logically, the contemporary removal of the Eastern threat to Europe should have relatively clear consequences according to this model. First, the NATO alliance itself should weaken and perhaps eventually collapse, in much the same way that the United Nations alliance against Germany in World War II collapsed and two of its dominant members, the United States and the Soviet Union, began to perceive each other as threats. Second, the withdrawal of significant U.S. power from Europe, because of the United States's own relative weakening as well as the disappearance of a Soviet threat, should undercut the other primary foundation for European integration. German reintegration and German economic expansion into Eastern Europe should then rekindle the concerns of France and others about Germany's potential threat to them. All of this may yet come to pass, but most analysts believe it to be too simplistic an analysis of developments in Western Europe.

In contrast to the simple realist interpretation, we can also outline a simple idealist/liberal one. In that model, Europeans have tired of and learned from centuries of internal conflict and have now put in motion a process of supplanting traditional European states with a European superstate. That process benefits from improved communication and transportation technologies that increasingly tie together the peoples of Europe and the world, in commerce and in other forms of interpersonal contact. The end of the Cold War and the collapse of the Soviet threat need not significantly retard this federalist (or at least confederalist) development; in fact, fear of the very internal European squabbling that the realists anticipate may drive far-sighted European leaders to still greater efforts at integration (for example, the Maastricht Treaty of late 1991). Again, this may be possible, but most analysts believe it to be far too simple an image.

Most analysts and close observers of developments in Europe have long believed that neither a single model nor any easy combination of the two adequately explains or foresees developments in Europe. Instead, an understanding of European integration, and of the evolution of human governance more generally, requires that we consider the interaction between the states and the individual citizens that is at the root of the respective models. A number of strains of integration theory, especially one called neofunctionalism, have attempted to do that. Their interpretations of what has happened and will happen in Europe quickly become much more complex and less definitive than those of the simplistic models.

This chapter will elaborate one such complex interpretation. It begins by giving more flesh to the analytical foundations of the liberal understanding. It then proceeds to interpret developments in Europe based upon that understanding, attempting not to lose sight of the realist insights concerning the importance of the state and its search for security.

LIBERAL GOVERNANCE

Let us imagine for a few minutes that liberalism had indeed triumphed globally and that generally rational but needy and demanding individuals were interacting freely with each other in the world. How might humanity organize its own governance in such a liberal world? That is to ask, what would analytically skilled and demanding citizens require of their government (Rosenau, 1990)? Such individuals would not accord legitimacy to forms of government simply because they had a long history, but rather would insist that government efficiently serve their basic needs, those that they could not reasonably satisfy themselves either individually or in free interaction with other individuals.

What are such needs? Substantively, they fall into categories such as (1) security (the primary reason historically for the existence of states and a collective need that will never disappear), (2) economics (minimally the guarantee of contracts and prevention of restraint of trade, but including also some assistance to economically disadvantaged groups), (3) environmental (the prevention of environmental exploitation and harm by those who do not bear the full costs of such action), and (4) cultural (the preservation and even nurture of various linguistic, religious, and social forms).[2] Analytically, the needs of individuals for government derive from the demand for goods that can only or most effectively be produced jointly (such as security, maintenance of free markets, redistribution of income, and protection of culture) and from the demand for protection against externalities generated by others (although we can conceptualize the demand for security in terms of externalities, we most often think here of environmental issues).

To begin such a consideration of the bases on which individuals in a liberal world would organize their governance is to move toward functionalism, an investigation of the functions that government performs for citizens and efficient structural approaches to performance of those functions. Functionalism has a long history—from Simeon Baldwin (1907) through David Mitrany (1943) and including Robert Keohane (1982)—of exploring how government can better satisfy the functional needs of people.[3] In a simple and somewhat caricatured version, functionalism foresees the movement of government from narrower to broader geographic jurisdictions. Given continued improvements in transportation and communication technology (technological advance drives much functionalist thinking), the scope of human activities does indeed widen, and it becomes increasingly efficient and, in fact, necessary to perform many

---

[2] With respect to this last set of needs, those who express doubts about the wisdom of the commitment of Wilsonian liberalism to collective self-determination as well as to individual freedom neglect the importance of cultural ties for those individuals. The model for self-determination in a liberal world should, of course, be closer to that of Quebec than to that of Bosnia; that is, it should be respectful of minorities within regions of self-determination and respected by peoples outside the region.

[3] Paul Taylor (1975: xix) also noted that functionalism has deep roots in liberal thought.

governmental functions more broadly. These functionalists argue that strengthening higher levels of government, or developing governmental capacity to perform specialized functions ranging from delivering mail to protecting the environment, gradually creates a web of government that will constrain traditional states.

More sophisticated versions of functionalism, notably neofunctionalism, recognize that these developments will not always be smooth (political change tends to be "lumpy") and that political entrepreneurs and visionaries will play key roles in pushing them along. More sophisticated functionalism should, but seldom does, recognize that efficient performance of functions in a liberal world will not always push governance outward in geographic scope. In some cases, especially with respect to issues in the cultural arena, governance may work best with a narrower scope. In many other cases, including the environment, geographic patterns of efficient governance will be highly complex and generally linked to regions that exhibit particular needs (such as watersheds or valleys with common air-quality concerns).

It therefore appears that in a truly liberal world, government would be highly complex, with governmental bodies of varying geographic scope and presumably with diverse resource bases, in a fairly constant state of flux so as to adapt to a technologically and otherwise changing world and to the (what we hope to be progressively improving) understandings and demands of an analytically skilled and highly mobilized population.

LIBERAL GOVERNANCE CONFRONTS THE POWER OF THE STATE

To rudely interrupt our thought experiment, however, liberalism has not triumphed globally, even though it may be posing an increasingly strong challenge to the generally anarchic (and, for liberals, increasingly archaic) state system that realists have long described. If we want to anticipate the future of governance, we must consider how the liberal vision might interact with the world that realists have long described with some accuracy.

Some, looking at the continuing strength of states and at the idealistic movements within Europe, have argued that the only real alternative to the contemporary European state system is a European superstate. The view that political union is the goal of the European Union (EU), formerly the European Community, has its adherents, especially among individuals involved in the process. For instance, Jacques Delors, president of the Commission of the European Union during the implementation of the single market (the big push in the 1980s and early 1990s for a truly common market), frequently urged attention to that goal (and in doing so prodded former Prime Minister Margaret Thatcher to wave caution flags in the name of British statehood). In 1988 Delors forecast that Brussels would eventually make 80 percent of key decisions and leave only 20 percent to state capitals.

Even member states appear to ratify such visions of a superstate when they support political union. For example, at the Paris summit in 1972 members agreed to create a (political) European union. Similarly, in Milan in 1985 a majority approved further discussions on European union (Hinsley, 1989: 1). In the Dublin summit of July 1990, members supported a new conference on political union. Discussions in 1991, culminating at Maastricht, created a treaty on "political union" for signature by member states, all of which have now ratified it.

Others, arguing that to believe in the willingness of states to ever turn over power to a superstate is to misunderstand the essence of states, believe that the future lies in a Europe-wide nation-building process (e.g., Deutsch et al., 1966; Inglehart, 1970). That is, they anticipate the eventual replacement of individual identity with particular states by a primary identity with Europe as a whole and believe that to be the only firm foundation of European integration. Many authors in this tradition foresee the ultimate emergence of a new European nation through a proliferation of transactions (such as trade, communication, and tourism) and through attitudinal transformations. This tradition has had less to say about the institutional structures that might characterize a state of integration.

Yet the data suggest that if either of these two processes are under way (state or nation building), they are at a *very* early stage. Even today, after more than thirty years of effort in Europe, the European Union administers only about 2 percent of the gross domestic product (GDP) of the member states, compared to the 40 percent that the average state controls (Daltrop, 1986: 125).[4] And in 1992 only 14 percent of the citizens in the EU reported that they often think of themselves as European; 51 percent declared that they never so characterize themselves (*Eurobarometer* No. 37, June 1992: A53).[5]

Such evidence calls into question the notions that either a superstate or supernation is really emerging in Europe. The initial Danish rejection of the Maastricht Treaty and, for that matter, the narrow margins of support for it elsewhere in Europe, add further doubt. More fundamentally, however, *the liberal vision itself casts doubt on such an outcome.* Would a superstate really serve the various needs of freely interacting, analytically skilled, and demanding citizens? Sophisticated functionalists have long doubted that it

[4] One could argue that a focus on budget ignores the powerful role of regulation. Yet the total administrative staff of the EU Commission numbers only 12,000 (one-third translators and interpreters), less than that of the French Ministry of Culture (*The Economist*, April 7, 1990: 61) and less than half of the British Department of Trade and Industry (*The Economist*, June 1, 1991: 48); regulatory bureaucracies tend to be very large.

[5] There has, of course, been progress on both state and nation building. As recently as 1977 the EU's institutions controlled only 0.7 percent of combined GDP. And majorities of the population in almost all member states consistently indicate support for European institutions and their strengthening. On the other hand, in 1988 16 percent of the citizens of the EU said that they often thought of themselves as European and only 44 percent reported that they never so characterized themselves (*Eurobarometer* No. 30, October 1988: 7).

would and have presented quite different visions of the future. David Mitrany (1943: 42) sketched his view:

> A territorial union would bind together some interests which are not of common concern to the group, while it would inevitably cut asunder some interests of common concern to the group and those outside it. The only way to avoid that twice-arbitrary surgery is to proceed by means of natural selection, binding together those interests which are common, where they are common, and to the extent to which they are common.

Both the failure of state- and nation-building efforts to proceed as some expected as well as the growing recognition that they may, in fact, not actually be the wave of the liberal future led in the 1970s to disillusionment with theorizing about European integration (Smith and Ray, 1993). They also led to a variety of efforts to outline an alternative vision of the European future, one much more consonant with our introductory thought experiment concerning liberal governance. Ernst Haas most decisively rejected the earlier traditions, arguing that they had three questionable properties:

> (1) the presumed predictability of the institutional outcomes of the integration process; (2) the tendency to treat the region undergoing integration as a self-contained geographical space; (3) the parallel tendency to regard that region's practices of increasing the centralization of joint tasks and concerns as an autonomous process following its own unique rules. (Haas 1976: 175)

Haas (1975, 1976) wrote instead of "asymmetrical overlap," attempting to convey highly complex patterns of governance in which various levels share policy-making responsibilities.

Even earlier, Leon Lindberg and Stuart Scheingold (1970: 307–10) concluded their masterful and eclectic analysis of *Europe's Would-be Polity* with favorable comments on the notions of Walter Yondorf concerning a "sector integrated supranational system." In addition, Donald Puchala (1972) identified similar developments as a "concordance system."[6]

More recently such notions have gone beyond scholars and have entered the public domain. Europeans sometimes refer to "Europe à la carte" or to "variable geometry." Even federalists go a considerable distance in recognizing

---

[6] See also Wolfram Hanrieder (1978). James Rosenau (1990) has written about "cascading interdependence" in a multicentric world. Richard Feinberg and Delia Boylan (1991) wrote of "modular multilateralism." Yale Ferguson and Richard Mansbach (1991: 379) argue that "history reveals a world that has always been a crazy-quilt of polities—foci of authority with varying scope and influence; distinct in some respects and overlapping, layered, and linked in others; competing and cooperating in a quest for allegiance of persons and control of stakes." If this is true, it suggests that the liberal vision elaborated here has long competed with the more realist one of state systems.

the power of this vision by elaborating the principle of "subsidiarity." Anne Daltrop describes it:

> Developments in modern society are leading to the gradual acceptance of a "multi-tiered" approach to government, with functions being carried out at the lowest tier compatible with both efficiency and accessibility for those whose needs it serves. A regional grouping like that of Western Europe can form a unit large enough to act as a necessary balance between the superpowers, but it must give each member state benefits which it can no longer achieve on its own. It must perform only those functions of government which cannot be carried out better at lower levels, closer to the individual citizens. (Daltrop, 1986: 180–81)

We will add to the terminological proliferation by calling this liberal but more realistic image of European integration (and future governance elsewhere) *complex governance*. That term emphasizes that we are talking about long-term structures of governance, not simply about some way-station on the road to traditional federalism in the form of a superstate (as the word integration popularly conveys). It also suggests that important insights into the evolutionary process that generate these structures might come also from a more general "neoliberal institutionalist" literature on interdependence, including the theory of complex interdependence (Keohane and Nye, 1977).

Attempts to synthesize liberalism with realism by positing the growth of a superstate or a supernation give away too much to the state-centrism of realism, on the one hand, while failing to recognize the real durability of states, on the other. It is more insightful to look at the European Union in the context of a larger and more fundamentally liberal evolution in human governance—not as the embryo of a superstate or a supernation, but as one organ, along with states, in the embryo of complex governance.

THE FOUNDATION: RESPECT FOR HUMAN RIGHTS

We have identified a liberal vision of complex governance, a future world of overlapping, multitiered, dynamic governance structures in which the state continues to play a critical role, as do regional institutions like the EU, but in which it becomes more and more difficult to identify dominant institutional structures. How might such an evolution proceed?

Integration theorists have elaborated many of the dynamics important to the interaction of existing structures such as states, citizen needs, policy entrepreneurs (and visionaries like Woodrow Wilson), and newly emergent institutions. For instance, we should cast aside any image of homogeneous "citizen demand." Instead, active interests will competitively seek to define the demand for goods and the appropriate level and form of governance.[7] Neofunctionalists have also drawn our attention to the role that policy entrepreneurs or visionaries play in bringing new structures into being, seldom without the support of large numbers of the citizens that those structures promise to serve. Similarly we should recognize that both old and new institutions themselves will play important roles in reshaping governance. For instance, we might expect to find that the EU would ally itself with levels of governance below the state (those in subregions) in an effort to garner support for its own innovations in governance. A large literature specifies, elaborates, and tests such aspects of what has historically been called integration, but may better be called evolution in governance.

Perhaps most fundamental and important, however, is that a liberal model of governance will only come into being in those regions of the world where existing governmental structures already respect and protect the rights of individuals to fully declare their governmental preferences and to act to transform government according to those preferences. Liberalism posits *freely interacting*, analytically skilled, and demanding citizens.[8] Democracy and the protection of human rights are essential. This suggests that efforts to push forward "integration" in regions that historically have not had democratic traditions or have not strongly protected such rights—whether they be less economically developed, like Central America or East Africa, or more economically developed, like Central and Eastern Europe—are unlikely to succeed (such efforts may, of course, also fail for other reasons). Some market integration may be possible in the absence of this foundation, but even that seems questionable in light of the historic failings of most economic integration efforts outside of Europe.

In part because of the shock caused by their dramatic violation in World War II, human rights have become an important focus of international law in the postwar period. The UN General Assembly approved the Universal Declaration of Human Rights in 1948. Both the International Covenant on Civil and Political Rights and the International Covenant on Economic, Social,

---

[7] The significance of the nongovernmental organization (NGO) role in European integration is controversial. For example, multi-national corporations (MNCs) actively supported the EU Commission in the decision to complete the single market by 1992. In 1983 they formed a Roundtable of European Industrialists, a group that reaches beyond the European Economic Community (its first chair was from Volvo). Wayne Sandholtz and John Zysman (1989) argue that such business pressure was indispensable to the acceptance of the Single European Act. Andrew Moravcsik (1991) disputes such claims, however, positing instead that state leaders (especially French President François Mitterrand) played the key role. Unfortunately, a full evaluation of the role of NGOs (or transnational interest groups) is well beyond the scope of this paper, and we will be able to provide only limited anecdotal information as we examine current European governance.

[8] Universities, those bastions of analytically skilled and demanding individuals, exhibit many of the characteristics of complex governance. The constant reexamination and readjustment of governance structures combined with the difficulty of keeping pace with rapid change in universities suggest some of the costs of complex governance.

and Cultural Rights opened for ratification in 1966 (Riggs and Plano, 1988: 245). John Ruggie (1983: 98) argues, however, that "only in the West European system does the relationship between the state and the individual, as embodied in the notion of human rights, firmly enjoy international legitimacy." And Jack Donnelly (1986) determined that only in Europe is there a strong "enforcement" regime in human rights, as opposed to weaker declaratory or promotional regimes. In contrast, Japan, South Korea, and the Philippines are the only Asian countries to have signed both UN Covenants.

Fourteen countries in Europe signed the European Convention on Human Rights (ECHR) in 1950 (Risopp, 1991). Almost simultaneously, European states created the Council of Europe, a main task of which is promotion of human rights. In 1993 all twelve members of the EU were among the twenty-four signatories of the ECHR. Many signatories incorporate the international rules directly into national legal systems—Greece, Spain, and Portugal have changed their constitutions to assure consistency. With the signing in 1975 of the Final Act of the Conference on Security and Cooperation in Europe (CSCE), thirty-five countries took a significant step toward further expanding the geographic scope within which at least official legal protection exists for basic individual human rights (although the scope and implementation procedures of the CSCE remain weak).

The EU relies upon these governance structures for the protection of human rights that extend considerably beyond the borders of the twelve members. The EU has, however, built on that foundation in its own way. For instance, Article F of the Maastricht Treaty stipulates that protection of human rights and maintenance of democracy are preconditions for membership in the EU (Michalski and Wallace, 1992: 34). Within the European Union, human rights law increasingly allows the individual both to stand up to states and to insist on changes in governance. As early as 1969 citizens of the EU began to use the European Court of Justice (to which individuals, not just states, can bring complaints) to challenge EU law (Risopp, 1991: 43–44).

We could portray human rights as yet another issue-area exhibiting an evolving pattern of governance—one in which the EU has taken an important role, but on which governance extends beyond the current borders of the EU. Human rights is, however, more than simply another issue-area in our discussion of emerging complex governance. The strengthening of regional and even global human rights regimes now provides a basis on which individuals and groups can challenge the traditional perogatives of states (or other levels of governance). Whereas most inter*national* law specifies the rights and obligations of states and leaves little room for individuals (historically it should have been called inter*state* law), human rights law places the individual at the center of attention. As Hedley Bull points out:

> Carried to its logical extreme, the doctrine of human rights and duties under international law is subversive of the whole principle that mankind should

be organized as a society of sovereign states. For, if the rights of each man can be asserted on the world political stage over and against the claims of his state . . . then the position of the state . . . has been subject to challenge. (Bull, 1977: 152)

The next sections of this analysis turn our attention to the patterns of governance that have been built in Europe on these foundations of respect for human rights and democracy. They consider the current patterns of European governance (beyond the state) in each of the substantive issue-areas we identified earlier (culture, economics, security, and environmental quality).[9]

PRESERVATION OF CULTURAL VALUES: NATIONAL/ETHNIC AUTONOMY

Most so-called "nation-states" are actually ethnically heterogeneous states. A study of 132 states found only twelve to be ethnically homogeneous. In twenty-five additional states a core nationality accounted for 90 percent or more of the total population (Jorgensen-Dahl, 1975: 653–54).[10] At the other extreme, the largest ethnic group in thirty-nine states constituted less than 50 percent of the population, and fifty-three states contained five or more significant ethnic groups.

Peoples want to use their own language, read and write their own literature, practice their own religion, and educate their children in their own cultural traditions. One of the most basic functions of democratic government is to facilitate their ability to do these things. Allocating cultural autonomy to geographically concentrated peoples is in principle quite straightforward; national self-determination theoretically allows all such peoples to control their own institutions. In practice, of course, there has long been a perverse tendency of peoples to deny that option to other peoples less numerous or less powerful than themselves (often because of security concerns or overlapping residence patterns).

In the twentieth century the principle of self-determination has motivated large numbers of changes in the institutions of governance, most notably decolonization and the breakup of European empires, both those with overseas holdings and those spread across contiguous nations in Europe. No principle is likely to be more important in determining the future of governance in Europe. And in spite of limited nation building at the European level, the reality is that older national groups are almost certain to retain the dominant loyalties of Europeans for the indefinite future.

---

[9] An earlier version of that discussion was outlined in Barry Hughes (1993).

[10] In a different count Gunnar Nielsson and Ralph Jones (1988: 1) argue that "only 30 of the world's 165 states would meet the test of near congruence between the members of a nation and the inhabitants of a state."

The implications of this are clear. Although other functions of government may move to broader institutions, those (such as education) that ultimately protect national identities will remain at, or be shifted to, local levels. In fact, the European Union, as well as individual states, has increasingly supported the devolution of such governance (Burgess, 1986). Belgium adopted a federal constitution in 1979 providing considerable autonomy to Flanders, Wallonia, and French-speaking Brussels (Daltrop, 1986: 117; Arlett and Sallnow, 1989). A Basque regional government took power in 1980. In the 1980s France granted Corsica its own assembly, and Spain allowed the Catalans, Andalucia, and Galicia to redevelop regional institutions. These peoples often rally around the concept of "subsidiarity," the idea that governance should gravitate to the lowest practical level.

Some of the nationality groups of Europe have advocated an international federalist approach to European governance, in which they, rather than traditional states, would be the basic units. A Bureau of Unrepresented Nations has, in contradiction of the name, represented them in Brussels since 1977. A few European parliamentarians also represent them. Bavaria suggests that a proposed European Senate organize its representation by region (nation), not state. The German Länder are already allowed to observe the Council of Ministers and seek the right to speak. As long as government in Brussels does not threaten, and even supports, local autonomy, some further concentration of governance at the European level is completely compatible with national demands (the EU and regional citizens can join forces in a challenge to the state). But any movement in the EU to centralize functions that threaten cultural autonomy would obviously engender the same intense grass-roots opposition that states have often faced.

ECONOMIC WELFARE

With respect to economic welfare, people place two very general primary demands on government. The first is that it facilitate their acquisition of substantial volumes of goods and services; the second is that it enforce some element of equity in distribution. People place other important (and often only instrumental) economic demands on government, such as protection of labor against abuse by employers or assurance of employment; we will not explore them here. Most important, we will ignore the role that states can play in economic bargaining with other states. If the world is moving toward competition among trade blocs, the EU will have an important mercantilist (realist) role that we do not adequately discuss.

In Europe, many see a connection between the acquisition of goods and the degree to which markets remain open. We therefore consider first the relationship between trade and governance. The primary reason for establishing the European Economic Community was, of course, to facilitate free trade in Europe. While the EU is sufficiently large to create a formidable trading bloc, it remains too geographically restricted to satisfy contemporary demands for free trade. That has been, of course, an important reason for expanding the community over time.

In addition to its own expansion, the EU has served increasingly as a leader in a still larger group of states with an interest in free trade. For example, the former European Community (EC) signed bilateral agreements for free trade with all European Free Trade Association (EFTA) members in 1972, and by 1984 all industrial goods moved tariff-free within the EC–EFTA area (Wallace, 1988). With the reintegration of Eastern European countries into the world economy, it seems nearly certain that additional members will soon join the EC–EFTA free-trade area. Poland, Czechoslovakia, and Hungary signed cooperation agreements with the former EC in late 1991. The new EU also plays an active and, in spite of agricultural issues, a generally supportive role in broader trade forums such as the General Agreement on Tariffs and Trade (GATT). The current boundaries of the EU are in no sense "natural" with respect to free trade.

Beyond the comparatively easy reduction or elimination of tariffs, further efficiency improvements in the combined economies of a set of states require even greater levels of coordination. Jacques Delors has advanced a vision of Europe in terms of three concentric circles. The EU constitutes the innermost circle, the EU and EFTA jointly populate the second (they concluded an agreement in 1991 on a European Economic Area that goes considerably beyond free trade), and the third incorporates those countries plus parts of Eastern Europe, Turkey, Malta, and Cyprus. This image has reopened a debate on the future of the EU that many frame in terms of "widening" versus "deepening."[11] The reality, however, is likely to incorporate both processes and is by no means restricted to the EU. Even within the EU it appears highly probable that groups of states will move toward greater economic coordination, such as monetary union, at different speeds.

Globally the movement toward that greater coordination can be seen in many forums. Within GATT, the Tokyo Round was the first to focus intensive discussion on nontariff barriers to trade, but the Uruguay Round carried the topic much further—it drew attention to what traditionally were considered domestic economic policies (such as agricultural subsidies). Similarly, the Organization for Economic Cooperation and Development (OECD) has investigated the microeconomic question of producer-subsidy equivalents across the agricultural policies of its members. The EU has, of course, gone furthest in reconciling domestic economic policies by deciding to complete a common market by 1992. Economic coordination in the EU is far in advance of that even envisaged elsewhere.[12]

---

[11] *The Economist* (February 3, 1990: 50); *Newsweek* (March 12, 1990: 38–40).
[12] Yet David Llewellyn (1988: 240) argues that on financial integration, "the specifically European dimension is largely irrelevant and overwhelmed by a global dimension."

Notwithstanding the differences in ambition and geographic scope of these efforts, they all have in common the recognition that further economic efficiency gains require both deeper and more extensive coordination of domestic economic policies. There is no reason to expect that the process should stop with the coordination of policies for 12 (EU), 19 (EU plus EFTA), 24 (OECD), 54 (CSCE), or any other fixed number of countries.

Beyond economic coordination, economic groupings can pursue greater equity among their members either in pursuit of strengthened community or as a calculated side-payment to disadvantaged groups in order to encourage their continued participation in structures that have greater efficiency as the primary goal. The pressures for greater equity exist at many levels of political organization. Within states like France, policies target poorer areas like Brittany or southwest France. Within the EU, the European Regional Development Fund has tried since 1975 to assist depressed areas; cross-national transfers have increased since the accession of Greece, Spain, and Portugal. On a broader scale, the EU assists (via trade preferences, aid, and investment) an assortment (sixty-six in 1990) of African, Caribbean, and Pacific states under the Lomé Conventions. Still broader arrangements channel funds from OECD members to countries around the world. In short, there are no obvious or natural boundaries on equity-enhancing schemes—the EU is simply one of several levels of governance with respect to them.

MILITARY SECURITY

Historically, reliance on balance of power among traditional states has dominated European efforts to assure security. Since World War II we see that strategy in the balance between NATO and the Warsaw Pact. The former European Community played a role in this postwar approach to governance in security (helping to define a roughly equal "pillar" in the North Atlantic alliance). In fact, from the realist perspective, this was the primary basis for the creation of the EC. Efforts to make the EC a strong military pole have historically had very limited success, however, beginning with the collapse in 1954 of the proposal for a European Defense Community.

The decline in tension between NATO and the Warsaw Pact during the era of detenté, and the more recent elimination of the threat posed by the former Warsaw Pact, have fundamentally changed the European security environment. The United States is substantially reducing its commitment to European security in the 1990s, requiring Europeans to face the issue of developing new security structures or strengthening old ones.

One early response to this new situation was the meeting of the Ministerial Council of the Western European Union (WEU) in June 1984, which set up a working group to consider the prospects for reactivating the WEU. All EU states except Greece, Denmark, and Ireland are members. So far the WEU remains little more than a shell (with a secretariat of only fifty in 1991). It organized a mine-sweeping operation in the Persian Gulf in 1987, however, and coordinated European involvement in the naval blockade of Iraq in 1990 and 1991. Although France and Germany have suggested desires to strengthen it and ultimately to bind it to the European Union, the United Kingdom and the Netherlands oppose EU–WEU fusion (*The Economist*, February 2, 1991: 48). Some members fear expansion even to Greece because of concerns that the WEU would then involve them in conflicts with Turkey. Thus it appears probable that membership will remain narrower than that of the EU.

A second and very different approach to security, something closer to collective security, has vied with the balance of power in its attractiveness to modern Europeans and helps explain the failure to pursue security cooperation within the EU. Since World War II much attention has specifically focused on controlling rivalry within the Franco–German dyad and on simultaneously expanding the geographic scope of European cooperation. The Council of Europe (now twenty-three members) symbolizes this thrust. Established in 1949 with headquarters on the French–German border in Strasbourg, the council set goals to support European cooperation, pluralistic democracy, and human rights.

With the Helsinki Final Act of 1975, the Conference on Security and Cooperation in Europe (CSCE) suggested the option of a still broader approach to European collective security. The CSCE process explicitly rejects the older bloc-to-bloc and spheres-of-influence approaches to European security. The basket of security measures of the CSCE process initially only emphasized the inviolability of European frontiers. Subsequently the emphasis shifted to peaceful change and interaction, as in the Stockholm Conference on Confidence-Building and Security-Building Measures and Disarmament in Europe (beginning in January 1984). The thrust of agreements on Confidence- and Security-Building Measures (CSBMs) is to move military postures toward nonprovocative defense and thereby control the problem at the root of the security dilemma—that defensive measures by one country can appear potentially offensive to others. This process extends the effort to reduce tensions and to dampen rivalry well beyond the Franco–German dyad and the WEU—it encompasses the critical German–Soviet and U.S.–Soviet dyads as well.

The CSCE now possesses only a rudimentary institutional structure. Yet the promise of the process suggests that provision of military security to Europeans may in part be served by governance with the geographic scope like that of the CSCE (fifty-four countries) rather than by strengthening the EU's political role. Reinforcing that broadening of approach to security, NATO supported in 1991 the establishment of the thirty-seven member North Atlantic Cooperation Council (NACC), bringing in partners from Central and Eastern Europe and from Central Asia. NATO now promotes the concept of "interlocking institutions" (Wörner, 1992), a kind of complex governance in the security arena that specifically links NATO to the UN, the CSCE, and the WEU. Nonetheless, the EU has a role to play even in the CSCE and the new NACC. Member countries have, for instance, coordinated their own positions and thereby been able to take leadership in CSCE sessions (von Groll, 1982).

No single organization is likely to organize the future security environment of Europe. NATO, the EU, the CSCE, the NACC, the WEU, and even the Independent European Programme Group, with its focus on rationalizing military procurement, are likely to share responsibility with states for pluralistic and complex governance in the security arena.

ENVIRONMENTAL QUALITY

Many environmental issues are classic common-property resource problems under conditions of increasing congestion. The geographic scope of the problems depends on how many people potentially have access to the common resource (such as water or air), and the scope of effective governmental arrangements will vary accordingly.

For instance, with respect to seas (both fishing and pollution issues), a wide range of institutional structures has evolved. The North East Atlantic Fisheries Convention of 1954 lists membership appropriate to its area of interest (Freestone and Fleisch, 1983). The Mediterranean Action Plan, sponsored by the United Nations Environmental Programme's (UNEP's) Regional Seas Programme, ties countries around that sea to a variety of cooperative efforts (Haas, 1989). And the countries surrounding the North Sea met in 1987 and again in 1990 to hammer out agreements on the reduction of dumping into that body of water (*The Economist*, March 3, 1990: 55–56).

The EU has had mixed success in dealing with these problems. For instance, the Common Fisheries Policy (CFP) has been highly divisive; debates on the issue were influential in Norway's referendum regarding EU membership (Freestone and Fleisch, 1983: 77). The CFP has, however, generally worked to limit the overfishing of European waters, and it gradually helped the member states reconcile the movement by the United Nations Conference on Law of the Sea (UNCLOS) to 200-mile exclusive economic zones with historic fishing rights in the North Sea. There have been other successes. In 1976 the Council of Ministers agreed on a directive to control discharges of dangerous substances into EU waters (Taylor, Diprose, and Duffy, 1986). The EU has adopted more than one hundred legislative acts on the environment since environmental policy became an issue in 1972 (Johnson and Corcelle, 1989: 2; Fouéré, 1987: 33). These address air, water, waste management, chemicals, noise, and endangered flora and fauna. One should not underestimate the importance of an existing and strong EU institutional structure in making possible interstate cooperation.

On many air and water pollution issues, however, the EU region is inadequately broad to deal with issues that cross the boundaries of European states. The United Nations Economic Commission for Europe has more appropriate geographic representation in many cases. For instance, in 1979 it sponsored the Convention on Long-Range Transboundary Air Pollution, which twenty-seven states ratified by 1989 (Soroos, 1989). Protocols in 1985 and 1988 set specific targets for control of sulphur emissions and nitrogen oxide (French, 1990).[13] Other problems, such as global warming, will require participation by still more. Similarly, the UNEP took the initiative within the Montreal Protocol of 1987 in restricting chemicals that deplete the stratospheric ozone layer (signed initially by twenty-four countries).

The OECD membership list contains most developed and industrial countries and has therefore not surprisingly instituted various studies on the environment. But the OECD may be too large, and its membership too dispersed, to take active leadership on environmental issues—that appears to be a role the EU can better play.[14] It did so by taking the lead in agreeing to completely phase out CFCs. Similarly, a binding directive of the EU in 1988 commits members to reduce significantly the emissions that cause acid rain (French, 1990: 32). The EU's aid program to Eastern Europe will target environmental problems there, as well as economic ones, thus constituting essentially a sidepayment for obtaining Eastern compliance with tougher Western standards.

In sum, the EU does not constitute a suitable structure of governance for most environmental issues. Its geographic scope is frequently too limited or simply inappropriate. Yet it can provide leadership to a broader Europe.

EUROPE AS A MODEL

A quick glance at North America, another region of democratic, pluralistic societies, suggests that we can see the same phenomenon of complex governance emerging there. In the realm of national/ethnic autonomy there is a devolution of governance in Canada driven by the desires of the French-speaking citizenry of Quebec (and by indigenous peoples). At the same time, Canada and the United States are implementing a free-trade area, now extended to Mexico (of which they are demanding much, including evidence of fundamental commitments to human rights).

In the environmental arena, agreements between the traditional states are of considerable importance, but so are regional arrangements such as

---

[13] Only seven of the EU states were among the twenty-one signatories of the sulphur emission protocol (Fouéré, 1987: 36).

[14] The OECD also faces pressures for expansion: Both Eastern European countries and Asian Newly Industrialized Countries (NICs) have expressed interest in membership (*The Economist*, March 3, 1990: 66).

those that link the domestic states and provinces bordering the Great Lakes and the Rio Grande. Traditional structures of governance in security remain largely, but by no means entirely, intact and state-centric (U.S. and Canadian officers staff the North American Air Defense Command in Colorado Springs). Even without the activity and growth of an organization like the EU, complex governance is gestating in North America, as well as in Europe.

CONCLUSIONS

This brief examination of European integration provides considerable support for the argument that the process underway is consistent with an emergence of governance based on liberal ideals. Governmental structures in pluralistic, democratic environments that respect human rights should ultimately adapt to the desires that citizens place on them for efficient production of a variety of public goods (while existing communities and institutions will strongly shape the process of evolution). In general, our review of European integration bears out the expectations for the evolution of what we have called complex governance.

Most fundamental, there is no question that institutional structures have become increasingly differentiated by issue-area and issue; both concentric and overlapping circles appear in the geographic scope of governance. On the issues related to culture or national/ethnic autonomy, some traditional states serve quite well, but a number of smaller national units have actually gained governmental capabilities in postwar Europe. On economic issues, traditional states, the European Community, the European Economic Area (EU plus EFTA), the OECD, and the Bretton Woods institutions (including the World Bank and International Monetary Fund) are interacting to define and redefine governance, most often broadening its scope. In the security arena, states remain predominant, but various European structures (like the WEU and the Council of Europe), broader alliances (notably NATO, extending into a larger group of countries that respect fundamental human rights), and even the CSCE and NACC contribute significantly to the security of European citizens (all more explicitly than does the EU). While there is no reason to believe that other structures will supplant the primary role of the state in this issue-area in the foreseeable future, the integration of the multiple states into other structures facilitates their increasing attention to domestic rather than international security. Finally, on environmental issues, the multiple regional groupings defined by seas, the European Union, the broader European continent (as defined, for example, by the United Nations), and even the CSCE supplement and increasingly supplant state governance.

This review also provides some support for our expectations concerning the dynamics of growth in complex governance. Most notable, the acceptance of human rights and democracy in Europe appears to have provided a foundation for ever more substantial challenges to the roles of existing institutions of governance. The countries into which the growth of complex governance is most likely to expand are those that share a similar foundation (especially those of the European Free Trade Agreement). The failure of Europe to react positively to Turkey's requests for more rapid inclusion may well owe less to the Islamic basis of Turkish society or even to the historic Greek–Turkish animosity than to the somewhat precarious status of human rights in the Kurdish areas of Turkey. In addition, although we have not extensively investigated the role of domestic and international interest groups, even this brief discussion is suggestive of the increasing grass-roots (domestic and transnational) pressure for changes in governance and the increasing responsiveness of existing institutions to it.

Furthermore, the EU has already begun to act as a seed and leader in establishing and strengthening a wide variety of governance structures with broader or at least (in the case of North Sea and Mediterranean pollution problems) alternative membership. It is not clear that the EU's current borders are "rational" for its freely interacting, analytically skilled, and demanding citizens with respect to any of the issues discussed here; nor is there any reason to expect that they ever will be, since the target is a moving one. Often, the natural borders of European governance on economic, security, and environmental issues lie considerably beyond its present membership.[15]

None of this discussion should in any way detract from the critical contributions that the EU has made in all of these issue-areas (or even more from the continuing and fundamental responsibility of states for governance in each). The EU remains the best-developed exemplar of governance above the traditional state. There is clearly reason for further strengthening of its institutions and policy coordination. Nonetheless, there is good reason to step back and view the EU not as the core of a superstate or supernation, but as an especially well-developed element in the embryonic but rapidly evolving phenomenon of complex governance.

One conclusion that we should *not* reach based on this discussion is that it is now time to throw out realism and to embrace liberalism with its alternative explanations of and expectations for world politics. In fact we began with the argument that neither a simplistic realism nor a simplistic and idealistic liberalism provides adequate insight of European integration. While this chapter has elaborated an interpretation of European integration that draws very heavily on liberalism, it has at no point called upon the reader to deny the great continuing importance of states and the logic of their interaction. That interstate interaction could yet fundamentally damage the fragile edifice of complex governance in Europe.

[15] Taking a somewhat more realist perspective, Jeffrey Harrop (1989: 195) argues that expansion of the Union is essentially complete and that its current size already exceeds the "optimal." He argues in terms of the difficulties of agreement among a larger number of more heterogeneous members.

Where democracy and the protection of human rights are well advanced, the importance of liberal insight concerning regional governance is very much evident. This discussion suggests, however, that it will probably be a very long time before governance based on liberalism prevails globally, in part because the prerequisite of strong support for democracy and human rights does not exist widely. The anarchic state system of realists still better describes most of the global system. Nonetheless, the complex governance evolving in large and powerful pockets of the global system demonstrates the growing strength of the liberal vision.

REFERENCES

Arlett, Sarah, and John Sallnow. (1989) "European Centres of Dissent," *Geographical Magazine* (September): 6–12.

Baldwin, Simeon E. (1907) "The International Congresses and Conferences of the Last Century as Forces Working towards the Solidarity of the World," *American Journal of International Law* 1: 565–78.

Bull, Hedley. (1977) *The Anarchical Society: A Study of Order in World Politics*. New York: Columbia University Press.

Burgess, Michael, ed. (1986) *Federalism and Federation in Western Europe*. London: Croom Helm.

Daltrop, Anne. (1986) *Political Realities: Politics and the European Community*, 2nd ed. London: Longman.

Deutsch, Karl W., et al. (1966) "Political Community and the North Atlantic Area," pp. 1–92 in Karl W. Deutsch et al., eds., *International Political Communities*. Garden City, N.Y.: Anchor Books.

Donnelly, Jack. (1986) "International Human Rights: A Regime Analysis," *International Organization* 40 (Summer): 599–642.

Eide, Asbjorn. (1986) "The Human Rights Movement and the Transformation of the International Order," *Alternatives* 11: 367–402.

Feinberg, Richard E., and Delia M. Boylan. (1991) "Modular Multilateralism: U.S. Economic Policy towards Southern Nations in an Age of Uneven Development," pp. 179–206 in Kenneth Oye, Robert Lieber, and Donald Rothchild, eds., *Eagle in a New World*. New York: HarperCollins.

Ferguson, Yale H., and Richard W. Mansbach. (1991) "Between Celebration and Despair: Constructive Suggestions for Future International Theory," *International Studies Quarterly* 35: 363–86.

Fouéré, Erwan. (1987) "Emerging Trends in International Environmental Agreements," pp. 29–41 in John E. Caroll, ed., *International Environmental Diplomacy: The Management and Resolution of Transfrontier Environmental Problems*. Cambridge: Cambridge University Press.

Freestone, David, and Anna Fleish. (1983). "The Common Fisheries Policy," pp. 77–84 in Juliet Lodge, ed., *Institutions and Policies of the European Community*. New York: St. Martin's Press.

French, Hilary F. (1990) *Cleaning the Air: A Global Agenda*. WorldWatch Paper 94 (January). Washington, D.C.: WorldWatch Institute.

Haas, Ernst B. (1976) "Turbulent Fields and the Theory of Regional Integration," *International Organization* 30: 173–212.

———. (1975) *The Obsolescence of Regional Integration Theory.* Berkeley: University of California Press.

———. (1964) *Beyond the Nation-State: Functionalism and International Organization.* Stanford: Calif.: Stanford University Press.

———. (1958) "Persistent Themes in Atlantic and European Unity," *World Politics* 10: 614–29.

Haas, Peter M. (1989) "Do Regimes Matter? Epistemic Communities and Mediterranean Pollution Control," *International Organization* 43: 377–403.

Hanrieder, Wolfram F. (1978) "Dissolving International Politics: Reflections on the Nation-State," *American Political Science Review* 72: 1276–87.

Harrop, Jeffrey. (1989) *The Political Economy of Integration in the European Community.* Aldershot, U.K.: Edward Elgar Publishing, Ltd.

Hinsley, Sir Henry. (1989) "The European Community: A Body-Politic or an Association of States?" *The World Today* 45: 1–3.

Hughes, Barry. (1993) "Delivering the Goods: The EC and the Evolution of Complex Governance," pp. 45–69 in Dale L. Smith and James Lee Ray, eds., *The 1992 Project and the Future of Integration in Europe.* Armonk, N.Y.: M.E. Sharpe.

Inglehart, Ronald. (1970) "Public Opinion and Regional Integration," *International Organization* 24: 764–95.

Johnson, Stanley P., and Guy Corcelle. (1989) *The Environmental Policy of the European Communities.* London: Graham and Trotman.

Jorgensen-Dahl, Arnfinn. (1975) "Forces of Fragmentation in the International System: The Case of Ethno-Nationalism," *Orbis* 19: 652–74.

Keohane, Robert O. (1982) "The Demand for International Regimes," *International Organization* 36: 325–55.

Keohane, Robert O., and Joseph S. Nye. (1977) *Power and Interdependence: World Politics in Transition.* Boston: Little, Brown.

Lindberg, Leon N., and Stuart A. Scheingold. (1970) *Europe's Would-be Polity: Patterns of Change in the European Community.* Englewood Cliffs, N.J.: Prentice-Hall.

Llewellyn, David T. (1988) "Financial Intermediation and Systems: Global Integration," pp. 239–60 in D. E. Fair and C. de Boissieu, eds., *International Monetary and Financial Integration—the European Dimension.* Boston: Kluwer Academic Publishers.

Michalski, Anna, and Helen Wallace. (1992) *The European Community: The Challenge of Enlargement.* London: The Royal Institute of International Affairs.

Mitrany, David. (1943) *A Working Peace System.* London: The Royal Institute of International Affairs.

Moravcsik, Andrew. (1991) "Negotiating the Single European Act: National Interests and Convention Statecraft in the European Community," *International Organization* 45 (Winter): 19–56.

Nielsson, Gunnar, and Ralph Jones. (1988) "From Ethnic Category to Nation: Patterns of Political Mobilization," paper presented at the Annual Meeting of the International Studies Association, St. Louis, Missouri.

Pentland, Charles. (1973) *International Theory and European Integration.* London: Faber and Faber.

Puchala, Donald J. (1988) "The Integration Theorists and the Study of International Relations," pp. 198–215 in Charles W. Kegley Jr. and Eugene R. Wittkopf, eds., *The Global Agenda*, New York: Random House.

———. (1972) "Of Blind Men, Elephants and International Integration," *Journal of Common Market Studies* 10 (March): 267–84.

Rawls, John. (1971) *A Theory of Justice*. Cambridge, Mass.: Harvard University Press.

Riggs, Robert E., and Jack C. Plano. (1988) *The United Nations: International Organization and World Politics*. Chicago: The Dorsey Press.

Risopp, Imke. (1991) *International Regimes—Back-Door to European Political Integration*. Unpublished master's thesis. Graduate School of International Studies, University of Denver.

Rosenau, James N. (1990) *Turbulence in World Politics: A Theory of Change and Continuity*. Princeton, N.J.: Princeton University Press.

Ruggie, John G. (1983) "Human Rights and the Future International Community," *Daedalus* 112 (Fall): 93–110.

Sandholtz, Wayne, and John Zysman. (1989) "1992: Recasting the European Bargain," *World Politics* 42: 95–128.

Smith, Dale L., and James Lee Ray, eds. (1993) *The 1992 Project and the Future of Integration in Europe*. Armonk, N.Y.: M.E. Sharpe.

Soroos, Marvin S. (1989) "Conflict in the Use and Management of International Commons," paper presented at the Tampere Peace Research Institute, Orivesi, Finland.

Taylor, D., G. Diprose, and M. Duffy. (1986) "EC Environmental Policy and the Control of Water Pollution: The Implementation of Directive 76/464 in Perspective," *Journal of Common Market Studies* 24: 225–46.

Taylor, Paul. (1975) "Introduction to David Mitrany," *The Functional Theory of Politics*. New York: St. Martin's Press.

Von Groll, Götz. (1982) "The Nine at the Conference on Security and Cooperation in Europe," pp. 60–68 in David Allen, Reinhardt Rummel, and Wolfgang Wessels, eds., *European Political Cooperation*. Boston: Butterworth Scientific.

Wallace, Helen. (1988) "The European Community and EFTA: One Family or Two?" *The World Today* 44: 177–79.

Wörner, Manfred. (1992) "A Vigorous Alliance—A Motor for Peaceful Change in Europe," *NATO Review* 40 (December): 3–9.

PART III

The Problematic Future Peace: Arms and Commerce as Contributing Factors?

No property of the international arena is given more emphasis in realist thought than the importance of force and security and its control. But theorists have differed greatly about the means to global stability, and these differences are seen clearly in the divergent emphases that realists and liberals give to two potential constraining factors—armaments and trade. Our next two chapters in this book take a fresh look at this old issue.

MILITARY POWER, ITS MANAGEMENT, AND INTERNATIONAL PEACE

To realism, perhaps no factor is more important than the relationship of the distribution of military capabilities and changes in that distribution to global stability. To many neorealists (for example, Mearsheimer, 1990; Waltz, 1992), the global dispersion of military capabilities throughout the system since World War II has contributed to world stability, for those weapons have become too dangerous to use safely. Awareness of this danger, together with the increasing numbers of actors who possess the most destructive weapons, was a bracing tonic, conducive to peace. The realist prescription "if you want peace, prepare for war" *was* seemingly supported by the advent of the longest period of great-power peace in history; to this school of thought (Gaddis, 1991), preparations for war *did* prevent the outbreak of large-scale violence during the Cold War.

In "Swords into Plowshares: Can Fewer Arms Yield More Security?" Robert C. Johansen critically analyzes these realist conclusions and finds the empirical and logical grounds for them lacking. Instead, he shows why liberal theories, drawing on the views of Dante in the fourteenth century, Erasmus in the sixteenth, Grotius in the seventeenth, and Rousseau, Hume, Kant, Paine, and Jefferson in the eighteenth, all reach the opposite conclusion in arguing that the price of settling international disputes by force is too high for both the victors and the vanquished, and why an alternative conception is unavoidable. Summarizing the strains of liberal thinking, Johansen clarifies why "idealist analysis provides criteria for assessing whether a military buildup is the result of perceptions of insecurity or the product of a drive for military supremacy to achieve political objectives by the threat or use of arms" (Kober, 1990: 12); in so doing, Johansen explains why in the liberal account arms competition *reduces* the security of individual countries and international stability generally.

Taking as his test case the superpower arms race during the Cold War, Johansen examines the impact of war preparations on, in succession, (1) the deterrence of war, (2) national security policies, and (3) the evolution of the international system, and he concludes that "one cannot demonstrate that high levels of U.S. (or Soviet) military preparations prevented" a war between them, or even "that the chronic military buildup laid as good a foundation for keeping peace today as might have been laid *without* it." Another lesson, he concludes, might more accurately be inferred—that arms races exacerbate the security dilemma. Johansen suggests why the liberal solution to this problem, embedded in the biblical warning that those who live by the sword shall die by the sword, is supported by strong evidence, as is its logical corollary that international security decreases when arms levels increase.

This assessment thus provides the backdrop to overcome the "intellectual inertia" surrounding this topic by "sketching an alternative to the traditional realist approach." In suggesting how theories of international politics might move "beyond doctrinaire realism," Johansen outlines the usefulness of (1) focusing "on processes of change, rather than on relatively static laws of state behavior," (2) understanding those processes "as social forces that are part of an emerging world society rather than as properties of states," and (3) studying how the processes creatively interact in tension between "pressures for integration, globalization, and centralization, on the one hand," and "forces for differentiation, particularization, fragmentation, and decentralization, on the other." This prescribes an escape from realism and takes Johansen far into the liberal school by concluding that, in the post–Cold War era, "the future of world peace will be influenced if not altogether decided by the extent to which the United States and other countries redirect their policies and institutions toward a deliberate multilateral diplomatic program aimed at ending chronic preparations for war and establishing stronger world institutions capable of presiding over peaceful change and enforcing a less war-prone code of international conduct."

The end of the Cold War has charged this historic liberal path to peace with a new vitality, especially given the recent agreements by the United States and Russia to implement deep cuts in their strategic arsenals. To the extent that these landmark achievements do not unravel and are followed by additional agreements to disarm voluntarily, the realist prophecy that arms reductions are imprudent is likely to be questioned further, and liberal theories about the decreasing utility of arms will be greeted with increasing enthusiasm. An old controversy therefore has re-arisen, and this, Johansen explains, will pull international relations theory into waters that have until recently been infrequently navigated.

Disarmament and arms control have served throughout history as vehicles to maintain (not eliminate) the balance of power. In the realist and neorealist accounts, the distribution of military might is critical to the preservation of the balance of power, which in turn helps to deter the hegemonic aspirations of a preponderant state bent on regional or world conquest. No analyst of the global scene questions the importance of this presupposition today. But, given its repeated history of failure, some authorities (for example, Claude, 1989; Hoffmann, 1992) wonder if an alternative exists to reliance on the balance of power mechanism, which realists assume "is the only possible and desirable option for deterring war" (Negretto, 1993: 517). "The balance of power, it can be argued, is the limit of any realist theory of international relations" since, as Martin Wight (1966) argues, to its vision "there is nothing further to theorize about after the discovery of the repetitive mechanisms of the balance of power" (Rosenberg, 1990: 285). In contrast to the liberal orientation, some forms of cooperation can ameliorate, perhaps even replace, balance of power jockeying for position and prominence.[1] This possibility is the object of analysis in this book's next assessment.

COMMERCE AND INTERNATIONAL CONDUCT

Lifted from the pages of Woodrow Wilson and, well before him, Immanuel Kant, Adam Smith, Karl Marx, and Richard Cobden is the liberal idea that international political relations are inextricably tied to international economic conditions and that freedom in the latter domain can facilitate freedom and peace in the former domain. As noted above, this idea has also gained re-newed currency in today's economically interdependent world that harbors hope for cooperation (Gasiorowski, 1986) alongside the fear that economic interdependence will operate as the breeding bed for instability (Uchitel, 1993). Liberal economic theories of international relations, such as those

---

[1] Yet, as Stanley Kober (1990: 13) clarifies, "It is incorrect . . . to say that idealism rejects the balance of power. In fact, idealism recognizes that in the face of a military threat, there is no alternative to maintaining a balance, or even a preponderance, of power. What idealism rejects is the idea that international peace is solely the product of a balance of power. For the idealist, a country can have friends as well as interests. The ultimate objective of idealism is to broaden the circle of friendship by fostering the spread of democratic values and institutions. In the meantime, recognizing the dangers of the world as it exists, idealism provides a mechanism for assessing the degree of threat posed by hostile regimes, in particular the threat posed by a military buildup."

associated with the "kapitalpolitik" of international political economy (Wallerstein, 1980), have once again become fashionable.

As Neil R. Richardson explains in "International Trade as a Force for Peace," this revival poses another challenge to realism, which generally treats economic factors as relatively unimportant in comparison to the military capabilities believed crucial to national security and national strength in the global balance of power. To the liberal tradition, the key to world order is less the balance of military power than it is the form of economic exchange and balance of fiscal power, for the latter operate at the superstructural level to shape the former. Hence, what Mark Zacher and Richard Matthew in Part I label "commercial liberalism" proceeds from the belief that open trading systems, less than military might, influence the prospects for peaceful politics. Once a country opens its markets to the world, democracy follows, for as the standard of living rises, so does the thirst for democracy, and democratic states behave less militantly than do closed economic and political systems. In addition, neoliberalism directly challenges "the doctrinal realist separation of domestic and international politics" (Rosenberg, 1990: 291). Even though it recognizes that states have "become international commercial agents in their own right (Hont, 1992: 42), rather than glorifying the state and mercantilism, neoliberalism escapes realism's "conservative ideology of the exercise of state power" by maintaining that the state's "economy is also part of a transnational whole which produces important *political* effects independently of the agency of the state" (Rosenberg, 1990: 296, 287).

Following the liberal belief that "if goods can't cross borders, soldiers will" (Buzan, 1984: 599), liberalism's advocacy of free trade and market mechanisms derives in part from its contention that state regulation of economic affairs and the state's control of international capital are partly responsible for retarded economic growth and secondarily for imperialism and war. As one observer summarizes liberal theory's position,

> For the idealist it is free trade rather than empire that sustains economic growth. One's trade must be protected against attack, but that is different from developing an exclusive economic zone that does not depend upon the goodwill of others. Idealists believe that the wealth of a nation depends not on the extent or characteristics of the territory directly under its control, but as Adam Smith states, "first, [on] the skill, dexterity, and judgment with which its labour is generally applied; and, secondly, [on] the proportion between the number of those who are employed in useful labour, and that of those who are not so employed." Since prosperity "seems to depend more upon the former of those two circumstances than upon the latter," it is important that the labor force of the most advanced country constantly improve its skills so that it can continue to produce innovative goods and services with high added value. Otherwise, it will inevitably fall behind. (Kober, 1990: 15)

Richardson evaluates the credibility of this prophecy in light of the economic trends that have transformed the international political economy in recent decades and assesses their implications for liberal theories of world politics. His review shows why the realist stress on the primacy of military might and on the state as an efficacious agent for development neglects the extent to which economic and domestic influences shape foreign policy and why this influence has expanded as the world has grown increasingly interdependent economically. As he describes, many states in the 1970s and 1980s, in conformity with liberal precepts, dismantled state management of their economies, opened their businesses to global competition by drastically cutting tariffs, privatized state-owned enterprises, and eliminated price controls over products. These free-market reforms thus overturned protectionist policies and forced domestic companies to compete in the international market, in contrast to the neomercantilist national economic policies that seek to promote national growth through government subsidies and trade protectionism. But these latter approaches have not been suspended altogether, as the costs and benefits of the two strategies remain a topic of controversy and debate in many national capitals.

Liberalism, Richardson explains, expands our understanding of these processes and controversies, and captures many of their consequences well.[2] In addition, neoliberal conceptualization, Richardson suggests, can provide a contribution to the theoretical interpretation of the issues around which this theoretical debate revolves, adding an account that goes beyond the explanation of prevailing practices that realism can provide.

Yet to Richardson neoliberalism, however beneficial, is not adequate by itself. Faith in its account was undermined by some trends since the 1960s in the area of international relations in which liberalism is dominant—in the international political economy. Here the record failed to support unambiguously the neoliberal claim that free markets are incomparably better than state interventionism in producing growth and peace (Colclough and Manor, 1991). Ironically, that phase in the evolution of the global political economy enhanced and reinforced the power of the state, which grew as competitive markets expanded. Moreover, studies of the political correlates of open international markets disclosed that, consistent with realpolitik thinking, "free trade [was] more likely within, rather than across, political–military alliances" (Gowa and Mansfield, 1993: 408).

Richardson's penetrating review of recent developments in the international political economy thus suggests that the "neoliberalism seemingly on the ascent at the moment" is, like all theories of world politics, a reflection

[2] Note that liberalism balances its interpretation by acknowledging that whereas capitalism and free trade produce many benefits, historically, capitalism also produced a brutal and exploitive global environment that was destructive, inegalitarian, and ineffective in providing public goods and basic necessities for the disadvantaged. Liberalism avers that it was against the abuses of unreformed and unregulated capitalism that communism and socialism originally arose, and, should these excesses of laissez-faire capitalism resume, the triumph of capitalism over its socialist alternative will likely prove short-lived; the movement toward democratic capitalism since 1989 did not necessarily put the final nail in the marxist coffin.

of its time and that these times are now rapidly changing in ways that may render neoliberalism less than complete and compelling. "Microeconomic changes are afoot," he continues, "that are beginning to change, once again, the meaning of trade" and with it possibly "trade's relationship to peace."

As Richardson elaborates, "modern interdependence" is taking on new, unprecedented characteristics. In the past, and especially in the 1970s and 1980s, liberal theory correctly captured the growing extent to which free trade had increased the mutual dependency and vulnerability of states in a way that, at least for the most active traders, reduced their incentives to wage war. But now global commerce is undergoing a transformation as firms are becoming mobile, sharing technologies and management, and forming alliances with competing multinational corporations, and the "liberal theory of international political economy has not confronted these new realities of corporate behavior." As a result, the pacificity that once was fostered among trading states whose economies had become interdependent and integrated (as liberal theory posited) may have begun to weaken. "The new corporate patterns are occasioning interstate rivalry and conflict."

However, Richardson also perceptively observes that at the same time, these new patterns are contributing to "new and stronger regimes." The elevated ties of economic integration are probably replacing the much weaker GATT to which they owe their continued liberalism. If this occurs, it will be fundamental because the fact that the major commercial states "are trying to collaborate," Richardson reasons, reflects "their growing realization that collective management is increasingly necessary to their prosperity." Hence "in the context of trade's newest connotations, it is becoming increasingly difficult," Richardson concludes, "to foresee circumstances in which the world's most active commercial states—including realism's 'great powers'—would war with each other."

In this sense, the liberal vision has been vindicated in a way that exceeds the most optimistic hopes of those who originally formulated the expectation that trade could operate as a force for peace. As international relations have grown more complex, so too has liberal theory evolved, and the recent changes in the behavior of global businesses and the new dynamics of global firms require that contemporary institutional liberalism be amended. In amended form, Richardson predicts that the liberal case that "trade promotes peace" will survive intact.

REFERENCES

Buzan, Barry. (1984) "Economic Structure and International Security: The Limits of the Liberal Case," *International Organization* 38 (Autumn): 597–624.
Claude, Inis L., Jr. (1989) "The Balance of Power Revisited," *Review of International Studies* 15 (January): 77–85.
Colclough, Christopher, and James Manor, eds. (1991) *States or Markets? Neo-Liberalism and the Development Policy Debate.* New York: Oxford University Press.

Gaddis, John Lewis. (1991) "Great Illusions, the Long Peace, and the Future of the International System," pp. 25–55 in Charles W. Kegley Jr., ed., *The Long Postwar Peace*. New York: HarperCollins.

Gasiorowski, Mark J. (1986) "Economic Interdependence and International Conflict," *International Studies Quarterly* 30 (March): 23–38.

Gowa, Joanne, and Edward D. Mansfield. (1993) "Power Politics and International Trade," *American Political Science Review* 87 (June): 408–20.

Hoffmann, Stanley. (1992) "Balance, Concert, Anarchy, or None of the Above," pp. 194–220 in Gregory F. Treverton, ed., *The Shape of the New Europe*. New York: Council on Foreign Relations Press.

Hont, Istvan. (1992). "Free Trade and the Economic Limits to National Politics: Neo-Machiavellian Political Economy Reconsidered," pp. 41–120 in John Dunn, ed., *The Economic Limits to Modern Politics*. Cambridge: Cambridge University Press.

Kober, Stanley. (1990) "Idealpolitik," *Foreign Policy* 79 (Summer): 3–24.

Mearsheimer, John J. (1990) "Back to the Future: Instability in Europe after the Cold War," *International Security* 15 (Summer): 5–56.

Negretto, Gabriel L. (1993) "Kant and the Illusion of Collective Security," *Journal of International Affairs* 46 (Winter): 501–23.

Rosenberg, Justin. (1990) "What's the Matter with Realism?" *Review of International Studies* 16 (April): 285–303.

Uchitel, Anne. (1993) "Interdependence and Instability," pp. 243–64 in Jack Snyder and Robert Jervis, eds., *Coping with Complexity in the International System*. Boulder, Colo.: Westview Press.

Wallerstein, Immanuel. (1980) *The Modern World System II*. New York: Academic Press.

Waltz, Kenneth N. (1992) "Nuclear Myths and Political Realities," pp. 49–58 in Charles W. Kegley Jr. and Eugene R. Wittkopf, eds., *The Global Agenda*. New York: McGraw-Hill.

Wight, Martin. (1966) "Why Is There No International Theory?" pp. 17–34 in Herbert Butterfield and Martin Wight, eds., *Diplomatic Investigations: Essays in the Theory of International Politics*. Cambridge, Mass.: Harvard University Press.

CHAPTER 10

Swords into Plowshares: Can Fewer Arms Yield More Security?

ROBERT C. JOHANSEN

Although we live in an age of unprecedented societal interdependence and interpenetration, an ancient principle still guides the security policies of many nations. It is the time-honored maxim: "If you want peace, prepare for war." Despite its widespread acceptance among realists, this guideline has little scientific foundation. It suggests one way to prevent some wars some of the time, but mounting evidence shows that this approach is not the *best* way to accomplish that goal, nor is it helpful in attempting to prevent all wars all of the time. Indeed, a quite different guideline seems more realistic today: If you want peace, prepare institutions to keep peace.

The purpose of this chapter is to explore the empirical and logical grounds for questioning the wisdom of this ancient maxim in today's world. This exploration focuses on three foundational themes in U.S. security policy. Because they are also widely shared throughout the world, the analysis applies broadly to most states and carries implications for the international system in general. These themes, constituting hallmarks of political realism, continue to exert a strong influence on the national security community. First, many people believe that U.S. preparations for war were the key to keeping peace during the Cold War. This belief is based on an assumption that the United States and the former Soviet Union would have fought a major war in the absence of such preparations. Yet historical evidence does not show that either of the two superpowers contemplated deliberate, large-scale military aggression (Garthoff, 1962, 1966, 1985; Kennan, 1982; Bundy, 1989; Nye, 1987; Wolfe, 1984; Sabin, 1989). Thus one cannot demonstrate that high levels of U.S. (or Soviet) military preparedness prevented it. Nor is it clear that the chronic military buildup laid as good a foundation for keeping peace today as might have been laid *without* it.

Second, U.S. policymakers in both political parties continue to favor relatively high levels of military spending, although somewhat diminished from previous years, because they believe that military preparations exert a generally pacifying, stabilizing effect on national security policies in today's uncertain world. Yet it is historically difficult to find sustained positive consequences flowing from chronic military preparations (Wallace, 1982; Mueller, 1989).

Third, realists believe that further military preparations will enable policy-makers to elicit as much peace as is possible from the international system. However, a plausible case can be made that realists' heavy emphasis on the centrality of military power *decreases* international security because this emphasis underpins and legitimizes an obsolescent, war-prone international system. Steps toward global demilitarization could produce more security than national military preparations if the benefits of reduced military expenditures and deployments would be organically tied to strengthening nonmilitary mechanisms and incentives for dispute settlement and multilateral enforcement. Indeed, *unless* systematic worldwide efforts are made to reduce nations' accumulation of arms, military emphases will impede measures urgently needed to enhance security through nonmilitary instrumentalities.

Before examining these three themes in detail and sketching an alternative to the traditional realist approach, it is essential to recognize that changes more fundamental than the end of the Cold War are underway. Indeed, to focus primarily on the absence of the Cold War is itself a symptom of intellectual inertia because this narrow focus emphasizes the singular importance of the state and mistakenly suggests that the disappearance of a militarily powerful contender to the world's leading military power, the United States, is the primary force ushering in a new era. However, the newness of this era can best be grasped by moving beyond doctrinaire realism in three ways: First, it is useful to focus on processes of change rather than on relatively static laws of state behavior. Second, these processes can be understood best as social forces that are part of an emerging world society rather than as the properties of states or clashing civilizations (Huntington, 1993), just as civil society may be distinguished from the state or broader civilizational themes in domestic political analyses. Third, the processes of social change are generating a creative tension between two powerful contending forces: Pressures for integration, globalization, and centralization, on the one hand, interact with forces for differentiation, particularization, fragmentation, and decentralization, on the other. These forces cannot be understood by focusing primarily on states and military power, as realists have done, to comprehend the multiple forms and functions of power in modern world politics (Zurn, 1993).

"Integration" is a process that brings more states or more dimensions of intersocietal relations within a boundary-crossing, overarching normative or institutional structure. The legal commitments by many countries from a variety of civilizations to refrain from developing nuclear weapons or to reduce emissions of chlorofluorocarbons in order to protect the ozone layer illustrate integration. In contrast, "differentiation" is a process that reduces the size of one or more states and increases the number of states, or that devolves power and authority to subnational political units, or that reduces the number or importance of social relations contained within a common normative or institutional framework. The fragmentation of the former Soviet Union and Yugoslavia or the deepening cleavages between Hindus and non-Hindus in India illustrate differentiation. Although this analysis focuses on international politics, integration and differentiation have psychological and sociological dimensions as well. To nurture more inclusive personal identities, for example, may be no less important to world peace than to build more inclusive institutions to represent all people fairly in global decision making.

Political realists have in the past dismissed processes of integration and differentiation, considering them relatively insignificant. In claiming that rational state actors and their military power are the important focal points for analysis, realists have discouraged imaginative action designed to nurture forms of integration and differentiation that would reduce people's reliance on military power. At worst, they have claimed that when wars are necessary, officials are duty-bound to conduct them effectively without being encumbered by moral constraints. This approach led to the heyday of nuclear overkill and exacerbated today's problems of nuclear proliferation and environmental degradation. At best, they have asked, "What makes this particular war legitimate or illegitimate?" They have not asked, "What can we do to make all wars unnecessary and illegitimate?" Yet no question is of more fundamental importance to the future of human security. As Kenneth Boulding (1989) suggested, to enhance security we need to move beyond the "threat power" of military prowess in order to use the more effective forms of "exchange power" (economic or productive power) and "integrative power" (persuasive and compassionate power) to bring people together.

The deficiencies of realism exacerbated the security dilemma throughout the Cold War, although they have become more widely recognized only since its end. For four decades, the United States legitimized the amassing of more military power than was necessary or wise. Those who pointed out the negative effects of an excessive faith in military power were largely ignored. To illustrate, the U.S. ambassador to the United Nations (and a defeated Democratic nominee for president) three decades ago delivered a speech before the United Nations entitled "Working toward a World without War." In this speech, informed by the Wilsonian legacy, Adlai Stevenson (1962: 18) said, "We do not hold the vision of a world without conflict. We do hold the vision of a world without war—and this inevitably requires an alternative system for coping with conflict. We cannot have one without the other." If steps would have been taken to implement such a vision, the world would have been much better prepared today for handling ethnic conflict and weapons proliferation.

Although realism has usefully stressed the power-seeking tendencies of the state, it has been less than helpful in learning how to bridle or change those tendencies—the task that Stevenson envisaged. Wilsonian liberalism anticipated the future in aiming for a collective institutional response to security threats, but it did not include sufficient sensitivity to the contesting forces of integration and differentiation, the sociology of conflict, the psychologically motivated inertia of human identities and acceptance of violence toward out-groups, and the economic bases for integration. Neoliberals have usefully pointed out that structural change can occur in the international system, but often they have not appreciated the deep political struggle required to implement a demilitarized code of international conduct.

To develop an effective policy for security enhancement requires extricat-ing ourselves from past intellectual orthodoxies and developing sensitivity to peoples' hopes and fears within states and within global society, in addition to noting the activities of states and state-to-state relations. As Charles Kegley has noted in his introduction, military power and military threats, although certainly important, constitute only one of several sets of serious security problems and opportunities.

The old decentralized state system and its accompanying threat pattern of relations simply cannot provide the integrative power required to protect the environment or to control weapons of mass destruction. Nor can it generate the exchange power required to orchestrate a prosperous global economy. The primacy of threat power exacerbates a dangerously unbalanced global social process in which societal interpenetrations and pressures for integration run far ahead of the establishment of new governing institutions capable of providing democratic control over the processes of centralization. As a result, people naturally resist centralization processes because decisions seem remote and unresponsive to their needs. Accepting a global norm against the spread of weapons of mass destruction, for example, may interfere with a society's drive to expand its national power. Similarly, accepting the principle of cutting carbon dioxide emissions may interfere with a society's economic growth. Danes, in voting against the Maastricht Treaty in 1992, worried that the regionally centralizing tendencies of Brussels bureaucrats in the European Union might not express their interests. In other contexts, such as the former Yugoslavia, people may feel that their own state does not reflect their needs, so they want to break away from it. This has been especially true recently when globalization brings modernization and secularization that threaten deep religious traditions. If the threat is severe, religious fundamentalism often results.

In brief, the drawbacks of integration, however perceived, may generate recurring pressures for differentiation. At the same time, the shortcomings of an overly decentralized political system in a world that is functionally interdependent generate pressures for integration. The state is only one of many actors in this process, whether the pressures are for more global gover-nance or more subnational control. The state's territorially limited definition of self and sovereignty makes it a sometimes obstructive force in the turbu-lence of social, economic, and psychological forces for which territorial bound-aries are less significant.

These contested processes of change in world society are likely to be long and difficult. Collective violence frequently will threaten, especially if more effective and democratic governance at the global level cannot be established soon to dampen the spread of destabilizing military technologies and to soften harsh economic disparities. At the same time, attempts to *force* integration will only heighten the resistance of those in both the North and South who fear they will be treated unfairly in local, national, regional, or global contexts. If large numbers of people feel alienated from increasing political integration because they are destitute, they will not support movement toward more global governance. Thus the future of world peace requires addressing "the structures of mass destitution" no less than the weapons of mass destruction. These are the structures that confine roughly three-fourths of the world's population to a position of economic and political inferiority in a system that increasingly resembles a form of global apartheid. They suffer destitution of one sort or another by being deprived of food or shelter, education or employment, clean water or healthy air.

Nearly a half century of realist education and highly militarized world policies have placed us at an enormous disadvantage intellectually, politically, and economically for correcting the existing imbalances and unrepresentative nature of institutions in global society. Nonetheless, the most promising formula for security enhancement now lies in new efforts to respect all people's rights and to facilitate their genuine control over as many of their own affairs as possible—the processes of differentiation and democratization. At the same time, it is politically necessary, as well as morally desirable, to provide integrative regional and global structures to relieve conditions of destitution, to guarantee rights to minorities or others against victimization, and to establish universal control over weapons of mass destruction and the handling of hazardous materials (such as weapons-grade fissionable material, dangerous radioactive wastes, and carbon dioxide emissions). Toward these ends, traditional military policies must be reviewed to determine their utility in both preventing war and building a more cooperative international system—the tasks to which we now turn.

THE IMPACT OF PREPARATIONS FOR WAR ON THE DETERRENCE OF WAR

Two historical experiences undergird the belief that high levels of military preparedness produce peace. First, many people believe that the military weakness of the countries opposed to German expansion in the 1930s and their willingness to appease Adolf Hitler at Munich in 1938 contributed to the coming of World War II. In brief, lack of military preparations encouraged war. Second, many observers believe that high levels of U.S. military preparedness, in particular the strategy of nuclear deterrence, contributed mightily to U.S.–Soviet peace since World War II (Mearsheimer, 1990).

These beliefs, although deeply held, rest on selective use of historical evidence, a disinclination to search for alternative explanations of how a more peaceful code of international conduct might have been achieved after World Wars I and II, and an unnecessarily restrictive estimate of possibilities for structural change in the international system. With regard to the Munich analogy, there can be no assurance that additional military preparations against Hitler in the 1930s would have produced a more durable peace than would have a different approach, employing cooperative international economic policies soon after World War I. A cooperative rather than a confrontational approach might have prevented Hitler's rise to power in the first place, or at least might have limited his ability to lead the German people down his destructive path. Hitler's political success, after all, grew out of a preparation-for-war mentality and a confrontational diplomatic ethos that emphasized preparations for war as an approach to peace. In contrast, two decades later a cooperative approach, using exchange power and integrative power to nurture the European Community, ended long-standing Franco–German animosities and expectations of war.

In brief, although realists can easily proclaim that marshaling more troops against Hitler in the late 1930s would have deterred him a bit longer, one cannot safely conclude that more intense preparations for war in the 1920s and 1930s would have been the most powerful means to prevent World War II. Less protectionist and more cooperative policies by Britain, France, and the United States might have averted the Great Depression and thereby the rise of fascism in Europe. Less preoccupation with relying on weapons for security and more intense preparations to arrest destitution and to ensure peace through peaceful means might have prevented the Second World War altogether.

In considering the peacemaking role of U.S. nuclear policies toward the former Soviet Union, John Vasquez (1991) has noted with precision that there is no logical or empirical foundation for the belief that nuclear deterrence has prevented nuclear war. His and others' analyses (see Mueller, 1988, 1989) have shown that the main element in U.S. security policy throughout the Cold War—nuclear deterrence—may have had nothing to do with nullifying what was perceived as the main threat to U.S. security, namely, nuclear war with the Soviet Union. To be sure, many other security consequences did flow from U.S. nuclear policies. It is possible that the nuclear deterrent and the fear of escalation from conventional to nuclear conflict did inhibit the two superpowers from engaging in conventional war. In addition, the nonnuclear preparations for war, which consumed roughly four-fifths of the military budget, were themselves a factor in both leaderships' calculations about whether to make war.

Yet one cannot make a compelling case for the idea that U.S. military preparations produced U.S.–Soviet peace unless one can show strong evidence that war between them would have been almost certain in the absence of those preparations or that war was a natural outcome of post-1945 international politics. Yet no evidence points to such conclusions. In fact, the opposite is true. To be sure, some historians believe that the period of peace between the United States and the Soviet Union was historically extraordinary. "How," John Gaddis asked in 1987, "does one explain why the great [military] conflict between the United States and the Soviet Union, which by all past standards of historical experience should have developed by now, has not in fact done so?" He concluded that, despite many influences on the long peace, nuclear weapons played the most decisive role in averting a third world war: "It seems inescapable that what has really made the difference in inducing this unaccustomed caution [about world war] has been the workings of the nuclear deterrent" (Gaddis, 1987: 217, 231).

Yet, was peace between Moscow and Washington truly a condition which "by all past standards of historical experience" could not have been expected? Russia and the United States have lived in peace not only in the age of nuclear deterrence, but throughout their entire histories. They have never fought each other, with one minor exception of U.S. intervention that occurred during the Russian civil war as the Bolsheviks were consolidating their revolution at the end of World War I. Although Moscow and Washington had severe ideological conflicts during the Cold War, the two societies have never been natural enemies in the traditional sense. They have no border conflicts, no irredentist ethnic minorities, no severe disputes over natural resources, no crusading religious or racial antagonisms. Moreover, they are geographically distant, except in the Bering Straits.

The post–Cold War opening of Soviet archives provides no evidence of Soviet intention to attack Western Europe or the United States at any time since 1945.[1] George Kennan reports that Soviet leaders *never* saw it in their interests to overrun Western Europe militarily. Moreover, he has "never believed that . . . they would have launched an attack on that region generally even if the so-called nuclear deterrent had not existed" (1987: 888–89). Mueller (1989) draws the same conclusion. To the extent that Soviet leaders did attempt to bully West Europeans, these tendencies were more pronounced soon after World War II, when the United States possessed a monopoly of

---

[1] Some authors, of course, have disagreed. Michael Mandelbaum (1989: A19), for example, believes that "the threat of Soviet aggression against Western Europe was credible precisely because it had already occurred—and indeed continues to this day—in Eastern Europe." The logical flaw of realism here is to assume that because Moscow established authoritarian control in Eastern Europe after the victory over German aggression in 1945, Soviet leaders later intended to attack Western Europe. A less dogmatic view would have observed that after establishing a buffer zone in Eastern Europe, including East Germany of course, Moscow may have felt sufficiently secure that it did not need to control Western Europe. Indeed, Moscow might well have calculated that it would be wise to refrain from attacking Western Europe precisely because the latter would have been too big a bite to digest, given Moscow's domestic problems and the likelihood that its Eastern European "allies" might rebel against Soviet control during a war with Western Europe.

nuclear arms and wielded its largest margin of military superiority over Moscow, than they were later on when Moscow was militarily stronger and U.S. threats to retaliate against Soviet misdeeds were less plausible. Moreover, Soviet intimidation, to the extent that it did exist in events like the Berlin crisis and the construction of the Berlin wall, was dampened more by Soviet officials' acquiring a deep sense of Soviet security and by the development of friendlier economic and political relations between Eastern and Western Europe than by the threat of overwhelming U.S. military power. The realist perspective has long been insensitive to these inconvenient realities.

Admittedly, U.S. military capability may have diminished any Soviet appetite for expansion. Similarly, the Soviet arsenal may have added to U.S. reluctance to roll back communism during the Hungarian uprising in 1956. Yet to acknowledge such influences on decision making does not establish that preparations for war were the only or even the most effective means of war prevention.[2] Nor does it confirm that the continuation of the U.S.–Soviet military buildup played a central role in war avoidance. Substantial evidence suggests that international security was not enhanced by U.S. decisions to escalate its deployments beyond a minimum nuclear deterrent or to develop a forward-based, deep-strike conventional arsenal and strategic doctrine (Boston Study Group, 1982; Johansen, 1980: 38–125, 1983, 1986). To the extent that one still chooses to assume that a policy of nuclear deterrence did deter nuclear war, a much lower level of military preparations presumably could have produced a similar deterring effect.

Even Moscow's deployment of far more weapons than necessary for a minimum deterrent does not show that the Soviet Union was preparing for a surprise attack on the West. Instead the excessive deployments were a product of the habitual accumulation of weapons that is prompted by the realists' claim that more military power is better than less and by the belief, which Washington legitimized by its own behavior, that peace can best be maintained through preparations for war. Insofar as the U.S. arms buildup reinforced belief in the utility of preparations for war, it discouraged Soviet leaders from abandoning their military habits. If no Soviet attacks on the West were in fact likely, then the expensive, habit-creating U.S. preparations for war may have added more to U.S. and European insecurity than to their security (Kaldor, 1981). Indeed, chronic military preparations probably prolonged the Cold War because they generated hostilities and obscured the disparities between the strengths of the Soviet and U.S. economies. These disparities could have become more visible much earlier if the single area of Soviet technological accomplishment, namely the military sector of the economy, would not have been given center stage and if U.S. economic growth would not have been hampered by the drain imposed on its economy by economically unproductive expenditures on arms.

[2] For historical and empirical studies on this point, see Wright (1965), Singer and Small (1979, 1968), Levy (1981), Wallace (1982), and Huth and Russett (1984).

One further reason for questioning the faith that many people have placed in military preparations as a deterrent to war arises from research on long cycles in international relations. Some scholars have noted that long-term changes in world leadership over the past five centuries have been punctuated by large-scale war, that long periods of peace at first accompany the new order established by an ascendant world leader during each new cycle, and that major challenges to the world's leading power often do not occur in spans as short as the period from 1945 to the end of the Cold War, during which the United States first established its dominance as world leader (Modelski and Modelski, 1988; Modelski, 1987).

Long-cycle theory suggests that U.S. preparations for war since 1945 have played a much smaller role in maintaining peace between the two superpowers than is commonly assumed. Avoidance of global war most likely would have occurred anyway, given reasonably good diplomacy.[3] The stability of the international system after the upheavals of 1914 to 1945 made the world safe for nuclear deterrence, rather than nuclear deterrence producing a safe international system. From this perspective, the preparations for war have not brought the peace; peace has made the military buildup tolerable. However, as the world moves into a less stable phase of the long cycle, war prevention will prove more difficult. Many clues suggest that the world will be moving in a less stable direction during the next half century, despite the short-term euphoria that some express about the United States being the only remaining superpower. As new powers emerge and U.S. resources fall short of U.S. global aspirations,[4] those seeking to contest U.S. dominance are likely to make relative gains, especially if the long cycle in world leadership is not interrupted through using integrative power to establish multilateral burden sharing and enforcement of global norms against the deployment and use of military power.

THE IMPACT OF PREPARATIONS FOR WAR ON NATIONAL POLICIES FOR SECURITY AND PEACE

The preceding section describes the common tendency to overestimate (1) the historical likelihood of a Soviet attack on the United States; (2) the deter-

---

[3] On this point, one of the keenest early analysts of nuclear deterrence has commented: "I have thought the likelihood of war sufficiently small during the entire period since the early 1970s that I am not inclined to attribute much of the success in avoiding nuclear war to any particular measures that were taken or not taken" (Schelling, 1989: 29). During much of the period before 1970, of course, the Soviet Union was hardly in a position to attack the United States and its allies because Moscow was preoccupied with recovering from World War II, strengthening its industrial base, and holding its own allies in line.

[4] Note that the United States did not even appropriate the resources to pay for an extremely brief war against Iraq, a small country of 17 million people with only modest industrial development and without a single effective ally or source of resupply.

ring effect of U.S. preparations for war on Moscow's leaders; and (3) the relative utility of more intense U.S., British, and French military preparations after World War I in preventing Hitler's rise to power. On the one hand, preparations for war have received too much credit for their possible contributions to peace and the deterrence of aggression. On the other hand, the utility of nonmilitary measures, designed to address the conditions that give rise to violence and that could help implement global demilitarization, receives too little emphasis. This analytic imbalance contributes to the second overall problem examined here. Although many people believe that military preparations provide the key to stabilizing and pacifying states' foreign policies within the balance-of-power system, in practice such preparations often discourage peaceful national security policies by one's adversaries and impede peace-building strategies within one's own country and its diplomacy.

This fundamental contradiction between belief and reality arises because of the tendency for people in one country to believe that *their* military preparedness will discourage would-be aggressors and lead to arms control, although an adversary's military preparations will engender war. Such a belief, which in practice is encouraged by realists, often focuses narrowly on short-term considerations and ignores the impact of military research and deployment on other countries and on the international system itself over the long run. From a national perspective, one's own military preparations easily appear to possess a positive utility that, from a global perspective, they lack.

Although chronic military innovation and production are understandable from the standpoint of a commander preparing for battle (because a commander cannot have too many weapons), they are not sensible from the standpoint of preparing for peace, because each increase in U.S. military capability usually becomes the prelude to a later increase in challenges to U.S. security. From a global perspective, almost all preparations for war, regardless of their locale, make someone nervous. One exception may be preparedness that is strictly defensive (Fischer, 1984), such as practiced by the Swiss Confederation. But the calculations guiding military planning even in the post–Cold War period have been insensitive to the overall impact of military policies that (1) legitimize the use of force, (2) stimulate counterarmaments or troubling resentments, (3) aim unabashedly to entrench a double standard in the international system for determining who may possess weapons of mass destruction, (4) inhibit prospects for establishing effective norms for arms control and nonproliferation of weapons, and (5) waste resources needed to alleviate conditions that encourage violence. Empirical studies of competitive arms buildups by states in conflict demonstrate that such competition leads more frequently to war than to peace (Wallace, 1982; Singer and Small, 1979). They fail to confirm the maxim counseling those who want peace to prepare for war.

Recent reductions in military spending by Washington and Moscow are important steps in the right direction because intense military preparations are, not surprisingly, more ominous than modest ones. Yet even today's less intense preparations for war are not coupled with serious policies to institution-alize a less militarized code of conduct universally. Today's military prepara-tions still occupy sufficient space in the minds of policymakers and in the budgets of legislators and manufacturers to crowd out alternative policy choices that could more profoundly decrease the prospects for war in the future. A historically analogous commitment of U.S. officials to develop coun-terinsurgency warfare early in the Kennedy administration, one should recall, encouraged the United States to become embroiled in war in Southeast Asia. Without these preparations and the capability to project military power thou-sands of miles from home, the United States would have avoided the Indo-chinese chapter in its military history, without any harm to its security.

Chronic preparations for war encourage excessive reliance on military instruments and undergird intellectual and budgetary inertia, which often shape policy planning far beyond the strategic realm itself. Two decades ago, for example, U.S. officials chose to deploy multiple independently-targetable re-entry vehicles (MIRVs) at a time when Moscow had none and therefore would have entertained proposals to ban such nuclear warheads completely. United States officials rationalized their deployments with arguments that such preparations for war were precisely what was needed to help prevent war (Johansen, 1980: 44–105, 1985). A decade later, after Moscow developed and deployed similar warheads, mainstream U.S. security analysts finally acknowledged what globally oriented observers had warned from the outset: Deployment of MIRVs, when copied by the Soviet adversary, would make deterrence less stable and the United States less secure than it would have been if MIRVs had never been built at all (President's Commission on Strategic Forces, 1983). Similar examples exist throughout the history of modern arms rivalries. Today U.S. officials continue to argue that new high-tech weapons must be developed against even uncertain future adversaries. The U.S. budget for developing new weapons for space warfare has increased while overall military spending has slowly declined since 1990. Even after the end of the Cold War, U.S. military expenditures for research and development of new weapons have been running 70 percent above levels of the 1970s and early 1980s (Stockholm International Peace Research Institute, 1991: 125). Yet many new weapons eventually are likely to haunt their makers, as future technolo-gies eventually move beyond "us" to "them."

Another manifestation of an uncritical acceptance of military preparations, which continues to influence today's security policy, is the belief that military expenditures enhance the prospects for arms control (Powell, 1989). John Gaddis (1989: 11), perhaps the leading historian of the Cold War, has written in an article entitled "Hanging Tough Paid Off" that Ronald Reagan "presided over the most dramatic improvement in U.S.–Soviet relations—and the most solid progress in arms control—since the Cold War began." He attributes this success to the Reagan administration's vast military buildup and diplo-matic toughness.

But the judgment that tough policies led to success in arms control can be considered compelling only if we ignore how Reagan's policies deliberately blocked many arms control possibilities that independent U.S. experts sought and Moscow then endorsed; only if we overlook how the Reagan administration reversed U.S. positions on agreements already drafted and moved the center of debate over arms control toward the extreme end of the political spectrum that favored a highly militarized, unilateralist foreign policy; and only if we think that Reagan's toughness had more to do with achieving arms control than did Mikhail Gorbachev's unprecedented, conciliatory arms control policies and asymmetrical concessions. The Reagan administration in fact sabotaged negotiations already far advanced when it entered office, refused to ratify important arms control treaties already signed by Moscow and Washington, and then finally agreed, in part to polish an image tarnished by the Iran–*contra* scandal and lack of progress in arms control, to a treaty banning intermediate-range nuclear arms in Europe (Warnke, Smith, McNamara, and Keeny, 1986).

One set of negotiations that "hanging tough" derailed were those leading toward a comprehensive nuclear test ban. By the time Reagan took office, the United States, Great Britain, and the Soviet Union had agreed on all of the most important points for a test ban, including the possibility of on-site inspection (Goldblat and Cox, 1988: 14–15). But realists in the Reagan administration suspended negotiations, reversed the policies of all previous presidents since Eisenhower, and flatly rejected an opportunity to achieve a total ban on nuclear weapons tests, regardless of their verifiability. As President Reagan explained, "A nuclear test ban is not in the security interests of the United States, our friends or our allies" (Gordon, 1986: A1).

There can be no doubt that Moscow wanted a comprehensive test ban. Because of U.S. opposition to Soviet overtures for strengthening verification of testing prohibitions, Moscow invited private U.S. scientists to the Soviet Union to calibrate seismographic equipment as a way of demonstrating its acceptance of necessary verification procedures. For a year and a half the Soviet government unilaterally stopped its nuclear testing and repeatedly invited the United States to reciprocate. Washington refused.

The U.S. rejection of a comprehensive test ban was not inconsequential. Most independent weapons experts agree that with a comprehensive test ban, which could have been in place since 1980, "further nuclear weapon development would be rendered largely impossible" (Goldblat and Cox, 1988: 37). The costly and destabilizing race for qualitative improvement of nuclear weapons could have ended nearly a decade earlier than it did. Moreover, had a test ban been implemented in the early 1980s, it could have been the bedrock for serious multilateral efforts to strengthen the nuclear nonproliferation regime, which might well have averted some of the proliferation problems that recently have become so unmanageable.

"Hanging tough" also prevented the achievement of a proposed 50 percent reduction in Soviet and U.S. strategic nuclear weapons that would have been possible if the Reagan administration had been willing to affirm that it would not violate the Anti-Ballistic Missile (ABM) Treaty, which Washington had previously signed and the Senate had ratified. But the Reagan administration refused to say that it would honor this legally binding treaty because the treaty stood in the way of developing space weapons for the Strategic Defense Initiative (SDI). Seen in this light, and with the knowledge that the costly SDI program for a space-based defense as advocated by Reagan was never a serious possibility anyway, it seems a surrealistic and unwarranted faith in military preparations to praise the Strategic Defense Initiative as "the successful bargaining chip it turned out to be" (Gaddis, 1989: 13).

Such unreflective acceptance of a heavy emphasis on military priorities has led to policies that have departed substantially from long-term interests. Reagan's rejection of Soviet proposals for a 50 percent cut in strategic nuclear weapons occurred because he wanted to terminate the Anti-Ballistic Missile Treaty in order to test components for the Strategic Defense Initiative. The Reagan administration's announced testing policies meant, in the words of Ambassador Gerard Smith, former director of the Arms Control and Disarmament Agency and chief U.S. negotiator for the ABM Treaty: "We are already in an anticipatory breach of contract" (Smith, 1984: A12). After conducting a detailed study, the U.S. Senate Committee on Foreign Relations (1987: 66) concluded that "the Reagan Administration's 'reinterpretation' of the ABM Treaty constitutes the most flagrant abuse of the Constitution's treaty power in 200 years of American history." These details remind us how easily observers in a political culture based on chronic military preparations accept the application of military pressure to an adversary, even though in reality it means a devastating series of reversals for arms control and cooperative foreign policies.

To the extent that the Reagan administration did achieve success in arms control—and indeed the ban on intermediate-range missiles in Europe was a positive achievement—this was probably due less to "hanging tough," as realists claim, than to the Reagan administration's eventual willingness to move away from its rigid policies. Only when the administration took a less confrontational posture, which was encouraged by Gorbachev and the U.S. Congress, did the prospect of an agreement move into view. It is simplistic, if not simply inaccurate, to attribute the Reagan administration's limited arms control success to "hanging tough." When high levels of military spending become normal, "selective inattention" to military costs and the utility of less militaristic diplomatic options often occur (White, 1984: 154). The partial picture that results then mistakenly appears to demonstrate that military prowess, rather than other factors, "did lead to [arms control] negotiations" and "did eventually pay off" in arms control (Gaddis, 1989: 14).

As a result, now that the United States faces no serious external military threat and possesses a golden opportunity to launch a diplomatic program to reduce permanently the role of military power in world affairs, its leaders and people fail to seize the opportunity. Although the end of the Cold War has to some extent reversed the excessive military expenditures of the Reagan and Bush administrations, the slowness of the reduction in military expenditures and the absence of any organically connected, comprehensive plan for initiating a process of global demilitarization are alarming. Such a plan might have utilized the creative tension existing between forces for integration and differentiation (in Central Europe and the former Soviet Union, for example) to establish public international control over weapons of mass destruction; it could still encourage political support for demilitarization with astute programs to address mass destitution and the many nonmilitary security threats that remain unattended.

What constitutes a reasonable level of military expenditures is, of course, a matter of debate. Yet almost no serious consideration has been given to imaginative suggestions such as those from former Secretary of Defense Robert S. McNamara or Lawrence J. Korb, former assistant secretary of defense, who have concluded that military spending could be safely cut by 50 percent over the next decade (Rosenbaum, 1989: 1). A detailed study by Jerome Wiesner, Philip Morrison, and Kosta Tsipis (1993) has demonstrated that only $115 billion (1990 dollars) could provide a more than adequate security policy for the United States. If one sought to change some security assumptions and to place more of the security burden on an upgraded UN capacity for peacekeeping and enforcement and the establishment of some universal, enforceable rules against highly threatening military deployments, even further cuts could be made in national military spending. Because U.S. forces "are now so large that for years to come they will have no rivals in power, once the geography of plausible combat is accounted for" (Wiesner et al., 1993: 15), the late 1980s and early 1990s were a propitious time to have taken action for system change because these years offered an unprecedented amount of international political fluidity and low security risks. Yet reductions in military spending have been much slower than were the dubious increases in the early 1980s. Even when the Pentagon's projected budget reductions are carried through 1995, the result (in constant dollars) after six years of contraction will place U.S. military spending approximately 20 percent *above* the 1980 level (SIPRI, 1992: 196).

Unless systematic efforts are made to reduce the role of military power in international and national affairs, global shifts in power, productive dynamism, and dissatisfaction will increase the difficulties of preventing war despite a vast array of technologically unequaled U.S. weapons. Indeed, Paul Kennedy (1987) provides abundant historical evidence that the effort by the United States to accumulate military power will sap its economic strength, as did similar efforts by all former leading powers over the past 500 years, until it eventually loses its leadership position. The relative decline of the United States as a world economic and political leader, at a time when it has poured historically unprecedented resources into preparations for war during the 1980s, lends plausibility to Kennedy's hypothesis.

Past and present national military priorities handicap both national and international efforts to institutionalize a less militarized code of international conduct. Less militarized mechanisms remain underdeveloped and unavailable for security enhancement. Although one can never know how history might have evolved under different conditions, it is instructive to imagine the economic benefits that might reasonably have flowed from avoiding the unnecessary military costs of fighting the war in Vietnam (1966–1972) and of the Reagan–Bush military buildups from 1980 to 1991, measured in terms of the amount that military spending exceeded the levels that would have been spent if military budgets had tapered off after the Korean War and become a flat line, adjusted only for inflation. The United States would have saved approximately $1.8 trillion (in 1990 dollars) without sacrificing one iota of its security. On the contrary, the United States could today possess a much stronger economy with a well-functioning infrastructure and with heavier investment and improved productivity. Even more important, U.S. economic strength could lead a strong world economy, and the combination of more extensive U.S. and world resources could have enabled Washington and others to offer to people in the former Soviet Union, Yugoslavia, Eastern Europe, and the developing world the assistance that they deserved, in return for progress in nuclear nonproliferation, collective security arrangements, and human rights guarantees for ethnic minorities. Such priorities could have been a much wiser form of "defense spending." Instead, during the unnecessary military buildup in the 1980s, the United States turned from the world's largest creditor nation into its largest debtor.

The inability of policymakers and citizens to prevail in launching policies for global demilitarization suggests that the greatest threat to the future of U.S. security may lie within the country—in its intellectual, moral, and economic inertia—rather than from without, because promilitary vested interests prevent the United States from taking realistic multilateral actions to manage future security threats, most of which are not amenable to the application of national military power.

The negative consequences flowing from collective acceptance of a long-standing overemphasis on threat power continue to shape intellectual and diplomatic agendas. For example, it may be historically less surprising, intellectually less innovative, and diplomatically less useful to note that the United States and the former Soviet Union lived in peace from 1945 to 1989 than to note that France and Germany have behaved peacefully toward each other after many decades of war and preparations for war against each other by using exchange power and integrative power rather than threat power. This lesson has relevance also for assessing, in the next section, how military preparedness affects the extent to which the international system itself takes on the customs of peace or war.

THE IMPACT OF PREPARATIONS FOR WAR ON THE EVOLUTION OF THE INTERNATIONAL SYSTEM

Two mutually reinforcing tendencies—to adopt a narrow, exaggerated focus on military threats to U.S. security (formerly from the Soviet Union and now from undetermined foes) and to overestimate the relative utility of U.S. armaments in building peace—lead to a third misunderstanding: Many policymakers underestimate the security dangers that are inherent not in one particular adversary or another, but in the balance-of-power system itself, especially over the long run. The prevailing realist view of national security underemphasizes both the war-prone conditions inherent in the international system and the prospects for changing that system. As indicated in the preceding section, realism expresses overconfidence about the ability of U.S. officials to maintain security through military preparedness. This may be especially true when security problems no longer arise from a stable, militarily conservative state like the formerly powerful Soviet Union. Instead they arise from diverse causes: ethnic, religious, and other social strife within weak states; the proliferation of weapons; population growth and economic inequities that will bring migratory and possibly violent pressures against prosperous countries; and ecological problems that no state can handle without shaping a structure of interests that will induce all states to work together. International insecurities arising from problems such as these all spring not from military unpreparedness, but from the unreliable and unfair system of international relations itself—a system whose inherent instabilities are exacerbated further by governments' military spending and deployments. Solutions to problems such as these require deemphasizing threat power and mobilizing exchange power and integrative power.

The balance of military power as a world security system never has and presumably never will be completely successful in eliminating major wars, regardless of how advanced the U.S. military may be. Yet because all-out war, even once a century, is no longer acceptable, neither is the current balance of power system. Inis Claude (1962: 92) noted three decades ago that "the suitability of the world for the operation of the balance-of-power system has been steadily diminishing for well over a century."[5] Joseph Lorenz (1992: 47–48) notes that "post–Cold War changes in the arrangements of power have altered the political landscape in ways that are fundamentally incompatible with the premises of balance-of-power theory." Even though the Cold War is over, the war system of international relations remains firmly in place. Just as the end of World War II opened the door to creating the United Nations, the end of the Cold War offers an excellent opportunity to graft a third generation of international organizations onto the existing UN system.

Yet merely to draw more frequently on UN peacekeeping without empowering institutions to enforce peaceful norms and facilitate global demilitarization does not reflect an appreciation of present opportunities for structural change. The United States spends 2,000 times as much annually on its own

---

[5] Although Claude (1989) has acknowledged that the balance-of-power system possesses a bit more stability than he earlier indicated, the fundamental tendencies to which he referred in his earlier study remain.

military preparedness as it does on UN peacekeeping. Washington has no plan for institutionalizing a new code of international conduct. Yet destructive technologies already available or likely to be near at hand in the future—whether chemical, biological, or nuclear—render the possibility of massive destruction easy, swift, and impossible to defend against through traditional means. Even bystanders in a major war will suffer economic and environmental damage of substantial proportions.

Traditional realist policies cannot suffice because today's security problems are more systemic than adversarial: Washington can easily destroy any adversary but it cannot, without worldwide cooperation, stabilize or pacify the international system. Systemwide constraints on violence and positive inducements to support nonmilitary yet coercive policing mechanisms for monitoring and enforcement are necessary to have an effective defense against security threats, whether arising from people who may seek nuclear or chemical weapons, plant suitcase bombs in the heart of a city, exert pressures for unwanted migration, employ instruments of environmental warfare, or practice policies that exacerbate economic dislocation. Military preparations aiming to provide the traditional mode of military defense do not meet the need to change the global security system. On the contrary, such anachronistic policies impede the domestication of the international system.

Despite ambiguity about the impact of preparations for war on discrete conflicts (Huth and Russett, 1984; Wallace, 1982; Kegley and Raymond, 1991; Levy, 1981; Singer and Small, 1979, 1968; Wright, 1965), negative systemic consequences are clear (Independent Commission on Disarmament and Security Issues, 1982; Falk, Johansen, and Kim, 1993). Governments' preparations for war legitimize a militarized code of international conduct and erode constraints on the use of force. They stimulate potentially alarming competitions between countries such as India and Pakistan, between China and Japan or other Asian neighbors, and between contesting regional powers in the Middle East and elsewhere. They build economic–technological–scientific–bureaucratic interests pressing for new destructive technologies and expanded arsenals, often with noxious side effects for democratic processes. Militarily, they habituate dependence on military instruments while inhibiting the growth of nonmilitary means for conflict management throughout the international system. Economically, they divert resources from human needs, which if unmet exacerbate conflict and perpetuate higher rates of population growth. Environmentally, they threaten the collapse of life support systems. Each of these three areas deserves brief elaboration because each bears directly on our ability to keep the integrating–differentiating dynamic peaceful while changing the international system.

Security Costs

Throughout this century, and especially since World War II, the idea that people can prepare for peace by preparing for war has deepened the militarization of culture and politics in virtually every corner of the globe. Even with the tapering off of world military expenditures since 1989, world society continues to devote far more productive skills and energies to military purposes than it did during the years leading to either the First or Second World War. Except for the successor states of the former Soviet Union, total world military expenditures since 1989 have declined only modestly when compared to the sharp increase in expenditures during the 1980s. Expenditures in 1990 were twice as high as the annual average of the 1960s. The overall growth in world military spending since 1960 continues to run ahead of the growth in world gross national product per capita since then (Sivard, 1991: 8).

Combat costs also cast doubt on the utility of military power. Estimates for the cost of the brief Gulf war against Iraq in 1991, for example, range from $50 to $100 billion for the U.S.-led effort alone (SIPRI, 1992: 252). The destruction in Iraq cost more than $250 billion. The Arab Monetary Fund estimated the war's cost to the region as a whole at $676 billion in 1990 and 1991 alone. Annual growth rates in the region averaged 7 percent during the four years preceding the war; after the war people faced a negative growth of 7 percent (Ibrahim, 1993: 14).

People in the bureaucratic, industrial, and research infrastructures devoted to the production and procurement of weapons in nearly every land justify their demands for resources by highlighting, if not exaggerating, the importance of military threats and military solutions. As a result, military production bears little connection to the actual threats that people face, as confirmed by the success of opposition to reducing U.S. military expenditures more sharply after 1989, despite the absence of security threats (SIPRI, 1993: 341–42). Moreover, because military purchases or innovations rarely occur at precisely the same moment or with symmetrical consequences among adversaries, they add to diplomatic tensions. The long-term trend in military technology has been to increase the amount of damage that one person or a small group can inflict on others. Overall, "it is difficult to think of any significant number of weapon developments in history which can be regarded in any sense as stabilizing in the long run" (Blackaby, 1986: 218; see also Fromkin, 1993: 4). Such a judgment deserves at least as much weight in developing a collective strategy to dampen global militarization as do realist prescriptions to accumulate more military power.

New efforts to achieve a comprehensive nuclear test ban are a positive step toward loosening the grip of past military priorities on security thinking. For as long as the United States refused to ban nuclear tests and insisted on developing new nuclear weapons, a truly effective nonproliferation regime could not be established. During those years Israel, India, South Africa, and Pakistan joined the ranks of those able to produce nuclear weapons. Iraq, Iran, Libya, and North Korea have made serious efforts to obtain nuclear weapons. Some realists have encouraged Ukraine to take control of the nuclear weapons that it inherited through the breakup of the Soviet Union (Mearsheimer, 1993). If it does, will neighbors like Germany be satisfied without nuclear weapons? If Ukraine and Germany have nuclear weapons, will Poland accept such conditions? If Kazakhstan would follow a Ukrainian example and take control of its nuclear weapons, what ripple effect would this have on Israel and other countries throughout Southwest Asia and the Middle East?

Even though the spread of nuclear weapons capabilities could vastly increase the human costs of future conflicts in some of the planet's most volatile regions, it has occurred with "surprisingly few diplomatic costs" to those acquiring nuclear capability (Spector, 1988: 4), in part because realists have discounted the importance of establishing international rules and supranational enforcement procedures to constrain military technology. Despite their possession of more destructive power than other countries, the United States, Russia, Britain, France, and China have refrained in most cases from imposing strong nonproliferation measures on potential nuclear powers for fear of undermining their own power positions. Moreover, the major nuclear weapons countries have set a dangerous precedent in treating nuclear weapons as key symbols of power and prestige, to which other rising powers are tempted to aspire. As a result, even a half-dozen years after the Cold War ended, no truly strong program is in place to ensure that nuclear weapons do not spread further.

The insecurities posed by ethnic and religious conflicts in the Balkans, the Middle East, South Asia, and Africa illustrate how forces outside of traditional realist agendas have become relevant to security policy. Many people holding traditional religious beliefs oppose centralizing pressures because they often bring threatening forms of modernization and secularization. Yet world society has a strong interest in overcoming the decentralizing forces that encourage the spread of dangerous weapons. Hindu extremists in India's Bharatiya Janata Party (BJP), for example, emphasize the development of a powerful Indian nuclear arsenal because they believe that nuclear weapons would make India safer within the subcontinent and more respected abroad. By refusing to adopt a serious program of demilitarization, including major changes in their own nuclear policies, Washington and other major military powers encourage BJP-like world views to go unchallenged. Indian nuclear policies, of course, make Pakistan unhappy. As this South Asian military rivalry continues, the economies of both countries will suffer, encouraging extremist politics such as occurred during the pre–World War II rise of fascism in Europe—a period, we should recall, during which realists still believed it would have been wise to put *more* money into weaponry.

Pakistan may turn for financial backing to friendly countries in the Middle East or North Africa that would be happy to gain some access to Pakistan's nuclear capabilities. Yet such a military path simply has no utility in the long run. The only solution to the prospect for proliferation is to establish enforceable norms against weapons of mass destruction, adequate inspection mechanisms, sufficiently strong incentives for compliance to ensure that no one can resist them, and global institutions built upon fair representation so that societies will feel committed to maintain minimal international stability.

The spread of technologies for producing aircraft and missiles also profoundly endangers global security by exacerbating the problem of uneven
growth of power among states, which some theorists believe is the most
fundamentally destabilizing problem of international relations in the contemporary world (Gilpin, 1981: 230). More than twenty Third World countries
currently possess ballistic missiles or are making serious efforts to develop
them. The prospect of stopping the further spread of destabilizing military
technologies is dim indeed unless serious steps are taken to achieve a universal
ban on testing and deployment of ballistic missiles. Yet such a ban cannot
occur, nor can the spread of other advanced military technology be halted,
as long as the world's greatest military power, already more secure than other
states, insists on preparing yet additional weapons.

United Nations constraints placed on Iraqi military developments after
the Gulf war suggest a promising multilateral direction, yet enforcement
difficulties highlight an unavoidable problem: Norms against deploying nuclear or chemical arms and missiles must be equitably applied. As long as
norms remain applicable to only one country in a region, they invariably will
stimulate resentment and will not elicit the universal support required for
their long-term success.

In sum, the continuing overemphasis on military preparedness has
stunted the growth of an international code of conduct that could gradually
reduce the role of military power in international relations. If we seek to
enhance security, our acknowledged inability to discern the precise relationship between a particular set of preparations for war and the likelihood of a
specific war must be given less weight than our ability to see clearly that
military competition generally in the decentralized balance-of-power system
needs to be curtailed and the system modified. Military rivalry and the existing
international system together constitute a permissive cause of war, if not
always a sufficient one (Stockholm Initiative, 1991). True realism would recognize today's security equation: Unbridled military competition plus an un-
transformed international system equals collective violence. Without system
transformation, the question is not *if* there will be violence, but only when
and where.

Economic Costs

Studies of the rise and fall of great powers demonstrate that their high levels of
military preparations over many years usually end in war or relative economic
decline (Kupchan, 1989; Kennedy, 1987; Kaldor, 1981; Wright, 1965). In
accord with these findings, U.S. and Russian military expenditures over four
decades slowed their economic growth substantially. The impact was devastating in the former Soviet Union and profoundly negative though less visible
in the much larger, stronger U.S. economy (Rosecrance, 1992: 65). Nonetheless, the ailing U.S. economy in the late 1980s and early 1990s had a ripple

effect, adding to economic stagnation and hardship throughout the world. By diverting potential resources from investment to military purposes and by ignoring nonmilitary security threats, Washington continues to sap its own economic strength and compounds long-term world economic problems. Many people favor substantial U.S. military expenditures now because they believe these enabled it to win the Cold War (Crowe, 1989). Yet a quite different lesson may be nearer to the truth: Washington should take precautionary measures to protect its economy against succumbing to the drag of military expenditures that eventually pulled down the Soviet Union, as they did all leading world powers for the past five centuries (Kennedy, 1987: xxiii).

Excessive world military spending continues to (1) draw skilled personnel out of the civilian sector of the world economy, (2) divert capital from productive investment into unproductive military activities, (3) contribute to inflationary pressures, (4) create significantly less employment than would an equal amount of nonmilitary spending by government or private consumers, (5) channel scarce revenues away from research and development on civilian needs in energy and ecology, and (6) cause disastrous effects on economic development programs (Dumas, 1986; Anderson, Frisch, and Oden, 1986; Oden, 1989; DeGrasse, 1983; Brzoska and Ohlson, 1986; Ball, 1988; Deger and West, 1987).

The most harmful overall impact of military expenditures on the global economy is that they prevent a concerted attack on poverty and other forms of destitution. Unattended, these will be likely to produce more insecurities than can be countered by any weapons that governments may add to their arsenals. The richest fifth of the world's people enjoy annual incomes that are fifty times larger, on the average, than the incomes of the poorest fifth of the world's people (Sivard, 1991: 5), producing inequities so painful and unjustifiable that they can hardly avoid leading people toward a politics of desperation.

Security enhancement requires hard-headed acknowledgment that resources are extremely scarce and urgently needed to address nonmilitary security threats and to provide the attractive benefits that will induce people in world society to support positive forms of political integration. If people are to support some global integration, they must receive benefits from restructuring. Money is needed to facilitate each demilitarizing goal, whether to provide multilateral peacekeeping while dampening the arms trade and weapons proliferation or to improve the quality of life while saving the planet from greenhouse gases. These security needs require international integration to facilitate intrusive inspection and enforcement, not a national military colossus on the sidelines or in space making threatening noises against potential proliferators and polluters. Because security enhancement now requires more integration than confrontation, the burden on economic policies is increased because they, not arms, provide the power to give as many countries as possible a positive stake in stable global governance. Order simply cannot be imposed on the world. It must rest on the consent of most of the world's governments and peoples, and this demands a more equitable global economic climate.

Because financial needs are severe and resources are scarce, further national military preparations seem to squander a precious ingredient of security. It may not be an overstatement to say that dollars allocated to buying more weapons inadvertently undermine security, because the opportunity costs of such allocations are so high. Changing realities suggest that doctrinaire realists may be military idealists who place unwarranted faith in the belief that military power is the guarantor of security when in fact it detracts from the achievement of genuine security.

Ecological Costs

Current military preparations also impede the global system's capacity to provide a sustainable life of dignity for all people. The world's armed forces are the single largest polluter on earth (Sivard, 1991: 5). In addition, when arms breed insecurities, governments invariably misdirect scarce resources. The industrialized countries devote ten times as much to preparing for war as they do to combating destitution. In the United States 60 percent of all federal funds for research and development flows into weapons research. The number of scientific personnel working on weapons research throughout the world in the 1980s exceeded the combined number working on finding new energy sources, improving human health and family planning, raising agricultural productivity, and controlling pollution (World Commission on Environment and Development, 1987: 298). As world military expenditures continue at a wasteful level, deserts expand, rain forests fall, carbon emissions increase, billions of tons of topsoil wash away, protein harvests from the seas decline, and population growth continues—all exacerbated by insufficient funds to take corrective action and by an aging international system perpetuated through the militarily competitive balance of power.

THE FUTURE OF WORLD SECURITY

When preparations for war are examined to discern their impact on deterring war against the United States and on making wise national security policies, the evidence fails to show that high levels of military preparedness have been constructive. The scales tip decidedly against preparations for war if one views them from a global social-change perspective and if one seeks not merely to deter a given war but also to pacify international relations and to transform the balance of military power into a balance of legally constituted political power. If systematic efforts were made to dampen worldwide preparations for war, tensions arising from competitive arms buildups would decrease, international rules for reducing arsenals could be more readily institutional-ized and reliably enforced, and resources could be husbanded to advance human and environmental well-being in ways that would increase nearly all societies' commitment to establishing integrative global governance for greater peace and justice.

Even today's relatively reduced military preparations still encourage soci-eties to target attention and resources on using military prowess to conduct diplomacy and fight rival states. Yet these means are not the most effective for enhancing security. Military preparations during the Cold War probably did less to deter attacks on the United States by the Soviet Union than they did to deter the United States, together with its allies and its opponents, from sensible efforts to be prepared in the 1990s to change the international system through peaceful management of the interactive, tumultuous processes of integration and differentiation that have recently become so visible. Yet such efforts appear to be the most important security need today.

Because of insensitivity to the systemic consequences of its behavior as the world's leading military power, the United States inadvertently continues, even in the post–Cold War world, to sustain the military patterns that are deeply ingrained throughout the world and yet are so harmful. Given the security threats attending the present degree of global militarization, eco-nomic dislocation, and ecological decay, it may not be an exaggeration to say that the political and attitudinal consequences of decades of U.S. military preparations have brought a greater threat to the future of U.S. security than has any adversary since 1945.

Realism's insensitivity to possibilities for positive change has produced a self-fulfilling dynamic of recurring insecurity in the real world. Unnecessarily militarized elements of past state behavior have been enshrined as prescrip-tions for achieving peace in the future. Realism has failed precisely in the area where, even according to its own exponents, it has the most to contribute: the sphere of great-power relations. While the great powers follow the maxim "if you want peace, prepare for war," they suffer enormous security losses and inflict tragic opportunity costs on those attempting to change the code of conduct as well as on the poor. Today's security challenges require weaving into the global social fabric some strands of liberalism found in Jeffersonian, Wilsonian, and Kantian legacies, which, respectively, can inspire essential efforts to democratize global governance as it mediates processes of integration and differentiation, to institutionalize cooperative, collective responsibility for global security, and to implement a code of conduct based on reciprocal rights and duties and on powerful incentives for compliance.

The future of world peace will be heavily influenced, if not altogether decided, by the extent to which the United States and other countries redirect their policies and institutions toward a deliberate multilateral diplomatic pro-gram aimed at ending chronic preparations for war and establishing stronger world institutions capable of presiding over peaceful change and enforcing a less war-prone code of international conduct.

REFERENCES

Anderson, Marion, Michael Frisch, and Michael Oden. (1986) *The Empty Pork Barrel: The Employment Cost of the Military Buildup 1981–85.* Lansing, Mich.: Employment Research Associates.

Ball, Nicole. (1988) *Security and Economy in the Third World.* Princeton, N.J.: Princeton University Press.

Blackaby, Frank. (1986) "On the Nature of SIPRI's Peace Research Studies," *Bulletin of Peace Proposals* 17 (No. 3–4): 217–28.

Boston Study Group. (1982) *Winding Down: The Price of Defense.* San Francisco: W. H. Freeman.

Boulding, Kenneth. (1989) *Three Faces of Power.* Newbury Park, Calif.: Sage.

Broad, William. (1993) "Russians Describe Extensive Dumping of Nuclear Wastes," *New York Times* (April 27): A1

Brzoska, Michael, and Thomas Ohlson, eds. (1986) *Arms Production in the Third World.* London: Taylor & Francis.

Bundy, McGeorge. (1989) "Revising the Bomb Thesis: Maybe War Is Simply Gone," *The Washington Post National Weekly Edition* (March 20–26): 36–37.

Claude, Inis. (1989) "The Balance of Power Revisited," *Review of International Studies* 15 (April): 77–86.

———. (1962) *Power and International Relations.* New York: Random House.

Crowe, William J. (1989) "Don't Cut a Winner," *New York Times* (April 10): A19.

Deger, Saadet. (1986) *Military Expenditures in Third World Countries: The Economic Effects.* New York: Routledge, Chapman, and Hall.

Deger, Saadet, and Robert West, eds. (1987) *Defense, Security and Development.* New York: St. Martin's Press.

DeGrasse, Robert. (1983) *Military Expansion and Economic Decline.* New York: Council on Economic Priorities.

Dumas, Lloyd J. (1986) *The Overburdened Economy: Uncovering the Causes of Chronic Unemployment, Inflation, and National Decline.* Berkeley: University of California Press.

Dumas, Lloyd J. and Suzanne Gordon. (1986) "Economic Conversion: An Exchange," *Bulletin of the Atomic Scientists* 42 (June/July): 45–48.

Falk, Richard A., Robert C. Johansen, and Samuel S. Kim, eds. (1993) *Constitutional Foundations of World Peace.* Albany: State University of New York Press.

Fischer, Dietrich. (1984) *Preventing War in the Nuclear Age.* Totowa, N.J.: Rowman & Allenheld.

Fromkin, David. (1993) "The Coming Millennium: World Politics in the Twenty-First Century," *World Policy Journal* 10 (Spring): 1–7.

Gaddis, John Lewis. (1989) "Hanging Tough Paid Off," *Bulletin of the Atomic Scientists* 45 (January/February 1989): 11–14.

———. (1987) *The Long Peace: Inquiries into the History of the Cold War.* New York: Oxford University Press.

Gardner, Richard N., and Joseph P. Lorenz. (1992) *Post-Gulf War Challenges to the UN Collective Security System: Two Views on the Issue of Collective Security.* Washington, D.C.: U.S. Institute of Peace.

Garthoff, Raymond. (1985) *Détente and Confrontation: American–Soviet Relations from Nixon to Reagan.* Washington, D.C.: Brookings Institution.

―――. (1966) *Soviet Military Policy: A Historical Analysis*. New York: Praeger.

―――. (1962) *Soviet Strategy in the Nuclear Age*. New York: Praeger.

Gilpin, Robert. (1981) *War and Change in World Politics*. Cambridge: Cambridge University Press.

Goldblat, Jozef, and David Cox. (1988) *The Debate About Nuclear Weapon Tests*. Occasional Paper No. 5 (August). Ottawa: Canadian Institute for International Peace and Security.

Gordon, Michael. (1986) "U.S. Again Says It Won't Join Soviet Moratorium," *New York Times* (August 19): A1.

Huntington, Samuel P. (1993) "The Clash of Civilizations?" *Foreign Affairs* 72 (Summer): 22–49.

Huth, Paul, and Bruce Russett. (1984) "What Makes Deterrence Work? Cases from 1900 to 1980," *World Politics* 36 (December): 496–526.

Ibrahim, Youssef M. (1993) "War Is Said to Cost the Persian Gulf $676 Billion in 1990 and 1991," *New York Times* (April 25): 14.

Independent Commission on Disarmament and Security Issues. (1982) *Common Security: A Blueprint for Survival*. New York: Simon and Schuster.

Johansen, Robert C. (1986) "The Reagan Administration and the U.N.: The Costs of Unilateralism," *World Policy Journal* 3: 601–41.

―――. (1985) "The Future of Arms Control," *World Policy Journal* 2 (Spring): 193–227.

―――. (1983) *Toward an Alternative Security System*. New York: World Policy Institute.

―――. (1980) *The National Interest and the Human Interest: An Analysis of U.S. Foreign Policy*. Princeton, N.J.: Princeton University Press.

Kaldor, Mary. (1981) *The Baroque Arsenal*. New York: Hill and Wang.

Kegley, Charles W., Jr., and Gregory A. Raymond. (1991) "Alliances and the Preservation of the Postwar Peace: Weighing the Contribution," pp. 270–89 in Charles W. Kegley Jr., *The Long Postwar Peace*. New York: HarperCollins.

Kennan, George F. (1987) "Containment Then and Now," *Foreign Affairs* 65 (Spring): 885–90.

―――. (1982) *The Nuclear Delusion: Soviet–American Relations in the Atomic Age*. New York: Pantheon.

Kennedy, Paul. (1987) *The Rise and Fall of the Great Powers*. New York: Random House.

Kupchan, Charles A. (1989) "Empire, Military Power, and Economic Decline," *International Security* 13 (Spring): 36–53.

Levy, Jack S. (1981) "Alliance Formation and War Behavior: An Analysis of the Great Powers, 1495–1975," *Journal of Conflict Resolution* 25 (December): 581–613.

Lichtenburg, Frank R. (1986) "Military R & D Depletes Economic Might," *Wall Street Journal* (August 22): 22.

Lorenz, Joseph P. (1992) "The Case for Collective Security," pp. 19–52 in Richard N. Gardner and Joseph P. Lorenz, *Post-Gulf War Challenges to the UN Collective Security System: Two Views on the Issue of Collective Security*. Washington, D.C.: U.S. Institute of Peace.

Mandelbaum, Michael. (1989) "Ending Where It Began," *New York Times* (February 29): A19.

Mead, Walter Russell. (1993) "An American Grand Strategy: The Quest for Order in a Disordered World," *World Policy Journal* 10 (Spring): 9–37.

Mearsheimer, John J. (1993) "The Case for a Ukrainian Nuclear Deterrent," *Foreign Affairs* 72 (Summer): 50–66.

———. (1990) "Back to the Future: Instability in Europe after the Cold War," *International Security* 15 (Summer): 5–57.

Modelski, George. (1987) *Long Cycles in World Policies*. Seattle: University of Washington Press.

Modelski, George, and Sylvia Modelski, eds. (1988) *Documenting Global Leadership*. Seattle: University of Washington Press.

Mueller, John. (1989) *Retreat from Doomsday: The Obsolescence of Major War*. New York: Basic Books.

———. (1988) "The Essential Irrelevance of Nuclear Weapons," *International Security* 13 (Fall): 55–79.

Nye, Joseph S., Jr. (1987) "Nuclear Learning and U.S.–Soviet Security Regimes," *International Organization* 41 (Summer): 371–402.

Oden, Michael Dee. (1989) "Military Spending Erodes Real National Security," *Bulletin of the Atomic Scientists* 45 (June): 36–42.

Powell, Colin L. (1989) "Why History Will Honor Mr. Reagan," *New York Times* (January 15): 27.

President's Commission on Strategic Forces. (1983) "Excerpts from Report of President's Commission on Strategic Forces," *New York Times* (April 12): A18.

Rosecrance, Richard. (1992) "A New Concert of Powers," *Foreign Affairs* 71 (Spring): 64–82.

Rosenbaum, David E. (1989) "Pentagon Spending Could Be Cut in Half, Ex-Defense Officials Say," *New York Times* (December 13): 1, 16.

Sabin, Edward P. (1989) "Threat Inflation: U.S. Estimates of Soviet Military Capability," *Peace & Change* 14 (April): 191–202.

Schelling, Thomas C. (1989) "Has Arms Control Worked?" *Bulletin of the Atomic Scientists* 45 (May): 29–31.

Singer, J. David, and Melvin Small. (1979) "Conflict in the International System, 1816–1977: Historical Trends and Policy Futures," pp. 57–82 in J. David Singer, *Explaining War: Selected Papers from the Correlates of War Project*. Beverly Hills, Calif.: Sage.

———. (1968) "Alliance Aggregation and the Onset of War: 1815–1945," pp. 247–86 in J. David Singer, ed., *Quantitative International Politics: Insights and Evidence*. New York: Free Press.

Sivard, Ruth. (1991) *World Military and Social Expenditures 1991*. Washington, D.C.: World Priorities.

Smith, Gerard C. (1984) "U.S. Close to Violating ABM Treaty," *The Washington Post* (June 20): A12.

Smith, R. P. (1977) "Military Expenditure and Capitalism," *Cambridge Journal of Economics* 1: 61–76.

Spector, Leonard S. (1988) *The Undeclared Bomb*. Cambridge, Mass.: Ballinger.

Stevenson, Adlai E. (1962) "Working toward a World without War," pp. 13–28 in U.S. Arms Control and Disarmament Agency, *Disarmament: The New U.S. Initiative*. Washington, D.C.: U.S. Government Printing Office.

Stockholm Initiative on Global Security and Governance. (1991) *Common Responsibility in the 1990's*. Stockholm: Prime Minister's Office.

Stockholm International Peace Research Institute (SIPRI). (1991, 1992, 1993) *SIPRI Yearbook: World Armaments and Disarmament*. Oxford: Oxford University Press.

Tullberg, Ruth. (1986) "World Military Expenditure," *Bulletin of Peace Proposals* 17 (No. 3–4): 229–334.

U.S. Senate Committee on Foreign Relations. (1987) *The ABM Treaty Interpretation Resolution*. Washington, D.C.: U.S. Government Printing Office.

Vasquez, John A. (1991) "The Deterrence Myth: Nuclear Weapons and the Prevention of Nuclear War," pp. 203–23 in Charles W. Kegley Jr., ed., *The Long Postwar Peace*. New York: HarperCollins.

Wallace, Michael D. (1982) "Armaments and Escalation," *International Studies Quarterly* 26 (March): 37–56.

Warnke, Paul C., Gerard C. Smith, Robert S. McNamara, and Spurgeon M. Keeny, "The Folly of Scrapping SALT," *Arms Control Today* 16 (May/June): 3–7.

White, Ralph K. (1984) *Fearful Warriors: A Psychological Profile of U.S.–Soviet Relations*. New York: Free Press.

Wiesner, Jerome B., Philip Morrison, and Kosta Tsipis. (1993) "Ending Overkill," *Bulletin of the Atomic Scientists* 49 (March): 12–23.

Wolfe, Alan. (1984) *The Rise and Fall of the Soviet Threat*. Boston: South End Press.

World Commission on Environment and Development. (1987) *Our Common Future*. New York: Oxford University Press.

Wright, Quincy. (1965) *A Study of War*. Chicago: University of Chicago Press.

Zurn, Michael. (1993) "What Has Changed in Europe? The Challenge of Globalization and Individualization," Paper prepared for a conference on "Competing Perspectives on World Order," Copenhagen, May 14–16, Harvard Center for International Affairs.

CHAPTER 11

International Trade as a Force for Peace

NEIL R. RICHARDSON[1]

Can international trade be a force for peace among states? Might mutual trade bind together the attitudes or objective interests of states such that they will be less apt to war with one another? Liberal theories generally answer this question in the affirmative. At least some realists suggest, contrarily, that trade can be a source of interstate disagreement or even bitter rivalry and, therefore, a force for war instead of peace.[2] As neoliberalism is seemingly on the ascent at the moment, and as trade relations may be in flux, it seems doubly opportune to revisit a central plank in liberal thinking about international relations.

Theories pertinent to the question at hand are—like all theories of world politics—reflections of their times. Theorists are usually inspired to think in terms of the happenings they sense around them. "When times change, the changes regularly generate attention to the potential need to adjust the theoretical lens through which events are viewed," writes Charles Kegley in his introduction to this volume.[3] In connection with the question of trade's relationship to peace, it is not only the resurrection of liberal theory and macroeconomic trade flux that make the issue timely. There are also microeconomic changes afoot that are beginning to change, once again, the very meaning of "trade."

---

[1] I want to acknowledge the valuable comments of John Vasquez on an earlier version of this chapter.

[2] Still a third view is that international trade is insufficiently important to weigh heavily—either positively or negatively—with respect to the grave issues of war or its absence. See, for example, Mark Gasiorowski and Simon Polachek (1982), Brian Pollins (1989), and Lois Sayrs (1990).

[3] Of course, contemporaneous inspiration is also a constraint; it is difficult to imagine abstractions of relationships that are not in evidence and perhaps never have been.

As the first two sections of this chapter briefly show, realist and liberal theories have long differed over the relationship between trade and peace. The chapter next turns to changes in global affairs that have led to revisions of realist and, especially, liberal thinking on the matter in recent decades. Thereafter, I describe two microeconomic phenomena that some observers suspect will come to redefine the meaning of world commerce. Finally, the implications of this for the proposition that trade is a force for peace are explored.

REALIST VIEWS

From Thucydides forward, realism has tended to dominate theoretical interpretations of world politics. Preoccupied with issues of the national interest, state power, and international power balances, many variants of realism touch upon issues of international trade only secondarily. On the other hand, realists universally acknowledge that a state's power is importantly (not to say exclusively) grounded in the economic foundations of its society. Just how foreign trade figures into the economic equation is another matter. In fact, there are two divergent realist dispositions toward the relationship between foreign trade and state power.

One of them reflects mercantilism, the now obsolete belief that a state's power is in direct proportion to its wealth (usually construed to mean its stock of gold or silver bullion). It was with such wealth, after all, that the state could purchase the services of mercenary soldiers, sailors, and arms. Consistent with the conception of national power as both a means and an end, mercantilism provided an economic rationale for the use of military power to acquire and protect colonies and trade routes. Once asserted, this power could be enhanced by trading practices that provided net economic benefit—accrual of yet more bullion—to the more powerful trading state. Thus did mercantilism's emphasis on generating wealth by means of favorable trade ties fit perfectly with realism's view of state power as both means and end.

For European states in centuries past, the quest for colonies as a means of trade-generated wealth was itself a cause of rivalry and sometimes war.[4] Thus did the mercantilist variant of realism prescribe imperial trade despite the prospect of international conflict among metropoles. And this result is unsurprising in that realism is founded on Hobbesian tenets of rivalrous conflict in a purely anarchic international system.

The mercantilist premise that accretions of state wealth are the means to power has long since been abandoned. But there is something to the mercantil-

---

[4] Although the prospect of resulting war was not lost on realists, they are not directly responsible for elaborating the theories relevant to this point. J. A. Hobson (1965) and V. I. Lenin (1939) were initial contributors to theories of imperialism and the prospect of war as a further consequence of rivalry over colonial acquisition.

ist legacy. One idea is that trade relations can be beneficial to some parties at the political expense of others. Albert O. Hirshman (1945) elaborated this theme in his pioneering study of Nazi Germany's trade policy with Central European states in the 1930s. Not only does the less dependent partner enjoy trade benefits under these circumstances, it also compromises the autonomy of its more dependent partners. This asymmetry is a further source of power potential, and, significantly, the dominant partner has also reduced the prospect to need to war with its dependencies.[5]

A somewhat different position is taken by those realists who extol the virtues of economic self-sufficiency. For them, the economic independence of the state is threatened by trade ties—at least intensive ones—because the economic benefits of trade can become addictive (Knorr, 1973, chap. 4); ideally, a state's economy should be self-sustaining. Moreover, for some realists the mere connectedness of states, to say nothing of their prospective interdependence, increases the probability of conflict among them (Waltz, 1971). And this threat to the peace is particularly great in the absence of a hegemonic guarantor.

The worry over interdependence also finds expression in neorealism, as crystallized by Kenneth Waltz (1979). The neorealist view is that "if interdependence grows at a pace that exceeds the development of central control, then interdependence hastens the occasion for war" (Waltz, 1979: 138). Yet, Waltz's peculiar definition of (systemic) interdependence is confined to relations between or among the great powers of the day, omitting all other states. Thus, his judgments cannot be of much assistance in the context of the broader assertion that trade inhibits war.

Although neorealism is unhelpful to this discussion, realism—to recapitulate—is of two minds on the question of whether trade is a force for peace. Some realists are inclined toward the mercantilist belief that trade is a most useful way in which to accrue state power in order to better fend off adversaries or, indeed, also a way to assert that power by means of asymmetrical trade advantage. Other realists emphasize the dangers of developing a reliance upon trade, asymmetrical or otherwise, and so emphasize the virtues of autarchy instead. Thus, for some realists, carefully limited foreign trade is valuable to the state, but, for others, even minimal trade may spark conflict.

LIBERAL VIEWS

Classical liberals, on the other hand, were quite single-minded on the question. They believed that free trade would be associated with the reduced

---

[5] See Klaus Knorr (1973, chap. 4) for a representative and admirably thorough discussion of the concepts of power and wealth and the relationships between them from this realist perspective. His sixth chapter turns to the exercise of power utilizing trade relations, including the prospect of pacifying other states.

likelihood of war. In Robert Keohane's (1990) view, there have been three strands of liberal justification for this, two of which survive intact in modern liberal theory.[6] The first line of argument, resting on domestic politics, characterized aristocracies as power seeking and mercantilist. Their ouster would create new, minimalist governments representing the bourgeoisie, which would be inherently uninterested in national power rivalries and eager to avoid war. Barry Buzan (1984: 600) points out that this prognosis was never tested because the emergent democracies quickly evolved into systems of mass politics replete with interventionist governments (see also Carr, 1939).

Complementing the domestically based expectation, "commercial" liberalism also advocated free trade as a force for peace. This internationally grounded rationale proceeds from the writings of Adam Smith and David Ricardo on the economic efficiencies of free market capitalism. Ricardo, in particular, showed how free trade among countries could benefit all parties and why this opportunity was so much more common than Smith had supposed. Thus, liberal thought to this day (for example, Rosecrance, 1986) continues to incorporate the relatively straightforward idea that free trade creates a harmony of commercial interests among states.

Relatively free trade has subsequently been observed on a widespread basis. Thus, unlike the liberals' domestic theory, the international rationale has been "tested." Indeed, both the prosperity and peace prevalent among the European powers in the late nineteenth and early twentieth centuries were widely attributed to free-trade practices disciplined by the British. And the return to mercantile protectionism during the Great Depression of the 1930s only reinforced the conviction that free trade was a vastly superior arrangement. Accordingly, free trade among major economies was renewed following the Second World War under the auspices of United States hegemony.

The third argument—"regulatory" liberalism—is also international in character. It stresses the crucial role that rules and international institutions can play in promoting peace among states. Moreover, the convenient marriage of commercial and regulatory liberalism is much in evidence in the conception of the Bretton Woods arrangements: Commercially derived harmonies of mutual interests would develop by adherence to rules overseen by international institutions that states create.

Within that framework, in the 1950s an institutionalized subset of these free-trade states developed what has become the European Union. These new institutions and policies embodied the neofunctionalist ideas of Karl Deutsch (1954, 1957), Ernst Haas (1958), and others. What they shared were regulatory liberal beliefs, of course. In addition, they expected that this coop-

---

[6] See Keohane (1990). Barry Buzan's (1984) treatment of liberalism organizes discussion around two strains of thought, the first comprising what Keohane terms the "republican" justification and the second including both Keohane's "commercial" and "regulatory" liberalism. A fourfold alternative is offered by Joseph Nye (1988: 246 ff.).

eration, once established, would be so mutually beneficial as to "spill over" into functionally different realms of activity.

Among European leaders, a principal impetus to undertake this experiment was to create very close economic interdependencies that, in turn, would generate both objective interests in, and favorable attitudes toward, maintaining peace among the continental powers twice devastated by recent wars. That trade could provide objective (that is, material) interests in peace was clear from Ricardo's time. About attitudes, on the other hand, Deutsch (1954) drew from Richard Van Wagenen:

> How do groups of men gain the status of security communities? . . . A *security community* is considered to be a group which has become integrated, where *integration* is defined as the attainment of a sense of community, accompanied by formal or informal institutions or practices, sufficiently strong and widespread to assure peaceful change among members of a group with "reasonable" certainty over a "long" period of time. (Van Wagenen, 1952: 10–11)

Thus could emerge what Deutsch and his associates (1957: 5–7) called a "pluralistic security community," defined as a group of states among which "there is real assurance that the members of that community will not fight each other physically, but will settle their disputes in some other way."

Notice that regulatory liberalism does not assert that a harmony of interests will emerge automatically. Rather, "international institutions need to be constructed both to facilitate the purposes that governments espouse in common and gradually to alter governmental conceptions of self-interest in order to widen the scope for cooperation" (Keohane, 1990: 181).

MODERN INTERDEPENDENCE

The liberalism widely observed in the 1950s and 1960s led many if not most states into increasingly close and complex interdependence by the 1970s (see Keohane and Nye, 1977). Students of integration had already posited the liberal benefits of institutionalized cooperation as establishing practices that might not otherwise take root. Becoming more prominent by the 1970s, however, were less formalized international institutions than those of Bretton Woods and the European Union.

These proliferating regimes seemed to some to have context-specific origins, but theorists sensed a broader pattern. As Keohane (1984, chap. 6) formulated it, both formal and informal international regimes serve to minimize their members' transaction costs, assure equality of information, and assure liability. That is, they pave the way for greater volumes of mutually advantageous transactions than would transpire in their absence. This, then, conceptualizes a rationale to account for so many new regimes.

An impressive variety of economic transactions has in fact blossomed in recent decades. Commodity trade has been joined by the rapid growth of trade in services. Direct foreign investment has grown even more rapidly than trade itself. Indeed, so much of today's trade is attributable to foreign investment that, in Dennis Encarnation's (1992: xi) words, "intracompany shipments between multinational parents and their foreign subsidiaries control international commerce among industrialized countries." Additional capital flows represent huge quantities of portfolio investment, including purchases of foreign government debt. On the twin bases of variety and volume, the density of international economic transactions has grown enormously in the past four decades.

Regimes, in turn, have developed in rough proportion to the volume and diversity of economic (and other) international transactions. And many believe that the increasing quantities of interactions have bred a qualitative change as well. John Ruggie (1983: 281) quotes Emile Durkheim (1895: 115) on the principle involved: "Growth in the volume and dynamic density of societies modifies profoundly the fundamental conditions of collective existence. . . ." For Durkheim, dynamic density refers to the quantity, velocity, and diversity of transactions that occur between members of the society.

Notice, then, how sharply the logic of interdependence departs from realist views. For interdependence theorists, the qualitative change that can result from quantitative growth in international transactions changes the international system itself, in substantial part because the volume induces (and is further encouraged by) the creation of regimes (see Keohane and Nye, 1987: 745–49). In this view, regimes are a mechanism of governance that states arrange as a way of facilitating those transactions. Regimes also incorporate norms, principles of behavior, and decisional processes, all of which mitigate interstate conflict. It is in this sense, then, that the more recent treatments of interdependence go well beyond either realist or classical liberal definitions of mutual vulnerability in their accounting for trade as a force for peace.

THE TRANSFORMATION OF GLOBAL COMMERCE

Meanwhile, two new economic activities have begun to thrive in the last decade.[7] First, firms are becoming increasingly mobile in a new, global context. In addition, they are fast forming alliances with competing firms. These two phenomena of microeconomics have macroeconomic implications as they spread. It remains to be seen whether modern conceptions of interdependence can accommodate these developments.

---

[7] These changes in the behavior of firms are major tenets in Robert Reich's (1991) *The Work of Nations*.

Let us begin with the new dimension to the mobility of the firm. As the world's leading industrial firms first developed, they became what Robert Reich (1991, chap. 4) calls "national champions." Owned and operated in their home states and enormous in scale, firms such as Krupp and Siemens in Germany, Du Pont and General Electric in the United States, and Fuji and Toyota in Japan symbolized the core identity with their countries. The idea is epitomized in the familiar phrase of then-president of General Motors, Charles Wilson (in U.S. Senate, 1953): ". . . for years I [have] thought what was good for our country was good for General Motors, and vice versa." This role of very large companies as the economic bedrock of their respective societies remained undiluted by the emergence of multinational operations on the part of manufacturers that burgeoned in the 1950s and thereafter.

By the 1980s, however, a new pattern of corporate behavior was developing. The rebuilding of Europe and Japan had reached maturity and industrialization was fast spreading to yet other economies. The old national champions faced intensified business challenges from other countries—a direct consequence of global commerce that continued to grow even faster in a liberal climate than did world product itself. Many of these firms therefore began moving their manufacturing and other advanced operations abroad in order to meet the cost structures of their new, foreign competition.

No longer were overseas subsidiaries just suppliers of raw materials and low-value components; subsidiaries were assigned sophisticated tasks of design, final assembly, and marketing. Capitalism's biggest firms were mobile as never before, and advances in communications made it technologically feasible to be so. Capital and ideas could also be moved from country to country instantaneously, so the advantages of keeping the more complex, high value-added tasks close to headquarters were quickly evaporating. By 1988, for example, some 17,000 international telephone lines were carrying data, video images, and engineering designs instantaneously around the globe (Reich, 1991: 111).

The second change under way for the old national champions is the rapid trend toward strategic alliances with foreign companies in the same industry. Some of these are long-term partnerships, anchored in equity ownership—thus, Ford now owns 25 percent of rival Mazda while Honda owns 20 percent of rival Rover. Other alliances are more transient and project-specific, giving rise to the term "virtual corporations" (Davidow and Malone, 1992). Generally speaking, there are two purposes these various alliances can serve. First, an alliance with a rival may serve to achieve economies of scale. The Chrysler–Mitsubishi assembly plant in Illinois produces virtually identical cars under different nameplates for the two companies.[8] Second, an alliance

[8] Originally the Diamond-Star assembly plant in Normal, Illinois, was equally owned by each firm. In 1991, Chrysler sold its half of the plant to Mitsubishi on the condition that certain Chrysler components continue to be used there and that Chrysler-badged vehicles continue to be produced there.

can allow each firm to complement the other's most distinctive talents and simultaneously learn from its partner's expertise.[9] In addition, these alliances are often complex: Mitsubishi works with Chrysler in North America and meanwhile cooperates in far-flung electronic and automotive ventures with Germany's Daimler-Benz and in automobile coproduction with the Volvo-Renault alliance in the Netherlands (see Kapstein and Toy, 1990).

Increased mobility and the proliferation of strategic alliances are corporate responses to the integration of the global economy. By the same token, these processes give further impetus to that integration. They again redefine the importance of the term "trade" in the discourse of international political economy. For what is literally traded—goods and services that cross state borders—remains relatively easy to measure. But such trade figures are now compounded threefold. As noted earlier, trade of recent decades has increasingly consisted of intrafirm transfers and to that extent represents one consequence of direct foreign investment as well. Now, in view of the twin dynamics of the 1980s, another compounding reflects the new face of a firm's mobility and, much more complicating, the network of alliances that veil the transfer or "trade" of technology and ideas.

"TRADE" AND PEACE

In this new light, the proposition that international trade is a force for peace merits reconsideration. One might suppose that, in keeping with classical liberal thinking or, more to the point, for reasons proffered by integration and interdependence scholars, a global economy that is still more tightly knit by recent trends in the behavior of firms would therefore be a more pacific one. But this logic would be too facile. Indeed, the purpose of this chapter is to suggest that this type of thinking does not take into account important changes afoot in the global economy.

It is not difficult to understand that the new corporate patterns can occasion interstate rivalry and conflict. One example is found in the competition for flat-panel display screen technology, now prevalent in laptop computers. In the future, this technology is expected to mushroom in sales for television sets, x-ray imaging, civilian radar, and other applications. Already, an alliance between Japan's flat-panel display manufacturers and U.S. computer firms is in place. Flat-panel developers in the United States are being squeezed out of existence by long-term alliances between the same Japanese and U.S. companies in which the latter are already dependent for continuously im-

---

[9] Vicki Golich (1992) elaborates on several types of gains available to manufacturing allies in the context of the commercial aircraft industry. She then adduces three models of corporate alliance structures.

proved memory chips and semiconductors. The computer firms simply will not consider switching to U.S. flat-panel suppliers, even if the latter can offer price or performance advantages over the Japanese products. On flat-panel display competition, the U.S. government has been passive.[10]

Washington has intervened instead on the issue of semiconductors, concluding difficult negotiations with Japan in 1986 that guarantee U.S. firms growing shares of chip sales in the Japanese market.[11] But this agreement illustrates the new mobility of major firms and the complexity of a situation the government did not understand. Texas Instruments, a U.S. company, is a major beneficiary of the semiconductor agreement. However, the U.S. government's hard-won gains for Texas Instruments may largely be siphoned into Taiwan because that is where the firm has invested $250 million to produce such chips (Reich, 1991: 159–60)!

These examples illustrate that the important changes discussed earlier—mobility and global alliances—are well under way. These cases also show that states are being drawn into disputes that are given new form by the growth of those global alliances. Finally, as we see in the semiconductor example, policymakers can all the more easily misunderstand the consequences of their acts—in this case, they are seemingly oblivious to the mobility of relevant firms—even as they futilely expend diplomatic goodwill in sometimes rancorous negotiations with other governments.

This, of course, is a recipe for interstate conflict. In the first place, the stakes are high. Both real economic interests as well as the symbolic importance of "national champions," which are presumed to deserve government support when seriously threatened, are at risk. Furthermore, the complexity of the new microeconomic behavior is likely to escape some policymakers and confound others.[12] Frustration over failed policy is one likely result (see, for example, Krauss and Reich, 1992). Resentment and hostility aimed at the policies of other states are others (see Encarnation, 1992). Thus, alarm in Washington over chronic imbalances in U.S. foreign trade with Japan routinely breeds complaints to the government in Tokyo. In short, interstate hostility and conflict bred of mismanaged commercial rivalry are already in evidence and seem all the more likely in the future.

---

[10] See the Corporation for Public Broadcasting (1992) program "Frontline: Why Japan Is Winning the War" for further details on proceedings leading up to the recent decision of the International Trade Commission.

[11] See Clyde Prestowitz (1988, chap. 2). The U.S. government also subsidizes Sematech, a semiconductor research and development consortium that is open only to U.S. firms.

[12] What is a member of the U.S. Congress to think when lobbied by the "Big Three" U.S. automakers for much higher tariff protection against Japanese minivans? Would the official know that Ford and Nissan jointly produce a minivan in the United States already? That the Dodge Colt minivan is imported from Japan? Would she or he appreciate that, because Japanese minivans have only a very small market share in the United States, Detroit would gain little from such a diplomatically costly decision? Few government leaders in the major trading states are likely to have such trade expertise.

If future "trade" (that is, commercial) relations will promote conflict, that propensity needs to be balanced by additional factors. Reconsider, for example, the growing magnitude of the stakes involved. This is a two-edged sword. Not only is there more reason for states to disagree, but there may also be more incentive to agree along lines adduced by initial theorists of interdependence. If international commerce creates greater efficiencies, then there is more wealth to share as well as to quarrel over.

Additionally, the accelerating trend of complex corporate alliances can generate integrative processes of several types. One is the multicultural sensitizing of the business people themselves (see Fayerweather, 1982). Another is the standardization of business practices and manufacturing processes (see Simison, 1991, for example). And a third prospect for integrative impact is in the politics of states.

Much is made of differences in state–society relations (for example, Katzenstein, 1978; Porter, 1990). Is government a partner in the national economy, following indicative planning or even industrial policy? Or is government seen as an adversary of the private sector? However a particular state may be characterized, the intensity of its concern with international commercial issues must eventually grow as its "national champions" become global players with "foreign" business allies. For a government to ignore this would be suicidal.

Indeed, even in the United States, where government traditionally stays at arm's length from the private sector, there is a growing realization that public policy—including coordination with other states—has become necessary. By contrast, such a convention as, say, the Group of 7 would not have met a warm reception even two decades ago. Yet, coordination of policy requires that norms (as well as policies) be substantially harmonized. It may require that decision-making processes (including dispute settlement) be established. In short, policy coordination necessitated by the growing density (and complexity) of valued transactions calls for regimes.

The ambitious agenda of the recently completed Uruguay Round of the General Agreement on Tariffs and Trade (GATT) reflects some of the newer commercial developments. It greatly expands the jurisdiction of GATT, incorporating provisions for both trade in services and the protection of intellectual property—including technology. But there is continuing uncertainty that the proposals incorporated into this document will ever be implemented broadly by the member states. Furthermore, the creeping protectionism of the last two decades, combined with the torturous path of the Uruguay Round negotiations themselves, has seriously compromised the credibility of GATT; its survival as a meaningful overseer of liberal trade remains in question. Lester Thurow (1992: 65), for one, has prematurely pronounced it "dead."

What may be emerging in its place are regional trade blocs, of which the European Union and the North American Free Trade Agreement (NAFTA) are the most prominent. These feature within-bloc commercial liberalization that goes well beyond GATT levels of achievement. Trade between the blocs or between bloc and nonbloc economies is another matter, however. It may be that GATT's legacy encourages the continuation of relatively free trade between blocs. The alternative, almost certainly, is not a return to high levels of protection across a broad range of goods; rather, it appears to be more of the managed trade that has been developing in the last decade among the industrial economies. Its critics will decry the "neomercantile" character of this possibility but, as Buzan (1984: 613–17) asserts, there is a real prospect that such protectionism can be benignly modest. Indeed, capitalism's largest firms will exert pressure to see that it is so because their alliance webs otherwise might be constrained.

If so, then the implication is straightforward for the original proposition linking trade to peace. Understanding that trade has for some time more properly referred to a variety of commercial transactions, we should now be cognizant also of the intricate webs that global businesses are creating. All of this implies much greater complexity and therefore both frustration and policy failure for states. By the same token, these patterns are producing a new economic fabric, one in which the identities of both national economies and firms themselves are breaking down. This is not only a cause of international interdependence; it is also a dawning new form of economic integration.

The rate at which governments can understand and then contend with these changes is problematic. Thus, the impact of commercial integration on interstate cooperation and conflict depends very importantly on a learning curve:

> International institutions need to be constructed both to facilitate the purposes that governments espouse in common and gradually to alter governmental conceptions of self-interest in order to widen the scope for cooperation. (Keohane, 1990: 181)

And, in this form, new and stronger regimes are emerging at regional levels, perhaps eclipsing the weaker GATT regime to which they owe their continued liberalism. Relations between them may evidence continued commercial rivalry, but the language of conflict is perhaps itself becoming defined in economic and commercial terms (see Rosecrance, 1986). War within the industrialized blocs is essentially unthinkable; by another name, the EU and NAFTA are also "security communities."

Furthermore, even if "trade wars" between blocs (and including Japan) become somewhat more likely with the demise of a GATT-inspired economic order, real war across major blocs seems highly unlikely. The major commercial states and other bloc members are very busy negotiating their differences over the management of their economies. The fact that they are trying to collaborate represents their growing realization that collective management is increasingly necessary to their prosperity. It also represents an intensification of initial integrative undertakings by the states themselves.

Meanwhile, as the new microeconomics of global firms becomes more widely appreciated, government leaders in the future may better understand the elusive and momentary properties of gains to be had from trade and other forms of contemporary international commerce. And, similarly, scholars may progress beyond characterizations of theory premised upon "absolute" and "relative" gains for states (see Grieco, chap. 6 in this volume). Theoretical lenses may be adjusted again to pertinent changes in the referent world. Thus, gains will often be defined as distributions within and across blocs of states. Moreover, the distribution of gains within a bloc will not bear on the likelihood of war among members of that bloc precisely because that likelihood will be nil in any case. The question of the links between trade and war will apply more restrictively to only those relations between states that do not belong to the same (or to any) commercial bloc.

Yet, quite apart from whether or when practitioners and scholars of world politics change their thinking, new and deadly interstate wars doubtless will exist, with some wars beginning even as other wars continue. Even the optimistic liberal and neoliberal theorists have not tried to deny this. The proposition that trade is a force for peace does not promise that the trading activity can be an iron-clad guarantee against war. Nevertheless, in the context of the newest connotations of "trade," it is becoming increasingly difficult to foresee circumstances in which the world's most active commercial states—including realism's "great powers"—would war with each other.

REFERENCES

Buzan, Barry. (1984) "Economic Structure and International Security: The Limits of the Liberal Case," *International Organization* 38 (Autumn): 597–624.

Carr, E. H. (1939) *Nationalism and After*. London: Macmillan.

Corporation for Public Broadcasting. (1992) "Frontline: Why Japan Is Winning the War," revised edition.

Davidow, William H., and Michael S. Malone. (1992) *The Virtual Corporation: Structuring and Revitalizing the Corporation for the 21st Century*. New York: HarperBusiness.

Deutsch, Karl W. (1954) *Political Community at the International Level*. New York: Random House.

Deutsch, Karl W., et al. (1957) *Political Community and the North Atlantic Area*. Princeton, N.J.: Princeton University Press.

Durkheim, Emile. ([1895] 1964) *The Rules of Sociological Method*. Edited by George E. G. Catlin. New York: Free Press.

Encarnation, Dennis J. (1992) *Rivals Beyond Trade: America versus Japan in Global Competition*. Ithaca, N.Y.: Cornell University Press.

Fayerweather, John. (1982) "A Review of the State of the Art," pp. 311–44 in John Fayerweather, ed., *Host National Attitudes toward Multinational Corporations*. New York: Praeger.

Gasiorowski, Mark, and Simon W. Polachek. (1982) "Conflict and Interdependence: East–West Trade Linkages in the Era of Detente," *Journal of Conflict Resolution* 20 (December): 709–29.

Golich, Vicki L. (1992) "From Competition to Collaboration: The Challenge of Commercial-Class Aircraft Manufacturing," *International Organization* 46 (Autumn): 899–934.

Haas, Ernst B. (1958) *The Uniting of Europe: Political, Economic, and Social Forces, 1950–1957.* Stanford, Calif.: Stanford University Press.

Hirschman, Albert O. (1945) *National Power and the Structure of Foreign Trade.* Berkeley: University of California Press.

Hobson, John A. (1965) *Imperialism: A Study.* Ann Arbor: University of Michigan Press.

Kapstein, Jonathan, with Stewart Toy. (1990) "Mitsubishi Is Taking a Back Road into Europe," *Business Week* (November 19): 64.

Katzenstein, Peter J. (1978) *Between Power and Plenty: Foreign Economic Policies of Advanced Industrial States.* Madison: University of Wisconsin Press.

Keohane, Robert O. (1990) "International Liberalism Reconsidered," pp. 165–94 in John Dunn, ed., *The Economic Limits to Modern Politics.* Cambridge: Cambridge University Press.

———. (1984) *After Hegemony: Cooperation and Discord in the World Political Economy.* Princeton, N.J.: Princeton University Press.

Keohane, Robert O., and Joseph S. Nye Jr. (1987) "Power and Interdependence Revisited," *International Organization* 41 (Autumn): 725–53.

———. (1977) *Power and Interdependence: World Politics in Transition.* Boston: Little, Brown.

Knorr, Klaus. (1973) *Power and Wealth: The Political Economy of International Power.* New York: Basic Books.

Krauss, Ellis S., and Simon Reich. (1992) "Ideology, Interests, and the American Executive: Toward a Theory of Foreign Competition and Manufacturing Trade Policy," *International Organization* 46 (Autumn): 857–98.

Lenin, V. I. (1939) *Imperialism: The Highest Stage of Capitalism.* New York: International Publishers.

Nye, Joseph S., Jr. (1988) "Neorealism and Neoliberalism," *World Politics* 40 (January): 235–51.

Pollins, Brian. (1989) "Does Trade Still Follow the Flag?" *American Political Science Review* 83 (June): 465–80.

Porter, Michael E. (1990). *The Competitive Advantage of Nations.* New York: The Free Press.

Prestowitz, Clyde V., Jr. (1988) *Trading Places: How We Allowed Japan to Take the Lead.* New York: Basic Books.

Reich, Robert B. (1991) *The Work of Nations: Preparing Ourselves for 21st Century Capitalism.* New York: Knopf.

Rosecrance, Richard. (1986) *The Rise of the Trading State: Commerce and Conquest in the Modern World.* New York: Basic Books.

Ruggie, John Gerard. (1983) "Continuity and Transformation in the World Polity: Toward a Neorealist Synthesis," *World Politics* 35 (January): 261–85.

Sayrs, Lois. (1990) "Expected Utility and Peace Science: An Assessment of Trade and Conflict," *Conflict Management and Peace Science* 11 (July): 17–44.

Simison, Robert L. (1991) "Nissan's U.K. Plant Teaches EC a Lesson," *Wall Street Journal* (July 23): A12.

Thurow, Lester. (1992) *Head to Head: The Coming Economic Battle among Japan, Europe, and America.* New York: Morrow.

U.S. Senate Armed Services Committee. (1953) *Confirmation Hearings on Charles Wilson as Secretary of Defense, February 18, 1953.*

Van Wagenen, Richard W. (1952) *Research in the International Organization Field: Some Notes on a Possible Focus.* Princeton, N.J.: Princeton University, Center for Research on World Political Institutions.

Waltz, Kenneth N. (1979) *Theory of International Politics.* Reading, Mass.: Addison-Wesley.

———. (1971) "Conflict in World Politics," pp. 454–74 in Steven L. Spiegel and Kenneth N. Waltz, eds., *Conflict in World Politics.* Cambridge, Mass.: Winthrop.

PART IV

Normative Constraints on International Conduct? Law and Morality in International Affairs

In order to survive, are states liberated to do whatever they deem most serves their interest in realizing that goal, including the use of force? Is *raison d'état* the only acceptable norm for national conduct? Or, instead, should states encourage the restriction of national autonomy through voluntary support for rules for international behavior that would police predatory practices and expansionist drives?

The problematic contribution of legal rules and procedures in regulating national behavior in international relations theory is the object of Harvey Starr's chapter, "International Law and International Order." Here, he first surveys the range of skeptical assessments of the functions of international law encompassed within the realist tradition, dissecting the critique along the basic divisions within it of its alleged limitations and functions. Against this argument about the relative irrelevance of international law in controlling states' behavior, Starr summarizes the liberal position that international law *is* relevant, and he identifies the propositions advanced by liberal theories in the Grotian tradition (see Bull, 1966; Cutler, 1991) about how international legal norms have demonstrably promoted international order, even in circumstances of a disorganized global community where realism maintains that that constraining influence will be weakest.

Stressing the interdependent nature of the international system and its impact on the formation of a truly global "society," Starr suggests why it is advantageous to view the relationship of international law to world order as a function of the system's changing and increasingly interconnected condition and of the level of consensus that prevails in this incipient society. His overview concludes (1) with an evaluation of the implications for a reconstructed theory of international relations that draws on a confluence of realist and liberal propositions in order to explain more clearly how rules for interstate behavior emerge to contribute to order in an anarchical system and (2) with an argument as to why this perspective can be used to synthesize realist and neoliberal views, as a truly international society along the lines that Grotius envisioned begins finally to crystallize.

Beyond the debatable place of international law in world affairs, perhaps on no issue are realism and liberalism believed to diverge more than with regard to the controversial place of morality in statecraft. At the extreme, "realists seemed to be arguing that there was no room for ethical considerations in a Hobbesian universe" (Hoffmann, 1987: 8) whereas, in contrast, liberals make normative concern and values their point of analytic departure and the center of their attention.

Consider first the realist perspective. To Machiavelli and Hobbes, in the latter's memorable phrase, international relations is "a war of all against all," and, because of this harsh reality, the morality that pertains to interpersonal relations in civil society is irrelevant. Extending this thesis, Max Weber argued that the international system prevents a monopolistic control of the use of force and therefore fosters the continual collusion of values with power, with the result that the two realms are doomed to divorce, and power prevails. Other realists' opinions on this issue, while diverse, generally concur with George F. Kennan's (1951) condemnation of moralistic approaches to international politics, arguing that the range of relevance of moral principles to the practice of statecraft is small (Oppenheim, 1991) and that what Morgenthau (1985: 584) termed the moral disease of "the crusading spirit" in politics *is* truly dangerous and misplaced.

This view is often contrasted sharply with the liberal tradition, which takes ethical values and their consequences as the bedrock of its perspective for analyzing how states should and do act. In this vision, international relations is inherently a domain of moral choice; for against "realism's tendency to be morally complacent, since it lacks the external standards of human rights that liberalism can use to criticize governments in power" (Keohane, 1992: 193), liberalism holds that the choices international actors make should be judged against a moral code, a conception of right and wrong.

Joel H. Rosenthal illuminates these differences on the controversial place of ethics in world affairs in "Rethinking the Moral Dimensions of Foreign Policy." After first describing the realist and liberal views of this topic in international thought, he finds danger in the tendency to exaggerate the differences, for this kind of dichotomization can lead to misunderstanding. To reduce the misunderstanding and steady the needle on our moral and theoretical compass, Rosenthal finds a common ground in the realist and liberal orientations that are often mistakenly regarded as incompatible. Reviewing the admittedly opposing premises associated with the two theories, he shows why the bifurcation is overdrawn because "most of the literature of the past fifty years is an unwitting and curious combination of the two approaches." Juxtaposing the realist and liberal assumptions about the role of morality in foreign policy, Rosenthal reveals why the points of convergence far exceed the points of divergence, particularly with respect to the attention both perspectives give to the importance of an international consensus about moral norms for the maintenance of order. In fact, his review shows that "realism and liberalism have always been in conversation," that "it is hard to imagine one without the other," and that both agree on the need to find a shared moral vision.

Contemplating the contemporary scene, Rosenthau convincingly argues why the hard choices and moral dilemmas of the post–Cold War "without the evils of 'communism' or 'capitalism' as self-justifying foils for one another" will inevitably bring the convergence of realism and liberalism into even tighter association because of the need for both perspectives "to make sense of the present and offer alternatives for the future." In this will be found the seeds for a further paradigmatic synthesis that, Rosenthal concludes, "by necessity" must incorporate "the insights of both realists and liberals. The hybrid exists, and in reality it has always been here. The challenge now is to relate the insights of these traditions to the problems of our age."

REFERENCES

Bull, Hedley. (1966) "The Grotian Conception of International Society," pp. 51–73 in Herbert Butterfield and Martin Wight, eds., Diplomatic Investigations: Essays in the Theory of International Politics. Cambridge, Mass.: Harvard University Press.

Cutler, A. C. (1991) "The 'Grotian Tradition' in International Relations," Review of International Studies 17 (January): 41–65.

Hoffmann, Stanley. (1987) The Political Ethics of International Relations. Seventh Morgenthau Memorial Lecture. New York: Carnegie Council on Ethics and International Affairs.

Keohane, Robert O. (1992) "International Liberalism Reconsidered," pp. 165–94 in John Dunn, ed., The Economic Limits to Modern Politics. Cambridge: Cambridge University Press.

Kennen, George F. (1951) American Diplomacy, 1900–1950. Chicago: University of Chicago Press.

Morgenthau, Hans J. (1985) Politics among Nations, 6th ed. Revised by Kenneth W. Thompson. New York: Knopf.

Oppenheim, Felix E. (1991) The Place of Morality in Foreign Policy. Lexington, Mass.: D. C. Heath.

CHAPTER 12

International Law and International Order

HARVEY STARR

My aim in this chapter is to outline a scheme by which we could think theoretically about international law, including its role in the international system, how it both reflects and contributes to order and "society" in that system, and finally how to distinguish and then reconcile realist and idealist (here "neoliberal") conceptions of international law. I will do this by first looking at the general relationship between law and "order," then at the more specific relationship between international law and international society. Next, I will outline realist and liberal (or Grotian, in Hedley Bull's [1977] terms) views of international law as law and then look at the functions of law in the anarchic society by stressing the interdependent nature of the international system. Finally, international law will be viewed as a mechanism for global order under changing conditions of interdependence. Realist and neoliberal responses to the question of how to manage interdependence will then provide a perspective that can be used in synthesizing these contending views of international law.

INTERNATIONAL LAW AND THE WESTPHALIAN STATE SYSTEM

Definitions of international law stress that it is composed of a body of *rules* that somehow govern states in their relations and that it delineates both the rights and obligations of states in these relations. A typical example is Bull (1977: 127): "International law may be regarded as a body of rules which binds states and other agents in world politics in their relations with one another and is considered to have the status of law." Key questions raised by such definitions concern *how* states that are sovereign, existing within the formally anarchic Westphalian system, can be "bound" by some "law" that has not been generated, is not interpreted, and cannot be enforced by a centralized, legitimate authority.

Such questions are really concerned with where law comes from, the nature of such law and thus on what basis such rules are binding, and why the subjects of international law would obey "law." These questions also highlight the central idea that law can only take on meaning given the context of the system or "society" within which it is supposed to operate, as that is shaped by the meanings attached by its units to its essential concepts (that is, "states," "sovereignty," and "anarchy").

Broadly, two approaches to law traditionally have been argued. Law may be based on transcendent, universalistic principles—they apply to all people at all times under all circumstances. The basis for obligation in this natural law perspective derives from the existence of universal principles (whether derived from divine sources or general laws such as those 'of the natural sciences that apply to all of nature), which are "self-evident to any individual exercising his 'right reason', or the moral faculty with which he was endowed" (von Glahn, 1992: 26). Alternatively, positivist theories of law maintain that law is what people say is law. The basis for obligation derives from self-interest, utility, and consent. The binding nature of rules comes from customary behavior, that is, the regularized and predictable practices of those who created the rules. This includes the articulation of expectations about rights and obligations (*opinio juris*). This view of international law corresponded well with concepts of the "social contract" as argued by such writers as Vattel in the eighteenth century and was particularly well suited to the nineteenth-century liberal utilitarianism of Mill and Bentham.

The dominant view of international law, as presented in contemporary international law and international relations texts, is positivist. However, the existence of an "eclectic" approach, which has attempted to combine the two by adding natural law to the self-interest and consent core of positivism, as found in the international law of human rights, should be noted. The positivist approach—that international law is what the subjects of international law agree the law is—has important consequences. It means that international law will reflect the *degree* of society in the international system in terms of what states find it in their interest to consent to and the degree of consensus that emerges. It reflects the various factors that lead states (and other actors) to obey international law and the conditions under which states find themselves constrained by international law, even if that constraint is self-constraint.

In the introduction to this volume, Charles Kegley notes that we must be concerned with "factors that promote change and continuity," that "circumstance and context also matter." The positivist view of international law drives us to consider the same assumption—that law is situational and reflects evolving politics, political structures, and dynamics of the system at some specific time in history. The consequences of a positivist view of international law for this chapter may be summarized for introductory purposes by observing that:

The perspective on international law provided here falls somewhere between the extreme views: that international law has no impact on the activities of states, and that international law can solve all our global problems. Following the approach of Stanley Hoffmann, we will look at international law as merely a magnifying mirror that "faithfully and cruelly" reflects the realities of world politics. (Russett and Starr, 1992: 466)

In the introduction Kegley also entreats us to ask, What is new? What is constant? The reflecting-mirror view of international law stresses certain constants. One is that international law is part of the environment or context of states. International law comprises one part of the set of "opportunities" and constraints within which states must act (see Most and Starr, 1989). In one of many feedback loops, the society of states in the international system creates law, but that law, in turn, becomes part of the context within which the society of states and its individual members must act, constraining them through a set of rules that alter the incentives, costs, and benefits of various possible choices and behaviors.

A second constant is the tension between the anarchy of the Westphalian system and the need for order (see Russett and Starr, 1992; Starr, 1994). The statesmen and leaders who fashioned the Peace of Westphalia in 1648 created agreements meeting the needs of the time. The Westphalian tradeoff stressed independence and autonomy, as against the lack of order inherent in the formal anarchy of a system of "sovereign" states. Yet, even then it was an international *system*. Any system is composed of a set of units and their interactions. For a system to exist, these interactions must also entail some degree of interdependence: Events and changes in one part of the system inevitably will have effects and consequences in other parts of the system, for reasons related to the mutual "sensitivity" and "vulnerability" of states as conceptualized by Robert Keohane and Joseph Nye (1989).

Thus, the international system, like any system, must deal with all the problems and opportunities generated by interdependence and, since Westphalia, must do so within the constraints of a formally anarchic structure. This is especially problematic, as there has always been a tension between the sensitivity and vulnerability of interdependence—which generate externalities and collective goods—and the concept of sovereignty. The legal principle of sovereignty holds that there exists no *authority* above that of the rulers of states and implies autonomy, noninterference, and equality. States thus find themselves facing a reality consisting of both interdependence and anarchy. International anarchy, according to Kenneth Waltz (1959: 160), consists of many sovereign states with no system of law enforceable by centralized authorities, thus generating a reliance on self-help, and with *each* state the "final judge of its own cause."

Bull (1977), while apparently recognizing both realities, argues that the international system reflects a "society" of states. From this derives the basic Grotian or liberal view of international law and international politics. All units in social life, existing within some society (which must be the case for units of people existing in an interdependent system), are seen to have three primary or elementary goals: security against violence, assurance that agreements will be kept, and stability of possession or ownership. Meeting such goals will bring about *order* within a social system.

In a classic work, Richard Rosecrance (1963) discusses the need for *any* system to have "regulators" to deal with disturbances within the system, with the demands of its units, and with problems that ultimately reduce to Bull's three basic components of order. A second important feedback loop must now be recognized. Through a complex set of economic, political, technological, and religious factors, a system of states arose, each of which was endowed with a special legal status—sovereignty. In so doing, the states had thrown off a set of putative regulatory mechanisms consisting of the spiritual hierarchy of the Catholic Church and the temporal hierarchy of feudalism culminating in the Holy Roman Emperor.

New regulatory mechanisms were needed. With a system of sovereign states to replace a vertical system of centralized authority, such mechanisms would, of necessity, be informal. Realists have stressed the balance of power as the informal mechanism most relevant to achieving and maintaining order in the Westphalian system and have dismissed (or undervalued) the regulatory capacity of a system of law that lacked centralized, authoritative enforcement capabilities.

In contrast, the liberal view gave international law a more prominent place in regulating order. Here is where the feedback loop emerges. The special condition of sovereignty created new conditions and requirements for regulatory mechanisms. It fostered the emergence of a system of rules and laws that could deal with the needs of states and that reflected the self-interests and consent (sovereignty!) of those states. Such laws, in turn, reinforced and further developed the concept of sovereignty as the legal basis for states and for the expansion of state power and control. States, needing mechanisms for order, created norms and rules—law—that permitted states to do *what they wanted to do*, to do so more efficiently, and to do so in such ways as to enhance the status of states.

The three basic elements of order presented by Bull indicate that order entails, in essence, the avoidance of chaos, capriciousness, and unpredictability. Patterns of activities that permit some degree of certainty and predictability, that rest on expectations of how others (and oneself) are supposed to behave, constitute *order*. Norms specify rules that make for predictability: They delineate boundaries; they serve as signposts for behavior; they routinize relations; they serve as a tripwire to focus attention on violations of expectations (Kegley and Raymond, 1990). Such consequences of norms are central to Bull's thesis. Because of the existence and impact of norms, order can exist either without formal, written rules or with only rudimentary rules.[1] To Bull,

---

[1] International law has been characterized by various scholars as a system of law that is primitive, incomplete, decentralized or imperfect. See also Michael Barkun (1968).

order is the basis of any society. Given this defintion of order, society can then exist without formal rules. Hence, there is not only an international system, but also an international "society" because there is an order based on sets of expectations of behavior and repetitive patterns of behavior. This order is encompassed not only in treaties and written international law, but in the informal norms of customary international law.[2]

I have tried to establish several points in this section. As a *system* of states, the international system has always needed regulatory mechanisms to foster order among its interdependent component units. I have tried to indicate that order—which implies society—can exist without a centralized authority or legal system and that order does exist in the international arena; this is the accepted wisdom that "anarchy" does not necessarily mean "chaos." All these constants, including the Westphalian tradeoff, must be seen within the context of any historical period. These contexts will reflect the changing interests of states, which are then reflected in the substance of international law. Such contexts and interests affect the way we address the central issue to be raised below: how to manage interdependence. By framing the issue in this way, we can better reconcile the differences separating realist and liberal theories on this dimension of world politics and be able to arrive at some form of realist–neoliberal synthesis.

DIVERGENCIES: BASIC VIEWS OF INTERNATIONAL LAW

The characterization of anarchy outlined above captures the basic realist view of international law (as represented by Morgenthau [1973] and Waltz [1959]). From a realist perspective, an international system is anarchic when there exists no legitimate authority that sits above the states in the system. Part of the realist view of international relations is that international law is irrelevant to how states will behave within this anarchic system. International law is irrelevant because it lacks the centralized enforcement mechanisms and capability that are seen to represent law. That is, to realists international law is of no consequence because it is not really law.

To realists, given that the anarchic system lacks centralized authority and states are endowed with the special legal status of sovereignty (which includes

---

[2] Recent studies have demonstrated the powerful impact of norms (what Gary Goertz and Paul Diehl [1992] call "decentralized norms") on the behavior of sovereign states in the formally anarchic international system. Changes in expectations of how states ought to behave, along with an understanding of the self-interest benefits that exist through self-constraint and compliance, have occurred in many important areas. John Mueller (1989) and James Ray (1989) have discussed changes in norms relating to slavery and to the use of force. Goertz and Diehl (1992) and David Strang (1991) have looked at norms of decolonization. Kegley and Raymond (1990) have looked at norms in regard to alliance behavior. Starr (1991) has investigated norms in regard to the diffusion of democracy in the international system.

a monopoly over the use of force), states must depend, ultimately, only on self-help against other states. Other states cannot be constrained by the threat of centralized enforcement; alliance commitments cannot be enforced as can domestic contractual arrangements. The structure of the anarchic system is thus *permissive*: War, or aggression, or coercion through the threat of force can occur because there is *nothing to stop it* (Waltz, 1959). The *opportunity for war* always exists within such a system.

According to the realist and neorealist account, given this structure of opportunities states must (or should) rely on self-help. A key component of realist thought, too often overlooked by neorealists, must also be included at this point—human nature. A strand of realism found in writers as diverse as Machiavelli, Hobbes, or Niebuhr focuses on human nature as "evil, sinful, power-seeking" (Dougherty and Pfaltzgraff, 1981: 85). With a permissive international system, and the inherent evil nature of humans, states must be prepared to defend themselves in a Hobbesian environment with the potential war of all against all. To do so statesmen must be concerned with power in terms of military capability. In Hans Morgenthau's (1973: 27) famous words, "International politics, like all politics, is a struggle for power."

These conditions also drive statesmen to a conservative answer in responding to the question of how much capability is sufficient to deal with worst-case scenarios. Never knowing how much is enough, realists conclude that states should seek to maximize their military power. This inevitable consequence of each state increasing capabilities to deal with international anarchy is known as the *security dilemma*, where any one state's security increases the insecurity of the others. The drive for more capability derives in part from the inability to distinguish intentions from capabilities; one must protect against capabilities because intentions are unknown. However, given that humans are evil, it would be best to prepare for the worst. The worst means that other states will be tempted to violate existing rules and *will* fail to comply with them when compliance compromises national interests. That is, states will choose to defect—to give in to the "rational" temptation to pursue short-term individual interests—rather than cooperate in the "prisoner's dilemma" situations that encourage noncompliance with agreements. Many such situations have been generated by the metaprisoner's dilemma of the anarchic international structure (see Snyder, 1971).

Within such a system, a positivist view that law is made by states and requires the consent of states is not assuring to realists. While a positivist view is consistent with the condition of sovereignty and the autonomy of states, it does nothing to ameliorate the security dilemma or guarantee the punishment for noncompliance required to make payoffs for defection so costly as to escape the prisoner's dilemma. A positivist view of law stresses self-interest and consent; to a realist this means that states do what they want to do.

It also means that law which lacks automatic and centralized coercive enforcement mechanisms cannot merit the name of "law." To realists, law corresponds to what Louis Goldie (1973) has called the "common model of the legal order." This model is based on a simple image of criminal law, law that is "command backed up by force" (Fisher, 1969). In this model, law consists of commands that prohibit certain kinds of behavior under the threat of coercive force to ensure compliance. Bull (1977) provides two responses to this view of law and its attendant claims that international law is not law. First, he argues that law does not require command and coercive sanctions to be regarded as law. Second, international law does entail sanctions, albeit informal ones.

In regard to Bull's first argument, Goldie (1973: 129) clarifies why the criminal law model is only one possible model of law. An alternative is the "facilitative" model, whereby law provides a citizen "with the procedures, with the means of doing the sorts of things he wants to do." This includes much of civil law, for example, the law of wills or the law of real property (as to procedures of transfer, sale, etc). That is, much of law has nothing to do with command and/or the coercive use of force.[3]

The facilitative view of law is closely related to states' need for order within an anarchic system. Much of international law has been created to facilitate coordination and cooperation among states, to allow them to do the things they feel a need to do. Because nothing is distributed equally in the international system, and because states must exist in a condition of interdependence with one another, they need to exchange goods and services, to communicate, and to coordinate their myriad transactions. For example, the international law on weights and measures, on international civil aviation, on the immunities and obligations of diplomats—all facilitate the interactions of states, permitting them to trade and to engage in the full range of economic, social, and political interchange required by each to satisfy the needs of their populations and the interests of their governments.

While the first model of law based on coercive command represents the realist view of "law" and thus the irrelevance of international law in the anarchic international system, this latter model of law is much more compatible with the liberal or Grotian view of the international arena. The Grotian view of a society of states recognizes that there is "neither complete conflict of interest between states nor complete identity of interest"; that "economic and social intercourse between one country and another" is most typical of overall international activity (Bull, 1977: 26–27).

The Grotian reality that states *are* linked with one another in an interdependent system, and must deal with one another on a continuing basis, under-

---

[3] Roger Fisher (1969: 154–55) adds that even some of the most important domestic law does not rest upon coercive command. He notes: "Governments regularly comply with adverse court decisions. This is true not only for constitutional law, administrative law, and tax law, but even for criminal law." He uses the example of the Supreme Court ordering the Truman administration to return the steel mills seized during the Korean War. He writes, "The Supreme Court had no regiments at its command. It had no greater force vis-à-vis the government than does the International Court of Justice. . . . Yet the steel mills were returned." Thus, command based on a superior coercive force is not required for law to act as law.

girds the claim that sanctions do exist even in the anarchic international arena and that international law can constrain state behavior in part based on such sanctions. This follows Bull's second response to the claim that international law is not law because it lacks centralized enforcement mechanisms. Such a defense of international law also relies on the concept of self-interest on which positivism is based. In the liberal vision, self-interest is seen within a mixed-motive game where all can win or all can lose. This contrasts to the realists' zero-sum orientation where what one wins must come at the expense of the others. Liberalism emphasizes that individual self-interest can be calculated only by taking the interests and reactions of the other states into account, as well as longer term collective interests; it makes *reciprocity* as a basis of international law the point of its departure.

To simplify a vast literature, obedience to international law or the self-constraint of states is thus based on the basic principles of reciprocity and precedent. Rules and norms constrain states because they are engaged in an indefinitely iterative game with multiple plays.[4] Acting under Robert Axelrod's (1984) "shadow of the future," states must be aware that short-term gains from breaking rules that they helped create may be offset by future costs imposed by other states. International law is based on a "golden rule" principle—rule-based behavior to others will beget rule-based behavior, whereas defection or noncompliance will beget noncompliance. Reciprocity includes fear of sanctions for rule-breaking behavior. International law recognizes both retorsion, "a lawful act which is designed to injure the wrongdoing state," as well as reprisals, "acts which would normally be illegal but which are rendered legal by a prior illegal act committed by the other state" (Akehurst, 1987; 6). The "shadow of the future" is expected to constrain rule violation, or defection, because

> . . . players can learn from past plays (history) and should be concerned with reciprocity in plays to come (future). Reciprocity is even more important when we recall that there are many games being played at the same time, that states interact in many issue areas at the same time, and that these are linked. . . . A state may defect in one game (for example arms control), but will have to worry about the other player's defection in another (retaliatory acts in trade, wheat sales, alliance fomation, military spending). The payoff matrix of costs and benefits thus will be affected by calculations of future costs and benefits. This menu will then affect the willingness of policymakers to defect. (Russett and Starr, 1992: 465)

As noted above, rules or norms may serve as boundaries and tripwires. They alert others to behavior considered unacceptable and permit others in

---

[4] See, for example, Robert Axelrod (1984), Thomas Franck (1989), Robert Keohane (1984), and Kenneth Oye (1986). Note, however, that works such as Keohane's or Oye's dealing with regimes, while also setting out the basic logic behind international law, almost never explicitly refer to international law.

the international society to respond. It is in the self-interest of states not to set a precedent that permits others to engage similarly in behavior considered unacceptable. It is in the self-interest of states not to cross lines that will bring about sanctions from others. Obeying international law is also in the self-interest of states because compliance brings with it a reputation as being a "law-abiding" member of the international society that others can trust and treat as dependable. Given the *informal* nature of this sanctioning system, such a reputation is important inasmuch as a state that regularly flouts international law cannot expect to benefit from the support of the society of states when it faces another rule-breaker (this happened to Iran in its decade-long war with Iraq; see Russett and Starr, 1992: 467–69).

In a reverse image from the need to coordinate, liberalism also emphasizes that it is in the self-interest of states to avoid the choas, uncertainty, unpredictability, and costs generated by a breakdown of order. By recognizing that states have overlapping, complementary, and even congruent interests in getting done the things they need to get done (interests that transcend fears for security in many situations), the liberal view sees international law as useful, necessary even, as international politics unfolds within a society of states.

THE FUNCTIONS OF INTERNATIONAL LAW
IN THE ANARCHIC SOCIETY

On the basis of these broad views of international law it should be clear that law goes beyond the criminal law model of command based on coercive force. In the absence of a formal coercive enforcement mechanism, international law nonetheless clearly does perform a variety of functions that help states create and maintain order within international society. International law facilitates the achievement of states' needs through its communications and management functions. By clarifying rights, responsibilities, and competencies, these functions demonstrably assist states in the coordination and cooperation required to achieve both self-interests and collective interests within an increasingly interdependent world.

But if the state system is also to be seen as a society, then, like any society, it requires rules or norms to constrain conflict and the use of force and to foster orderly conflict resolution. For example, in his exposition of the Grotian anarchical society, Bull (1977) notes that as with any society, the society of states has attempted to impose restrictions on the use of force—confining war only to sovereign states and then restricting its spread through laws of neutrality and belligerency, restricting the reasons or the just cause for the use of war (*ius ad bellum*), and restricting the manner in which a just war could be conducted (*ius in bello*).

Thus, international law serves a variety of *conflict-related* functions, from the realist-oriented instrument of direct control (but with only informal sanctioning mechanisms) to limiting the conditions under which a justified conflict can originate, to regulating the legal means of conflict, and to serving a central role in the range of processes involved in conflict prevention, management, and resolution. In this lattermost role international law can be used to channel conflict through a number of mechanisms and procedures for dealing with conflict.[5] International law can be seen as a method of bargaining, employing processes of claim and counterclaim, whether in informal negotiations or in the formal processes of arbitration and adjudication. In this way international law can substitute for the use of force or violence as a means of contesting outcomes (reflecting Anatol Rapoport's [1960] concept of how to engage in a "game" rather than a "fight").

While the conflict-related functions of international law are self-evidently important to order, one purpose of this essay is to emphasize the facilitative, management, and coordination functions of international law. William Coplin (1966) has been a major exponent of international law as a system of quasi-authoritative communications. As he explained, international law serves as an instrument of communication and, as such, perhaps the primary device for *socializing* policymakers as to the nature of the prevailing consensus in the international system and its changing expectations regarding the rights and duties of international actors.

Hence, the communication function should be seen as a prerequisite for the facilitative function, as the set of expectations to be communicated includes the rules necessary for the simple coordination of behavior required in order to get things done. This is analogous to the classic "rules of the road," such as the rules specifying the side of the road on which to drive or which color light means stop and which color means go. These rules inform all drivers both what they should do and what to expect others will do. In the same manner international law serves to establish and facilitate routine interactions among states.

Just as important is the way international law can help to coordinate the search for solutions to common problems, which is usually referred to as the management function of international law. The needs for coordination and management reflect *the* key role of international law in world order. The growing sensitivity and vulnerability of interdependence reflect the existence of, and the need to deal with, global issues that fall in the category of "collective goods" (see Russett and Starr, 1992, chaps. 16, 17). Collective goods characterize extreme forms of interdependence. They produce special prob-

---

[5] For example, Article 33 of the UN Charter sets out a range of conflict resolution processes that states should pursue before submitting a dispute to a UN organ such as the Security Council or the General Assembly: "negotiation, inquiry, mediation, conciliation, arbitration, judicial settlement, resort to regional agencies or arrangements, or other peaceful means of their own choice."

lems for states, which, in turn, require special types of solutions with special types of mechanisms.

Economic interdependencies and ecological issues that involve both "free-rider" and the "tragedy of the commons" problems (Hardin and Baden, 1977) require political, social, and legal mechanisms to produce the cooperation or collaboration needed to deal with problems that *cannot* be solved by the laissez-faire workings of the market. The market failures of such a system are generated by the externalities inherent in interdependence, where being sensitive and vulnerable to jointly supplied and nonexcludable goods make some states "forced riders" (Russett and Starr, 1992). Interdependence, externalities, and collective goods can thus generate highly conflictual situations. In such classic prisoner's dilemma situations, sovereign states, looking out for their individual, short-term, "myopic self-interest" (Keohane, 1984; 96), will rarely be able to solve such problems and will usually make them worse.

In attempting to devise policies that could deal with the dilemmas generated by collective goods, analysts initially developed two broad approaches: some form of enclosure or privatization, by which goods are made private and owners given the responsibility for their care, and coercion through some form of centralized authority. However, recent theory and research (e.g., Keohane, 1984; Oye, 1986; Ostrom, 1990; Rosenau and Czempiel, 1992) have demonstrated that such dilemmas can be addressed and solved through the cooperation and collaboration of individuals or groups, without solutions imposed from some higher authority, and with the relevant participants willing to engage in self-regulation (and enforcement!) in order to achieve some good or to protect an existing common-pool resource.

All this should be familiar to students of international regimes. It is in the theory, practice, and consequences of regimes that international law finds its most important impact on order in the global system. Questions of regime emergence, maintenance, and effectiveness have all been addressed before in the study of international law. For example, the two primary sources of international law are treaties and custom. These two processes are directly analogous to the discourse about negotiated or spontaneous regimes.[6] International law is a central component of regimes, one of a number of regime elements alongside formal and informal rules, both state-based and those deriving from nonstate actors. The attention paid to regimes derives from the

---

[6] The idea of imposed regimes is not especially relevant to a positivist view of international law. However, it does resonate in discussions of how Third World countries have viewed, and dealt with, a system of international law created by their Western colonial masters before they became independent. As noted above, most work on regimes ignores previous thought on international law. Though it is not as pronounced, the regime literature also downplays important aspects of previously developed integration theory. For example, models of negotiated, spontaneous, or imposed processes of regime creation are analogous to the neofunctionalist integration model of Ernst Haas, Karl Deutsch's social communication model, and the federalist model of integration, respectively.

same concerns noted above: clarifying what states have what rights to what behavior, as well as their obligations. Regimes and international law are used to change the structure of the games in which states are engaged, either by altering the payoffs or by changing the nature of the choices. Even the informal sanctions of international law, perhaps as imposed by the international organizations involved in regimes, can alter the costs and benefits of cooperation or defection.

Arthur Stein (1983) helps us conceptualize the different functions of international law as well as understand why some regimes are relatively easy to create and successfully manage while others are more difficult. He identifies regimes of "common aversion," where the purpose is to coordinate behavior in order to avoid negative outcomes. These are regimes that deal with the coordination function, with such "traffic light" issues as having pilots and air traffic controllers in the international civil aviation regime all capable of communicating in the same language (English). Because of the coordination focus, these regimes have been relatively easy to form (and often develop along the same lines as does customary international law).

Stein (1983: 123) differentiates the preceding type of regimes from regimes of "common interest," which require collaboration to deal with prisoner's dilemma situations or "to deal with the collective suboptimality that can emerge from individual behavior." Both types of regimes are contingent on states following their self-interests while also recognizing that their self-interests are imbedded in broader collective interests. While regimes of common aversion need only to facilitate coordination, regimes of common interest require management, in which states agree to constrain themselves and agree to the ways in which the collectivity will institutionalize power to monitor behavior, assess and generate both payoffs and sanctions, and deal with conflict resolution. These activities can be quite difficult (e.g., consider the protracted Uruguay Round negotiations).

It is important to recall that international law facilitates international communication, including diplomacy. Diplomacy generates treaties, that is, more international law. Both law and diplomacy create intergovernmental organizations (IGOs), which, of course, facilitate more diplomacy as well as more international law (either formally or through custom). In sum, international law is fundamentally important in the creation, maintenance, and operation of regimes, which generate and promote even more international law.

GLOBAL ORDER: CONTINUITY, CHANGE, AND POSSIBILITIES FOR SYNTHESIS

Charles Kegley asks the questions: What is new? What is constant? The anarchic structure of the international system is one constant. A second is the need to reconcile the tension between that structure and state sovereignty with the nature and consequences of interdependence. Realism suggests one view of how to manage the interdependence of the system; neoliberalism in the guise of Grotian international society suggests another. The contemporary answers provided by neoliberalism also draw from "what is new?" in the international system. While many pages could be devoted to this question,[7] a useful way to summarize what is new is found in Keohane and Nye's (1989, chap. 2) characterization of "complex interdependence."

What Is New? The Conditions of Complex Interdependence

The first aspect of complex interdependence draws attention to the multiple linkages that connect states and, in so doing, takes cognizance of the whole range of transnational relations that bypass the high-level decision makers of governments and the whole range of nonstate actors in the international system. What is new is the increasing consequence of nonstate actor behaviors, a consequence that can be explained by the growth of interdependence and the ability of even the "smallest" or "weakest" actors to have an impact on a system linked by networks of vulnerability (see Ward and House, 1988). What is new are the technologies of James Rosenau's (1990) "microelectronic revolution," which increase the ability of individuals and groups to penetrate the "hard shell" of the sovereign state, create multiple channels of communication, and, through new forms of communication and transportation, produce ever greater levels of interdependence among all international actors (see also Goodman, 1993). What is new is the whole multicentric system identified by Rosenau, composed of "sovereignty-free" actors who interact with states and form an important part of the environment within which states exist.

The second component of complex interdependence follows from the argument that there is no consistent hierarchy of issues—there are multiple issues, they cut across traditional domestic–foreign distinctions, and military security does *not* dominate the hierarchy. In conjunction with the first aspect of complex interdependence, there is a newly consequential transnational relations, which blurs the lines that realists claim separate domestic and foreign politics. This separation is crucial to a number of components of realism, including national interest defined as power, the lack of universal moral principles, and the "autonomy of the political sphere" (Dougherty and Pfaltzgraff, 1981: 99–100).

---

[7] For another perspective on "what is new?", see Mark Zacher (1992) and Zacher and Matthew in chapter 5 of this volume for arguments that the international system is in "a process of fundamental change." As the essays by Barry Hughes (chap. 9) and J. Martin Rochester (chap. 8) in this book explain, while interdependence effects provide the basis for changes in the "patterns of governance," other factors, such as the cost of war among great powers, are also likely to be important to the maintenance of order in the twenty-first century (see Kegley and Raymond, 1994).

Of more consequence is the increasing importance of economic, ecological, and social issues in all areas of the world, especially since the end of the Cold War. As Kegley notes in the introduction, "different problems are likely to replace the threat of East–West ideological discord and military aggression." The end of the Cold War, rather than meaning the end of history, means that different issues will be of importance to different states at different times. Accordingly, what is new is that the issue of "how to manage interdependence" means more than alliances and balance of power being used to deal with security interdependence.

This last statement becomes even more crucial when the final component of complex interdependence is noted: "Military force is not used by governments toward other governments within the region, or on the issues, when complex interdependence prevails" (Keohane and Nye, 1989: 25). How will interdependence be managed among states that have given up the option of military force and that are connected by powerful bonds of economic, social, political, and technological interdependence? What is new are ever-growing "zones of peace," the products of Deutschian integration processes called "security communities" (Deutsch et al., 1957).

What is also new is the spread of democracy throughout the globe (see Starr, 1991). Democracy, it has been shown, is a key component to successful integration and the creation of security communities (Russett and Starr, 1992, chap. 14). Research has demonstrated that pairs of democracies do not go to war against one another. Thus, it is in groups of democracies that form Deutschian security communities that the realist perspective, and its approach to managing interdependence, are the most *irrelevant* in terms of conceptualization and explanation. Bruce Russett (1993) indicates how the newly emergent group of democracies might have a significant impact on the system. When the international system consisted mostly of autocratic or authoritarian states, it would have been very risky for democracies to behave on the basis of democratic norms, norms resembling those advocated by liberal proponents such as Immanuel Kant and Woodrow Wilson. However, Russett notes:

> Perhaps major features of the international system can be socially constructed from the bottom up; that is, norms and rules of behavior internationally can become extensions of the norms and rules of domestic political behavior. . . .
> A system composed substantially of democratic states might reflect very different behavior than did the previous one composed predominantly of autocracies. . . . A system created by autocracies several centuries ago might now be re-created by a critical mass of democratic states. (Russett, 1993: 281)

What Is Constant? A Possible Synthesis

The tension between realism and neoliberalism parallels the tension in the Westphalian tradeoff between sovereignty and interdependence. The state system structure has always been anarchic, and yet states have always had to manage some degree of interdependence. There has always been a need for order, and the solutions have all rested on some variety of decentralized, informal sanctioning mechanisms. Realism's version of "how to manage interdependence" derived from a view of the Westphalian tradeoff, which stressed autonomy over interdependence and viewed power as control over military capabilities. This perspective culminated in the balance of power as the key mechanism for the maintenance of world order. The balance of power was generally conceived of as a deterrence process that threatened transgressors with unacceptable costs and was based on fluid and flexible alliances as well as domestically created military capability.

Neoliberalism's version of "how to manage interdependence" is, on the other hand, based on a set of changing conditions that stress the interdependence side of the Westphalian tradeoff. Neoliberalism thereby embraces a very different notion of "power." Its alternative vision is one centered on sensitivity, vulnerability, and bargaining among states that have largely eschewed the use of the military option. As the state system has developed (matured?) and greater ties of interdependence have emerged, informal sanctioning mechanisms, also based on deterrence processes, have developed. International law has depended on self-interest and reciprocity—fear of the costs others could impose on rule-breakers. In the twentieth century, the deterrence processes of the balance of power have evolved under conditions of increased interdependence, the growth of democracy, the emergence and growth of zones of peace, and norms against the use of force. Peacetime alliances have attempted to maintain order through collective defense. Universal international organizations have applied collective security with growing success and relevance. Both collective defense and collective security work on the same principle of deterrent sanctions as does the balance of power.

The elements of a synthesis by which realist and liberal perspectives may be joined are now manifest. Realism and neoliberalism can be brought together by viewing them as different positions on a continuum rather than as exclusively rival approaches. With the same anarchic system structure, the same decentralized sanctioning mechanisms, and the same deterrence process that characterized the balancing mechanisms of realism, the neoliberal can point to changing conditions that now provide a setting in which international law, international organizations, and regimes can play a central role. What were dreams to Grotius are the realities of the contemporary world.

Clearly the realist perspective was more accurate during certain historical periods and under certain interpretations of the Westphalian tradeoff. Yet, as I have sought to demonstrate in this chapter, some of the conditions affecting that tradeoff have changed, while others touch on aspects of realism and liberalism that require each other's account to provide a fuller explanation of how international law contributes to world order. Therefore, rather than setting realism and neoliberalism up as exclusive and contending explanations, rather than asking which perspective or model is "right" or "wrong," this chapter has directed us to follow the advice of Benjamin Most and Harvey Starr (1989: 181), and instead ask, "Under what conditions does each model/ theory work?"

REFERENCES

Akehurst, Michael. (1987) *A Modern Introduction to International Law*, 6th ed. London: Allen & Unwin.

Axelrod, Robert. (1984) *The Evolution of Cooperation*. New York: Basic Books.

Barkun, Michael. (1968) *Law without Sanctions: Order in Primitive Societies and the World Community*. New Haven, Conn.: Yale University Press.

Bull, Hedley. (1977) *The Anarchical Society*. New York: Columbia University Press.

Coplin, William D. (1966) *The Functions of International Law*. Chicago: Rand McNally.

Deutsch, Karl W., et al. (1957) *Political Community and the North Atlantic Area*. Princeton, N.J.: Princeton University Press.

Dougherty, James E., and Robert L. Pfaltzgraff. (1981) *Contending Theories of International Relations*, 2nd ed. New York: Harper & Row.

Fisher, Roger. (1969) *International Conflict for Beginners*. New York: Harper & Row.

Franck, Thomas M. (1989) "The Strategic Role of Legal Principles," pp. 295–304 in Bruce Russett, Harvey Starr, and Richard Stoll, eds., *Choices in World Politics: Sovereignty and Interdependence*. New York: W. H. Freeman.

Goertz, Gary, and Paul F. Diehl. (1992) "Toward a Theory of International Norms," *Journal of Conflict Resolution* 36 (December): 634–64.

Goldie, Louis F. E. (1973) "International Law and the World Community," pp. 127–40 in F. H. Hartman, ed., *World in Crisis*, 4th ed. New York: Macmillan.

Goodman, Allan E. (1993) *A Brief History of the Future*. Boulder, Colo.: Westview Press.

Hardin, Garrett, and John Baden, eds. (1977) *Managing the Commons*. San Francisco: W. H. Freeman.

Kegley, Charles W., Jr., and Gregory A. Raymond (1994) *A Multipolar Peace? Great Power Politics in the Twenty-First Century*. New York: St. Martin's Press.

———. (1990) *When Trust Breaks Down: Alliance Norms and World Politics*. Columbia: University of South Carolina Press.

Keohane, Robert O. (1984) *After Hegemony*. Princeton, N.J.: Princeton University Press.

Keohane, Robert O., and Joseph S. Nye (1989) *Power and Interdependence*, 2nd ed. Boston: Scott, Foresman.

Morgenthau, Hans J. (1973) *Politics among Nations*, 5th ed. New York: Alfred A. Knopf.

Most, Benjamin A., and Harvey Starr. (1989) *Inquiry, Logic and International Politics*. Columbia: University of South Carolina Press.

Mueller, John (1989) *Retreat from Doomsday*. New York: Basic Books.

Ostrom, Elinor. (1990) *Governing the Commons*. Cambridge: Cambridge University Press.

Oye, Kenneth A., ed. (1986) *Cooperation under Anarchy*. Princeton, N.J.: Princeton University Press.

Rapoport, Anatol. (1969) *Fights, Games, and Debates.* Ann Arbor: University of Michigan Press.

Ray, James Lee. (1989) "The Abolition of Slavery and the End of International War," *International Organization* 43 (Summer): 405–39.

Rosecrance, Richard. (1963) *Action and Reaction in World Politics.* Boston: Little Brown.

Rosenau, James N. (1990) *Turbulence in World Politics.* Princeton, N.J.: Princeton University Press.

Rosenau, James N., and Ernst-Otto Czempiel, eds. (1992) *Governance without Government: Order and Change in World Politics.* Cambridge: Cambridge University Press.

Russett, Bruce. (1993) "Can a Democratic Peace Be Built?" *International Interactions* 18 (no. 3): 277–82.

Russett, Bruce, and Harvey Starr. (1992) *World Politics: The Menu for Choice,* 4th ed. New York: W. H. Freeman.

Snyder, Glenn H. (1971) "'Prisoner's Dilemma' and 'Chicken' Models in International Politics," *International Studies Quarterly* 15 (March): 66–103.

Starr, Harvey. (1993) "How to Manage Interdependence? The State in a Multi-Centric/Transnational World," in Brian Toyne and Douglas Nigh, eds., *International Business Inquiry: An Emerging Vision.* Columbia: University of South Carolina Press.

————. (1991) "Democratic Dominoes: Diffusion Approaches to the Spread of Democracy in the International System," *Journal of Conflict Resolution* 35 (June): 356–81.

Stein, Arthur A. (1983) "Coordination and Collaboration: Regimes in an Anarchic World," pp. 115–40 in Stephen D. Krasner, ed., *International Regimes.* Ithaca, N.Y.: Cornell University Press.

Strang, David. (1991) "Global Patterns of Decolonization, 1500–1987," *International Studies Quarterly* 35 (December): 429–54.

von Glahn, Gerhard. (1992) *Law among Nations,* 6th ed. New York: Macmillan.

Waltz, Kenneth N. (1959) *Man, the State and War.* New York: Columbia University Press.

Ward, Michael D., and Lewis L. House. (1988) "A Theory of the Behavioral Power of Nations," *Journal of Conflict Resolution* 32 (March): 3–36.

Zacher, Mark W. (1992) "The Decaying Pillars of the Westphalian Temple: Implications for International Order and Governance," pp. 58–101 in James N. Rosenau and Ernst-Otto Czempiel, eds., *Governance without Government: Order and Change in World Politics.* Cambridge: Cambridge University Press.

CHAPTER 13

Rethinking the Moral Dimensions of Foreign Policy

JOEL H. ROSENTHAL

There would seem to be no greater gulf between realist and liberal theories of international relations than in their respective views of the proper role of morality in foreign policy. In fact, morality has traditionally been a defining characteristic. Realists earn their label by emphasizing consequences over moral principles and necessity over choice. Liberals begin with opposite premises, emphasizing duty over consequences and moral imperatives over expediency.

Yet a close study of the literature on morality and foreign policy in the contemporary era shows that the traditional distinctions, while useful and valid, are often overdrawn. While self-professed realists and liberals have indeed begun with different assumptions about human nature, international society, and the possibilities of moral action, their views on the role of morality in foreign policy can and should be considered together. Most of the literature of the past fifty years is an unwitting and curious combination of the two approaches.

Perhaps no other topic within international relations is as prepared for conscious reconstruction as this one. The realist/liberal hybrid suggested by Charles W. Kegley Jr. in his introduction to this volume and elsewhere (Kegley, 1992, 1988) already exists in this area. It needs only to be made more clear.

REALIST ASSUMPTIONS ABOUT THE ROLE OF MORALITY IN FOREIGN POLICY

Realist theories begin with a tragic view of human nature and experience. Realists emphasize the ubiquity of egoism, conflict, and anarchy: Insecurity, both on the individual and group level, leads to inevitable struggles for power

317

(Smith, 1986; Donnelly, 1992). They begin, with Hobbes (1947: 82–83), in a world where life is "nasty, brutish, and short." Behind the thin veneer of civilization is the natural state of man—"the war of every man against every man." With this in mind, realists dwell on the problem of power. As one scholar has put it, "as far as political motivation goes," realists argue that "the will to power outweighs the will to good" (Little, 1993).

Realists are well known for their profound skepticism over the possibilities for moral action in international affairs. This skepticism stems both from their assessment of human nature and their observation of international society. According to realist theory, a natural *animus dominandi* (will to power) combines with a lack of central authority and enforcement mechanisms in international society to create a perpetual security dilemma. Power maximization—and therefore enhanced security—becomes all. In a world where history proves that the strong usually do what they will and the weak do what they must, "necessity" leaves little room for "choice." In this view, moral imperatives are limited and easily derived: The morally preferable decision is one that results in a favorable outcome for the state.

In the classical, purest form of realism expressed by Machiavelli, moral considerations beyond *raison d'état* (reason of state) are not only inherently suspect, but often counterproductive. For Machiavelli, the road to disaster begins with good intentions. One of Machiavelli's cardinal lessons for the prince is that a leader must learn to deal with the world as it is, not as he wishes it to be (Forde, 1992).

Realists carry their skepticism to issues such as universality and the problem of agency (the means by which a moral course can be determined and carried out). George F. Kennan (1985–1986: 207) states flatly, "there are no internationally accepted standards of morality to which the U.S. government could appeal if it wished to act in the name of moral principles." Hans J. Morgenthau (1954: 9) is just as blunt in his often-cited *Politics among Nations* where he writes, "universal principles cannot be applied to the actions of states." It is not that the realists question the existence and essential goodness of universal principles such as those proclaimed in the Universal Declaration of Human Rights or the Helsinki Final Act; it is the difficulty of equitable enforcement and the propensity for such proclamations to result in hyperbole that cause the realists' pessimism. Universal maxims spell trouble for the prudent statesmen whose task it is to make distinctions, draw lines, and implement policy. Realists fear that the very grandiosity and ambition of universal principles doom the statesman to hypocrisy.

The problem of universality and consistency extends to the problem of reconciling individual moral beliefs to the reality of social experience and the moral behavior of groups. Reinhold Niebuhr's book *Moral Man and Immoral Society* (1932) suggests the problem in its title. Niebuhr (1932: xi) undoubtedly went too far in his assertion that "a sharp distinction must be drawn between the moral and social behavior of individuals and social groups . . . and that this distinction justifies and necessitates political policies which a purely individualistic ethic must always find embarassing." Yet Niebuhr identifies a central problem in relating morality to international affairs. What standards or yardsticks can be used in evaluating moral judgments? Can the behavior of states be evaluated according to the same standard as the one for individuals? And how should one account for different statuses of statesmen, soldiers, and private citizens? Are there legitimate distinctions to be made between "duties of station" and "duties of conscience"? (Little, 1978). If so, or even if not, how does this affect our understanding of the moral dimensions of foreign policy?

Colin S. Gray, a contemporary unreconstructed realist, makes much of this point. He argues that "deontological reasoning [the ethics of duty], by and large, is inappropriate for polities." Quoting Morgenthau he states: "Realism, then, considers prudence—the weighing of consequences of alternative political actions—to be the supreme virtue in politics. Ethics in the abstract judges action by its conformity with the moral law; political ethics judges action by its political consequences" (Gray, 1993: 4; Morgenthau, 1954: 10).

According to Gray (1993: 4), realists are, by definition, consequentialists. He writes: "The moral or religious sanction behind law, 'thou shalt not steal' *because it is wrong to do so*, in political ethics finds its functional equivalent in consequentialist logic: 'thou shalt not steal thy neighboring state's border province' *because the cost of so doing* (which probably exceeds any guilt) *is likely to exceed the gain.*"

Yet if realists are consequentialists, it must be added that most realists since Machiavelli have not entirely abandoned moral principle beyond its incarnations as "prudence" and "national interest." As Morgenthau (1951: 33; see also Smith, 1993b) writes: "The choice is not between moral principles and national interest devoid of moral dignity, but between one set of moral principles divorced from political reality and another set of principles derived from political reality."

Realism must be understood as a product of the societies that have produced it. The varieties of realism produced by Thucydides, Machiavelli, and Hobbes all bear the marks of societies struggling for survival. Similarly, the revival of realism in twentieth-century America owes much to the Manichean struggles of the "free world" against totalitarianism and communism. It is no coincidence that Hans Morgenthau's treatise on modern realism, *Politics among Nations*, appeared in 1948. It brought to an idealistic United States the hard lessons of realpolitik; as such, it was an apt primer for the Cold War struggle.

Morgenthau and his realist colleagues sought to educate students and statesmen as to what had gone wrong in the wake of World War I. The Arbitration Movement of the early 1900s, Wilsonian idealism, and the moralistic–legalistic approach to international affairs symbolized by the Kellogg-Briand Pact of 1928 all bore the marks of the same flaw. Each initiative failed the first test of realism: Each failed to distinguish between the desirable and the possible. Cold War realism was meant as an antidote to utopianism and a lesson in the proper conduct of power politics.

When realism evolved into the "neorealism" of the 1970s and 1980s, explicit discussion of morality as an element in foreign policy went into eclipse. Within mainstream international relations theory, the focus turned away from historical–political analysis and studies of statesmanship to structuralism and regime theory. Beginning with realist premises regarding human nature and the nature of the international system, neorealists such as Kenneth Waltz, Robert Keohane, and John G. Ruggie emphasized the explanatory power of systemic theory (Waltz, 1979; Keohane, 1983, 1986; Ruggie, 1983). Imprecise terms such as "national interest" and "prudence" were bypassed in favor of terms and methods that promised more theoretical rigor. The overarching objective was to extend the insights of realism to more consistent analyses of state behavior (Keohane, 1986). Morgenthau's maxims had been internalized by a generation of theorists and practitioners: The challenge now was to refine the theory to deal with the pressing issues of deterrence, interdependence, and economic development.

LIBERAL ASSUMPTIONS

Liberals begin with a different view of man and his fate. For liberals, the human condition is subject to improvement. Man is not fated to conflict—reason and the rational application of universal principles offer the path to harmonious social order. In the liberal world view there is no *animus dominandi* that is not subject to the ameliorating effects of rationality and/or moral duty (Smith, 1992).

Generally thought of as heirs to the Enlightenment (although their roots can be traced to earlier times), liberals strive for the perfectibility of man and overall human progress. They believe in the efficacy of social institutions—institutions that are created by imperatives of right reason and sustained by rational principles. Liberals place great faith in the positive effects of education and of other social institutions that promote individual fulfillment and social harmony.

For our purposes, the best statement of the liberal position is Immanuel Kant's essay "Perpetual Peace" ([1795] 1970). While Kant does share the realist observation that international society is essentially anarchic, he argues for the pursuit of perpetual peace. In fact, like the realists, Kant presents a partially prudential view: War has become so destructive that it has outlived its purpose as an instrument for political gain. Mankind would soon realize that its very survival depends on an evolution away from war, and this is where Kant's moral imperative makes its appearance. Man has a moral duty to seek peace, even if the immediate prospects are uncertain. Kant sets out to outline how such an evolution—an improvement of the human condition—might take place (Bok, 1990).

Kant's political *modus vivendi*, requring a qualitative improvement of man and his institutions, is the ultimate expression of liberal tenets. First, it affirms the centrality of individual human liberty as the hallmark of the liberal system, and it finds the natural protection of this liberty in the democratic state. Kant's vision is of a world of peaceful democratic states. It is a world where citizens and statesmen are unlikely to go to war since they are surrounded by equally enlightened peoples, in league through mutually beneficial commerce and other interests. The recent political science literature on the reluctance of democracies to fight one another is based on this idea.

A defining characteristic of liberals is their desire to reform the anarchic state of international relations (Smith, 1992). This desire is premised by a belief that it is possible to do so, primarily through structural reform. Liberals believe that by strengthening the philosophical foundations of internationalism, as well as the institutions that facilitate and encourage the practice of international cooperation, rivalry and conflict can be overcome. For liberals, ideas can be transformed into workable structures. Hence, Woodrow Wilson's 1917 pledge to make the world safe for democracy became the Fourteen Points in 1918 and the League of Nations Charter in 1919.

Liberals also differ from realists in their mode of moral reasoning. Liberals value reason over experience and principles over consequences (Donaldson, 1992). Liberals are moved by deontological imperatives—the requirements of moral duty. They insist on the universalizability of moral principles and the notion that they are accessible through reason. Liberals reject any calculation that resembles "the end justifies the means." All moral action must be rooted in a calculation that is true to a universalizable moral principle.

In the twentieth century, liberals have had a number of opportunities to exert influence on the question of morality and foreign policy. The most obvious examples have been the events surrounding the three great conflicts of the century: World War I, World War II, and the Cold War.

Prior to World War I, the growing Arbitration Movement—emerging with some force out of the Hague Peace Conferences of 1899 and 1907—was the brainchild of liberals. Realists such as Alfred Thayer Mahan argued that arbitration may lead men to "the belief that war is so entirely wrong that beside it no other tolerated evil is wrong." But liberals such as Andrew Carnegie responded with proposals for a League of Peace, arguing, "It is the crime of destroying human life by war and the duty to offer or accept peaceful arbitration as a substitute that needs to be established, and which, we think, those of the Church, the universities, and of the professions are called upon to strongly emphasize." For liberals of that era, such as the journalist Hamilton Holt, the "peace problem" was "nothing but the ways and means of doing *between* nations what has already been done *within* the nations. International law follows private law" (Chambers, 1991: 8, 11, 18).

After World War I a generation of internationalists followed in this tradition. International law and organization became a field of academic study and a growing area for the practice of foreign policy. Following from Wilson's

Fourteen Points and proposed League of Nations, liberals sought a postwar order that featured, among other things, a World Court, naval arms control, and the renunciation of war as an instrument of statecraft.

The common thread of the liberal approach is the fundamental belief in individual human liberty, safeguarded by domestic and international institutions—all of which are governed by reason and universalizable standards. As Wilson states at the conclusion of his Fourteen Points speech:

> An evident principle runs through the whole programme I have outlined. It is the principle of justice to all peoples and nationalities, and their right to live on equal terms of liberty and safety with one another, whether they be strong or weak. Unless this principle be made its foundation no part of the structure of international justice can stand.

The liberal world order is one where free people live in democratic states that trade and interact freely. This liberal–internationalist view later became the basis for the United Nations, providing the rationale and impetus for the adoption of its charter in San Francisco in 1945. It remains a forceful influence today in current references to a "new world order."

POINTS OF DIVERGENCE AND CONVERGENCE

The unalterable philosophical differences between liberals and realists cannot be brushed aside. Where liberals believe in the ideas of perfectibility and progress—that history moves in a linear fashion toward higher levels of civilization—realists see no such pattern. Where liberals place faith in the improvement of both individuals and institutions, realists find the human condition unchangeable. And where liberals see morality and foreign policy in terms of the imperatives of duty, realists see them in terms of consequences. Yet this said, it would be a mistake to leave the description there. With the issue of morality and foreign policy, realists and liberals need each other: The two schools virtually define one another.

The best example is provided by Hans J. Morgenthau himself. Even Morgenthau—the prototypical modern realist—took up a number of themes dear to the liberals. Although in *Politics among Nations* he argues that national interest is defined in terms of power, he also acknowledges the normative content of realism and the importance of many liberal and international concepts. *Politics among Nations* and the realist literature it inspired are far from nihilistic in tone or content. It is all about reconciling morality and power—and ensuring the survival of a just and humane world based on individual human freedom. Foreign policy and "power politics" are not ends in themselves; they are, rather, means to achieving a purpose—the establishment and protection of a just society (Myers, 1991).

Realism's warnings regarding the limits of rationality and the verities of human nature should not be mistaken for an advocacy of cynicism and amorality.

Albeit with lower expectations than their liberal colleagues, realists share similar objectives: (1) to encourage the ameliorating influence of international law and diplomacy; (2) to recognize and promote the virtue of moral restraint; (3) to strengthen the weight of international moral norms; and (4) to explore institutional reforms to deal with changing circumstances.

Realist theory tries in a number of ways to deal with the "morality" factor in international affairs. After dispensing with the first problem of morality—self-righteous moralism that serves as a mask for self-interest—realists do probe into the structural problems of international morality and the existential dilemmas of moral choice. The most quoted passage on this subject belongs to Morgenthau:

> . . . if we ask ourselves what statesmen and diplomats are capable of doing to further the power objectives of their respective nations and what they actually do, we realize that they do less than they probably could and less than they actually did in other periods of history. They refuse to consider certain ends and to use certain means, either altogether or under certain conditions, not because in the light of expediency they appear impractical or unwise, but because moral rules interpose an absolute barrier. (Morgenthau, 1954: 254)

Morgenthau then goes on to cite a list of codified moral restraints that prove his point. Among his examples he includes the previously mentioned Hague Declarations of 1899 and 1907 and Geneva Conventions of 1949 as evidence for his argument.

Even though Morgenthau expends considerable effort and in fact makes his reputation by exposing their shortcomings, he also recognizes the significant influence of these restraints and other moral imperatives—influence that is reinforced not only by a vague notion of moral duty, but also by the considerable weight of supporting public opinion. The relationship between moral restraint and public opinion is introduced and accounted for, yet not in any theoretically rigorous way. Few if any realists develop the connection any further than to note its existence. But again, this concern puts Morgenthau and the realists in touch with liberal concerns about democracy and democratic values.

A similar fuzziness clouds the realist analysis of the moral nature and function of sovereignty, as well as the moral significance of mechanisms such as the United Nations. Realists do discuss the liberal dream of a peaceful confederation of nation-states willingly cooperating and even ceding sovereignty in areas of mutual interest. In fact, Morgenthau devotes a full one-third of *Politics among Nations* to assessing this dream. Yet for the realists, the liberal world order remains a dream—a vision that may represent the desirable, but not the immediately possible.

For Morgenthau and the realists, the establishment of world order—and, more specifically, a world state—depends first on the establishment of a world community (that is not likely to arrive any time soon).

Such a world community implies a community of shared moral values. Taking up this theme in his recent book, Robert McElroy (1992: 22–23) notes, "Morgenthau believed that a substantive international morality can exist only to the degree that an international society provides consensual moral standards that are universally accepted." Zbigniew Brzezinski (1993: 231), a noted realist himself, puts it this way in his most recent book: "In a world of fanatical certitudes, morality could be seen as redundant; but in a world of contingency, moral imperatives then become the central, and even the only, source of reassurance. Recognition of both the complexity and the contingency of the human condition thus underlines the *political* need for shared moral consensus in the increasingly congested and intimate world of the twenty-first century."

It is in this attention to moral consensus and the establishment of international moral norms where realism most actively touches on liberalism. This aspect of realism is not lost on most self-described realists. As the noted neorealist Robert G. Gilpin writes:

> Whereas [idealists] tend to believe that technological advance, increasing economic interdependence, and the alleged emergence of a global community are transforming the nature of international relations, I for one lean toward a belief in Morgenthau's *perennial forces* of political struggle and the limits they place on human perfection. To me at least, this moral skepticism joined to a hope that reason may one day gain greater control over passions constitutes the essence of realism and unites realists of every generation. (Gilpin, 1986: 321)

Skepticism and hope; reason and passion; self-interests and the common good; national interests and global responsibilities—these tensions have been the hallmarks of realist thought throughout the generations.

THE CONTEMPORARY SCENE

Honest discussion of morality and foreign policy requires equal consideration of realism and liberalism. If realism were indeed the cynical amoralism it is frequently portrayed to be, it would be of little use. Statesmen would be loath to use it, citizens would refuse to support it, and theorists would ignore it. By the same measure, if the liberal idealism of Kant and Wilson were a sufficient moral guide, the lesson of realism would not resonate so loudly and persistently. Realism and liberalism have always been in conversation; it is hard to imagine one without the other.

It is interesting to note that the United States, a relatively youthful participant in world history, has played a pivotal role in defining the way in which much of the world thinks about morality and foreign policy today. The unique role of the United States in combining morality and foreign policy in such a self-conscious way should be noted, but it should be the beginning and not the end of discussion. This is particularly true now that the influence of anticommunist *raison d'état* in the West has gone the way of the Marxist–Leninist *raison d'état* in the East. Both are now gone, and their reflexive appeals to the "necessity" rationale for all policy decisions must now yield to more nuanced views and substantive analyses.

As the historian Gaddis Smith (1993a) points out, the end of the Cold War opens a new era of hard choices. These choices will assuredly evoke moral dilemmas. Without the evils of "communism" or "capitalism" as self-justifying foils for one another, and without a dire bipolar balance of terror dominating the geopolitical calculus, moral principles beyond "necessity" will inevitably come into play.

A current and yet perennial example is the issue of humanitarian intervention. Under what conditions and by what mechanisms is such intervention morally permitted? Where might it be *required*? And by what principles and standards should these judgments be made? The 1993–1994 intervention in Somalia and subsequent failure to intervene decisively in the former Yugoslavia offer interesting test cases. Decisions to intervene or not to intervene are, by definition, exercises in moral and political judgment.

Ethnic violence, regional conflict, demographic shifts, economic rivalries, and environmental protection are now at the center of the international agenda. New motivations and restraints have emerged in dealing with these issues, primarily the reality of limited resources and the difficulties of sustaining cooperation among new allies. And along with these new elements, old considerations tied to particular national interests remain powerful and often decisive. Given this mix of changing and enduring interests, many choices will need to be justified in new or at least different terms.

Will the end of the Cold War result in a strengthening of the shared values of the world community? Realists and liberals may have different opinions on this, but both would agree that a discussion of the status of the "world community" (such as it exists) is essential. Realists and liberals alike are asking the questions: How will the end of bipolar "necessity" policies affect the status of the world community? And how will the world community accommodate the aspirations and beliefs of diverse cultures, many with their own moral traditions and each with its unique history?

The realist argument against liberalism has been as much about the fallacies of positivism and rationalism as about the proper role of morality in foreign policy. Similarly, the liberal argument against realism has focused more on philosophical assumptions (regarding moral duties, the nature of the international system, and the idea of progress) than on practical applications. These differences are bridged in the continuing attention given to assessments of the power of morality, mores, and norms as factors in international politics. However, where realists see these ideas as ameliorating forces, lessening the more dangerous aspects of the struggle for power, liberals see them as instruments for achieving a real "perpetual peace." Where the realists believe that at best the bleeding may perhaps be stopped, the liberals believe that a cure is possible.

The insights of both liberals and realists will be needed to make sense of the present and offer alternatives for the future. The fact that these two approaches begin from different philosophical premises does not undermine their utility for those who see virtues in both. For similar reasons, realists and liberals alike are interested in exploring more areas of normative agreement. Their respective critiques of the role of morality in foreign policy—including its possibilities and limitations—will be essential in considering the hard choices that are already evident in the post–Cold War era.

WHERE THE REALIST/LIBERAL PARADIGM LEAVES US

Can the realist/liberal paradigm be enhanced? How might it suggest pathways for the future study of ethics and international affairs or, more specifically, the role of morality in foreign policy? The recent literature has produced three identifiable approaches, all of which build upon the hybrid discussed above.

The first is a comparative historical approach, best exemplified in the recent book *Traditions of International Ethics*, edited by Terry Nardin and David R. Mapel (1992). This book catalogs the major Western traditions of international ethics, pointing out major distinctions between them. It describes the central premises of each tradition (such as realism, liberalism, and marxism) and relates them to perennial issues in international relations, such as self-determination and intervention.

This book serves the useful function of setting out terms for analysis and comparison. The first problem in discussing morality in foreign policy is the lack of a common vocabulary. This book, and this type of study, enable cross-tradition discussion; that is, they clarify the methods used in coming to judgment while they illustrate both the particular and universal characteristics of each tradition.

Traditions of International Ethics is a pioneering work in what should be a growing field of comparative study. It begins with a description of fundamental theoretical arguments and includes attention to historical contingency and human agency. Much work of this type needs to be done on non-Western traditions, the most obvious being Islam and the Asian traditions dominated by Confucian thought.

A second approach begins with specific issues and discusses them in terms of national and international moral norms (Beitz, 1988; Jones, 1991). These issues typically include sovereignty and intervention, self-determination, human rights, the use of force, and distributive justice. The list is driven by empirical political realities, and its treatment is primarily descriptive. The idea underlying this approach is to illustrate the ways in which moral norms have influenced decision making in the realm of foreign policy.

As the intellectual historian Dorothy V. Jones illustrates in her recent book *Code of Peace: Ethics and Security in the World of Warlord States* (1991), the nations of the world themselves have forged an evolving consensus on ethical principles that serve as the normative foundation of international relations. These principles, which have arisen out of the hard-won lessons of war and peace throughout world history, and especially the twentieth century, include the sovereign equality of states, the presumption of nonintervention, the recognition of human rights, the principle of self-determination, and provisions for cooperation among states.

This approach is most readily recognized in analysis of documents such as the United Nations Charter, the Universal Declaration of Human Rights, and the work of the Geneva Conventions. As declarations of prescriptive principles of desirable behavior to which most nations can and do agree, the norms expressed in these documents can serve as benchmarks for both realists and liberals by which to measure political acts.

Not all international moral norms have been codified into universally understood and accepted documents. However, as Jones points out, there is enough evidence to assert that these norms do indeed exist and that they carry considerable weight. More work needs to be done to analyze how and where they are effective and by what means they might be strengthened (e.g., Kegley and Raymond, 1990).

A third approach is the development of case studies to complement the historical and principle-based approaches. It is difficult and perhaps counterproductive to discuss principles without examples, just as it would be incoherent to discuss examples without regard to some general organizing principles. Inevitably then, in discussing morality and foreign policy, one must get down to cases.

The issue of morality and ethics is ultimately about choice, and the study of choice makes sense only within reasonably well-defined parameters. Case studies present all the complexities of political and moral judgment. More often than not, morality and foreign policy concern the sorting of competing moral claims. It is difficult if not impossible to appreciate the sometimes subtle and sometimes overwhelming force of these competing imperatives divorced from cases. Excellent case studies have recently been written on topics such as humanitarian aid, covert action, intervention, the obligations of multinational institutions, international business practices, terrorism, and many others (McElroy, 1992; Carnegie Council, 1990). These works are valuable supplements to theoretical excursions in the field and powerful illustrations of the moral dimensions of foreign policy.

There is a growing literature in ethics and international affairs, much of it focusing on the question of morality and foreign policy. By necessity, all of this literature incorporates the insights of both realists and liberals. The hybrid exists, and in reality, it has always been here. The challenge now is to relate the insights of these traditions to the problems of our age.

REFERENCES

Beitz, Charles R. (1988) "Recent International Thought," *International Journal* 43 (Spring): 183–204.

Bok, Sissela. (1990) "Early Advocates of a Lasting Peace: Utopians or Realists?" *Ethics & International Affairs* 4: 145–62.

Brzezinski, Zbigniew. (1993) *Out of Control: Global Turmoil on the Eve of the Twenty-first Century.* New York: Charles Scribner's Sons.

Carnegie Council. (1990) Case Study Series. New York: Carnegie Council on Ethics and International Affairs.

Chambers, John W., II, ed. (1991) *The Eagle and the Dove: The American Peace Movement and Foreign Policy 1900–1922.* New York: Syracuse University Press.

Donaldson, Thomas. (1992) "Kant's Global Rationalism," pp. 136–57 in Terry Nardin and David R. Mapel, eds., *Traditions of International Ethics.* New York: Cambridge University Press.

Donnelly, Jack. (1992) "Twentieth-Century Realism," pp. 85–111 in Terry Nardin and David R. Mapel, eds., *Traditions of International Ethics.* New York: Cambridge University Press.

Doyle, Michael W. (1986) "Liberalism and World Politics," *American Political Science Review* 80 (December): 1151–69.

Forde, Steven. (1992) "Classical Realism," pp. 62–84 in Terry Nardin and David R. Mapel, eds., *Traditions of International Ethics.* New York: Cambridge University Press.

Gilpin, Robert G. (1986) "The Richness of the Tradition of Political Realism," pp. 301–21 in Robert O. Keohane, ed., *Neorealism and Its Critics.* New York: Columbia University Press.

Gray, Colin S. (1993) "Economic Well-Being and Global Security: A Strategic Perspective," paper presented at conference on "Ethics, Security and the New World Order," National Defense University, February, Washington, D.C..

Hobbes, Thomas. (1947) *Leviathan.* Oxford: Oxford University Press.

Jones, Dorothy V. (1991) *Code of Peace: Ethics and Security in the World of the Warlord States.* Chicago: University of Chicago Press.

Kant, Immanuel. ([1795] 1970) "Perpetual Peace: A Philosophical Sketch," in Hans Riess, ed., *Kant's Political Writings.* New York: Cambridge University Press.

Kegley, Charles W., Jr. (1992) "The New Global Order: The Power of Principle in a Pluralistic World," *Ethics & International Affairs* 6: 21–40.

————. (1988) "Neo-Idealism: A Practical Matter," *Ethics & International Affairs* 2: 173–97.

Kegley, Charles W., Jr., and Gregory A. Raymond. (1990) *When Trust Breaks Down: Alliance Norms in World Politics.* Columbia: University of South Carolina Press.

Keohane, Robert O., ed. (1986) *Neorealism and Its Critics.* New York: Columbia University Press.

———. (1983) "Theory of World Politics: Structural Realism and Beyond," pp. 503–40 in Ada Finifter, ed., *Political Science: The State of the Discipline*. Washington, D.C.: American Political Science Association.

Kennan, George F. (1985–1986) "Morality and Foreign Policy," *Foreign Affairs* 64 (Winter): 205–18.

Little, David. (1993) "The Recovery of Liberalism: *Moral Man and Immoral Society* Sixty Years Later," *Ethics & International Affairs* 7: 171–201.

———. (1978) "Duties of Station and Duties of Conscience: Are There Two Moralities?" in Donald G. Jones, ed., *Private and Public Ethics: Tensions between Conscience and Institutional Responsibility*. New York: Edwin Mellen Press.

McElroy, Robert W. (1992) *Morality and American Foreign Policy: The Role of Ethics in International Affairs*. Princeton, N.J.: Princeton University Press.

Morgenthau, Hans J. (1954) *Politics among Nations*, 2nd ed. New York: Alfred Knopf.

———. (1951) *In Defense of the National Interest*. New York: Alfred Knopf.

Myers, Robert J. (1991) *Speaking Truth to Power: The Quest for Equality in Freedom*. New York: Carnegie Council on Ethics and International Affairs.

Nardin, Terry, and David R. Mapel, eds. (1992) *Traditions of International Ethics*. New York: Cambridge University Press.

Niebuhr, Reinhold. (1932) *Moral Man and Immoral Society: A Study in Ethics and Politics*. New York: Charles Scribner's Sons.

Ruggie, John G. (1983) "Continuity and Transformation in the World Polity: Toward a Neorealist Synthesis," *World Politics* 35 (January): 261–85.

Smith, Gaddis. (1993a) "What Role for America?" *Current History* 92 (April): 150–54.

———. (1993b) *Woodrow Wilson's Fourteen Points: A Seventy-fifth Anniversary Reconsideration*. New York: Carnegie Council on Ethics and International Affairs.

Smith, Michael Joseph. (1992) "Liberalism and International Reform," pp. 201–24 in Terry Nardin and David R. Mapel, eds., *Traditions of International Ethics*. New York: Cambridge University Press.

———. (1986) *Realist Thought from Weber to Kissinger*. Baton Rouge: Louisiana State University Press.

Waltz, Kenneth N. (1979) *Theory of International Politics*. Reading, Mass.: Addison-Wesley.

PART V

International Relations Theory and the Global Future

In many respects, the seven preceding essays in Parts II–IV share an interest in critically evaluating realist approaches to peace. Each factor or dimension of world politics that these essays treat describes a pressing but perennial controversy, about which resurrected liberalism presents a challenge to the realpolitik path to world order. Moreover, these essays all center on the larger question begging for greater scholarly evaluation, which is how theoretical inquiry might expand in order to broaden understanding about international relations. To pursue this broader theory-building concern, our last contribution places the controversies assessed above into context and assesses the implications in light of the changes the future might bring.

"Great things are achieved," Giuseppe Mazzini noted in 1910, "by guessing the direction of one's century." Yet, as James Lee Ray reminds us in "Promise or Peril? Neorealism, Neoliberalism, and the Future of International Politics," because prediction is most perilous, to prepare theoretically for the future requires preparing for uncertainty.

Indeed, only the foolhardy would presume to forecast confidently the shape of the world to come. These are hard times for prophets. Whether realists or liberals, political pundits are not doing well these days, given the cascade of events since 1989 unforeseen by *any* scholarly tradition. And there is little reason to expect that forecasters will do much better in the near future. We simply do not have a reliable method for either confidently characterizing the changes that will shape the world's future or for framing a coherent theory that can explicate their meaning. Since we do not know how accurately to describe or predict the changes that will occur, we do not as yet have agreement as to the kind of theory of world politics that will best advance our understanding. Whether it is appropriate to take idealism out of mothballs and allow it to temper the hard-nosed realism that until recently has steered theorizing remains problematic (see Baldwin, 1993).

How, then, might we visualize the future, given the difficulty of distinguishing long-term secular trends from short-term, temporary perturbations? And which theoretical orientation can best help us understand international behavior under conditions pervaded by uncertainty about the prospects for both propitious and destabilizing changes (Havel, 1993; Hoffmann, 1992)?

At the heart of the issue, and critical to the liberal posture, is the question of whether progress is to be expected in international relations. Many realists abandon hope that human effort in the realm of international politics can significantly change the world, given their expectation that conflict is endemic because humans are more interested in being relatively better-off than others rather than being simply well-off (see Snidal, 1993, and Grieco's chapter in this book). This inherent pessimism about a country's innate desire for advantage and relative gains with its competitors ultimately disposes realist theorists to resist the Enlightenment faith in historical progress. By contrast, those who adhere to the liberal creed believe that given the proper reforms and incentives, bickering and bloodshed can yield to a system in which cooperation and peace can predominate—that competition can yield to collaboration in environments in which what is perceived as good for another country can be good for one's own.

Whichever expectation is fulfilled will have much to do with the kinds of theories of international relations that will be fashioned and gain acceptance. Should brutality and warfare capture tomorrow's headlines, realism will flourish. But should cooperative endeavors and concerted action to contend with the common problems facing humanity expand, then liberalism will find itself a home in which many theorists are likely to find comfort.

Professor Ray describes the setting in which this theoretical debate is likely to unfold. To estimate the prospects for historical progress (and the future of realist and liberal interpretations of world history), Ray turns to the evidence produced by scientific analysis of historical patterns. Comparing the Cold War with the two world wars that preceded it in this century, he also explores the implications of those three global wars for theories of international politics. Showing the "blow" that the idealists' liberal faith in democracy as a force for peace received from World War II and the ways in which the Cold War further reduced the influence of liberalism, Ray notes that these liberal interpretations are only now beginning to recover in the years immediately following the Cold War's demise.

Fastening his scope on two indicators that speak to possibilities—the abolition of slavery and the potential obsolescence of international war—Ray shows why this record inspires hope and why "the end of the Cold War shows signs of breathing new life into the liberal or Wilsonian idea that regime type plays a key role in the explanation of international conflict." However, he cautions that whereas these achievements attest to the capacity for progress, they do not assure that progress is inevitable. The possibility of reversals is potent. Should such reversals materialize, they would undermine confidence in the new liberal theories of world politics and make realism's despair about international change and cooperation appear justified. Therefore, Ray concludes that euphoria about the post–Cold War is unwarranted, and that should the future bode a return to the grim properties that have governed world politics throughout most of its history, neoliberalism might prove to be "a fad, a product of ephemeral enthusiasms. . . . The neoliberal moment in the international system may be brief." Yet despite this, Ray suggests why realism and neorealism will not provide an adequate basis for explaining the future, and why, therefore, "the predominant [realist] paradigm is in need of important modifications to which neoliberalism can contribute."

This sober warning about the dangers of premature speculation brings the preceding discussions about the neoliberal challenge to realist theories full circle. It invites the reader to take cognizance of the circumstantial and intellectual forces that drive paradigmatic revisions and revolutions. In conjunction with the book's other essays, Ray's essay forces a contemplation of the ways in which liberal principles might be constructively integrated with realist premises. This reintegration, many of the essays in *Controversies in International Relations Theory* suggest, is possible because "in important ways realism never did break with idealism" (Rosenberg, 1990: 296), and "realist and idealist theories share a common set of assumptions" (Jones, 1992: 186). Hence, within their divergent depictions of world politics might be found the clues to uncovering whether and in what circumstances cooperation might take precedence over conflict (Stein, 1991) and how, in a Hegelian dialectical fashion, a successor paradigm might evolve that incorporates elements of both and moves beyond them. "Realism and neoliberalism," Ray submits, "can be synthesized, with encouraging results."

As scholars and students attempt to arm themselves intellectually to deal with the future of world politics, they will need to reexamine habitual theoretical premises. The essays in *Controversies in International Relations Theory: Realism and the Neoliberal Challenge* provoke awareness of that need. If in suggesting "how idealism can go hand in hand with realism" (Isaacson, 1992: 82) they inspire critical reassessments of theoretical orthodoxies and encourage an effort to build a more sophisticated theoretical framework, this book will have succeeded in its overarching purpose.

REFERENCES

Baldwin, David A., ed. (1993) *Neorealism and Neoliberalism: The Contemporary Debate*. New York: Columbia University Press.

Havel, Vaclav. (1993) "The Post-Communist Nightmare," *New York Review of Books* 51 (May 27): 8–10.

Hoffmann, Stanley. (1992) "Delusions of World Order," *New York Review of Books* 39 (April 9): 37–43.

Isaacson, Walter. (1992) "Sometimes, Right Makes Might," *Time* (December 21): 82.

Jones, Erik. (1992) Review of Arthur A. Stein, *Why Nations Cooperate*, *SAIS Review* 12 (Winter/Spring): 186–88.

Rosenberg, Justin. (1990) "What's the Matter with Realism?" *Review of International Studies* 16 (April): 285–303.

Snidal, Duncan. (1993) "Relative Gains and the Pattern of International Cooperation," pp. 181–207 in David A. Baldwin, ed., *Neorealism and Neoliberalism: The Contemporary Debate*. New York: Columbia University Press.

Stein, Arthur A. (1991) *Why Nations Cooperate: Circumstance and Choice in International Relations*. Ithaca, N.Y.: Cornell University Press.

CHAPTER 14

Promise or Peril? Neorealism, Neoliberalism, and the Future of International Politics

JAMES LEE RAY

In 1989, the Berlin Wall fell, and the Soviet Empire in Eastern Europe fell apart. All of the regimes that the Soviets had propped up in that part of the world disintegrated with rather amazing speed once it became clear that the Soviets would not support them with military force. By the end of 1991, the "Soviet empire" in the form of the Union of Soviet Socialist Republics had also fallen apart, and at this writing it is not clear whether this process of disintegration has reached its conclusion. In other words, "Russia" itself is threatened by separatist groups that want to dismantle the Russian Federation.

These events, and the end of the Cold War, have created a situation reminiscent of the end of the world wars of this century. "Like World Wars I and II, a consequence of the event [i.e., the end of the Cold War] was that a major empire was dismembered, important political boundaries in Europe were reorganized, and several nations were politically transformed" (Mueller, 1991: 6). The Soviet Union did not lose a military conflict as Germany did in both of the "real" world wars, but the political regime that held the empire in Eastern Europe and within the USSR together has become discredited in a way that is at least reminiscent of the ruination of the regime and ideology that supported Germany in its two world wars, setting the stage for a restructuring of the international system almost as fundamental as that which occurred after World Wars I and II.

The world wars had obvious and profound impacts on the academic field of international politics. So, too, did the Cold War, and it is predictable that the end of the Cold War will have important impacts on that field. It is, from a historical point of view, premature to speculate about what those impacts will be. But as Bruce Russett (1993: 280) has recently observed, "Social scientists sometimes create reality as well as analyze it." How the end of the Cold War ultimately will be judged to have affected international relations theory will depend to some extent on "premature" speculation and analysis of its impact in these years immediately following its demise. I embark here on an attempt to describe what I believe are the implications of the end of the Cold War for international relations theory, based in part on comparisons of the Cold War with the world wars that preceded it. But description will be mixed with prescriptive statements regarding what I hope (and prefer) the impact might be and the logical or theoretical bases for those hopes.

THE IMPACT OF THE WORLD WARS ON THE FIELD OF INTERNATIONAL RELATIONS

According to James Dougherty and Robert Pfaltzgraff (1990: 2), "No systematic development comparable to that in internal political theories of the state occurred in international theory before World War I." World War I brought international politics forcefully to the attention of American (and British) scholars, who are credited with inventing the modern field of international politics.[1] This is a debatable claim, and recently such analysts as Torbjorn Knutsen (1992) and Chris Brown (1992) have argued rather persuasively that there is an integrated theoretical tradition in the field of international politics with obvious connections to the contemporary field that goes back at least as far as such writers as Machiavelli, Rousseau, Hume, and Kant.[2]

Nevertheless, it is clear that American scholars have played a role in the development of the contemporary field of international politics roughly proportionate to the role that the United States has played in the international political system and that between the world wars, the "dominant approach" among American scholars of international politics "was to embrace what was international and to condemn what was national, and to evaluate events of the day by reference to the extent to which they conformed to the standards established by international legal norms and the League of Nations" (Dougherty and Pfaltzgraff, 1990: 6). In short, American writers, joined by some British academics of kindred spirit, developed a "utopian" literature that argued for policies and theories stressing the importance of international law,

---

[1] Martin Hollis and Steve Smith (1990: 16, 17) argue that international relations is a "discipline which, although helped by many contributions from elsewhere, has taken shape largely in Britain and America." They also assert that the First World War "led to the establishment of the subject."

[2] Dougherty and Pfaltzgraff (1990: 2) are not unaware of the contributions of those writers.

international organization, and ethical principles in the field of international politics.[3]

This "utopianism" or "idealism" received a devastating blow from events surrounding the onset of World War II and the predominant interpretations of those events after the war, from which it is only now, as this volume suggests, beginning to recover. And there is no question that "idealistic" theories and the policies idealistic theorists advocated deserved *some* of the criticisms they received in the wake of World War II.

Nicholas Murray Butler and James Shotwell, for example, both influential writers in the field of international politics (and both associated with the Carnegie Endowment for International Peace), played notable roles in the launching of the Kellogg–Briand Pact of 1928, which "outlawed" international war. The U.S. Senate approved the treaty in 1929 by a vote of 85 to 7. President Hoover declared that "the Treaty for the Renunciation of War will be felt in a large proportion of all future international acts" (De Conde, 1963: 512).

That prediction was overly optimistic, and the effort to eliminate international war simply by getting governments to make legal commitments to avoid it was "idealistic" and "utopian" in the pejorative senses of both of those terms. But the general rejection of idealist principles, specifically those having to do with reliance on international organizations (and, to a lesser extent, international law), was arguably illogical and so unjustified. The League of Nations did fail to prevent World War II. But the failure did not necessarily result from flaws in the ideas on which the League was based. Rather, the League failed because the organization and the principles upon which it was founded were not supported by the most important states in the system, with the United States not joining the League at all. The remaining major powers had neither the commitment nor, without the United States, the overwhelming power that might have deflected Japan's attack on Manchuria, Italy's attack on Ethiopia, and various predatory moves by Germany in the 1930s. In short, the "lesson" that should have been learned from the experience of the 1930s regarding the League was arguably *not* that reliance on such international organizations is a mistake but rather that it is a mistake not to support an organization *like* the League of Nations.

And that was precisely the lesson that seemed to be learned by the foreign policy-making establishment in the United States. After World War I, Woodrow Wilson's attempt to get the U.S. Senate to ratify the Treaty of Versailles, and join the League, was rebuffed by the Senate after a long and bitter struggle. The contrast with what happened after the launching of the United Nations when the charter was signed by fifty nations in June 1945

---

[3] "The emergence of International Relations as a separate field of study was closely related to the . . . First World War. . . . [T]here was a widespread view that the overwhelming lesson of the war was that military force could no longer achieve its objectives" (Hollis and Smith, 1990: 17).

could hardly have been more stark. "After six days of formal debate, the Senate approved the charter on July 28 by the landslide vote of 89 to 2" (De Conde, 1963: 638). Clearly, the American political establishment had "learned" not that the League of Nations was a mistake or that the principles upon which it stood had been exposed as misguided. Instead, the U.S. Senate felt that the lack of support from the United States for the League and its principles had been a grievous mistake that must not be repeated.

Meanwhile, though, enthusiasm among academic specialists in international relations for international organizations or for the liberal, idealistic principles on which the UN was founded was notably lower after World War II than it had been after World War I. Certainly the general thrust of realism in the post–World War II period was toward greater self-reliance and away from cooperative ventures like the United Nations. Hans J. Morgenthau in his *Politics among Nations*, an example obviously not selected at random, asserted the following with respect to the United Nations:

> The erection of a structure of international government upon what proved to be no political foundation at all has been a failure which threatens to come crashing down and bury the peace of the world beneath its ruins. The United Nations is like a building designed by two architects who have agreed upon plans for the second floor, but not upon those for the first. . . . In consequence, not only does the second floor become an unlivable abode, but the whole structure threatens to disintegrate. (Morgenthau, 1948: 383–84)

REALISM, REGIME TYPE, AND THE LESSONS OF WORLD WAR II

Another lesson that apparently was learned by American theorists of international relations from the process leading to World War II was that regime type does not matter. In other words, from the realist point of view (and ultimately the neorealist perspective as well), a state is a state is a state, and for the purpose of understanding the foreign policies of states, or how they interact, one need not and should not focus on what type of political regimes states have.

The denunciation of the idea that democracy is a force for peace, which is a fundamental aspect of modern realism in international political thought, was launched even before World War II in *The Twenty Years' Crisis* by E. H. Carr. Carr (1939, 1946: 143) acknowledges that "the victory of the democratic countries in 1918 created an almost universal opinion that democracy was the best form of government." But one of the more effective, best-remembered passages in this book is a condemnation of "Wilsonians" and the tendency of the "English-speaking peoples," that is, the United States and Great Britain, to identify what is in their own national interest with "universal right." Carr (1939, 1946: 79–83) explains that "theories of international morality are . . .

the product of dominant nations or groups of nations. For the past hundred years, and more especially since 1918, the English-speaking peoples have formed the dominant group in the world; and current theories of international morality have been designed to perpetuate their supremacy."

Carr (1939, 1946: 79) here justifiably emphasizes the point that "theories of social morality are always the product of a dominant group which identifies itself with the community as a whole." But he also exemplifies, and makes his own contribution to, the discrediting of the Wilsonian idea that democracy is a key to peace; this anti-Wilsonian theme became an important feature of realism as it emerged from World War II.

The antidemocratic bent of realism was certainly solidified by the founder of modern realism. In the first edition of *Politics among Nations*, Morgenthau (1948: 187) explained that "when in the course of the nineteenth century democratic selection and responsibility of government officials replaced government by the aristocracy, the structure of international society, and with it, of international morality underwent a fundamental change." A good democrat or a Kantian might anticipate that this assertion is a prelude to the development of a thesis to the effect that democratically elected leaders face effective ethical constraints with which aristocratic leaders, whose positions of power are theirs by birthright, are not forced to deal. But Morgenthau's argument is to the contrary. "Where responsibility for government is widely distributed among a great number of individuals with different conceptions as to what is morally required in international affairs . . . [i.e., in democratic regimes]," Morgenthau (1948: 189) asserts, "international morality as an effective system of restraints upon international policy becomes impossible." In short, in Morgenthau's view, "the democratic selection and responsibility of government officials destroyed international morality as an effective system of restraints."

But probably the most effective and influential realist argument against the idea that democracy is a pacifying factor of importance appeared in *Man, the State and War* by Kenneth Waltz (1954). An essential thesis of that still-influential book is that the "second image, the idea that defects in states cause wars among them" (Waltz, 1954: 83), is fundamentally flawed. In a chapter that still bears close scrutiny by liberals or neoliberals in danger of overconfidence, Waltz (1954: 101) points out that in 1791 Thomas Paine asserted with respect to the French Revolution that "Monarchical sovereignty, the enemy of mankind, the source of misery, is abolished. . . . Were this the case throughout Europe . . . the cause of war would be taken away." Waltz (1954: 118) traces the evolution of this argument to Woodrow Wilson who, in his message to Congress asking for a declaration of war against Germany, stated that "a steadfast concert for peace . . . can never be maintained except by a partnership of democratic nations." The basic problem with all of these arguments of the second-image type, according to Waltz, is that they assume that the conflicting units can be "perfected," and perfection is impossible for states as well as men. Waltz concludes:

> A world full of democracies would be forever at peace, but autocratic govern-
> ments are warlike. . . . *Capitalist* democracies actively promote war, *socialist*
> democracies are peaceful. Each of these formulations has claimed numerous
> adherents, and each adherent has in turn been called to task by critics and
> by history. (Waltz, 1954: 121)

Waltz goes on to point out that the hopes that *socialism* would bring
peace to humankind were dashed by divisions and conflicts among socialist
states, such as Tito's split with Stalin. In criticism of the idea that democracy
has important pacifying potential, he points not to divisions and conflicts
among democratic states, but to aggressive U.S. policies with respect to
Mexico, Spain, and the Philippines, arguing that "the optimism of nineteenth
century liberals was confounded by the First and Second World Wars" (Waltz,
1954: 121). Although the inconsistency of disparaging the peace-producing
potential of socialist states by pointing to conflicts among them while expressing equally dubious opinions about the pacifying potential of democratic states
on the basis of their conflict proneness vis-à-vis autocratic states is apparent to
contemporary readers familiar with the thesis about peace among democratic
states, I think Waltz is nevertheless correct in his assessment that the liberal
faith in democracy as a key to peace was severely damaged by the First and
Second World Wars. The First World War was fought, according to the leader
of what became the most powerful state in the victorious coalition, to make
the world safe for democracy. It failed to do that, and its failure in that respect
became obvious quite rapidly. Perhaps even more important, Adolf Hitler was
elected democratically. That turn of events can be and has been interpreted as
devastating to the idea that democracy is a guarantor of peace.

The democratic election of Hitler is in fact an important reminder of the
limits of democracy as a force for peace. But that example is also arguably a
shaky foundation for the rejection of the pacifying potential of democracy (and
of other liberal principles), which the process leading to the Second World
War, and the war itself, seems to have produced among theorists of international relations, and more broadly. Hitler's rise to power might have, as
logically, been utilized as an example in support of the idea that autocracy,
especially in major powers, is dangerous and destabilizing. Instead, for reasons
I will not guess at here, the historical lessons learned by international relations
theorists about the relationship between regime type and international politics
focused more intently on the democratic process that brought Hitler to power
rather than on the thoroughly antidemocratic regime he established and
through which he carried out his foreign policies, which were crucial to the
onset of World War II.

THE IMPACT OF THE COLD WAR ON RADICAL AND LIBERAL
SYMPATHY FOR DEMOCRACY

Charles Kegley, in the introduction to this volume, rightly asserts that the
ascendance of realism in the international relations field and the relative

decline of liberal theoretical ideas about international politics both occurred after the Second World War not only because of the lessons learned from that war, but also because of the onset of the Cold War. "Realism," he points out, "found a hospitable home in which to flourish during the conflict-ridden fifty-year system between 1939 and 1989 when the lust for power, appetite for imperial expansion, struggle for hegemony, a superpower arms race, and an obsession with national security were in strong evidence." Evidence supporting the idea that this "correlation" between the Cold War environment and the dominance of realism is indicative of a causal connection can be gleaned from a review of what happened, theoretically speaking, to the field of international relations in the 1970s, another decade (like the 1990s) during which the Cold War "ended." The Vietnam War wound down, Nixon went to China, SALT I was ratified and détente was established with the Soviet Union, and OPEC brought international economic problems to the fore. Probably the most characteristic theoretical document of that decade was *Power and Interdependence* by Robert Keohane and Joseph Nye (1977). Although not totally incompatible with realism, *Power and Interdependence* did contain important antirealist themes, criticizing, for example, realist emphases on the primacy of military force and national security issues and the utility of treating states as unitary rational actors. One reviewer (Michalak, 1979: 150) suggested that it "may well become the *Politics among Nations* of the 1970s," implying not that it was "realist" in tenor, but that it provided a prominent, perhaps even predominant, theoretical alternative to realism appropriate to the 1970s.

But thanks to such seminal events as the seizing of American hostages by Iran, the Soviet invasion of Afghanistan, and the election of Ronald Reagan in 1979, the Cold War did not stay ended. It was probably not coincidental that the rebirth of the Cold War occurred jointly with a resurgence of realism, marked most prominently by the appearance of neorealism in *Theory of International Politics* (Waltz, 1979). Perhaps the renewal of Cold War tensions also accounts to some extent for the reception accorded to another book published in the same year, volume four of R. J. Rummel's *Understanding Conflict and War: War, Power, Peace* (1979). The thesis of that volume, and indeed of the whole five-volume set, was that "a necessary condition of violence between two states is that at least one be totalitarian or authoritarian" (Rummel, 1979: 278). Ultimately, Rummel's contributions regarding the democratic peace proposition have received some recognition. For example, in the wake of the second ending of the Cold War, the *Journal of Conflict Resolution*, the *Journal of Peace Research*, and *International Interactions* devoted special issues to "democracy and peace,"[4] and in each Rummel is cited with regularity.[5] However, as the Cold War was being reborn in the

[4] See Bruce Bueno de Mesquita, Robert Jackman, and Randolph Siverson (1991); Nils Petter Gleditsch (1992); and Steve Chan (1993).

[5] However, cited more often are rather derivative articles such as Rummel's (1983, 1985) rather than the five-volume work in which he developed his ideas about the relationship between regime type and international conflict.

early 1980s, Rummel's five volumes of *Understanding Conflict and War* appeared (from 1975 to 1981), and they evoked very little reaction. As Rummel himself (1989: 324) observed: "I did not expect it [i.e., the five volumes of *Understanding Conflict and War*] to be a hit. I was not prepared however for [*Understanding Conflict and War*] being so widely ignored."

The Cold War's negative impact on the reception accorded to liberal ideas regarding the relationship between regime type and international conflict occurred not only because its harsh atmosphere made realist ideas seem more plausible in general. The Cold War also reduced the influence of liberalism because of its impact on many analysts who might have, under other circumstances, been inclined to be more sympathetic. Specifically, the Cold War turned both ideological "radicals" and "liberals" against some liberal ideas regarding the peace-producing potential of democracy.

The impact on radicals, both on individual scholars and on their influence as a group, derived more specifically from one of the more tragic episodes of the Cold War, that is, the Vietnam War. It was a war fought by the democratic United States ostensibly in favor of democracy in South Vietnam. (No matter how skeptical one might be about that war, and the extent to which allegiance to democracy motivated it, one would have to admit that the United States, by encouraging elections in South Vietnam in the middle of warfare, went to some trouble to make it look like it was a struggle on behalf of democracy there.) I believe that analysts from widely divergent points on the ideological spectrum could agree on the statement that the war's length, brutality, and futility combined to give democracy a bad name. It certainly increased the influence within the international relations field of radical analysts like Noam Chomsky (1969, 1973), Richard Falk (1968a, 1968b), Gabriel Kolko (1969), and Harry Magdoff (1969).

In simple terms, the major message of all their works was that democracies, or at least capitalist, market-oriented democracies, are extremely bellicose. The Vietnam War created an atmosphere in which defenders of democracy, at least among academic theorists of international politics, were not notable in number. On the contrary, the Vietnam War as well as the broader context of the Cold War, with its central contest between democracy in the United States and dictatorship (of the proletariat) in the Soviet Union, provided an environment in which "research attributing major importance to political democracy seemed propagandistic to many peace researchers who subscribed to a 'third way' in the Cold War and disliked anything that smacked of one-sided propaganda for 'the free world'" (Gleditsch, 1992: 374).

J. David Singer (1969: 40–41), for example, vigorously defended that idea that the Cold War confrontation was symmetrical—generated by similar processes on both sides—and that the clash of ideas regarding the relative virtues of democracy or socialism was superficial. The essential problem, in his view, was not dictatorship in the Soviet Union or capitalism in the United States, but the fact that "threat-perception arises out of a situation of armed hostility, in which *each* [emphasis added] body of policymakers assumes that the other entertains aggressive designs; further each assumes that such designs will be pursued by physical and direct means if estimated gains seem to outweigh estimated losses." "Abstract political dogmas," or "the ideological utterances of Marx or Locke, Lenin or Jefferson, Manuilski or Wilson," were in Singer's view not central to an understanding of the Cold War conflict.

It is not surprising then that Singer and coauthor Melvin Small were skeptical when they addressed the hypothesis that regime type plays an important role in the explanation of international conflict. They reported first that between 1816 and 1965, international wars involving democracies were not dissimilar from wars involving only undemocratic states in terms of longevity and fatalities. They acknowledged that, with a couple of debatable exceptions, there had been no wars between democratic states, but they concluded that this was probably due to the fact that "war is most likely between neighbors," and "bourgeois democracies do not border upon one another very frequently" (Small and Singer, 1976: 64).

However, the finding that wars involving democratic states have not been significantly different from wars involving only autocratic states with respect to their length and number of battle deaths is only tangentially relevant at best to an evaluation of the hypothesis regarding the rates at which different types of political regimes become involved in war (Small and Singer [1976: 61] were aware of this problem). Even if democratic states had been, over the time period analyzed, 99 percent less likely to become involved in wars than autocratic states, the wars in which they did become involved might still have been equivalent in length and severity to those involving only autocratic states. More important, from a review of a partial list of bordering democratic states, Small and Singer conclude that democracies do not border on one another very frequently. They do not estimate what proportion of democratic dyads border on each other *compared to* the analogous proportion of autocratic states. (They could not; the data necessary for such an analysis were not available.) They assert that "as we can see from this listing, the incidence of geographic contiguity between democratic states is quite small" (Small and Singer, 1976: 67), even though in fact it is not possible to see anything of the sort because no basis of comparison is provided.

Nils Petter Gleditsch (1993: 21) demonstrates quite persuasively that for most of the time period from 1816 to 1986, "the average distance between democracies was well *below* the system distance and for the period after World War II the two distances are roughly the same." So, according to Gleditsch, "The idea that democracies tend to be particularly far apart can be dismissed out of hand." Gleditsch here deals with the geographic relationship between pairs of states in terms of the distance between their capitals, which is not precisely the notion that Small and Singer (1976) had in mind when they speculate about the extent to which democratic states are contiguous. But utilizing a measure of proximity or contiguity from the University of Michigan Correlates of War project, which more closely approximates the notion that Small and Singer (1976) address, Stuart Bremer (1992, 1993) has demonstrated quite conclusively that the absence of war between democratic states cannot be accounted for by a lack of contiguity among them.

I think it is fair to infer from the tenuous relationship between the evidence they provide and the conclusions they reach that Small and Singer (1976) were rather intent on discrediting the idea that democracy has any important peace-producing effect. From this and other work, it is apparent that Singer in particular is convinced that the problem of international war cannot usefully be addressed with a focus on the types of states that exist in the international system. Small and Singer (1976: 68), for example, conclude with the statement that "perhaps the recognition that all governments, democracies and autocracies alike, are prone to war will turn our attention away from rival domestic systems to the conflict-generating properties of the system in which we all must live."[6]

One might infer, in addition, from the tone of this discussion that my point is that pressures from the academic community to be politically correct had the unfortunate effect of blinding analysts of the Cold War period to the peace-producing virtues of democracy. But such an argument would be based on hindsight in a way that would be clearly unfair to international relations analysts and theorists who lived through the Cold War period. Even more important, such a criticism would be misguided even though based on hindsight (which, despite the cliché to the contrary, is never "20-20"). Democratic states may be relatively peaceful in their relationships with *each other*; their relationships with autocratic states can, however, clearly be quite conflictual. Furthermore, democratic states in their relationships with autocratic states can often be hypocritical, self-righteous, and aggressive. It is certainly possible that decision makers in the United States during the Cold War who were encouraged to be even more convinced of the relative virtues of democracy than they already were might have made for a more dangerous confrontation with the Soviet Union. It was that danger about which Singer and like-minded peace researchers were concerned, probably with justification.[7]

The point here is to explain why not only (typically more conservative) realists, as well as radicals, but also "liberals" who might, all else being equal, have been otherwise inclined, ignored or avoided ideas regarding the peace-producing potential of democracy because of the impact of the Cold War. That impact on at least one substantial sector of peace researchers and quantitatively

---

[6] Similarly, an essay by Singer and Karl Deutsch on the relative virtues of bipolarity and multipolarity (Deutsch and Singer, 1969: 324) concludes that both types of systems are inherently dangerous: "Multipolar systems are . . . self-destroying. . . . *If the spread of nuclear weapons could be slowed down or controlled*, a transition from the bipolar international system of the early 1950s to an increasingly multipolar system in the 1960s might buy mankind some valuable time to seek some more dependable bases for world order."

[7] As Singer (1989: 220) points out, while there may have been some tendency within the international relations academic community during the Cold War to avoid propagandistic (or politically incorrect) views regarding the virtues of democracy, there were also substantial political costs to pay for adopting a "non-Manichean approach to the Cold War."

oriented scholars of international politics is reflected clearly in an essay by John Vasquez (1987). Vasquez reviews the findings of the Correlates of War project, but the scope of his essay is broader. He considers the work of many analysts whose only connections to the COW project involved a shared interest in the causes of war and/or a common reliance on data generated by the project. In that quite wide-ranging essay on empirically oriented research regarding international conflict, Vasquez never mentions liberal ideas regarding the role of democracy, or regime type, in processes leading to international war.[8]

INTERNATIONAL RELATIONS THEORY AFTER THE END OF THE COLD WAR

Interest in those liberal ideas among associates of the COW project, among the broader empirically oriented international relations community, and among international relations theorists in general, was soon to develop. (Any review of the COW project now could hardly avoid discussing an already lengthy list of works devoted to examination of the proposition that democratic states do not fight wars against each other.) But the rather sudden flowering of this interest, occurring jointly as it has with the end of the Cold War, serves as a credible basis for skepticism. Perhaps the demise of totalitarianism in the Soviet Union (not to mention the demise of the Soviet Union itself) and the associated disappearance of the tension, the arms race, and the threat of cataclysmic nuclear war have produced a reaction in the form of "neoliberalism" that is understandably euphoric, but also hasty and naive.

Anyone who has asserted for public attribution, and in the dramatic year of 1989, that moral progress might lead international war to become as obsolete as slavery (Ray, 1989) will be familiar with such arguments. Since that assertion was based in part on the observation that democratic states do not fight wars against each other and that democracy is becoming more prevalent, I have noted with interest the often acerbic reaction to Francis Fukuyama's (1989) thesis regarding the "end of history" as well as related criticism of John Mueller's (1989) theme regarding the obsolescence of war, which was developed

---

[8] This lack of attention or interest in such ideas on the part of Vasquez, and many others, even as recently as 1987, might be reflected most intriguingly in the fact that while Vasquez never refers to democracy or regime type as an important factor to consider in the analysis of international war, he does cite Rummel (1979), but only on a marginal matter. According to Rummel (1989: 323), the most important conclusion of Rummel (1979) is that "the fundamental variable relating to the occurrence of international . . . war . . . is political rights, civil liberties, and economic freedom within nations. The less freedom within two nations, the more likely violence is between them; and between democracies, war should not occur at all." In other words, Vasquez (1987) did not fail to discuss such ideas because he had not been exposed to them.

in a book published in that same pivotal year. Furthermore, I acknowledge that some of the criticisms regarding the neoliberal reaction to the end of the Cold War are not devoid of merit.

Certainly one of the most visible sources of such criticism is the essay by John Mearsheimer, "Back to the Future." His prediction that "the demise of the Cold War order is likely to increase the chances that war and major crises will occur in Europe" (Mearsheimer, 1990: 52) seems already borne out in many ways. Consider, for example, the internal unrest involving right-wing fanaticism in Germany, the demise of Czechoslovakia, ominous statements by Hungarian government officials regarding Hungarian minorities in neighboring states, Romanian irredentism involving Moldova, and, perhaps most important, the 1992 reversals in the movement toward unity within the European Union as well as the murderous wars among the republics of the former Yugoslavia. Even more central to our concerns here is Mearsheimer's assertion that "the possibility always exists that a democracy will revert to an authoritarian state. Liberal democracies must therefore worry about relative power among themselves. . . . Lamentably, it is not possible for even liberal democracies to transcend anarchy" (Mearsheimer, 1990: 50).

In short, there are certainly no guarantees (as Mearsheimer rightly points out) that the "march of democracy" to which Kegley refers in the introduction will continue. As Samuel Huntington (1991) has observed, two previous "waves" of democratization have been followed by setbacks, with new autocratic governments replacing several more democratic ones. Democracy is certainly not secure in Russia or in the other republics of the former Soviet Union. The Chinese government has resisted democratic reforms in a determined and, so far, apparently effective fashion.[9] In 1992, Freedom House, in its annual review of the world, announced that "India, the world's most populous democracy, fell to Partly Free for the first time since martial law was declared in 1975" (McColm, 1992: 5). In rough and admittedly marginally exaggerated terms, the former Soviet Union, China, and India have total populations of 300 million, 1.2 billion, and 1 billion, respectively. Together, their 2.5 billion people constitute almost half the population of the world. With a continuation of autocracy and/or serious setbacks for democracy certainly possible in all three places (not to mention in a whole series of new, fragile democracies in Asia, Africa, and Latin America), confidence in the continuation of the global "march of democracy" has to be tentative at best.

Another reason to be skeptical about what the future will hold for neoliberal notions about international politics arises from an analysis of what occurred in the aftermath of the Napoleonic Wars in the nineteenth century, as well as the two world wars of this century. William Riker's (1962: 32–33) *size principle*, according to which "participants create coalitions just as large as

---

[9] However, for a fairly optimistic assessment of China's political future, see Andrew Nathan (1993).

they believe will insure winning and no larger," is certainly congruent with realism as it is applied to international politics. In other words, Riker, in his discussion of the implications of the size principle for international relations, treats states as the most important actors, assumes that states can be treated as unitary rational actors, and maintains that states calculate their interests in terms of power—three essential characteristics of realism, according to Keohane (1983). And the implication of the size principle that grand coalitions will fall apart is supported by Riker's analysis of the fate of the grand coalitions that emerged victorious from the Napoleonic Wars, World War I, and World War II—that is, they fell apart in short order (Riker, 1962: 69–71).

The implications of this argument for the aftermath of the Cold War are obvious. For the moment, all the major powers of the world constitute a kind of grand coalition, whose unity has been demonstrated most dramatically in its response to Iraq's attack on Kuwait in August 1990. But if history is an accurate guide with respect to the fate of such grand coalitions, that unity will be short-lived. The grand coalition will break up; serious divisions within it are bound to show up sooner rather than later. It is possible that China's sale of sophisticated nuclear technology to Libya and Iran or North Korea's export of missiles to Iran, for example, is an early indication of unity among the antidemocratic states in the international political system.

The same pessimistic prediction might be based on a more traditional balance-of-power model. At this time the United States is clearly the most powerful state in the system. One can reasonably expect a coalition against the United States to spring up as a counterweight. Such a prediction is at least implicit in Kenneth Waltz's (1991: 670) recent observation that the U.S. invasion of Panama in 1989 was clearly illegal, and that the United States is better than most nations, but not as much better as many Americans believe. "In international politics," Waltz concludes, "unbalanced power constitutes a danger even when it is American power that is out of balance." In other words, in Waltz's view, the invasion of Panama by the United States is the kind of high-handed action one would expect from a major power unchecked by a counterbalancing coalition (self-perceptions of some Americans about the United States being different from ordinary power-seeking states notwithstanding), and such high-handedness will likely evoke such a coalition in the not-too-distant future.

The U.S. invasion of Panama suggests another reason why the neoliberal moment in the international system may be brief. As Robert Rothstein has noted, "the implicit message of the democracies-do-not-fight-democracies school might seem to be that existing democracies ought to use violence against nondemocracies in order to end the scourge of war—violence to achieve nonviolence" (Rothstein, 1991: 48). It was an explicit part of the rationale for George Bush's mission in Panama to "restore democracy" there.

In this book's introduction, Charles Kegley harks back rather nostalgically to the Wilsonian roots of neoliberalism. Yet he also warns that it should be remembered, in pondering those roots and the possible fate of contemporary neoliberalism, that President Wilson himself exhibited a strong interventionist streak, not only in World War I, but also in his authorizing invasions (and occupations) of, for example, the Dominican Republic, Haiti, and Mexico; he also continued the occupation of Nicaragua. If the American intervention in Panama proves to be a precedent for future missions, surely the United States will provoke a backlash that will undermine many neoliberal tenets regarding respect for international law and international organization, as well as the global trend toward democracy.

But the pessimism exemplified by Mearsheimer's "Back to the Future," as well as the nostalgia for the alleged relative tranquillity of the Cold War, provides a one-sided view to which neoliberalism can provide some useful balance. It might be pointed out, for example, that pessimism always appears more profound, even though pessimistic projections are certainly not always accurate. As John Kenneth Galbraith (1972: 6) once observed," [It] requires neither courage nor prescience to predict disaster. . . . Historians rejoice in crucifying the false prophet of the millennium. They never dwell on the mistake of the man who wrongly predicted Armageddon." More recently, Francis Fukuyama (1994: 29) makes virtually the same point when he states that "a Cassandra proved wrong . . . is never held accountable; indeed, such people retain an aura of moral seriousness for their tragic sense of human history. Naive Pollyannas, by contrast, are routinely held up to ridicule." John Mueller (1992) presents an impressive list of notable people who, during the Cold War, confidently predicted Armageddon in the form of cataclysmic nuclear war. (Somehow they did not appreciate the peace and tranquillity of the nuclear confrontation while it was occurring.) Hans Morgenthau, for example (to pick him out again in a nonrandom fashion), declared in 1979 that "the world is moving ineluctably towards a third world war—a strategic nuclear war. I do not believe that anything can be done to prevent it. The international system is simply too unstable to survive for long" (cited in Mueller, 1992: 69).[10]

Admittedly, many liberals, or idealists, made similar predictions during the Cold War. Also, even if some of the pessimism during the Cold War was excessive, it is still possible that some of the reactions to the end of the Cold War have been unjustifiably optimistic. Partially in self-defense, though, I would point out that Mueller's (1989) book regarding the obsolescence of international war, Fukuyama's (1989) article regarding the global trend toward democracy and the "end of history," and Ray's (1989) argument about the possible implications of the demise of slavery for the future of international war were all published *before* the fall of the Berlin Wall, the end of the Soviet

---

[10] Now, predictably, "the end of the cold war has brought a flood of glum views of the future. The tone . . . has ranged from pale gray to nearly coal black discussing the replacement of the Soviet Union by four new nuclear powers, the bloodbath in Yugoslavia, the grim future of democracy in Russia, the Iraqi demonstration that neither the United States nor the United Nations is qualified to prevent fearsome slaughters in the Third World, and the specter of nuclear or chemical war coming closer and closer" (Singer and Wildavsky, 1993: 8).

Empire in Eastern Europe and the disintegration of the Soviet Union, and the reasonably democratic election of Boris Yeltsin in Russia. The point is that none of these works were produced in the aftermath of the most dramatic episodes marking the end of the Cold War—that is, those episodes with the greatest potential for producing unwarranted euphoria. And in the case of Fukuyama's "End of History" in particular, its timing perhaps makes it deserving of more credit than it is typically accorded for a prescient appreciation of the strength of the democratizing trend that was yet to manifest itself in numerous dramatic ways.[11]

PREDICTING THE END OF THE COLD WAR

This is not to say that Fukuyama or anybody else predicted specifically that democracy was on the verge of coming to the Soviet Union and Eastern Europe or that the Cold War was about to end. According to John Gaddis (1992–1993: 18), the absence of such predictions in the international relations literature indicates the bankruptcy of the field. "One might as well have relied upon stargazers, readers of entrails, and other 'pre-scientific' methods for all the good our 'scientific' methods did. . . . Clearly our theories were not up to the task," Gaddis concludes, "of anticipating the most significant event in world politics since the end of World War II."

This is at least a partially misguided criticism. More specifically, it might be a valid criticism of the predominant paradigm of realism or neorealism, but it is arguably an inaccurate indictment of neoliberalism. It is true that realism and neorealism are ill-equipped to deal with events like the end of the Cold War. Neorealism in particular, "based as it is on the presumed symmetry of relations between the United States and the Soviet Union . . . and on a lack of attention to internal factors, assumed too much about the ability of politico-military factors to maintain the balance" (Crockatt, 1993: 71). Nor did liberals, or neoliberals, or anybody else in the international relations field show any significant degree of foresight regarding the internal transformation of the Soviet Union (or the disintegration of its empire). Regime transition has never been of much interest to analysts of international politics. That topic has been more closely associated with the subfield of comparative politics. In my view, one lesson that should be learned from the end of the Cold War, and from the way it ended, is that international relations analysts should focus more of their attention on regime transitions and on their relation-

---

[11] As Fukuyama (1992: 17) himself has pointed out, "The pessimists have been wrong in virtually every prediction they have made in the past decade—that Communism would never try to democratize, that the Kremlin would never give up Eastern Europe, that the Soviet Union would never break up."

ships to international politics, viewing those transitions as part of a global process in a way that comparative politics specialists are unlikely to do.

But to suggest, as Gaddis (1992–1993) does, that all international relations theories proved to be equally useless because they produced no specific accurate forecasts regarding the end of the Cold War is almost precisely analogous to an argument that the absence of accurate predictions from meteorologists in the years from, say, 1985 to 1991, that Hurricane Andrew would hit south Florida in August 1992 indicates that the field of meteorology is bereft of useful theories and that its practitioners have no real understanding of hurricanes.

Meteorologists, in fact, understand hurricanes quite well and, in retrospect, can explain quite convincingly the process that produces them and why they hit when and where they do. What they cannot do is to predict specifically, years or even months in advance, when and where a major hurricane will occur.[12] While it is not inconceivable that international relations theorists might, on occasion, generate accurate forecasts of events like the end of the Cold War, surely there will consistently be surprises of significant dimensions in global politics, just as it is unlikely that meteorologists will ever be able to tell us this year specifically when and where the major meteorological events of next year will occur.

However, just as meteorologists can explain hurricanes quite well in theory, and in retrospect, international relations theory is not without concepts and theories that "postdict," as it were, the end of the Cold War, without depending entirely on post hoc reconstructions. Surely, Rummel's theory of international conflict as developed in *Understanding Conflict and War*, for example (or any of the theoretical frameworks focusing on the peaceful nature of relationships between democratic states) imply that if the autocratic protagonist in a conflict like the Cold War moves toward democracy, antagonism between the parties to that conflict should decrease significantly. Keeping this in mind, as well as the fact that even in retrospect neither realism nor neorealism is able to anticipate or explain the end of the Cold War in this way, provides a strong basis for an argument that, at the very least, the predominant paradigm in international relations is in need of important modifications to which neoliberalism can contribute.

CONCLUSION

The two world wars had obvious impacts on the field of international relations. World War I gave birth to the contemporary academic specialization as we know it. It also gave a strong impetus to an "idealistic" or "utopian" approach to

---

[12] It might be argued that meteorologists, though, did predict, for example, when and where Hurricane Andrew would hit Florida in the days before August 26, 1992, thus indicating a level of understanding of the phenomena meteorological theory addresses significantly superior to that attained by analysts of international politics. But political scientists, too, have demonstrated an ability to generate short-range forecasts at a level of accuracy that is within the range of that achieved by meteorologists (Ray, 1992: 160–61).

international politics. However, the events leading up to World War II and the predominant postwar interpretation of those events dealt idealistic approaches a severe blow. Realism and neorealism have held sway ever since. The Cold War helped to solidify the predominance of realist approaches, not only among conservatives naturally inclined in that direction, but also among radicals and liberals who might otherwise have been more receptive to arguments that democracy can make an important contribution to international peace.

The end of the Cold War shows signs of breathing new life into the liberal or Wilsonian idea that regime type plays a key role in the explanation of international conflict. The rather sudden explosion of interest in the notion regarding the historical absence of war between democratic states in the wake of the end of the Cold War, though, suggests that neoliberalism might be a fad, a product of ephemeral enthusiasms. Neorealists argue, persuasively, that even if democratic regimes are peaceful in their relationships with each other, there is no guarantee that democratic regimes, especially nascent ones among the republics that made up the former Soviet Union or in Eastern Europe, will stay that way. Also, in the recent history of international politics, grand coalitions that have emerged as victors in general, systemic wars like the Napoleonic Wars in the nineteenth century and the world wars of this century have fallen apart very quickly. Both the size principle and more traditional balance of power analyses suggest that the same type of divisive process may have an impact on the currently unified major powers in the wake of the Cold War. Also, Wilsonianism has, historically, an interventionist dimension that could undermine the current neoliberal resurgence.

In the introduction, Charles Kegley calls for a "melding" of realism and neoliberalism. The end of the Cold War is an example of the kind of event that suggests a need for such a synthesis of approaches. The neoliberal idea that relationships between democratic states will be peaceful is borne out by the normal, even friendly relationship between the United States and the Soviet Union before its demise and the similarly less conflictual relationships between the United States and the republics of the former Soviet Union, which have instituted reforms in the direction of democracy. Even in retrospect, neorealism, with its emphasis on the impact of system structure as opposed to regime type, is hard-pressed to deal with such a turn of events.

Nevertheless, Waltz (1986: 66) points out that anarchic systems are "regulated, so to speak, by the 'rationality' of the more successful competitors. . . . Either their competitors emulate them or they fall by the wayside. . . . Competition spurs the actors to accommodate their ways to the most acceptable and successful practices." These points are not made specifically in the context of a discussion of regime transitions, but Waltz himself has demonstrated that the general point is applicable in such a context.[13] In short, neorealism pro-

---

[13] Waltz (1993: 50) argues, for example, that "the political and economic reconstruction attempted by the Soviet Union followed in part from external causes. . . . Gorbachev realized that the Soviet Union could no longer support a first-rate military establishment on the basis of a third-rate economy. Economic reorganization, and the reduction of imperial burdens, became an externally imposed necessity, which in turn required internal reforms."

vides a rationale for treating regime transitions as part of a global process, a step in the direction of modifying international relations theory in such a way as to make it better able to cope with the post–Cold War world.

Randall Schweller (1992: 237) investigates the age-old realist "theme of international politics, that uneven rates of growth are the fundamental cause of . . . war." He finds support for the hypothesis that "power transitions" (Organski and Kugler, 1980) are an important cause of conflict. But he also reports interesting evidence in support of the neoliberal idea that regime type matters. Specifically, his analyses reveal that "only nondemocratic regimes wage preventive wars against rising opponents. Declining democratic states . . . do not exercise this option. Instead, when the challenger is an authoritarian state, declining democratic leaders attempt to form counterbalancing alliances; when the challenger is another democratic state, they seek accommodation" (Schweller, 1992: 238).

Bruce Bueno de Mesquita and David Lalman (1992) provide another example of the potential compatibility of the realist and neoliberal approaches. Bueno de Mesquita's (1981, 1985) work over the last decade has important realist and neorealist elements, with its focus on states as important actors that can be treated as rational, expected utility calculators and its emphasis on power calculations, the fungibility of military power, the distribution of power among the states involved (potentially as well as actually) in a given dispute, and alliance ties (Ray, 1995).[14] Now, however, in *War and Reason*, Bueno de Mesquita and Lalman (1992) have developed a model of international interactions that retains virtually all of the realist and neorealist elements of Bueno de Mesquita's previous work, but that also incorporates domestic political factors, among the more important examples of which is regime type. From this model they derive the proposition that "democracies confronting one another are less likely to engage in violence than are mixed dyads" and conclude from their analysis of the evidence that "democracies are unlikely to fight with one another" (Bueno de Mesquita and Lalman, 1992: 158). Realism and neoliberalism *can* be synthesized, with encouraging results.

REFERENCES

Bremer, Stuart A. (1993) "Democracy and Militarized Interstate Conflict, 1816–1965," *International Interactions* 18 (No. 3): 231–50.
———. (1992) "Dangerous Dyads: Conditions Affecting the Likelihood of Interstate War, 1816–1965," *Journal of Conflict Resolution* 36 (June): 309–41.

[14] For these reasons, Keohane (1983: 512) refers to *The War Trap* (Bueno de Mesquita, 1981) to be among "some of the finest work" of the realist genre, and Alexander Wendt (1987: 351) designates Bueno de Mesquita's "Toward a Scientific Understanding of International Conflict" (1985a) as the definitive "discussion of the philosophy of science underlying neorealism."

Brown, Chris. (1992) *International Relations Theory: New Normative Approaches.* New York: Columbia University Press.

Bueno de Mesquita, Bruce. (1985a) "Toward a Scientific Understanding of International Conflict," *International Studies Quarterly* 29 (June): 121–36.

_____. (1985b) "*The War Trap* Revisited: A Revised Expected Utility Model," *American Political Science Review* 79 (March): 156–77.

_____. (1981) *The War Trap.* New Haven, Conn.: Yale University Press.

Bueno de Mesquita, Bruce, and David Lalman. (1992) *War and Reason.* New Haven, Conn.: Yale University Press.

Bueno de Mesquita, Bruce, Robert W. Jackman, and Randolph M. Siverson, eds. (1991) "Democracy and Foreign Policy: Community and Constraint," special issue of *Journal of Conflict Resolution* 35 (June): 179–381.

Carr, Edward Hallett. (1939, 1946) *The Twenty Years' Crisis, 1919–1939.* New York: Harper Torchbooks.

Chan, Steve, ed. (1993) "Democracy and War: Research and Reflection," special issue of *International Interactions* 18 (No. 3).

Chomsky, Noam. (1973) *For Reason of State.* New York: Pantheon Books.

_____. (1969) *American Power and the New Mandarins.* New York: Pantheon Books.

Crockatt, Richard. (1993) "Theories of Stability and the End of the Cold War," pp. 59–81 in Mike Bowker and Robin Brown, eds., *From Cold War to Collapse: Theory and World Politics in the 1980s.* Cambridge: Cambridge University Press.

De Conde, Alexander. (1963) *A History of American Foreign Policy.* New York: Charles Scribner's Sons.

Deutsch, Karl W., and J. David Singer. (1969) "Multipolar Power Systems and International Stability," pp. 315–24 in James N. Rosenau, ed., *International Politics and Foreign Policy,* 2nd ed. New York: Free Press.

Dougherty, James E., and Robert L. Pfaltzgraff Jr. (1990) *Contending Theories of International Relations,* 3rd ed. New York: Harper and Row.

Falk, Richard A. (1968a) *Legal Order in a Violent World.* Princeton, N.J.: Princeton University Press.

_____. (1968b) *The Vietnam War and International Law.* Princeton, N.J.: Princeton University Press.

Fukuyama, Francis. (1992) "Rest Easy: It's Not 1914 Anymore," *New York Times* (February 8): Section 4, p. 17.

_____. (1994) "Against the New Pessimism." *Commentary* 97: 25–29.

_____. (1989) "The End of History?" *The National Interest* 16 (Summer): 3–18.

Gaddis, John Lewis. (1992–1993) "International Relations Theory and the End of the Cold War," *International Security* 17 (Winter): 5–58.

Galbraith, John Kenneth. (1972) *The Great Crash 1929.* Boston: Houghton Mifflin.

Gleditsch, Nils Petter. (1993) "Democracy, Opportunity and War," paper presented at the Annual Meeting of the International Studies Association, March 23–27, Acapulco, Mexico.

_____, ed. (1992) "Focus on Democracy and Peace," special issue of *Journal of Peace Research* 29 (November): 369–434.

Hollis, Martin, and Steve Smith. (1990) *Explaining and Understanding International Relations.* Oxford: Clarendon Press.

Huntington, Samuel P. (1991) *The Third Wave: Democratization in the Late Twentieth Century.* Norman: University of Oklahoma Press.

Keohane, Robert O. (1983) "Theory of World Politics: Structural Realism and Beyond," pp. 541–78 in Ada Finifter, ed., *Political Science: The State of the Discipline*. Washington, D.C.: American Political Science Association.

Keohane, Robert O., and Joseph Nye. (1977) *Power and Interdependence*. Boston: Little, Brown.

Kolko, Gabriel. (1969) *The Roots of American Foreign Policy*. Boston: Beacon Press.

Knutsen, Torbjorn. (1992) *A History of International Relations Theory*. Manchester: Manchester University Press.

Magdoff, Harry. (1969) *The Age of Imperialism*. New York: Monthly Review Press.

McColm, R. Bruce. (1992) "The Comparative Survey of Freedom: 1992," *Freedom Review* 23 (Jan.–Feb.): 5–6, 11–12.

Mearsheimer, John J. (1990) "Back to the Future: Instability in Europe after the Cold War," *International Security* 15 (Summer): 5–56.

Michalak, Stanley J., Jr. (1979) "Theoretical Perspectives for Understanding International Interdependence," *World Politics* 32 (October): 136–50.

Morgenthau, Hans J. (1948) *Politics among Nations*. New York: Knopf.

Mueller, John. (1992) "Quiet Cataclysm: Some Afterthoughts about World War III," *Diplomatic History* 16 (Winter): 66–75.

―――. (1991) "Is War Still Becoming Obsolete?," paper presented at the Annual Meeting of the American Political Science Association, August 29–September 1, Washington, D.C.

―――. (1989) *Retreat from Doomsday: The Obsolescence of Major War*. New York: Basic Books.

Nathan, Andrew J. (1993) "China's Path from Communism," *Journal of Democracy* 4 (April): 30–42.

Organski, A. F. K., and Jacek Kugler. (1980) *The War Ledger*. Chicago: University of Chicago Press.

Ray, James Lee. (1995) *Democracy and International Conflict*. Columbia: University of South Carolina Press.

―――. (1992) *Global Politics*, 5th ed. Boston: Houghton Mifflin.

―――. (1989) "The Abolition of Slavery and the End of International War," *International Organization* 43 (Summer): 405–40.

Riker, William. (1962) *The Theory of Political Coalitions*. New Haven, Conn.: Yale University Press.

Rothstein, Robert. (1991) "Democracy, Conflict and Development in the Third World," *The Washington Quarterly* 14 (Spring): 43–63.

Rummel, R. J. (1989) "Roots of Faith II," pp. 311–28 in Joseph Kruzel and James N. Rosenau, eds., *Journeys through World Politics*. Lexington, Mass.: Lexington Books.

―――. (1985) "A Test of Libertarian Propositions on Violence," *Journal of Conflict Resolution* 29 (September): 419–55.

―――. (1983) "Libertarianism and International Violence," *Journal of Conflict Resolution* 27 (March): 27–71.

―――. (1979) *Understanding Conflict and War: War, Power, Peace*, Vol. 4. Beverly Hills, Calif.: Sage Publications.

Russett, Bruce. (1993) "Can a Democratic Peace Be Built?" *International Interactions* 18 (No. 3): 277–82.

Schweller, Randall L. (1992) "Domestic Structure and Preventive War: Are Democracies More Pacific?" *World Politics* 44 (January): 235–69.

Singer, J. David. (1989) "The Making of a Peace Researcher," pp. 213–30 in Joseph Kruzel and James N. Rosenau, eds., *Journeys through World Politics*. Lexington, Mass.: Lexington Books.

———. (1969) "Threat Perception and National Decision Makers," pp. 39–48 in Dean G. Pruitt and Richard C. Snyder, eds., *Theory and Research on the Causes of War*. Englewood Cliffs, N.J.: Prentice-Hall.

Singer, Max, and Aaron Wildavsky. (1993) *The Real World Order*. Chatham, N.J.: Chatham House.

Small, Melvin, and J. David Singer. (1976) "The War Proneness of Democratic Regimes, 1816–1965," *The Jerusalem Journal of International Relations* 1 (Summer): 50–69.

Vasquez, John. (1987) "The Steps to War," *World Politics* 40 (October): 108–45.

Waltz, Kenneth N. (1993) "The Emerging Structure of International Politics," *International Security* 18 (Fall): 44–79.

———. (1991) "America as a Model for the World? A Foreign Policy Perspective," *PS: Political Science and Politics* 24 (March): 667–70.

———. (1986) "Reductionist and Systemic Theories," pp. 47–69 in Robert O. Keohane, ed., *Neorealism and Its Critics*. New York: Columbia University Press.

———. (1979) *Theory of International Politics*. Reading, Mass.: Addison-Wesley.

———. (1954) *Man, the State, and War*. New York: Columbia University Press.

Wendt, Alexander. (1987) "The Agent–Structure Problem in International Relations Theory," *International Organization* 41 (Summer): 335–70.

Index

About the Contributors

MICHAEL W. DOYLE is professor of politics and international affairs at Princeton University. He has also taught at the Johns Hopkins University. His book publications include (with Fred Hirsch et al.) *Alternatives to Monetary Disorder* (1977), (with Arthur Day, editors) *Escalation and Intervention* (1986), and *Empires* (1986). Recent journal articles have been published in *Philosophy and Public Affairs*, the *American Political Science Review*, and the *Review of International Studies*.

JOSEPH M. GRIECO is professor of political science at Duke University, co-director of the Duke University Program in International Law and Institutions, and a member of the Board of Editors of *International Organization*. His research concentrates on theories of international relations and problems of international political economy. He is the author of *Between Dependency and Autonomy: India's Experience with the International Computer Industry* (1984) and *Cooperation Among Nations: Europe, America, and Non-Tariff Barriers to Trade* (1990). He has published essays in *World Politics*, *International Organization*, and the *Journal of Politics*.

OLE R. HOLSTI is the George V. Allen Professor of International Affairs at Duke University, where he has been chairman of the department of political science (1978–1983) and director of undergraduate studies (since 1992). He has also taught at Stanford University, the University of British Columbia, and the University of California at Davis. He has served as an officer in several professional organizations, including the International Studies Association as president (1979–1980), and as a member of the editorial boards of *International Studies Quarterly*, *The Journal of Politics*, *Western Political Quarterly*, *American Journal of Political Science*, *Journal of Conflict Resolution*, *International Interactions*, and *The American Review of Politics*. He is also a contributing editor for *Running Journal*. Holsti's publications include eight books, and his articles have appeared in *The American Political Science Review*, *World Politics*, *International Studies Quarterly*, *Diplomatic History*, *Public Opinion Quarterly*, *The Journal of Politics*, *Journal of Conflict Resolution*, *Science*, and elsewhere. He has received five National Science Foundation grants, a Guggenheim Fellowship, the Nevitt Sanford Award of the International Society of Political Psychology, and two teaching awards: a Pew Faculty Fellowship at Harvard University and the Howard Johnson Distinguished Teacher Award.

BARRY B. HUGHES is professor at the Graduate School of International Studies, University of Denver, and serves that institution as vice provost for graduate studies. His primary research interests are in international politics; computer simulation models for economic, energy, food, and population forecasting; and global futures. The larger concern that ties these interests together is the crafting of effective international responses to long-term global change. He has authored or coauthored books on *The Domestic Context of American Foreign Policy* (1978), *World Modeling* (1980), *World Futures* (1985), *Disarmament and Development* (1990), *Continuity and Change in World Politics* (second edition, 1994), and *International Futures* (1993). He has also developed or contributed to the development of several computer simulations of global futures, including the International Futures model that accompanies his book by that title.

ROBERT C. JOHANSEN is Senior Fellow and director of graduate studies at the Kroc Institute for International Peace Studies at the University of Notre Dame, where he is also professor in the department of government and international studies. A specialist in U.S. security and arms control policies, and in peace and world order studies, Johansen has taught previously at Manchester College and Princeton University and is past president of the World Policy Institute, contributing editor to the *World Policy Journal*, and a member of the board of directors of the Arms Control Association in Washington, D.C. His publications include *The National Interest and the Human Interest: An Analysis of U.S. Foreign Policy* (1980), *Toward an Alternative Security System* (1983), and *The Constitutional Foundations of World Peace* (with Richard Falk and Samuel Kim, 1993). He has published articles in a wide range of journals, including *World Politics, World Policy Journal, International Interactions, Bulletin of Peace Proposals, Political Studies, Alternatives,* and *Third World Quarterly,* as well as periodicals including *The Atlantic Monthly, Harper's,* and *The New York Times.* In 1992 and 1993, Johansen conducted research on the utility of military and nonmilitary power while a Visiting Scholar at the Center of International Studies at Harvard University.

THOMAS J. JOHNSON is a doctoral candidate in the School of International Service, The American University, where he has taught world politics and theories of international politics. He is currently writing a dissertation on the Sophistic roots of realist theory. He is also a member of the research staff of the United States Institute of Peace.

CHARLES W. KEGLEY JR. is Pearce Professor of International Relations at the University of South Carolina, where he served as chairman of the department of government and international studies from 1981 to 1985 and as codirector (with Lawrence S. Eagleburger) of the Byrnes International Center from 1985 to 1988. Elected president of the International Studies Association (1993–

1994), he has held faculty appointments at Georgetown University, the University of Texas, the People's University of China, and Rutgers University, and he was a Pew Faculty Fellow at Harvard University. Among his three dozen book publications, he has recently published (with Gregory A. Raymond) *A Multipolar Peace? Great-Power Politics in the Twenty-first Century* (1994) and *When Trust Breaks Down; Alliance Norms and World Politics* (1990); (with Eugene R. Wittkopf) *World Politics: Trend and Transformation* (5th ed., 1995), *The Global Agenda* (4th ed., 1995), *The Future of American Foreign Policy* (1992), and *American Foreign Policy: Pattern and Process* (4th ed., 1991). In addition, he edited *The Long Postwar Peace: Contending Explanations and Projections* (1991) and (with Kenneth W. Schwab) *After the Cold War: Questioning the Morality of Nuclear Deterrence* (1991). He has published articles in a wide range of scholarly journals, including *The Journal of Peace Research, International Studies Quarterly, International Organization, Ethics & International Affairs, The Jerusalem Journal of International Relations, Alternatives, USA Today, Harvard International Review, Comparative Political Studies, International Interactions,* and *The Journal of Politics.*

RICHARD A. MATTHEW recently received his Ph.D. from Princeton University and is currently a Killam Postdoctoral Fellow in the Institute of International Relations, the University of British Columbia. He has taught at the University of Victoria and the University of British Columbia. His publications include an edited volume entitled *The New Pacific Interface: Japan's Relations with North America* (1989) and articles on regional patterns of international relations in the Asia–Pacific area and North America. He organized a Colloquium on International Relations and Political Theory at Princeton (1986–1988) and a Conference on Environmental Change at the University of British Columbia (1993). He is currently completing a book entitled *Politics Divided: Justice, Interest and World Political Order* and editing a volume on environmental change and conflict. Matthew recently has begun research on two projects, the first dealing with democracy and republicanism in world politics and the second with environmental refugees as a moral problem in international relations.

NICHOLAS G. ONUF has taught at the School of International Service, The American University, since 1970. He has also taught at Columbia University, Georgetown University, Howard University, Johns Hopkins University's Nitze School of Advanced International Studies, Ritsumeikan University (Japan), and The University of Colombo (Sri Lanka). His book publications include *World of Our Making* (1989) and (with Peter Onuf) *Federal Union, Modern World: The Law of Nations in an Age of Revolutions, 1776–1814* (1993). He is currently writing a book on republicanism in international thought and, again with his brother, a second volume of *Federal Union, Modern World.* His articles have appeared in a wide range of scholarly journals.

JAMES LEE RAY is professor of political science at Florida State University, where he has served as director of the international affairs program since 1985 and director of the peace studies program since 1987. He is a specialist on the causes of war, various aspects of international political economy, regime transition, and American foreign policy in Latin American and the Middle East. He has taught at the State University College at Fredonia (New York) and the University of New Mexico, where he served as chairman of the department of political science from 1982 to 1984. His publications include articles in *International Interactions, International Organization, International Studies Quarterly*, and *The Journal of Conflict Resolution*. Ray's books also include authorship of *The Future of American–Israeli Relations* (1985) and *Global Politics* (1992). His current writing focuses on additional analyses of contending explanations of major power peace, with a special emphasis on the relevance of such explanations to an understanding of contemporary relationships involving the European Union, and he has recently authored *Democracies and International Conflict*, published by the University of South Carolina Press in 1995.

NEIL R. RICHARDSON is associate professor of political science at the University of Wisconsin-Madison. He has also taught at the University of Texas-Austin and at Hebrew University of Jerusalem. The author of *Foreign Policy and Economic Dependence* (1978), Richardson has had many book chapters and articles appear in *The American Political Science Review, International Studies Quarterly, The Journal of Politics, The Jerusalem Journal of International Relations, The Sage International Yearbook of Foreign Policy Studies*, and *Social Science Quarterly*. He is currently writing a book on the difficulties encountered by states in the industrialized world as they attempt to guide their economies.

J. MARTIN ROCHESTER is professor of political science and a Fellow in the Center for International Studies at the University of Missouri-St. Louis. He has chaired the political science department at UM-St. Louis and has served twice on the Governing Council of the International Studies Association. A specialist in the area of international organization, he has published the following books and monographs: *International Institutions and World Order: The International System as a Prismatic Polity* (1974); *The Global Condition* (with Frederic Pearson, 1988 and 1992); and *Waiting for the Millennium: The United Nations and the Future of World Order* (1993). His scholarly articles have appeared in such journals as *International Organization*, the *American Political Science Review*, the *Journal of Peace Research, International Studies Quarterly*, and *Western Political Quarterly*. His current research focuses on the prospects for reform of the United Nations.

JOEL H. ROSENTHAL is director of education and studies at the Carnegie Council on Ethics and International Affairs in New York, where he oversees the council's research and publication program in ethics and international affairs. He is also editor of the Carnegie Council's annual journal *Ethics & International Affairs*. Rosenthal is the author of *Righteous Realists: Political Realism, Responsible Power, and American Culture in the Nuclear Age* (1991), as well as numerous articles on ethics and foreign policy.

HARVEY STARR is the Dag Hammarskjold Professor in International Affairs at the University of South Carolina. In 1991 he became editor of *International Interactions* and was elected president of the Conflict Processes Section of the American Political Science Association for the 1992–1995 term. He has also taught at Indiana University, serving as chairman of the department of political science from 1984 to 1989. He specializes in the areas of international relations theory, international conflict, alliances, and foreign policy analysis. His current research interests include geopolitics, the diffusion of international phenomena, and the relationship between domestic factors and international conflict (democracy and war; war and revolution). He is author or coauthor of eight books and monographs and over forty journal articles or book chapters. His most recent books are *Inquiry, Logic and International Politics* (1989, with Benjamin A. Most) and *The Diffusion of War: A Study of Opportunity and Willingness* (1991, with Randolph M. Siverson). The fourth edition of *World Politics: The Menu for Choice*, with Bruce Russett, was published in 1992.

KENNETH N. WALTZ is Ford Professor at the University of California, Berkeley. During the 1992–1993 academic year, Prof. Waltz was a visiting scholar at the Department of International Relations at the London School of Economics. He earned his A.B. from Oberlin College (1948) and his M.A. and Ph.D. from Columbia University (1950 and 1954). He is a past president of the American Political Science Association (1987–1988) and a Fellow of the American Academy of Arts and Sciences. He has written *Man, the State, and War: A Theoretical Analysis* (1959), *Foreign Policy and Democratic Politics: The American and British Experience* (1967, reissued 1992), and *Theory of International Politics* (1979). He is coeditor and coauthor, with Robert Art, of *The Use of Force*, now in its fourth edition, and coeditor (with Steven L. Spiegel) of *Conflict in World Politics* (1971). His "Nuclear Myths and Political Realities" won the Heinz Eulau award for best article in the *American Political Science Review* in 1990.

MARK W. ZACHER is professor of political science at the University of British Columbia, where he served as director of the Institute of International Relations (1971–1991). He has also taught at Cambridge University. He has authored *Dag Hammarskjold's United Nations* (1970), *International Conflicts and Collective Security 1946–1977* (1979), *Pollution Politics and International Law* (with Michael M'Gonigle, 1979), *Managing International Markets* (with Jock A. Finlayson, 1988), and has coedited *Canadian Foreign Policy and the Law of the Sea* (1977) and *Canadian Foreign Policy and International Economic Regimes* (1992). He will soon complete *Governing Global Networks:*

International Regimes for Shipping, Air Transport, Telecommunications and Postal Services and *Common Enemies and International Change: International Collaboration in Response to Nuclear, Environmental, Health and Translation Crime Threats.* His articles have been published in *International Organization, Ocean Development and International Law,* the *Journal of International Affairs,* and elsewhere.